The Treason Trials, 1794

Figure 1. Sir James Eyre, Chief Justice of the Court of Common Pleas, 1793–1799. (By permission of the Masters of the Bench of Gray's Inn.)

THE TREASON TRIALS, 1794

ALAN WHARAM M.A.
Barrister-at-Law

Leicester University Press
Leicester and London

Distributed in the United States and Canada by St. Martin's Press, New York

Leicester University Press
(a division of Pinter Publishers)
25 Floral Street, Covent Garden, London WC2E 9DS, United Kingdom

Editorial offices
Fielding Johnson Building, University of Leicester,
Leicester LE1 7RH

Trade and other enquiries
25 Floral Street, London WC2E 9DS, UK
and Room 400, 175 Fifth Avenue, New York, NY 1   10, US

First published in 1992

© Alan Wharam, 1992

Distributed exclusively in the United States and Canada by St. Martin's Press, Inc., 175 Fifth Avenue, New York, NY 10010, USA

Alan Wharam is herby identified as the author of this work as provided under Section 77 of the Copyright, Designs and Patents Act, 1988.

British Library Congress Cataloguing in Publication Data

A CIP catalogue record for this book is available from the British Library

ISBN 0 7185 1445 9

Library of Congress Cataloging in Publication Data

Wharam, Alan.
   The Treason Trials, 1794/Alan Wharam.
      p. cm.
   Includes bibliographical references and index.
   ISBN 0-7185-1445-9
   1. Hardy, Thomas, 1752-1832 – Trials, litigation, etc. 2. Tooke, John Horne, 1736-1812 – Trials, litigation, etc. 3. Trials (Treason) – England – London. 4. Jacobins – Great Britain. I. Title.
KD372.T74W48 1992
345.42'0231 – dc20
[344.205231]

                                                                              92-15182
                                                                              CIP

Typeset by Saxon Printing Ltd, Derby
Printed and bound in Great Britain by Biddles Ltd, Guildford and King's Lynn

In Memory of
Philip Anthony Brown M.A.
and
Thomas Kenny V.C.
both of the Durham Light Infantry

CONTENTS

List of figures

For contemporary maps of London, readers are referred to *Rocque's Atlas (1746–47)*, republished as *The A to Z of Georgian London* (Harry Margary) 1981; and *Horwood's Atlas (1792–99)*.

PREFACE

A long time ago, an uncle of mine, who seems to have been regarded as the black sheep of the family, was despatched to the colonies; he settled in Rhodesia, and brought up his family in very difficult circumstances. In 1965, their government declared unilateral independence, whereupon the Attorney-General, Sir Elwyn Jones, told the House of Commons that there was 'abundant authority' for saying that what had occurred was treasonable. The nature of this 'abundant authority' was never disclosed, so anyone seeking to rebut the charge was left with no alternative but to review the entire body of legislation and case law since 1351; this I endeavoured to do in an article which was published two years later.[1]

It became apparent to me, while I was preparing this article, that the Treason Trials of 1794 were an episode of great importance in our legal history – there had never been a case like this before, there has never been one like it since – but, short of reading the reports in full, there was no way of finding out anything about them. They did not appear in the Notable British Trials series, and references to them in standard history and legal textbooks were perfunctory and inaccurate. Here, I thought, was a gap waiting to be filled, a book waiting to be written.

Twenty years elapsed before I could resume my research. By this time, Professor Goodwin had published his book, *The Friends of Liberty*, including a detailed account of the events of the 1790s. Otherwise, even writers who had specialised in the history of the period had little more to say.[2] The gap in the literature was all the more remarkable because the evidence given at the trials covered many important events in the 1780s and early 1790s – evidence which was given on oath, most of it (surprisingly) unchallenged, and supported by a mass of documents, many of which have been forgotten; and all available in print for anyone who cared to read the State Trials.

The accused included a variety of talented men: there was Thomas Hardy, the shoemaker, who was believed by the government to be hatching a revolution in the back room of his shop at No. 9 Piccadilly; there was the Revd John Horne Tooke, priest and politician, pamphleteer and philologist, who was thought to be organising an insurrection from his house at Wimbledon; Thomas Holcroft, the novelist and playwright; John Thelwall, poet and lecturer; Stewart Kyd, barrister-at-law; Augustus Bonney, attorney; the Revd Jeremiah Joyce, tutor to the sons of Earl Stanhope; John Richter, gentleman; and John Baxter, a labourer then, later to become an historian.

Leading counsel for the Crown was Sir John Scott, the son of a Newcastle coal merchant; leading counsel for the defence was Thomas Erskine, son of the Earl of Buchan; and presiding over the trials was Chief Justice Sir James Eyre, the son of a country parson.

Among the men who were to stand in the witness box that autumn, among the King's messengers and spies, the tradesmen and shopkeepers, the shoemakers and cutlers, were Richard Brinsley Sheridan the playwright and William Sharp the engraver, the Rt. Revd Richard Beadon DD, Bishop of Gloucester, the Duke of Richmond, Charles James Fox, and William Pitt himself.

My original intention was to write a book along the lines of the Notable British Trials, with a short introduction and biographical sketches of the leading personalities, followed by the transcript, or at least substantial parts of the transcript, of the cases; but it soon became clear that this was beyond anyone's capacity. The trials of Hardy and Horne Tooke alone occupy nearly 1000 closely printed pages in the State Trials – and they were tied up with other trials in London, Edinburgh, Dublin and the provinces; and both leading counsel, at least four of the defendants, and many of the witnesses have been the subject of substantial biographies.

So I have tried to give in outline an account of the trial, conviction and transportation of the 'Scottish martyrs' in Edinburgh; and of the events which led the Law Officers of the Crown to embark on a prosecution for treason. As far as the biographical sketches are concerned, I have restricted myself to four characters – the two leading advocates, and the two principal defendants. The description of the trials themselves has necessarily been reduced to a summary, and inevitably I have had to be selective; but I hope that I have managed to preserve and convey the atmosphere of the Court of Justiciary and the Old Bailey in those critical days of our history two hundred years ago.

SOURCES AND ACKNOWLEDGEMENTS

This book is about the Treason Trials which were heard at the Old Bailey in 1794 and other related cases, verbatim reports of which are to be found in the State Trials (St.Tr.) edited by Howell in 30 volumes, 1816–26. Many historical documents, including the minutes of the Edinburgh Convention of 1793, are printed in these reports.

Other principal sources are as follows.

Adolphus: John Adolphus (1768–1845) was the son of a German immigrant. He was admitted solicitor in 1790, but spent most of the next decade writing a *History of France* (referred to as Adolphus (France)) and the first 3 volumes of a *History of the Reign of George III* (Adolphus (England)). Early in the Nineteenth century, he was called to the bar, and became a leading criminal advocate. In his old age, he resumed work on the *History of the Reign of George III*.[1]

Bayne-Powell: *Eighteenth Century London Life*, by Rosamund Bayne-Powell, 1937; a very detailed account.

Bindman: In 1989, the British Museum held an exhibition called 'The Shadow of the Guillotine: Britain and the French Revolution'; the catalogue for this exhibition was compiled by David Bindman, Professor of History of Art, Westfield College, University of London; many contemporary documents, pictures, etc., were exhibited and are reproduced in the catalogue. Citations in parentheses refer to exhibit numbers.

Blackstone: William Blackstone (1723–1780) was the first Vinerian Professor of Law at Oxford. His *Commentaries on the Laws of England* (Bl.Comm.) were published in 1765; they soon became a standard students' textbook, and their contents can usually be regarded as accurate statements of the law at that period.

Brown: Philip Anthony Brown (he always signed himself thus, even in his letters to his mother) graduated from New College Oxford in 1909 and taught at Newcastle University (in association with the WEA), at Durham University and the London School of Economics. On the outbreak of war, he enlisted in the Duke of Cornwall's Light Infantry, leaving the manuscript and proofs of his book, *The French Revolution in English History*, with his friends, Mr and Mrs J. L. Hammond. In the summer of 1915 he was commissioned into the 13th Battalion of the Durham Light Infantry, which in the autumn of that year was posted to La Houssoie, a quiet stretch of the front between Armentières and Lille – 'a mild enemy in front of us, I think', he wrote to his mother on 3 November; late on the following evening, he and a Durham coal-miner, Private Thomas Kenny, were on patrol in no man's land in thick fog when they were seen by the enemy who opened fire and wounded Brown in both legs. In spite of the fog and heavy enemy fire, Kenny struggled for two hours to bring Brown back to the English lines, and eventually succeeded, but Brown died a few minutes later. Kenny received the VC and, after being promoted to Sgt-Major, returned to County Durham, where he had twelve children and survived until 1948. Brown's book was published in 1918 and reprinted in 1965.[2]

Campbell: John Campbell practised at the English bar for many years; he held the offices of Solicitor-General, Attorney-General, Chief Justice of the Court King's Bench and Lord Chancellor. His extensive *Lives of the Chancellors*, one volume of which was devoted entirely to Lord Eldon, and much of another to Lord Erskine, were written in 1845–47, and two supplementary volumes on Lords Lyndhurst and Brougham were published after his death in 1861. He also wrote a series of *Lives of the Chief Justices* of the Court of King's Bench.[3]

Cartwright: Frances Cartwright's *Life and Correspondence* of her uncle, Major John Cartwright, was published in 1826.

Cockburn: Lord Cockburn, a Scottish judge, wrote a detailed account and commentary of the Scottish sedition trials, which was published, under the title *An Examination of the Trials for Sedition in Scotland*, in 1888.

Cone: *The English Jacobins*, by Carl B. Cone, Professor of History at the University of Kentucky, was published in 1968.

Croly: *The Life and Times of George IV*, by the Revd George Croly, was published in 1830.

Dictionary of National Biography (DNB).

Eldon: Lord Eldon compiled his *Anecdote Book* in 1824–27; this was made available to his biographers, but was not printed and published until 1960.

Ferguson: Alexander Ferguson published a biography of Henry Erskine in 1882; this contains much material relating to Henry's brother, Thomas, and the Erskine family.

George: *London Life in the Eighteenth Century*, by Dorothy George, a research scholar of the London School of Economics; a very detailed work, published in 1925.

Goodwin: *The Friends of Liberty: the English Democratic Movement in the Age of the French Revolution* (Hutchinson; 1979). Albert Goodwin, born in 1906, was the son of a Sheffield edge-tool forger; an Oxford graduate, he was for a time on the staff of Prof. Veitch at Liverpool University (see below); he was the author of various books on eighteenth century history, and wrote *The Friends of Liberty* when he was Emeritus Professor of Modern History in the University of Manchester.

Hall: Walter P. Hall wrote his *British Radicalism 1791–1797* as a Ph. D. thesis for Columbia University; it was published in 1912, and reprinted in 1976.

Hardy: Thomas Hardy's *Memoir* was published in 1832 and reprinted by David Vincent, *Testaments of Radicalism*, in 1977. It should be noted that Hardy wrote in the third person, referring to himself as Hardy.

Hone: Dr J. Ann Hone, senior lecturer at the Canberra College of Advanced Education, published *For the Cause of Truth: Radicalism in London, 1796–1821* in 1982; it contains much material from the Home Office records for this period.

Schama: Simon Schama, Professor of History at Harvard University, published his book *Citizens* in 1989; this book deals in detail with the French Revolution, and I have relied on it, unless otherwise stated, for events occurring in France in the years 1789–1794.

Stanhope: towards the end of the Nineteenth century, Ghita Stanhope was writing a biography of her ancestor, the Third Earl of Stanhope; following her death, this was completed by C.P. Gooch, and published in 1914.

Stephens: Alexander Stephens published his *Memoirs of John Horne Tooke*, in two volumes, in 1813.

Thompson: E. P. Thompson, who held posts at Leeds and Warwick Universities, published his monumental *The Making of the English Working Class* in 1963 (reprinted by Penguin Books, 1980).

Twiss: Horace Twiss published his *Life of Lord Eldon*, in 3 volumes, in 1844.

Veitch: George S. Veitch (1885-1943) wrote his book, *The Genesis of Parliamentary Reform*, when he was a Research Fellow of Liverpool University; the book was published in 1913 and reprinted in 1964; Veitch spent most of his working life at Liverpool University, where he was Professor of History from 1923 to 1943.[4]

Vincent: see Hardy, *supra*.

A few other sources will be found in the notes.

The author and publishers have been unable to trace the copyright holder of the material reproduced in Appendix III from *Songs of Many Wars*, edited and arranged by Kurt Adler and published by Howell Hosking, Soskin, New York, and would be grateful for any information that would enable them to do so.

If this was a legal text-book, references would be given for every quotation and every fact stated; but in order to keep the annotation within reasonable limits I have in general omitted citing references from the State Trials and other Eighteenth and Nineteenth century sources.

I am grateful to the Cambridge University Library for providing me with photocopies of the reports in the State Trials; to the Leeds Polytechnic Library; to the Leeds University Law Faculty Library; to the Leeds Central Reference Library; and in particular to that remarkable institution, the Leeds Private Library (founded 1768), and its librarians, Geoffrey Forster and Graham Neal, and their staff: much of this book has been written on a 'strong oaken table' which was presented to the Library in the year of its foundation and was standing there while the events described herein were taking place. I am also grateful to John Beaumont of the Leeds Polytechnic Law School; to Alec McAulay of Leicester University Press and Professor Aubrey Newman of the History Faculty of Leicester University; to Mr R. E. Williams and Dr Alex Sakula for their help on medical matters; to the copy editor, Jane Holden; and the staff of Pinters. Thanks also to Dorothy for making sure that the text was right, and to Helen and Susan for their encouragement.

Abbreviations

I have as far as possible avoided the use of legal terminology, except that I have employed the conventional abbreviations for the Law Officers of the Crown and the Judges; these follow the names of the individuals, e.g. Smith J.

A.-G. and S.-G.	Attorney- and Solicitor-General
B. and CB	Baron and Chief Baron of the Court of Exchequer
J. and CJ	Justice and Chief Justice of the Courts of King's Bench and Common Pleas (JJ in the plural). (For a note on the courts, see Appendix II)
LC	Lord Chancellor

CHAPTER 1

THE BACKGROUND: REFORMERS AND REVOLUTIONARIES

There were in those days, wrote Frances Cartwright in the biography of her uncle, the Major, two political factions: the Tories, who believed in the divine right of kings; and the Whigs, who believed in the divine right of noblemen and gentlemen. Anyone who did not fall into these categories had no share in the government of the country; rotten and pocket boroughs were under the control of the aristocracy, and the right to nominate their members of the House of Commons could be bought and sold on the property market[1] – the doctrine of 'no taxation without representation' was a sham since the majority of taxpayers had no say in the taxes which were imposed upon them.

When James II had fled from the kingdom in 1688, leaving the country without either Crown or Parliament, the Prince of Orange summoned a Convention – 'the fountainhead', said Macaulay,[2] 'from which the authority of all future Parliaments must be derived'. It was supposed to represent the nation, but to all outward appearance it was just like any other parliament and, although it discussed various possible constitutional reforms, no suggestions were put forward for reforming Parliament itself. The settlement of 1688 was regarded as sacrosanct; very few chose to look beyond it to see how it could be reconciled with the earlier laws and constitution of the country, or even with the ordinary principles of logic and common sense. When there were complaints of scandal and corruption in government, the cry was that the nation should revert to the purity of 1688. The settlement itself, it seems, was never questioned. It was not until the year of the American Revolution that this tradition was broken by Major John Cartwright.

Major Cartwright was so-called because he was for many years the Major, and in practical terms the commanding officer, of the Nottinghamshire Militia. His career had started in the Navy, and as a boy he had fought under Lord Howe in the Battle of Quiberon Bay. When the American War broke out, Lord Howe, who was now Commander-in-Chief, invited him to accept a post on his flagship. But, as he had already openly given his support to the rebels, Cartwright felt bound to turn the offer down; he also declined the offer of a command in the American Navy on the ground that he would never fight against his own country.

In 1776, in a pamphlet called *Take Your Choice*, Major Cartwright advocated universal suffrage and annual parliaments, and schemes for reforming Parliament soon became more popular. Petitions from county associations were being presented to Parliament and some were so strongly worded that they were being compared to those which had been submitted at the time of the Great Rebellion; there were rumours that the reformers were prepared to take up arms,[3] and Lord George Gordon, MP for Ludgershall, boasted, under the protection of parliamentary privilege, that he had 160,000 Scotchmen[4] under his command, and that if the King did not cut their taxes, they would come and cut off his head.[5]

Towards the end of 1779, the Revd Christopher Wyvill convened a meeting of Yorkshiremen to petition Parliament for reform, and in 1780 he organised a convention of several county associations. This convention had no constitutional status, but the City of London gave it respectability by placing the Guildhall at its disposal and the Lord Mayor presided.[6] At the trials in the following decade, there was much discussion as to whether the convention which met in Edinburgh in 1793 and was to be reconvened in 1794 was, like the Guildhall meeting of 1780, an assembly to petition Parliament, or, like the Convention of 1688, to re-model the constitution or, like the National Convention of France, to usurp the functions of government.

Proposals for reform varied, but were mostly along the lines of abolishing the rotten and pocket boroughs, and giving representation to the new industrial towns – suggestions which were eventually enacted half a century later in the Great Reform Act. Some reformers, however, supported Major Cartwright's plans for universal suffrage, and in April 1780 he founded the Society for Constitutional Information to propagate his views. In the same spring, a committee of the electors of Westminster (where all male residents already had the vote) drew up a report recommending, *inter alia*, annual elections, universal adult male suffrage, poll by ballot, and the payment of wages to members.[7] And on 3 June the Duke of Richmond introduced into the House of Lords a bill 'for declaring and restoring the natural unalienable and equal rights of all the Commons of Great Britain to vote in the election of their representatives in Parliament.'

This far-reaching suggestion was rejected without a division. It was indeed not a day that the Duke would have chosen for introducing a measure of this type since proposals for relaxing the laws against Roman Catholics were also under discussion in Parliament, and these were bitterly opposed by the Protestant Association, led by Lord George Gordon. On the previous day, the Association had held a mass meeting in St George's Fields from whence they marched, with colours flying and wearing blue cockades, and accompanied by a band of Scotch bagpipes, to Westminster; they surged into the lobby of the House of Commons and assaulted peers on their way to the House of Lords, and interrupted the Duke in the middle of his speech.

During the next few days, the crowd plundered the houses of Roman Catholics; they attacked Newgate (see Figure 2), which was to London what the Bastille was to Paris – 'a place which for its security seemed to be equal to a

Figure 2. Newgate Prison: 'a place which for its security seemed to be equal to a prison in the centre of the Earth'; destroyed in the Gordon Riots and rebuilt, then finally demolished in the twentieth century. (By permission of the Museum of London.)

prison in the centre of the earth'; 'built in such a manner as to justify the idea that it was impregnable to armed force'[8] – they set fire to the Keeper's house, attacked the prison itself, and released all the prisoners. 'Everyone who was in London at the time', said Lord Loughborough CJ in his charge to the grand jury in the case of *R. v. Gordon*, 'must remember, that it bore the appearance of a town taken by storm; every quarter was alarmed; neither age, nor sex, nor eminence of station, nor sanctity of character, nor even an humble though honest obscurity, were any protection against the malevolent fury and destructive rage of the lowest and worst of men.' The house of Lord Mansfield CJ[9] in Bloomsbury Square was burnt down. An attempt was made to divert the New River to prevent its use in fighting fires, and a plan was made to seize the Bank of England. However, King George III,[10] who had been working unremittingly throughout the crisis, was able to assemble a force, and the Guard shot 60 or 70 rioters. By Friday 9 June, large bodies of troops had been mobilised and eventually order was restored; Lord George Gordon himself was arrested and sent to the Tower.

It was, and indeed it still is, for the provision has never been repealed, an express term of the Bill of Rights that Protestants are entitled to bear arms for their own defence; but the Riots left a lasting impression on the mind of the government which was not easily erased.

In spite of this interruption, proposals for reform were continued. The younger William Pitt, the son of the Earl of Chatham, was now a leading advocate for reform, and so was his brother-in-law Lord Mahon, the heir of the Earl of Stanhope. Following the death of her eldest son at Eton, the Countess of Stanhope had taken Lord Mahon to Switzerland, where he was educated at Geneva. Returning to England in 1774, it happened that they were passing through Paris when Louis XV died, and they witnessed the funeral procession of the no longer *bien aimé* king coming at full gallop to the royal tomb at St Denis while the crowd 'hooped (*sic*) and holloed as if they had been at a horse race instead of a funeral procession'.

The Stanhopes were closely associated with the Chathams and shortly after his return to England Lord Mahon married William Pitt's sister, Hester. They lived at Chevening in Kent and had three daughters; William used to visit his nieces – Hester, the eldest, was the tomboy, 'the Jackey Girl', he used to call her; Griselda was 'the book devourer'; and Lucy, 'the beauty'. Lady Hester died in 1780, and the widower then married her cousin, Louisa Grenville, by whom he had three sons. In the same year, he became a Member of Parliament; he and Pitt worked in close collaboration, and his unswerving integrity was a political asset, as were his stentorian voice and his wild gesticulations.

Another meeting of the county associations was held in 1781, and in May 1782 Pitt introduced a reform bill into the House of Commons; following its rejection, a meeting of the leading reformers was held on 18 May at the Thatched House Tavern in St James's Street. This was a regular meeting place for politicians, but this particular meeting is the one which came to be referred to as *the* Thatched House meeting. The minutes were taken by William Pitt in his own writing;[11] the Duke of Richmond was there, as were Lords Surrey and Mahon; so were the Lord Mayor of London and Alderman Wilkes, and Major Cartwright, William Tooke, Horne Tooke, and an attorney called John Frost. The meeting resolved unanimously that it had become necessary to petition Parliament for a substantial reformation of the House of Commons. Further petitions were presented to Parliament, and further motions were introduced into the House of Commons, but little further progress was made at that time.

✻   ✻   ✻

At the time of these events in England, similar developments were taking place in Ireland.[12]

In 1782, a settlement was reached between England and Ireland, under which Ireland achieved what would later have been described as 'Dominion status'. The Irish Parliament had almost unfettered powers, but it had the same sort of defects as its English counterpart, and in the early 1780s movements were under way to reform it. There was in Ireland a long-standing tradition of forming military units, known as the Volunteers; they were usually commanded by Protestant gentry, and most of the rank and file were middle-class businessmen and farmers – membership provided opportunities for parading in resplendent uniforms and taking part in social activities. In 1783, provincial conventions of Volunteer delegates were held at Lisburn and Dungannon, and in the winter another convention met in Dublin. The latter was a much more formidable meeting than the London convention: it represented most of Ireland; it consisted predominantly of Volunteers; and it was presided over by their commanding officer, the Earl of Charlemont. It was seen as a real rival to the constitutional Irish Parliament and it recommended various reforms which were embodied in a bill which was presented to Parliament, but rejected. Another congress, again representing most of the country, met for several weeks in the autumn of 1784, but after that, for some years, the reform movement lost impetus and the Volunteers began to dwindle.

One incident occurred during 1783 which had lasting repercussions in the following decade. One of the leaders of the Volunteers, Colonel Sharman, wrote to the Duke of Richmond to ask his advice on the problems of corruption in Ireland. The Duke replied on 15 August: much of his letter[13] dealt with Irish matters, but the gist of his proposals is summarised in the following passage:

> I am more and more convinced that *the restoring the right of voting universally to every man, not incapacitated by nature for want of reason, or by law for the commission of crimes*, is the only reform that can be effectual and permanent. I am farther convinced that it is the only reform that is practicable.

The Dukes of Richmond were of royal blood, being descended from the bastard son of Charles II by Louise de Keroualle, Duchess of Portsmouth; the

Figure 3. Horne Tooke in 1791, by an artist called Thomas Hardy, thought to be no relation of the shoemaker. (By permission of the Wimbledon Society.)

text of the letter was printed and widely circulated; and when the members of the reforming societies were put on trial one of their principal lines of defence was that they were simply trying to put the Duke of Richmond's plan into effect.

           ❊   ❊   ❊

The delegate for Surrey at the Guildhall convention was the Revd John Horne Tooke (see Figure 3), who was also a member of the Society for Constitutional

Information. By the early 1780s he had established a reputation as a formidable pamphleteer, an authority on the law and the constitution, a persistent litigant, and a thorn in the flesh of the government.

He was born John Horne, on 25 June 1736, one of seven children of a poultry dealer who had a shop in Newport Market, Westminster. Frederick, the Prince of Wales, kept his court at Leicester House nearby, and John, who was two years older than the little Prince George, used to play, once or twice a week, with the future King. Rather surprisingly, I have found no reference to this boyhood friendship when, half a century later, one was accused of compassing the death of the other.

One of John's brothers became a successful market gardener and introduced the pine-strawberry from North America (and vandals invaded his garden, stole the runners, and undersold him at Covent Garden); one sister married Dr Demainbray, Prince George's tutor, and their son became the superintendent of the Royal Observatory at Kew; another sister married a wine merchant, and their son, John Wildman, became a brewer in Chelsea and was a great support to his uncle in later years. John himself was evidently the favourite child, and his parents spared no expense in his education, sending him for two years to Westminster School, and then in 1744 to Eton.

It was while John was at Eton, during a scrap with another boy who had a knife in his hand, that the knife pierced John's eye, and he lost the sight in it, although as the years went by the injury became imperceptible. Otherwise, little is known about his time there; there are no records of any academic achievements or of any escapades, although one friend recalled that he had never been in such awe of anyone as John Horne.[14] Some of his aristocratic contemporaries (William Pitt the elder and Lord North were at Eton at about the same time) ridiculed his humble origin, but he told them that his father was an eminent turkey merchant and that seemed to satisfy them, for at that time England enjoyed a large share of the Levant trade, and turkey merchants had a reputation for credit and wealth.

There followed three years at St John's College, Cambridge, where Horne was friendly with Richard Beadon, who later became the Master of Jesus College and a bishop; and then a spell as an usher at a school in Blackheath, where he fell in love with a girl who lived in the same house, but the affair was broken off by some 'formidable yet unexplained obstacle', and he never married.

John Horne's father wanted his son to enter holy orders and he was ordained at about this time; but John himself wanted to go to the bar, and he became a member of Inner Temple. It was here that he met John Dunning, the son of a tradesman from Devonshire, who later acted professionally for him, and Lloyd Kenyon, a Welshman who had been brought up in an attorney's office, and was to become Chief Justice of the Court of King's Bench. The three spent much time together, and used to dine at a little eating-house near Chancery Lane, for 7½d each; Horne and Dunning used to give the waitress 1d, but Lloyd Kenyon, 'who always knew the value of money', gave her ½d or a promise.

After he was ordained, Horne obtained the living of New Brentford, a thriving village on the banks of the Thames in Middlesex, where he remained for eleven years. He carried out his work as a parish priest conscientiously: his sermons were plain and practical; he visited the sick; he studied the works of Boerhaave[15] and prepared medicines for those of his parishioners who could not afford an apothecary; and he won the respect of the neighbouring gentry to such an extent that one of them employed him to take his son on a tour of Europe. But at the same time he began to take an interest in public affairs. John Wilkes, then the Member of Parliament for Aylesbury, was illegally arrested for denouncing the Government, and Horne sprang to his defence, castigating all and sundry in a stream of letters and pamphlets, and in particular attacking Lord Mansfield, who was then regarded, as he still is, as one of our most eminent judges:

> Your lordship's firm and persevering conduct has effected what our laws never could. And an Englishman is under the necessity of being absolutely free from faults and indiscretions – which is difficult – or your friend – *which is impossible.*

He was lucky to escape prosecution.

Then another gentleman in Brentford invited Horne to take his son to Italy, so, leaving his parish in the care of a curate, he set off again. Wilkes by now had been expelled from Parliament and was living in self-imposed exile in Paris where he was squandering his own and his wife's fortunes, and the two men met there. Wilkes recognised Horne as a man of outstanding talents who was likely to be of use to him in the future, and so it fell out. Soon after Horne's return to Brentford, there was a by-election in Middlesex and Wilkes came back to contest it. Horne was able to distinguish the candidate's profligate personal life from his political beliefs, and he devoted himself to the cause: he canvassed all round the county, on foot and on horseback; he pledged himself to the full amount he was worth and obtained the use of the two best inns in Brentford; he addressed the electors, and declared that in a cause so just and holy, he would dye his black coat red. His opponents stirred up physical violence and hired ruffians to attack the crowds; one man died, and Horne went in person, accompanied only by a night constable, to find the murderers (one of them was a giant, nicknamed 'the infant') and arrested them in an alehouse near Covent Garden. Wilkes was elected, but the result was declared void and Colonel Luttrell was put up against him; he polled 296 votes against 1143 for Wilkes, but he was declared the duly elected member – and when the furious mob attacked him, it was Horne who went to his rescue.

Horne now became involved in a series of legal proceedings. There was *Bigby* v. *Kennedy* – the case of the widow Bigby: her husband had been murdered by the Kennedy brothers, in circumstances so atrocious that it was confidently expected that they would be convicted and executed; and so they would have been but for the charms and influence of their sister Poll who managed to secure their pardon; so the widow revived the ancient 'appeal of blood'[16] against them in order to obtain compensation. Horne knew that the King's pardon was of no avail in this procedure, and he retained John

Dunning, now a Serjeant, at his own expense, to argue the case for the widow; but Mansfield CJ threw so many obstacles in the way that she was unable to proceed.

In the same year there was a libel action brought against Horne by George Onslow, arising out of a poisonous letter in the press which may, or may not, have been written by Horne. The case was tried before Mansfield CJ himself, and the jury brought in a verdict for the plaintiff with £400 damages, but Horne appealed and the case was argued before the Twelve Judges who ruled that the Chief Justice had misdirected the jury and set the verdict aside. Horne was delighted at the result: he had publicly proved that Lord Mansfield was not infallible, and from then onwards he took every opportunity to belittle him.

In 1769, he was involved in the case of Doyle and Valline, two Spitalfields weavers, which gave rise to his first conflict with James Eyre, who, a quarter of a century later, was to preside over his trial for treason. The two weavers had been involved in a riot, and had been sentenced to death in accordance with the usual formula – 'You shall be taken from hence to the place whence you came, and from thence to the usual place of execution'. Eyre was the Recorder of London, and he added an extra clause to the sentence, namely that the execution should take place 'at the most convenient place near Bethnal Green Church', no doubt as a deterrent to the neighbourhood. As soon as Horne heard about this, he denounced it as a palpable variation and warned that anyone who obeyed the warrant would be guilty of murder. The Sheriffs took counsel's opinion and petitioned the Crown, and the Twelve Judges were consulted; in the end the two men were executed at Bethnal Green, but from that day on, until the abolition of public executions, the mode of passing sentence was altered to prevent any variation between the judgment and the order for execution.

Horne and Eyre were involved in another dispute at about the same time. The City of London addressed a remonstrance to the King, complaining of the misdeeds of his ministers, and when this was rejected, Horne prepared another remonstrance. In normal circumstances this would have been read to the King by the Recorder, but Eyre refused to accompany the delegation to the Palace on the ground that the Address was libellous, so it was read by the Town Clerk.[17] Eyre was summoned to the Common Council and told that he would no longer be consulted or employed in the affairs of the City; the King, however, looked on his conduct in a different light, and soon afterwards appointed him a Baron of the Court of Exchequer.

Many political associations were springing up at this time and in 1769 Horne founded the Society for Supporting the Bill of Rights, to conserve the constitution as it had been established in 1688, and to support Wilkes and anyone who had been wrongly imprisoned for political offences, notably a printer called Bingley whose case established the doctrine, which is still today a fundamental principle of our law, that a man cannot be compelled to incriminate himself – 'the right to silence'. Under Roman law, a man could be compelled to disclose his own guilt; a refusal to answer amounted to contempt of court, and he could then be imprisoned until he did answer. Although this practice had been abolished by statute in 1673, Mansfield CJ directed that Bingley was to answer certain questions, and on default to be committed for contempt. Horne was delighted to have another opportunity to confront the Chief Justice; he investigated the law and advised Bingley to stand firm, and eventually Mansfield CJ was obliged to yield and Bingley was discharged.

Horne had also been giving Bingley financial support and assumed that the Bill of Rights Society would do likewise, but when it was moved that £500 should be raised for him, Wilkes voted against the proposal and also accused Horne of embezzling the funds which had been raised for the widow Bigby and the Spitalfields weavers. The two men embarked on an acrimonious correspondence in the press, trading insult for insult over a period of many months; and the Society was dissolved and replaced by the Constitutional Society[18] which consisted of many of the original members, but without Wilkes and his friends.

Horne was now 37. He had given up all hope of preferment in the Church; he was so notorious that his application to Cambridge to proceed to the degree of Master of Arts, which would normally have been conferred as a matter of routine, was opposed by many senior members of the University. However, it was supported by Dr Beadon and eventually granted.

His parents were now both dead; some of his friends were encouraging him to go to the Bar; and so, in 1773, he resigned his living and rented a house nearby in Windmill Lane, where he prepared himself for his new profession.

However, his plans were interrupted. Horne had a friend called William Tooke who had purchased an estate at Purley, in Surrey; his neighbour, Mr de Grey, was the lord of the manor and the two men became involved in litigation about fish ponds and rights of common, and an attempt was made to settle the dispute by Act of Parliament. So in 1774 a bill was introduced to enable de Grey to inclose various commons and fields, and Tooke cross-petitioned on the ground that the proper procedures had not been followed. De Grey's supporters were determined to rush the bill through all its stages until, on the day before it was due to be read for the last time, Tooke came to Horne to seek his advice. Horne devised a desperate measure; he wrote an anonymous address, under the title 'Strike but Hear!' in which he libelled the Speaker of the House, and had it published by Henry Woodfall in the Public Advertiser on the following morning. When the House sat, Woodfall was summoned to the bar, and he said that he had been authorised to disclose the name of the author – 'It was Mr John Horne, who was at that very moment in the gallery, ready to answer for himself.' Many Members hated Horne and were delighted that he had delivered himself into their hands, but the supporters of the bill began to be alarmed, for they realised that his action was in some way connected with it. So Horne came down to the bar where he declared his real motives; he was taken into custody and detained for some days – but the proceedings on the bill were stopped, the offending clauses were omitted, and resolutions were passed to prevent precipitate action in future.

The problem of Tooke's estate was soon overshadowed by a much more serious crisis. Horne had always maintained that the doctrine of 'no taxation without representation' applied to the colonies as it did, in theory, to Great Britain; he was one of the first to express his concern at the treatment of the Americans, and he decided to take the first opportunity to act in the boldest and most resolute manner against the measures which were being taken. The opportunity came at a meeting of the Constitutional Society on 7 June 1775; news of the battle of Lexington had just been received, and he proposed a resolution that:

> A subscription should be immediately entered into...for raising the sum of £100, to be applied to the relief of the widows, orphans, and aged parents, of our beloved American fellow subjects, who...[had been] inhumanly murdered by the king's troops at or near Lexington and Concord.

After the motion had been carried, Horne added his signature, and the resolution was sent to the press.

No government could have been expected to ignore such a publication. However, the events which had taken place in America were, at that stage, more in the nature of riots and it was not until two years had passed, and the disorders had developed into a general rebellion, that the Crown decided to take action. Horne appeared on a charge of seditious libel at the Guildhall on 4 July 1777. The case was tried before Mansfield CJ; Wilkes, in his capacity as an Alderman of the City, was sitting beside him on the bench.

The defendant opened the case by raising various points of law, leading on to an attack on Mansfield CJ's conduct in the Onslow case. This developed into a three-sided argument between the judge, Thurlow A.-G. and the defendant – Gurney, the shorthand writer, lost his way at one stage and simply inserted in square brackets 'Here some promiscuous altercation ensued'. Eventually, however, the Attorney-General was able to proceed with the case. His opening address to the jury was brief and to the point; the evidence was restricted to the formal proof of the publication of the documents in question, and lasted little more than 20 minutes, and most of this was taken up in cross-examination of Woodfall, the printer, about his previous relationship with the defendant.

Horne then addressed the jury for some four or five hours, on a variety of topics ranging from murder and sodomy to the prosecution of Prynne in the Court of Star Chamber and the massacre of Glencoe; from time to time he discussed events in America and the charge on which he was before the Court. He then endeavoured, without success, to call the Attorney-General as a witness; but he did call three other witnesses, including a subaltern who had served in America and had been present at the Battle of Lexington, according to whom, the colonists had fled before the British had opened fire.

Horne was convicted, and sentenced to 12 months' imprisonment and a fine of £200. He appealed to the House of Lords, briefing Lee and Dunning to argue the case on his behalf, but the appeal was dismissed. He served his term in the King's Bench Prison in St George's Fields. For £500 paid in advance, but later converted into a weekly tenancy, he found accommodation in a small house 'within the rules'[19] and there he was visited by his friends, and they instituted a regular meeting every Wednesday at the Dog and Duck nearby. Horne had previously been very abstemious, but now began to indulge himself with a few glasses of wine. Before long, he contracted jail fever,[20] for which in those days red wine was the recognised cure; and he regularly felt better on Wednesdays and Thursdays, after which his health declined until the following feast-day. So he had recourse daily to claret, which cured him completely of the fever, but had the unfortunate side effect of inducing gout,[21] from which he suffered occasionally until his death.

After his release from prison, aged 43, Horne applied to Inner Temple to be called to the bar. Several attorneys had promised to brief him, and the profession regarded him as well qualified to practise; but he had earned the hostility of those in power, and particularly of Lord Mansfield, and his application was rejected, on the excuse (according to Stephens) that he was a clergyman.[22] Angry and frustrated, he turned his attention to agriculture and bought a farm in Huntingdonshire, where he drained the fields, introduced better strains of grass, and grew cabbages for his cattle. Unfortunately, he suffered a violent attack of ague and had to abandon his scheme. So he returned to London and rented a house in Richmond Buildings, Dean Street, Soho, where he soon recovered, and where he was nearer to the centre of government and politics, and he frequently attended debates in both Houses of Parliament. It was here, under the date 1780, that his biographer first mentions the two Harte girls, Mary and Charlotte; they were then at boarding school, but lived with Horne during the school holidays, and then for the rest of his life. These two girls were Horne's illegitimate daughters: he looked after them when they were young; they looked after him when he was old. I have been unable to discover anything about their mother except that Horne was making financial provision for her for the rest of his life.

At this period Horne was passing much of his time with his friend William Tooke at Purley; it was now coming to be assumed that he was to be Tooke's heir, and it was in 1782 that he adopted the new surname, and he will now be referred to as Horne Tooke, the name by which he is usually known. He was also engaged at this time in writing his first book. He had always been interested in language, and in 1786 he published the first volume of *The Diversions of Purley* which consisted of a detailed account of the etymology and parts of speech of the English language, and took the form of a dialogue between the writer and Dr Beadon. He maintained his interest in politics, and continued to give his support to the young Prime Minister; like Pitt, he was a moderate reformer – some of those who wished to reform the government, he used to say, would travel in the coach as far as Windsor, but he would be set down at Hounslow. He advocated annual elections by all who were charged for taxes or rates at £2 p.a.; each elector, on casting his vote, was to pay two guineas out of which the elected members were to receive a salary of £400. He and Pitt both joined the Constitutional Club, and wore its blue and scarlet uniform with buttons inscribed 'King and Constitution'; and at the general election of 1788 he gave unstinted support to Pitt against the opposition in the person of Fox.

*   *   *

The British had had several centuries of parliamentary experience, the French had virtually none; nevertheless, in the spring of 1789 some six million French taxpayers were registered and voted for 'primary assemblies', which in turn elected delegates to 'general assemblies', who finally elected the six hundred members of the Third Estate to represent the commons of France. It was a remarkable achievement and led to the meeting of the Estates General at Versailles in May. On 20 June, the Third Estate found that the door of their chamber was barred against them, so they met in a tennis court nearby, and swore an oath never to separate until they had drawn up a constitution. Some three weeks later, the National Assembly, as the Estates General was now known, drew up a Declaration of Rights. On 13 July, riots broke out in Paris, and the crowd marched to the Bastille and assaulted it on 14 July; within a few weeks, it was demolished, and bits of stonework were distributed as souvenirs – Horne Tooke acquired a piece and kept it in his study. On 15 July, the Marquis de Lafayette was invited to accept the command of the Paris militia, which soon became the National Guard; and three weeks later, on 4 August, the feudal system was abolished and the nobility surrendered their hereditary rights.

In Great Britain, the Revolution was greeted with widespread enthusiasm. On 4 November 1789, the Society for commemorating the Revolution (i.e. the Glorious Revolution of 1688) held its annual dinner to celebrate the birthday of William of Orange. In the morning, Dr Price, who had written a book called *Observations on Civil Liberty* in support of the American colonists, preached a sermon at the Old Jewry on 'The Love of our Country' during which he produced his definition of liberty: it consisted in three parts, he said – the right of liberty of conscience in religious matters; the right to resist power when abused; and the right to choose our own governors, to cashier them for misconduct, and to form a government for ourselves.[23] Price went on to declare: 'I could almost say, "Lord, now lettest thou thy servant depart in peace, for mine eyes have seen thy salvation." After sharing in the benefits of one revolution, I have been spared to witness two others, both glorious'.

Later in the day, with the third Earl of Stanhope (whose father had recently died) in the chair, Dr Price moved an Address to congratulate the National Assembly of France on its successful revolution; this was forwarded to Paris under the signature of the Earl, and further correspondence ensued between the Society, the French Assembly, and various provincial societies in France.[24] Burke, who declared that Price's sermon was in a strain which had not been heard in the kingdom since 1648, was known to be composing a reply to the Address, and the Earl sent him a 30-page pamphlet to forestall the arguments which he was thought to be advancing; many copies of this were printed and distributed, and a French translation, *Apologie de la Revolution Française*, was widely circulated in France.

On the first anniversary of the fall of the Bastille, a magnificent meeting was held in the Champs de Mars, attended by the king and his family, the National Assembly, M. de Lafayette riding on a white horse, and a vast concourse of people, including 50,000 Guardsmen from all over France, who all took the oath of allegiance 'To King, to Law, and Nation'.

In London, on the same day, 632 gentlemen met for dinner at the Crown and Anchor in the Strand; they all wore cockades, and a stone from the Bastille was on the table – at one stage, a waiter climbed up on the table and lifted the stone up to his head to the applause of the company. Earl Stanhope presided and made a speech in favour of the Revolution, and Sheridan moved a resolution rejoicing in the establishment and confirmation of liberty in France. This was greeted with vehement applause, but Horne Tooke, who, for once, was having misgivings about the Revolution, moved an amendment expressing satisfaction that the subjects of England had a much less arduous task than the French, and only needed to improve their constitution. A copy of the resolution was sent to Paris, accompanied by a letter from the Earl, and was received with acclaim in the National Assembly. The Assembly, and many provincial societies in France, replied to the Earl; the reformers of Nantes held an Anglo-Gallic festival on 23 August and sent their president, M. Français, to London, where he stayed with the Earl and was received by a committee of the Revolution Society under the chairmanship of John Hurford Stone, who was soon afterwards to settle in France and take French citizenship.

At about the same time Burke published his *Reflections on the French Revolution*; it immediately became very popular but he used some unfortunate phrases – his reference to the 'swinish multitude' was particularly tactless and unpopular.

There were many replies to the *Reflections*. There was the schoolmistress Mary Wollstonecraft, who wrote *The Vindication of the Rights of Man*; there was her future husband, William Godwin,[25] the son of a dissenting minister from the Fens, who worked for 18 months from five in the morning to midnight in bachelor lodgings in London to produce his *Political Justice*. There was the young Scotchman, James Mackintosh, who, in *Vindiciae Callicae*, advocated the abandonment of all appeals to precedent and tradition to rely on justice and reason. But it was Paine's *Rights of Man* that was the best known.

CHAPTER 2

THE NEW SOCIETIES AND THE *RIGHTS OF MAN*

Thomas Paine (see Figure 4) had been born in Thetford in 1737, the son of a Quaker staymaker; he had been a sailor, staymaker and exciseman before taking an active part in the American Revolution. He was now back in England, living at the Angel, Islington. His *Rights of Man, Part I* was published in March 1791; much of it was simply a reply to Burke, but it also contained an outspoken criticism of monarchy and aristocracy, and of the doctrine that the Revolution settlement of 1688 was sacrosanct. He attacked the fundamental principles of the English constitution; indeed, he denied that there was any such thing as an English constitution, pointing out that the Act which declared that Parliament should sit for seven years showed that there was no constitution in England, and that Pitt's bill for the reform of Parliament was based on the same erroneous principle: 'The right of reform is in the nation in its original character, and the constitutional method would be by a general convention elected for the purpose.' The book received immediate acclaim. Only a week after it was published, the Society for Constitutional Information passed a resolution to thank Paine for:

> his most masterly book...in which not only the malevolent sophistries of hireling scribblers are detected and exposed to merited ridicule, but many of the most important and beneficial political truths are stated in a manner so irresistibly convincing, as to promise the acceleration of that not very distant period, when usurping borough-sellers, and profligate borough-buyers, shall be deprived of what they impudently dare to call their property – the choice of representation of the people.

By now, opinions in England were becoming polarised between the ardent reformers and the equally ardent supporters of Burke and the Constitution. The reformers were coming to be associated with the Dissenters, who were increasing their demands for the removal of their legal disabilities. It had not escaped their notice that the principle of religious equality had been treated as fundamental, both in America and in France: article X of the French Declaration of Rights, as translated in Paine's book, read – 'No man ought to be molested on account of his opinions, not even on account of his *religious* opinions, provided his avowal of them does not disturb the public order

THOMAS PAINE.

Figure 4. Thomas Paine, by Romney and engraved by William Sharp, the friend of Horne Tooke and regarded as the finest engraver of his time. (By permission of the Trustees of the British Museum.)

established by law' – thus religious freedom had been achieved in Catholic, despotic France whilst, a century after the Glorious Revolution, many English protestants were still disabled. The Church of England in turn began to regard itself as being under threat and 'Church and King' clubs were being set up to support the constitution. The antagonism between the two parties spilled over into violence, or threats of violence, on 14 July 1791.

In Manchester, that 'great, nasty, manufactoring town',[1] the self-styled Constitutional Party threatened to pull down the house 'in which the popular party assembled over the heads of its members...; the brains of every man who assembled there would much be improved by being mingled with brick and mortar';[2] however, it so happened that one of the leading reformers, a cotton merchant called Thomas Walker, was also the borough-reeve for the year, and he was able quell the disorder.

In Birmingham, another of the new industrial towns, in the worst outbreak of violence of the period, a crowd gathered round the hotel in Temple Row where a dinner was being held to celebrate the fall of the Bastille, and later set out to destroy the meeting-houses of the Dissenters. They probably intended to kill Joseph Priestley, who was the leading dissenting minister and also a chemist and physicist, and, although he himself escaped, they burnt down his house and his laboratory; there were rumours that papers were found in his house that showed that he was conspiring to burn the churches, blow up Parliament, cut off the King's head, and abolish taxes. After order was restored, a royal proclamation was issued, calling for the rioters to be arrested and brought to justice, and they were put on trial at Warwick Assizes. At first there were signs that the Crown would have difficulty in securing convictions, but prosecuting counsel and Perryn B., who told the jury that Dr Priestley, in both his private and public character, was an honour to society, took a firm line; four of the ringleaders were convicted, and two were executed.[3]

In London, the Society for Constitutional Information met to celebrate Bastille Day, and received and read in translation an address from Nantes:

> To the Friends of Liberty, assembled together at London on the 14th July, 1791, to celebrate the French Revolution.
> The Free Citizens from the banks of the Loire address their testimonies of brotherhood and good-will to the noble sons of liberty who inhabit the happy shores of the Thames.

After referring to the French nobility who were 'carrying the poison of their calumny into foreign parts', and to the Pope, 'Let the great ultra Montane Bramah excommunicate us; his impotent thunders will only serve to enkindle the fires which in France consume his effigy', the address culminated in the hope that

> we shall see the two first nations of the earth, England and France, united together in a holy league, to avenge the human race of those unpunished outrages which have disgraced it during so many ages.

A few weeks later, a meeting was arranged 'of the friends of universal peace and liberty' – probably the Society for Constitutional Information and other associated societies – to take place in the Crown and Anchor, to celebrate the anniversary of the abolition in France of 'the feudal system of injustice and tyranny, on the 4th August 1789'; but they were prevented from meeting 'by the interference of *certain unnamed and skulking persons*, with the master of the tavern, who informed us, that, on their representations, he could not receive us *there*'. However, the meeting was held about a fortnight later, and an Address was published, rejoicing at the French Revolution as a most happy event, and expressing astonishment that their own government should prefer to associate with the most despotic powers in Europe. And in November, the Revolution Society held its annual dinner; it was Dr Price's last appearance, and the old man clambered on to the table to propose a toast – 'The Parliament of Britain; May it be come a National Assembly'.

New societies were being founded and looked to the Society for Constitutional Information, and to Horne Tooke in particular, for guidance and advice; in the autumn of 1791, it seemed that the Society was taking over the functions of leading the opposition to the government – a fact which did not escape the notice of the Parliamentary Committee of Secrecy which was set up three years later.[4]

There had been a by-election at Westminster in 1790 and Horne Tooke had stood against the candidates of both main parties, Fox and Lord Hood; he attacked the enormous sums which had been spent in the two previous elections in bribery, violence and murder, and after the election he petitioned against his opponents, complaining of deliberate outrage and armed violence, and that no attempt had been made to inflict punishment, secure redress, or prevent a repetition of similar outrages in future. The petition was dismissed, and Fox sued for and was awarded the costs of contesting it.

Horne Tooke used to be consulted on a variety of topics and, sometime in 1790, a Mr Gow, a watch-maker, had called upon him and told him that his brother and several passengers on an American ship had been captured by a corsair and taken into slavery in Algiers. Mr Gow had come to seek his advice and assistance in securing their release. Horne Tooke's advice was to apply to the Privy Council, which would afford redress; when he was told that this had already been tried, Horne Tooke said that there was only one other course, and that was to ransom the captives. He opened a fund, to which he himself contributed, and persuaded others to do likewise. The plan was successful, and some time later, Gow's brother, still dressed in Algerian clothes, came in person to thank Horne Tooke. This led to Horne Tooke's first meeting with Thomas Hardy, a shoemaker who was in business at No. 9 Piccadilly (see Figure 5); when Hardy heard what had happened, he also called upon Horne Tooke, but for a very different purpose – namely to seek his advice as to the wording of the constitution of the London Corresponding Society.

Within three years, Hardy's handwriting was to be known throughout the land, and the government had formed the opinion that he was the mastermind behind a plot to overthrow the constitution.

Thomas Hardy was able to trace his ancestry back to a Frenchman who was the cup-bearer to King John of France; they had both been captured by Edward the Black Prince and taken to England. At an entertainment, the King of England, Edward III, asked his own cup-bearer to fill a glass of wine to the worthiest in the company, and he did so and presented it to his master. The cup-bearer to the King of France took this as an insult to his master, and struck his English counterpart on the ear, upon which the King of France

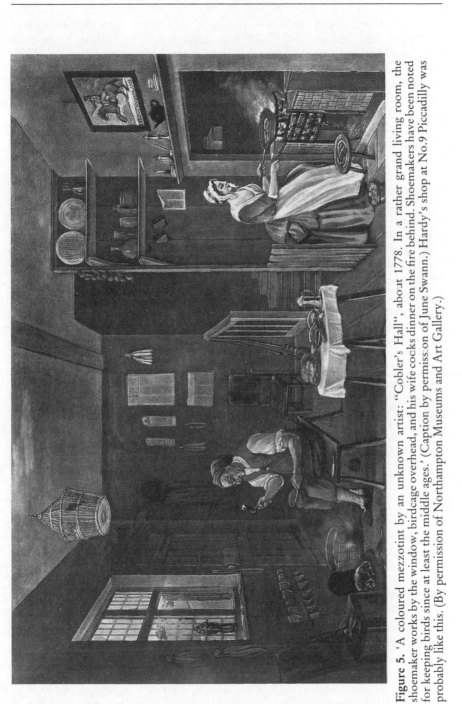

Figure 5. 'A coloured mezzotint by an unknown artist: "Cobler's Hall", about 1778. In a rather grand living room, the shoemaker works by the window, birdcage overhead, and his wife cocks dinner on the fire behind. Shoemakers have been noted for keeping birds since at least the middle ages.' (Caption by permission of June Swann.) Hardy's shop at No.9 Piccadilly was probably like this. (By permission of Northampton Museums and Art Gallery.)

called out *'trop, trop hardi'* – too, too audacious – but the King of England exclaimed *'sera deshormais Hardie'* – in future he will be Hardie. So he took the name Hardie, and *Sera deshormais Hardie* became the family motto. The King of Scotland was also a prisoner in England, and when he was released he took Hardie with him and gave him some land at Corresgarff in Mar. There the Hardies flourished until they quarrelled with the Clan of Grant and murdered the chief of the Clan, and as a result their estates were forfeited.

Thomas Hardy's father was a prosperous merchant seaman, who married the daughter of Thomas Walker, a shoemaker. Thomas himself was born on 3 March 1752 in Larbert, about a mile from the forest of Torwood where there was a huge oak tree with a hollow trunk in which Sir William Wallace, the Scottish patriot of the thirteenth century, had planned many of his exploits; Thomas often visited this tree when he was a boy.

Walter died at sea; it was thought that he had left enough to enable his widow and three children, of whom Thomas was the eldest, to live in comfort, and to give him a suitable education for the clerical profession; but the family's affairs fell into bad hands, and the widow was left destitute. So her father took Thomas under his care, and sent him to school to learn reading, writing and arithmetic; at that time, the price of tuition was 1d a week.

Thomas Walker also taught his grandson his own business, and he then sought work in Glasgow, a beautiful and populous city which had a flourishing trade with America. Many adventurers were setting up factories in America, and one of them was proposing to establish a shoe-factory at Norfolk, Virginia. He recruited workmen from Glasgow, and entered into an agreement with Hardy to superintend the enterprise for five years; however, as Hardy was not yet 21 and unable, therefore, to enter into a legally binding contract, his family interfered and prevented him from going. Not long afterwards, at the beginning of the American War, Norfolk was burnt to the ground by the British forces.

Hardy later found employment as a bricklayer at the iron works at Carron. The Carron Company had just established their foundry for cast iron, and needed a large work-force to construct their buildings. While Hardy was working on a house for the general manager, Thomas Roebuck, the scaffolding collapsed and the men fell into a cellar. One was killed and others were seriously hurt; Hardy was carried home, badly bruised, but soon recovered. He decided, however, not to return to bricklaying, and recommenced the trade of shoemaking with a man who had just settled in Scotland from London. Hardy's curiosity was aroused, and he made up his mind to see the metropolis; so he took a passage on board a smack and after 11 days, on 23 April 1774, he reached London. He was a total stranger in the capital, with no more than 1/6d in his pocket, but he had a letter of introduction to Mr John Kerr, with whom he lodged the first night, and who introduced him to other acquaintances. Hardy assured the readers of his *Memoir* that he was:

> from his earliest years, of a sedate and serious turn of mind, avoiding all those scenes of dissipation, which, too often, lead astray the youthful and unwary, to the ruin of both their morals and their constitutions. It must, however, be owned, that a

disposition to what is falsely called a life of pleasure, affords adventures, which, when afterwards related, conduce greatly to the entertainment of certain readers; but such as peruse these pages must expect nothing of the kind. The life of a plain, industrious citizen affords nothing of the light or the ludicrous circumstances which compose a great part of the frivolous reading of the present day.

Hardy soon became acquainted with many Dissenters. At that time the Scottish colony in London had a Presbyterian chapel in Crown Court, and Hardy became a member of the congregation. When the minister died, in 1784, candidates to replace him came from all over Scotland and England, and for two years they preached in turn, but met with little approval. One candidate, however, the Revd James Chambers, gave great satisfaction, and it was Hardy who wrote to him to ask if he would accept a call if one were given him. Chambers replied that he would accept, provided that the call was signed by the majority of the congregation. Hardy discussed the matter with some friends, and they convened a meeting; it was well attended, and Hardy was appointed chairman. He told them why the meeting had been called and, after some discussion, it was adjourned. Another meeting was held and a deputation was appointed to wait upon the elders, with a request that they should convene a general meeting of the Church to consider giving Chambers a call. However, the Elders refused to comply and insinuated that there was something wrong with him. The supporters of Chambers regarded this as a calumny, and the congregation was split into two factions – the elders and their supporters on one side, and the friends of Chambers on the other. The latter entered into correspondence with many ministers in Scotland, who knew Chambers, to find out if his moral character was good, and many certificates of his reputation were received. At the same time, the Elders were ransacking all quarters to discover something that would justify their allegations, and eventually succeeded in discovering that Chambers had two wives, one in Scotland, and one in England. A meeting of both parties was then called, with Chambers present, so that the whole affair could be thoroughly discussed, and the result was that both sides became pretty well satisfied of the truth of what had been said. Hardy did not take the story any further, but it may be presumed that Chambers did not receive the call.

Hardy was also the innocent cause of another embarrassing incident at the Chapel.[5] He was a friend of Lord George Gordon, and invited him to come one Sunday to hear a young man from the Highlands of Scotland preach the sermon. Unfortunately, the highlander was unable to come, and another man preached, who actually read his sermon, which so displeased Lord George that he interrupted him in the middle, telling him that it was contrary to the rules of the Kirk of Scotland to read a sermon from the pulpit. However little they may have liked the preacher, this extraordinary interruption gave great offence to the congregation. Lord George knew no one present, very few knew him, and Hardy himself had been detained at home by illness in his family. Lord George called for Hardy, who had invited him, and who he supposed had played him a trick; the congregation, on the other hand, thought that Hardy had sent him to create a disturbance: the poor man was in an awkward position, although he was in fact innocent of the whole affair. Once again, Hardy failed to tell his readers the final outcome of this episode.

In 1781, Hardy married Lydia[6] Priest, the youngest daughter of a carpenter and builder in Chesham in Buckinghamshire, and they lived together 'in spite of all the tricks of fortune, in the most perfect state of connubial happiness', and she bore him six children, who all died young.

Hardy carried on his business with varying success. He became friendly with Col. Smith, the son-in-law and private secretary of John Adams, the first Ambassador from the United States to England. He supplied Col. Smith with boots and shoes, and was encouraged by him to emigrate, but something always occurred to stop him from going abroad.

Towards the end of 1791, Hardy was offered a partnership with a currier and leather cutter, who promised to supply leather and provide a market for as many boots and shoes as he should make. He agreed to this proposal, and took the house which was soon to become so famous, No. 9 Piccadilly.[7] He started to carry out his side of the bargain, but he had hardly settled into his new house when his partners deserted him and broke their contracts. He had no capital of his own, but a friend came to his assistance and enabled him to carry on his trade. Number 9 was at the east end of Piccadilly, a fine site for a shop. Every evening, at eight o'clock, the mail-coaches for Bath, Bristol and the West Indies, for Exeter and Lisbon, set out from the Gloucester Coffee House; over fifty stage-coaches left the White Horse Cellar nearby every day for the West Country.[8] Within a few minutes' walk were St James's Palace, and Buckingham House where the Royal Family usually lived when in London, and Carlton House where the Prince of Wales had his establishment, and the Opera House in Haymarket.

Nevertheless, Hardy began to feel the pressure of taxation and the rising cost of living[9] which he attributed to the corruption of the so-called representatives of the people in Parliament. He asked himself whether the cause of the people was hopeless, or could the nation set itself free? He studied the tracts which had been published by the Society for Constitutional Information, and he devised a plan for establishing a new Society to tell the people how their rights had been lost and might be recovered. He drew up a set of rules for this Society, and he submitted them to three friends at supper one night. They approved of his scheme, and decided to meet weekly at a public house, and to invite others to join them to promote the objects of the Society.

The first formal meeting was held on 25 January 1792[10] at the Bell, in Exeter Street, off the Strand. There were nine men present. They met after work and, after their usual supper of bread and cheese and porter, they smoked their pipes and talked of the hardness of the times, and eventually the conversation turned to the topic for which they had assembled, namely parliamentary reform. Hardy produced the rules and preamble which he had drawn up, and it was proposed that all who wished to become members should subscribe their names, and endeavour to promote the objects of the Society. To this proposal, all except one agreed (and he became a member at the next meeting).

Hardy produced a book which he had bought for the purpose, in which the members set down their names, and, as in the journeymen's clubs in London, they paid a subscription of 1d a week.

There was some discussion about the name of the Society: Hardy recommended the London Corresponding Society, and that was the name which was adopted; he was then appointed secretary and treasurer. There was 8d in the treasury that night, but within a fortnight the sum had increased to 4/1d. The name of the father of the Society remained unknown at the time; some thought it was Horne Tooke or Paine, but this did not worry Hardy as he feared that it might be disadvantageous if it became known that such an obscure person was its founder. The first chairman was Maurice Margarot, who was, as his name suggests, of French origin; his father was a wine merchant who carried on business in Devonshire, and it was there that Maurice, who had been born in 1745, was brought up until he went to Geneva University. He was employed in the family business and had travelled to Portugal and the West Indies, as well as in France.[11]

During the spring of 1792, Hardy and Margarot prepared a constitution for the Society; on 2 April, a draft was submitted to Felix Vaughan, a member of the Society and a barrister, for his professional opinion. It was a lengthy document. It started with a preamble, reminiscent of the American Declaration of Independence – 'that all men are by nature free, equal and independent of each other', etc. – and went on to recite some of the grievances of the people: the Corn Act, which artificially raised the price of bread for the benefit of the landowners; the Game Laws, which robbed everyone of their constitutional rights and subjected them to 'the brutality of a bashaw[12] in the form of a country justice'; the Excise Laws; the Mutiny Act; the Impress Service (i.e. the press gang); and above all, the failure to have proper representation in Parliament. The body of the constitution then set out the procedure for admitting members: candidates were to be proposed by members, and could only be admitted if they gave satisfactory answers to certain questions, e.g. 'Are you convinced that every man...ought to have a vote for a representative and not more than one vote? Will you, by all justifiable means endeavour to promote a reform in the parliament of this country...?'

An important feature of the constitution, in which it resembled the Jacobin Clubs in France, was the provision for expansion. The Society was to be divided into divisions, each of which was not to exceed 30 members; once a division had more than 16 members, it was entitled to split so that the Society should spread throughout the country. There was also a well-drafted disciplinary procedure, under which any member believed to have acted improperly could be prosecuted before a jury of other members.

The text of the constitution was then embodied in an Address to the Nation at large, dated 24 May 1792, in which the writers went on to declare:

We find that the constitution of our country (which was purchased for us at the expense of the lives of our ancestors) has, by the violence and intrigue of criminal and designing men, been injured and undermined in its most essential and important points; but particularly in the House of Commons, where the whole of the supposed representation of the people is neither more nor less than a usurped power, arising either from abuses in the mode of election and duration of Parliaments, or from a corrupt property in certain decayed corporations, by the means of which the liberties of this nation are basely bartered away for the private profit of members of parliament.

In the whole country, 257 members (a majority of the House) were elected by less than a thousandth of the people, whereas Sheffield, Manchester, Birmingham, Leeds and Wolverhampton had no electors or representatives at all. And they went on to say 'that while we boast the best constitution, the mildest laws, the freest government, we are in fact slaves'. They called for An Honest Parliament, an Annual Parliament, and added optimistically: 'Soon then we shall see our liberties restored, the press free, the laws simplified, judges unbiassed, juries independent, needless places and pensions retrenched, immoderate salaries reduced, the public better served, taxes diminished, and the necessaries of life more within the reach of the poor, youth better educated, prisons less crowded, old age better provided for, and sumptuous feasts at the expense of the starving poor, less frequent.'

Hardy sent the draft of the Address, unsigned, to the Society for Constitutional Information for its views and after Horne Tooke had read it, he inserted Hardy's name at the end and sent it straight off to the press. The London Corresponding Society then had copies printed as handbills and sent a copy to Henry Dundas, the Secretary of State, with a covering letter in which Hardy claimed his protection and added that, unless he specifically withheld it within ten days, it would be assumed.[13] Copies of the covering letter were kept and these were seized, along with the Society's other papers, two years later, but rather surprisingly it was never mentioned at Hardy's trial, either by the prosecution or by the defence.

Hardy also showed the Address to Col. Smith, who said tersely, 'Hardy, the government will hang you'.

Other societies were springing up. In Sheffield, a Constitutional Society was founded in 1791 by 'four or five mechanics of good character' at the Cock in the Square;[14] William Broomhead, a cutler and scissor finisher, was its secretary, and its numbers grew rapidly. It so happened that a freed slave, Gustavus Vassa, was living with Hardy at 9 Piccadilly, and was writing his Memoirs there; Hardy wrote a letter about him and the slave-trade to a Shefffield clergyman; and this led in turn to correspondence between the Sheffield Constitutional Society and the London Corresponding Society.

In the spring of 1792, a Constitutional Society in Manchester was in correspondence with Horne Tooke and the Society for Constitutional Information, to seek their advice on the publication of an abridged edition of the *Rights of Man* – 'I wish you, as a friend of Paine's, and of mine, would be kind enough to take care that Paine's reputation is not mangled by mangling his book'.

On 19 April a group met at the Three Tuns Tavern, Southwark, and resolved to form themselves into a society to be known as the Friends of the

People; Charles Grey, who was to take the Great Reform Bill through Parliament forty years later, was a member, as were many other Members of Parliament. They passed a declaration that they were wearied with the unmeaning names of Whig and Tory, and of Ministerial and Oppositional parties. And there were other societies in London – the Aldgate Friends of the People, the Constitutional Whigs at Frith Street, and some more Friends of the People who met at Furnival's Inn.

At this period the Society for Constitutional Information was meeting on Friday evenings at No. 4 Tooke's Court. Horne Tooke was a regular attender, as were Major Cartwright; Paine's solicitor, John Bonney; Stewart Kyd, a barrister; William Sharp, the engraver; Thomas Holcroft, the novelist and playwright; the Revd Jeremiah Joyce, a dissenting minister; John Richter, a manservant; and a man who was always described simply as Mr Banks, probably Thomas Banks, the celebrated sculptor who was known as a violent democrat.[15] On 27 April they wrote to the Friends of the People; the letter contained the sort of language which was customary from this body, e.g.:

> When this society, sir, contemplates that flood of light and truth which, under a benign Providence, is now sweeping from the earth despotism in all its forms, and infringements of rights in all its degrees, to make way for freedom, justice, peace, and human happiness; and when it sees your society announce itself to the world as the Friends of the People, it rests assured that this new institution abundantly partakes of that light, that it embraces that truth, and it will act up to the sacredness of that friendship which it professes, by nobly casting from it, with disdain, all aristocratic reserves, and fairly and honestly contending for the people's rights in their full extent.

The letter was unsigned, but sent to the Friends of the People in the name of Major Cartwright, who was in the chair that evening.

The next meeting of the Friends was held on 12 May, under the chairmanship of the Rt. Hon. Lord John Russell; they evidently realised that they were getting into deep waters, and Lord Russell himself wrote back:

> ...We wish to reform the constitution because we wish to preserve it. We must beg leave...to decline all future intercourse with a society whose views and objects...we cannot help regarding as irreconcilable with those real interests on which you profess to inform and enlighten the people.

There was no such hesitation on the part of the 'nest' of societies, as the Attorney-General was later to describe them, which were being formed at Norwich, a city which, with a population of 30,000 or more, was one of the largest in the country outside London. In the county, peasants were losing their land and their rights of common under enclosure acts and were flocking into the town where the principal industry was the manufacture of worsteds; there had been an extensive export trade to Europe, the East Indies and North America, and the artisans had built their houses in every available space – timber-framed, three-storeyed buildings with continuous windows on the top floor to provide light for the workers. But the trade had been hit by the American War, and by competition from the new cotton mills.[16]

A meeting of the delegates of the Norwich United Constitutional Societies was held at the Wheel of Fortune, St Edmund's, on 24 March, and they wrote to the Society for Constitutional Information, saying that their societies consisted of 'some hundreds' with new societies forming. Another society at Norwich, known as the Revolution Society, wrote to the Society for Constitutional Information on 26 April; this letter contained an outright attack upon the settlement of 1688:

> It is willing to hope the redress of every existing grievance at the hands of a government resulting from an extraordinary convocation, in 1688, of all who had at any preceding time been elected representatives of the people assisted by the hereditary counsellors of the nation, and a peculiar deputation from the metropolis,[17] which National CONSTITUTING Assembly cashiered for misconduct a king of the House of Stuart.

While these societies were being formed, Paine was writing Part II of his *Rights of Man*, which was dedicated, on 9 February 1792, to M. de Lafayette. It contained much material relating to the monarchical system, with passages such as: 'Hereditary succession is a burlesque on monarchy. It puts it in the most ridiculous light, by presenting it as an office which any child may fill. It requires some talents to be a common mechanic; but, to be a king, required only the animal figure of a man – a sort of breathing automaton.' Once again, the book was an immediate success, but Paine was hated venomously among the aristocrats and loyalists, who wore 'Tom Paine' nails in their boots to trample him underfoot; he was burnt in effigy in towns and villages throughout the country, and tokens were struck showing him suspended from a gibbet.[18] It was at about this time that there was an attempt to set fire to the House of Commons by hanging an old pair of breeches, stuffed with combustible material, in the ceiling of a room under the House, and the Public Advertiser published a skit in which it was stated that Paine would be unable to attend the enquiry about the fire because his breeches had gone to be re-seated.[19]

A few weeks after his book was published, Paine wrote to the Society for Constitutional Information, to warn them that he had been informed that the government was intending to prosecute him, and asked for their help in bringing out a cheap edition of his book – 'a nation (as well the poor as the rich) has a *right* to know what any works are that are made the subject of a prosecution'. The letter was read at a meeting of the Society on 18 May, its first meeting to be held at the Crown and Anchor which was to be its venue from then onwards. The Society resolved to give Paine all the assistance it could, and to have 3000 copies of his letter and of their own resolutions printed. The following week, they ordered 6000 more copies to be printed and distributed – 1200 each to Sheffield and Norwich, and 200 to the other societies. About this time, the Society paid 12 guineas for printing, and 9/11d for the despatch of a parcel to Sheffield, and 8/3d for the same to Norwich.

The following week, it was decided to distribute many more, including 1200 to Manchester and 400 to Scotland. A letter from the London

Corresponding Society was then read which included a reference to *The Rights of Man*:

> It gives us infinite satisfaction to think that mankind will soon reap the advantage of Mr Paine's labours, in a new and cheaper edition of *The Rights of Man*.
>
> We are, however, no ways surprised at the report of a prosecution being commenced against his works, for, by the doctrine substituted for law in England, that truth constitutes the libel, the very many truths in both volumes of *The Rights of Man*, render them completely libellous.

The Society for Constitutional Information ordered that the letter should be published in the press.

The government was evidently becoming increasingly concerned at the spread of literature which they regarded as subversive and, on 21 May, the Crown issued a proclamation for suppressing publications.[20] The King himself addressed the House of Lords, and it was on this occasion that the Prince of Wales made his maiden speech,[21] declaring himself a firm supporter of the government – 'it would be treason to the principles of his mind, if he did not come forward and declare his disapprobation of those seditious publications which had occasioned the motion before his lordships'.

The royal proclamation was debated in the House of Commons on 25 May, and this led to Paine writing to Secretary Dundas on 6 June.

> Sir, as you opened the debate...on the proclamation for suppressing publications, which that proclamation (without naming any) calls wicked and seditious, and as you applied those opprobrious epithets to the works intituled RIGHTS OF MAN, I think it unnecessary to offer any further reason for addressing this letter to you.

He repeated and defended what he had said in his book, and pointed out that he had lived in different countries, and under different systems of government, and was therefore a better judge of the subject than Secretary Dundas could be. He then dealt with the Prime Minister in forthright terms:

> But it is needless now to talk of mere theory, since there is already a government in full practice; established upon that theory, upon the Rights of Man, and has been so, for almost twenty years. Mr PITT, in a speech of his some short time since, said, 'That there never did, and never could exist, a government established upon those rights, and if it began at noon, it would end at night.' Mr PITT is not yet arrived at the degree of a school boy in this species of knowledge....
>
> The system of government purely representative, unmixed with anything of hereditary nonsense, began in America.... So powerful is the representative system...that America was enabled thereby totally to defeat and overthrow all the schemes and projects of the hereditary government of England against her....

Then he set out the accounts of the annual expenditure of the United States. In those days the total expenditure of Congress and the federal government, including £4006.16.0 for firewood, stationery and incidental expenses, amounted to £66,275.11.0. He repeated his own budget proposals, which had already been set out in Part II of *The Rights of Man*, for the establishment of old age pensions and marriage and family allowances, and the payment of

Members of Parliament, to be financed out of savings made by curtailing the expenses of government, and concluded this part of the letter by referring to a passage in his book, 'which Mr Dundas (a man rolling in luxury at the expense of the nation) had branded with the epithet "wicked"':

> ...the poor laws, those instruments of civil torture, will be superceded.... The hearts of the humane will not be shocked by ragged and hungry children, and persons of seventy and eighty years of age begging for bread... Widows will have a maintenance for their children, and not be carted away, on the death of their husbands, like culprits and criminals....

According to his budget, there would still have been a surplus of nearly £1½m which could be employed for disbanding and pensioning the Army and Navy; and he finished the letter: 'I am, Mr Dundas, not your obedient humble servant, but the contrary, Thomas Paine'.

A copy of this letter was in the hands of the Society for Constitutional Information at their meeting of 8 June, and they arranged for its publication and distribution throughout the country. A week later, when Horne Tooke was in the chair, they received a letter from the London Corresponding Society who said that they had opened a subscription for Paine's defence so they resolved to open their own subscription for him. On 22 June, Horne Tooke reported that an information had been filed against Paine; Mr Favell, the treasurer, 'having a great many similar concerns on his hands', asked to be excused from receiving the subscriptions, so they were paid to Mr Bonney instead.

The following week, the Society arranged to distribute copies of the letter: 1200 each to Manchester, Norwich and Sheffield; lesser numbers to various other towns throughout the country, to affiliated societies in London and to private individuals, and '700 Mr Johnson, St Paul's Church-yard, for different parts of the country'.

It was now July, but very few people in England dared to celebrate Bastille Day that year.

CHAPTER 3

REVOLUTION, REGICIDE AND WAR

In France, the king was still on the throne; by the Constitution of 1791, he had power to appoint a ministry, and to make war and peace; he was the commander-in-chief of the armed forces; and the nation was to provide 'for the splendour of the throne' at the expenditure of 1m sterling a year. But since his abortive attempt to flee the country, he was now a virtual prisoner in the Tuilleries. It was against this background that Joel Barlow, an American agent then travelling in Europe, addressed a letter to the French people, in which he poured ridicule upon the Constitution, declared that in place of the maxim that 'The King could do no wrong' there should be a new one, 'That Kings can do no good'; and recommended the establishment of a republic.

During the spring of 1792, Prussia and Austria entered into an alliance and France declared war on the latter in April. Prussia was waiting to invade; riots and rebellions and counter-rebellions were in progress in the provinces. On 20 June, 1792, the anniversary of the Tennis Court Oath, a massive procession took place in Paris; the crowd planted a tree of liberty[1] in the Garden of the Capuchin near the Tuilleries; they danced *La Carmagnole* and sang *Ca ira*;[2] they forced their way into the palace and compelled the king to put on a red cap of liberty.

M. de Lafayette hurried back to Paris from the northern frontier to try to calm the situation, and offered the king the support of his men; and about the same time Charles Barbaroux, the deputy for Marseilles, formed a scheme of his own and sent home for 500 men to join him. On 5 July the Marseilloises, as they were called in those days, set out, bringing with them Roger de Lisle's famous song which was soon to oust *Ca ira* in popularity. Rumour went ahead of them – they had been terrorising the south of France; they came from the gaols of Genoa and Corsica; their progress towards Paris was marked by robbery, rape and murder.[3] On 29 July they reached Paris, and they dined[4] that evening at the *Cadran Bleu,* the Blue Dial, in the Champs Elysées (places were set for 1200, it was said). Quarters were found for them in the southeastern outskirts of the City and from there, on 10 August, they marched to the Tuilleries. They crossed the river unopposed, and the king and the royal family abandoned the palace and took refuge with the Assembly which was sitting in the Riding School near by. The Marseilloises, and men from Brest and Alsace, assaulted the palace and killed the Swiss Guards who attempted to defend it, and later in the day the Assembly moved that the king, the 'hereditary representative', be suspended and that a National Convention be summoned. This was the Revolution of 10 August 1792.[5]

A few days later, the royal family was transferred to the Temple, where the king was to remain for the rest of his life. And a few days after that, a machine for decapitating criminals, like the one which had so long, long ago fallen into disuse in Halifax,[6] was set up in the Place de Carrousel; it was sometimes called the Louisette after the surgeon who advocated its use, sometimes the 'national razor', but is more usually known by the name of its designer, Dr Guillotin.

Although a Convention had been summoned, the Legislative Assembly continued to sit. The Prussians and Austrians were invading France from the east, but in the midst of this turmoil, on 26 August, the primary elections for the Convention were held, and on the same day the Assembly conferred citizenship on the 'chief Foreign Friends of Humanity' – including George Washington, Thomas Paine, Horne Tooke and Joseph Priestley. A few days later, Paine was elected by the Pas de Calais to a seat in the Convention, and Priestley was elected by Orne and Rhône-et-Loire; Priestley declined the honour, but Paine accepted.

*   *   *

It was at about this time that Horne Tooke left his house in Richmond Buildings, and went to live in Wimbledon, 'a neighbouring village', where he resided for the rest of his life. He had always been interested in gardening, and he wished to spend the remainder of his days in cultivating his flowers, managing his fruit trees, and 'regulating the economy and disposition of his esculents'; the rearing of cauliflowers and cabbages, the planting of gooseberries and currants were matters in which he took great delight. His house, big enough for a large family, was detached and pleasantly situated, with two fields in front where he kept a couple of cows. The two Miss Hartes, still children, lived with him; and he had a small but valuable library. Henry Dundas, the Secretary of State, bought a house next door, their two gardens separated only by a ha-ha.[7]

He was 56 now, and in poor health. Ever since his youth he had suffered from a malady which, said Stephens, 'proved extremely inconvenient. This consisted of a difficulty in performing one of the natural functions of nature, which obliged him to have recourse to a peculiar management, in order to transact business without interruption or engage in the usual amusements of life.' In spite of his ill-health, he was strong and athletic, and of middle height; his eye was particularly expressive, said Stephens – 'it had something peculiarly keen as well as arch in it; his look seemed to denote a union of wit and satire'. When he first looked at a stranger, he seemed to take a *peep into his heart*. His dress 'savoured of the old school', and added an air of dignity to his conversation. He had discarded the black garb of the priesthood, as well as the blue and silver of the Grand Tour of Europe. His coat was of a dark brown

English broad-cloth, with no collar, while his cuffs were adorned with a row of steel buttons; his waistcoat was handsomely tamboured; his stockings were of silk; he wore long ruffles at his wrists; and his hair was long and powdered.

His regular Sunday dinner parties started at about this time; his guests might arrive as early as 11 a.m., but more usually, early in the afternoon; if the weather was fine, they walked round the gardens. Dinner was served at 4 p.m., in the parlour looking over the common. The host led the company through the hall, where the chairs were covered in coats and hats; at the table, he usually placed strangers or the most distinguished guests near to himself. The dinner was always excellent and substantial. Both white and brown meats were served; at the top of the table there was fish – turbot, soles or cod – all with their appropriate sauces; and this was followed by a fillet of steak; in the centre there was a tureen of soup, and at the bottom a round of beef or a sirloin. As side dishes, there were the products of his garden; and there were excellent white pies and puddings. The host, although he had a hearty appetite and always ate well, now found time for his jokes and gibes. After the cloth was removed, various wines were served, usually Madeira, sherry or port, accompanied by fruit which Horne Tooke had grown in his garden: Alpine strawberries, Antwerp raspberries, and Dutch currants in the summer; grapes, grown on a high south-facing wall, in the autumn; apples and pears – charmaentel, jargonel, the chrisan, brown bury – followed on during the winter, well-preserved into the spring.

One curious feature of these parties was the total absence of any silverware; the food was always served in earthenware or china, but the spoons, etc., were of pewter. The reason for this was that Horne Tooke's house had been broken into through the roof and the thieves made off with most of the plate, which was never recovered. On the morning after the burglary, Horne Tooke went to London with the surviving silver and deposited it at his bank. From that day on, no article of silver was kept or seen at his house.

Horne Tooke presided at these weekly feasts and took an active part in the various topics of conversation and whenever a serious dispute arose, an appeal was made to his judgment. He preferred not to offend either party by making a peremptory decision (unless it was on some issue of law, or the constitution, or religion); instead, where possible, he settled the argument by a joke, and was usually sufficiently skilful as to resolve the question and set the table laughing.

✵ ✵ ✵

In September, Horne Tooke wrote a letter to Petion, the mayor of Paris, in which he said that he had raised £1000 for France and asked for the name of some person in London to whom money could be given in the assurance that it would be remitted to Paris without delay or fraud: 'We can now begin the patriotic contribution towards our patriotic gift of £1000 sterling; and I have no doubt but in time it will amount to several thousands'.[8]

Paine, accompanied by John Frost, set out to Paris, taking this letter with them, and on 20 September, the very day on which the French declared themselves a Republic (and the day on which the new French army withstood the attack of the Prussians at Valmy), Frost sent Horne Tooke a long account of their arrival in Paris:

> My dear Sir;– we arrived safe at this place yesterday to dinner; and, having met with no interruption on our journey, by night or by day, since we left Dover, except delay at Abbeville, Amiens, Clermont, and for want of horses, which the emigrants have wore out. Paris is now quiet, though it was illuminated, and the guards under arms from an apprehension of the people visiting the Temple to destroy Louis and his wife; the latter braves it, and will to the last; the former is insensible to his fate.... Mr Paine made his appearance in the National Assembly last night, which excited great curiosity among both men and women, and occasioned no small interruption. The first who embraced him was Cambon, who last night made a most excellent speech on the subject of the jewels, plate, &c. found in the churches, &c. in order to have them melted, as hitherto most infamous use had been made of them, by pawning them to the Jews, &c. to raise money for the emigrants. This motion was become the more necessary, as, a few nights ago, that is, on the morning of Tuesday, 40 men armed, entered the Thuilleries, and carried off 30 millions of livres. The gates of Paris have been shut, and a search made: more than a million has been found. The treachery of Louis is so great, that the indignation of the people cannot be wondered at. He has anticipated the civil list a year and a half, and mortgaged his domains for six years. The bankers, and others who have advanced the money, will be ruined.

Frost said that he would forward a detailed account of 10 August, and went on to give a description of the military operations which were being carried on by the Prussians and Austrians, before returning to his and Paine's affairs:

> We dine today with Pethion. Paine has entered his name on the roll of parliament, and went through the forms of office with a great deal of nonchalance.... Mr Paine is in good spirits; and indeed the flattering reception he has met with all through France, could not fail of it. It is more than I can describe. I believe he is rather fatigued with the kissing.... Always your's, J. F.

One topic was omitted from this letter: during the first week in September, in the first outbreak of the Terror, over a thousand men had been massacred in the prisons of Paris, including two hundred priests and some Swiss Guards who had survived 10 August and were being held in captivity.

On 21 September, Hardy wrote to the Society for Constitutional Information, proposing that they should join the London Corresponding Society in sending an address to the French National Assembly to 'assure that suffering nation that we sympathise with them in their misfortunes...and that should those in power here dare...to join the German band of despots, united against liberty, we disclaim all concurrence therein....'

On 25 September, in the 'First year of the Republic',[9] Paine wrote a letter to the People of France, which was later published and distributed by the London Corresponding Society:

> Fellow Citizens:– I receive with affectionate gratitude the honour which the late National Assembly has conferred upon me, by adopting me a citizen of France; and the additional honour of being elected by my fellow citizens a member of the National Convention....

I am well aware that the moment of any great change, such as that accomplished on the 10th August, is unavoidably the moment of terror and confusion... But let us now look calmly and confidently forward, and success is certain. It is no longer the paltry cause of kings, or of this, or of that individual, that calls France and her armies into action. It is the great cause of ALL. It is the establishment of a new aera, that should blot despotism from the earth, and fix, on the lasting principles of peace and citizenship, the great republic of man....

When the bagatelles of monarchy, regency, and hereditary succession 'shall be exposed, with all their absurdities, a new ray of light will be thrown over the world, and the revolution will derive new strength by being universally understood....

Let us begin the new aera by a greatness of friendship, and hail the approach of union and success. Your fellow citizen, Thomas Paine.

Paine's letter, like Frost's, contained no reference to the September massacres.

On 1 October, Boncher Rene wrote to Horne Tooke on behalf of the mayor of Paris, thanking him for his letter and saying that he would forward the name of some person through whom money could be transmitted to France; Horne Tooke received this letter on 9 October, and shortly afterwards another letter from Petion himself:

Brothers and Friends;– Liberty is a bond which ought to unite all men, and which will one day unite all nations. There are preparing those great revolutions which disseminate useful truths. Thus the philosophical societies make all despots tremble. You have the glorious advantage of deserving the hatred of your government. The league of tyrants will never be able to resist the power of reason....

Your fellow citizen, Petion. 6th October, first year of the French Republic. Society of the Friends of the Revolution.

By the time this letter was read out at the Old Bailey, two years later, Petion had fled to Bordeaux, and his dead body, half eaten by dogs,[10] had been found in a cornfield.

Horne Tooke was now a French Citizen, and about this time he wrote to the President of The Convention:

Mr President. Thirty years ago I travelled in France when she was enslaved. I received a thousand civilities, and I was chagrined at her destiny. I now come to acquit myself of a small part of my former debt to France, in her state of freedom. I entreat her to accept these 4000 livres, and to apply them to the expenses of the war against all the tyrants who have dared, or shall dare, to attempt against her liberty, without excepting anyone, were it even of my own country. As to the debt of honour newly contracted as a French citizen, it will be the object of the rest of my life to acquit myself of it faithfully and with great zeal.

In the meantime, Hardy and Margarot had written an address to the French nation:

Frenchmen! While foreign robbers are ravaging your territories, under the specious pretext of justice; cruelty and desolation leading on their van, perfidy with treachery bringing up their rear, yet mercy and friendship impudently held forth to the world as the sole motives of their incursions, the oppressed part of mankind forgetting, for awhile, their own sufferings, feel only for yours, and with an anxious eye on the event, fervently supplicating the Almighty Ruler of the Universe to be favourable to your cause, so intimately blended with their own.

Frowned upon by an oppressive system of control, whose gradual, but continued encroachments, have deprived this nation of nearly all its boasted liberty, and brought us almost to that abject state of slavery, from which you have so emerged, 5000 British citizens, indignant, manfully step forth to rescue their country from the opprobrium brought upon it, by the supine conduct of those in power....

Though we appear so few at present, be assured, Frenchmen, that our number increases daily; it is true, that the stern uplifted arm of authority at present keeps back the timid, that busily circulated impostors hourly mislead the credulous, and that court intimacy, with avowed French traitors, has some effect on the unwary, and on the ambitious. But, with certainty, we can inform you, friends and freemen, that information makes a rapid progress among us.... Men now ask each other, what is freedom? what are our rights? Frenchmen, you are already free, and Britons are preparing to become so!...

Seeking our real enemies, we find them in our bosoms; we feel ourselves inwardly torn by, and ever the victims of a restless, all-consuming aristocracy, hitherto the bane of every nation under the sun! Wisely have you acted in expelling it from France.

Warm as are our wishes for your success...a sense of our duty, as orderly citizens, forbids our flying in arms to your assistance; our government has pledged the national faith to remain neutral:– in a struggle of liberty against despotism, Britons remain neutral! O shame!...

Dear friends, you combat for the advantage of the human race. How well purchased will be, though at the expense of much blood, the glorious, the unprecedented privilege of saying, mankind is free! Tyrants and tyranny are no more! Peace reigns on earth! And this is the work of Frenchmen.

This address was signed on 27 September and Hardy visited M. Chaveline, the French Ambassador, to find out whether he would transmit it to Paris; he agreed to do so, and a deputation waited upon him on the following day, when the Address was read to him. He forwarded it to Paris, where the Convention ordered it to be printed and copies to be sent to each of the eighty-four departments, and to be read at the head of the Armies of France; it was also printed in the Paris newspapers, and in this form returned to England. When Barlow heard about this, he sent Hardy a copy of his own Letter to France, along with a covering letter in which he said that his observations were of general application, and that the present disposition in Europe towards revolution was founded in a current of public opinion too strong to be resisted, and too sacred to be treated with neglect.

On 11 October, Hardy's Address was read at a meeting of the Society for Constitutional Information who appointed a committee to draw up their own address to the National Convention; this was read and approved on 9 November:

Servants of a Sovereign People, and Benefactors of Mankind:– We rejoice that your revolution has arrived at that point of perfection which will permit us to address you by this title; it is the only one which can accord with the character of true legislators. Every successive epoch in your affairs, has added something to the triumph of liberty; and the glorious victory of the 10th August, has finally prepared the way for a constitution, which we trust you will establish on the basis of reason and nature....

From bosoms burning with ardour in your cause, we tender you our warmest wishes for the full extent of its progress and success. It is indeed a sacred cause...; but it is our real opinion, that we now speak the sentiments of a great majority of the English nation....

At the same meeting, the Society appointed Frost (who had now returned to England) and Barlow to take the Address to Paris, along with a gift of 1000 pairs of shoes, and a promise of a further 1000 pairs a week for six weeks.

In reality, however, the attitude of the public in England was now hardening against France. Sir Samuel Romilly, who in 1789 had expressed the opinion that the French Revolution was the most glorious and happiest event that had ever taken place, now, in September 1792, wrote 'one might as well think of establishing a republic of tigers in some forest of Africa as of maintaining a free government among such monsters'.[11]

In the autumn of 1792, the government decided to prosecute Paine for Part II of *The Rights of Man* as a seditious libel. He was still in France and the case came on for trial in his absence before Kenyon CJ in the Court of King's Bench on 18 December. Paine had written a letter, dated Paris, 11th November, First Year of the Republic, which the Attorney-General read to the Court; the writer said that his duty to the National Convention of France prevailed over his duty to return to England to stand trial, and he deliberately went out of his way to aggravate his guilt by saying that the government of England was the greatest perfection of fraud and corruption that had ever taken place. Thomas Erskine was briefed for the defence, but Paine was found Guilty.[12] As he was abroad, no sentence was imposed.

In the meantime, Frost and Barlow had reported back from France to the Society for Constitutional Information, dating their letter on 29 November, 'at the Bar of the Convention'; they said that they had executed the Society's commission and had presented the Address, which had been received with universal applause: 'After which, the president gave us the kiss of fraternity in behalf of the French nation which we returned in behalf of our society. The scene was truly interesting to every feeling of humanity, and drew tears from a crowded assembly'. In addition to reading the Address, they had told the Convention that innumerable societies were forming in every part of England, Scotland and Ireland, and predicted that it would not be long before there would be a national convention in England; and they added that the 1000 pairs of shoes were now in Calais.[13] Accompanying the report was a translation of the president's answer:-

Brave children of a nation which has given lustre to the two worlds, and great examples to the universe; you have addressed us with something more than good wishes, since the condition of our warriors has excited your solicitude....

Your islands, it is said, were severed from the continent by a great convulsion of the globe; but liberty, established on the two shores of the narrow sea which divides us, will repair the breach, and restore the two nations to the harmony and friendship for which nature has designed them....

It was not only from Paris that the Society for Constitutional Information received fraternal letters. On 2 December 1792, the Committee of

Correspondence of the Society of Friends of Liberty and Equality at Laôn wrote a letter to thank the Society, presumably, for the shoes:

> Generous Republicans:– The philanthropic gift that you have presented to the warriors of France, announces, with energy, the great interest you take in the sacred cause which they are defending.
> Accept the thanks of a society that does honour to itself in esteeming you.
> The time, perhaps, is not far distant, when the soldiers of our liberty shall be able to testify their gratitude to you. Then their arms, their blood itself, shall be at the service of all your fellow citizens.... Then France and England shall together form a treaty of union as lasting as the course of the Seine and the Thames....

Four days later, the Society of the Friends of Liberty and Equality at Mâcon wrote to the Society, evidently in reply to one congratulating them on the revolution of 10 August, starting with the words:

> Yes, citizens, our brethren and friends, the 10th August, 1792, shall be distinguished in the annals of the world as the day of the triumph of liberty;

then, after setting out the imperfections of their first constitution, they went on:

> From thence, the necessary day of the tenth of August 1792. From thence, a second revolution, but a revolution which is only a completion of the first, which has received our vows and our oaths, and which we will bless for ever....
> Let intrigues, tools and tyrants calumniate us; we despise them, too much to condescend to answer them and seek for their esteem.... We behold the brave English adopt our principles, become our friends...soon they will become our allies, and, uniting our efforts, we shall go on to deliver the universe from the yoke of tyrants....

About a fortnight later there came a letter from the Committee of Correspondence of another Society; it commenced as follows:

> Apt, the 17th December,
> First year of the French Republic.
> The popular and republican society of Apt, department of the mouths of the Rhone, to the popular society, sitting at London.
> LIVE FREE, OR DIE!
> Citizens, Brethren and Friends:- How glorious it will be for France and England to have formed a confederacy destructive of tyrants, and to have purchased at the price of their blood, the liberty of Europe – we say more, of the whole universe....
> You will soon lift yourselves up against that perfidious court of St James's, whose infernal policy, like to that which found its tomb in the Thuilleries, has made so many victims in our two nations.... The popular societies of France desire ardently the epoch that shall permit them to address their vows to the national assembly of Great Britain, and to offer to the soldiers of the liberty of your nation, arms, bayonets, pikes.

All these letters were found among the papers of the Society for Constitutional Information.

✳   ✳   ✳

In Part I of *The Rights of Man*, Paine had commented on the free, straight speaking of members of the French National Assembly: 'Their parliamentary language...is free, bold and manly.... If any matter or subject respecting the executive department, or the person who presides in it (the King), comes before them, it is debated on with the spirit of men, and the language of gentlemen.'

The French National Assembly had now been replaced by the Convention, of which body Paine was a member; and in December, the King was put on trial for his life. Members of the Convention were using the sort of language which Paine had so admired. 'If you have to decide on the fate of Louis', said Jean Bon St André, 'it is because you are a revolutionary assembly, created by the French Nation in a state of insurrection.' Barrère, who was to be banished a few months later, said:

> 'Nothing was wanting to immortalize that assembly, but to have delivered France from the calamity of kingly government, and to have relieved you from the duty of judging the last of your kings. Invested, from your origin, with the most unlimited confidence by your fellow citizens, you hesitate in the first step. Am I then no longer in the midst of that national convention, whose honourable mission it was to destroy kings and royalty?'

Paine himself, as far as his limited knowledge of French would allow, tried to parry the attacks on the King by suggesting that he should be sent to America, and was at once roundly condemned by Marat as a Quaker who did not believe in the death penalty.

These and many similar speeches were printed in the *Moniteur* and copies were being imported into England, and a large number – many hundreds – were sold regularly by M. Joseph Deboffe, a Swiss bookseller in Gerrard Street, Soho.

On 17 January, the King was condemned to death. On the very next day, St André, who was in England, 'being considered by us as one of the most judicious and enlightened friends of human liberty', was admitted as an honorary member of the Society for Constitutional Information. One week later, Citizens Barrère and Roland were likewise admitted, and the resolutions for their admission were ordered to be published in the papers.

There was at that time a young attorney in London, John Adolphus; in later years he was to become a leading member of the Old Bailey Bar, and a leading historian of the period. Half a century later, he had these comments to make on the English radicals who were corresponding with France that autumn:

> Their obsequious adherence to French principles, and their applause of all the excesses that flowed from them, formed a strange instance of perverted depravity. Their congratulations on the invasion of the Tuileries were not restrained by the massacres of September; nor were their admission of some conspicuous regicides as honorary members, and the introduction of their ferocious harangues on their records withdrawn, when they saw the catastrophe and the cruelties to which they led the way.

The King of France was executed on Monday 21 January. Immediately, there was a surge of sympathy for him on this side of the Channel, and pictures of him taking his final farewell of his family, and of the scene of his execution, appeared in prints and on mugs and medals.[14] On 24 January the French and British ambassadors left their respective host countries; on Friday 1 February, France declared war on Great Britain. On that same evening, the Society for Constitutional Information held its regular weekly meeting at the Crown and Anchor, and resolved that the speeches of Citizens St André and Barrère be inserted in the books of the Society and that the resolution to that effect be published in the newspapers.

They were treading on dangerous ground. All those who were present at the Crown and Anchor that evening were exposing themselves to very serious risk, although in fact none of them was ever prosecuted for adhering to the enemy. It was also on 1 February that the London Corresponding Society wrote to the Friends of the People, chiding them for failing to give their whole-hearted support to the sentiments which they had expressed in their address to the National Convention of France. It was a fortnight before Edward Curteis, on behalf of the Friends, replied; his letter contained a clear warning as to the risks attached to any continued correspondence with France: 'On this subject all farther remark is now become unnecessary, as every good citizen must now feel himself precluded from all political intercourse with France...by a war, the principle of which we utterly disapprove, the inevitable evils of which we deeply deplore, and at the consequences of which we tremble.' The Society seems to have taken heed of this warning.

The government now thought it desirable to cut off supplies of arms and provisions from the enemy, so a bill was introduced for that purpose, and followed the pattern of acts which had been passed in previous wars. The new Traitorous Correspondence Bill covered not only commercial dealing and investment in French land or public funds (which were to become treasonable), but also the insurance of ships and goods belonging to the enemy, and travelling on enemy territory without a licence (which became subject to imprisonment). In spite of the existence of a state of war between the two countries, the bill was hotly contested, but was passed and received the royal assent on 7 May.

CHAPTER 4

SEDITIOUS CONSPIRACY

Although Hardy was concentrating on France, he was not neglecting other societies at home. During August and September 1792, he wrote to Lambeth, Manchester, and Stockport to 'Seize with joy the first opportunity of commencing an acquaintance and correspondence with men who act on a similar plan' to himself. A reply from Stockport inquired how a new parliament was to be chosen? 'Can we expect it from the present order of things? Would not all the evil be done away at once by the people assembled in convention?'

It was at about this time that a new paper, *The Patriot*, was established at Sheffield, and in October its editor wrote a letter to the secretary of the Stockport society, to advise them how to choose men to go as delegates into the villages, and how they should approach different kinds of people: as 'Sir Robert Walpole (one of the elders and fathers of corruption) very justly observed, every man has his price in the way of being bought'. The farmers of Lancashire, 'ignorant as the brutes they ride to market', could be aroused by the mention of tithes, shoemakers by the price of leather, and inn-keepers by the standing army which was frequently billetted in taverns. The editor then wrote to the Society for Constitutional Information to request its support for Stockport. This letter was considered by the Society at the Crown and Anchor during November and their answer contained a passage to which the prosecution attached considerable importance in the subsequent criminal proceedings:

> We rejoice with you in the increase of the members and societies of freedom.... Freedom, though an infant, makes herculean efforts; and the vipers, aristocracy and monarchy, are panting and writhing under its grasp. May success, peace, and happiness attend those efforts.

In November, a new society in Norwich, the Society for Political Information, wrote to Hardy to ask (and this was another passage subsequently stressed by the prosecution), 'whether the generality of the societies mean to rest satisfied with the duke of Richmond's plan only; or, whether it is their private design to rip up monarchy by the roots, and place democracy in its stead'. The London Corresponding Society were suspicious of this letter, and feared that they might be led into a trap; it was a fortnight before a reply was sent, and it bore simply the initials 'M.M. Chairman'. The letter was much more carefully worded than many; Margarot regretted that he had never heard of the Society for Political Information.

Simultaneously with the establishment of reforming societies, loyalists, usually calling themselves Church and King Clubs, were spreading throughout the country, and these were now co-ordinated by John Reeves, a barrister, already known as the author of a *History of English Law*. Reeves had just returned to England after serving a term as the Chief Justice of Newfoundland, and is believed to have had close contacts with the Home Office and the Treasury Solicitor. On 20 November 1792, he set up his organisation, ironically, at the Crown and Anchor; it was known as the Association for protecting Liberty and Property against Republicans and Levellers, it included many members of parliament and the peerage, and its object was to establish a network of societies to invite information relating to subversive activities, and to respond to the misleading doctrines of the *Rights of Man*. The Association used to meet, apparently, on the same day, but on a different floor, as the Society for Constitutional Information.[1]

It was in reply to Reeves that Margarot and Hardy wrote and published an Address on 29 November, declaring that it was indeed their intention to obtain a restoration of their lost rights: 'If at the revolution [in 1688] this country was adequately represented, it is now so no longer, and therefore calls aloud for reform'; and rejoicing in the revolution which had taken place in France – 'they have driven out the family that would have destroyed them, they have scattered the mercenaries who invaded their freedom, and have broken their chains on the heads of their oppressors'.

The government had been receiving reports of discontent among the working classes from many parts of the country, and on 1 December the Crown issued another Proclamation and mobilized the militia in ten counties.[2] In London, the Tower was fortified; in Manchester, a mob attacked and wrecked the offices of the *Manchester Herald*, and then tried to assault Thomas Walker's warehouse. Parliament was in recess when the Proclamation was issued, but was reconvened on 13 December, when the King announced its terms in the House of Lords. The government were also taking an increasing interest in the activities of the London Corresponding Society, which was having difficulty in finding premises in which to hold its meetings; it had no regular home, but committee meetings were often held in the Beaufort Building in the Strand, in a room fitted with benches and desks as in a school, and the president's chair at the end of the room in a sort of pulpit raised three feet off the floor. It was believed that spies were infiltrating the membership, so Margarot wrote a letter to Henry Dundas, the Secretary of State:

London, 4th December, 1792
No 10 High-street, Marybone.

Sir;–.... Confiding in the justice of our claim, in the merits of our peaceable demeanour, and our ready obedience to all the laws of our country, we imagine ourselves clear from all charge or imputation of sedition, rebellion, conspiracy or treason; and that in pursuing what no one can deny to be our *right*, we are entitled to every protection and support of government. – I therefore, in behalf of my fellow citizens, this day call upon the king's ministers to protect and uphold us in the pursuit of our *constitutional* rights; and require, that in future, our lawful and well regulated assemblies, may be no more disturbed or interrupted by the saucy interference of usurped authority, by men unnamed, working with threats upon the fears of uninformed publicans, and boasting of SECRET orders and warrants – as though Britain was fallen under a despotic government, and liable to be ruled, not by laws, but by proclamations, and to be subservient to ministerial dictates, written on a drum head, and proclaimed by the mouth of the cannon.

Equally known by his activity as by his knowledge of the laws, an honest magistrate, whose *spies* had well informed him of the nature of our meetings, has acknowledged that they were *peaceable*, innocent, and CONSTITUTIONAL, and further admits the necessity of a reform:– at your hands, sir, I therefore, demand justice and protection for the society against all ruffians, who, let loose on the public, have dared, or shall henceforward dare, like the satellites of ancient sanguinary tyrants, assume to themselves the double office of making laws and executing them. Certain that such an iniquitous system cannot originate in a British cabinet, we exclaim, may perdition light equally upon such vile miscreants, and upon their employers!

Were we, according to the hackneyed custom, to recur to precedents, we should say, that Mr Pitt, and the duke of Richmond, have themselves traced out the path which we now pursue, that they themselves have asserted the rights of Britons, to a fair, equal, and adequate representation in parliament – that they, themselves, had invited us to associate and discuss our rights; and we might add, that in so doing, they spoke, they acted like honest men – they were not then in office.

The writer went on to add that, if prosecutions were commenced against members of the Society, he would deem it a favour, and indeed claim it as a right, that they should be commenced against him.

Instead of delivering this letter in person to the Secretary of State's office, Margarot had it delivered at the General Post Office and an official receipt was obtained; copies of the letter and of the receipt were then printed and published.

Then there were Baxter's divisions, composed of the silk-weavers of Spitalfields. Spitalfields had been the centre of the silk-weaving industry for over a century, since the Huguenots had fled from France after the revocation of the Edict of Nantes and had settled there. For a time they had flourished, but in the middle of the Eighteenth century they had faced increasing competition from silk-mills established elsewhere in England, and from throwing-mills powered by water;[3] the industry became notoriously depressed and the district was the scene of frequent riots.

At a meeting of the London Corresponding Society, held at No. 8 Queen Street, Seven Dials on 7 February, it was reported that these divisions were very poor, and Margarot said that they must be preserved, going on to add, according to Lynam, a government spy, when giving evidence against Hardy, 'for they will be of great service if we go to war'. England and France had been at war for a week now, and at the trial Lynam was closely cross-examined as to what Margarot had said, but he persisted that the word 'war' had been used, and added that Margarot had said that the country would rise against the present government.

While the various divisions of the London Corresponding Society were meeting in private houses, the Society for Constitutional Information continued to hold its regular Friday dinners at the Crown and Anchor. Horne Tooke was a regular attender, but usually went home early, a point which was to become significant at his trial.

The meeting of 12 April was well attended. The Society had recently received a letter from the United Political Parties at Norwich, which considered three specific proposals – first, a petition to Parliament:

> 'We think ourselves under that degrading necessity to state our grievances to the House of Commons, with a request for redress, and should they refuse to grant our reasonable petition, we have still got (no thanks to them) a formidable engine, that will convey the insult to the remotest parts of the kingdom';

secondly, an address to the King: '... We are dubious of its good consequences'; and thirdly, a convention: 'and oh! that the period was arrived! – but in the present state of affairs, alas! it's impracticable'. In a postscript, the writer, J. Broughton, at St Mary's Church, added that there were thirty or forty separate societies in Norwich, besides many in the country villages. In his reply, dated 16 April, the secretary discussed the alternative suggestions: he regarded any petition to the Crown as hopeless, and was sure that a petition to Parliament would receive an absolute negative, but 'as to a Convention, we regard it as a plan the most desirable and most practicable, so soon as the great body of the people shall be courageous and virtuous enough to join us in the attempt'.

On 29 April, the Society for Constitutional Information held its anniversary dinner, with Lord Sempill in the chair. Lynam was present and recorded that the members talked very boldly, and laughed at the fears of the public – they were sure that a revolution would take place; and they drank toasts – The rights of man; May we never be ashamed to assent to those principles we wish to enjoy; May despotism be trampled under the hoofs of the swinish multitude; May the world be our country, and doing good our religion; Freedom to France, and peace to all Europe; Thomas Paine.

This was hardly a suitable time for pressing for parliamentary reform, but debates on this subject were taking place during the spring. A petition for reform was read at a meeting of the London Corresponding Society on 7 March, and copies were circulated to delegates to leave in coffee houses to receive signatures; five weeks later, it was reported that 2000 signatures had been obtained, and the Society resolved to stick bills up in the night, to inform the public where the petitions could be found for signing.

A leading advocate for reform was Sir Philip Francis; he had been a clerk in the War Office, from which humble position he had been sent to Bengal as a commissioner for regulating the affairs of India. He was an outspoken member of the House of Commons, and on 10 April he made a speech advocating a radical reform in the representation of the people; Margarot and Hardy wrote to thank him, and Francis replied on the following day, but he was not sanguine about the proposals:

> With respect to a parliamentary reform, the utmost that can be done by a few individuals in the House of Commons, and all that can be expected from them is, to take every favourable occasion to agitate the question, and to bring the subject as often as they can into public view and discussion.

The Society was also in correspondence with Fox, who wrote to them on 2 May: he said that he would present their petition if they so desired, but he thought it desirable that it should be presented by someone else, as he had always been an avowed enemy of universal representation.

A full-scale debate on the reform of the House then followed, opened by Grey who presented his argument in the form of a petition from the Friends of the People; Pitt replied on behalf of the government, saying that his own plans for reform had been taken over by 'wicked persons' who aimed at subversion. John Wharton called for the restoration of the constitution of 1688, but the time for parliamentary reform had passed, and the motion was defeated by 282 votes to 41.[4]

Meetings of the London Corresponding Society were desultory during the summer of 1793. However, thanks were given to Mr Wharton for his speech in the House of Commons, and the Society for Constitutional Information had 10,000 copies of the speech printed.

It was also during the summer that the London Corresponding Society had further correspondence with H. Buckle from Norwich. In a letter which the Society received on 25 June, Buckle, commenting on the suggestion which had already been put to the Society for Constitutional Information and their reply, said that he found their ideas congenial to his own, namely:

> An address to the king – futile; a petition to parliament (as a conquered people) – tolerable; a national convention (if circumstances admitted) best of all....
>
> Alas! where is the majesty of the people? An indifferent observer would suppose it to centre in stars and garters, ribbons and costly apparel, palaces, coaches and horses, with all the trumpery of futile amusements; and were it not for their accursed consequences, we could bear with it; but when we consider how many sweat, and toil, and starve, to support it, how can we be persuaded but that there is a contrivance between the land owners and the merchant to hold the people in vassalage?... but a rumour is spread from the south, and it is terrible to tyrants; it stings their mind – it galls their flesh – and like Pashur, are a terror to themselves, lest the people should assert their rights.

A month later, on 25 July, Hardy and Margarot replied. They said that they had sent in a petition, signed by near 6000 persons and then went on:

> We firmly pursue our purpose...under the eye of the court, in the middle of the metropolis, and in the very nest of place and pension hornets, the tavern where

Reeves, the tool of the junto, holds his inquisitorial tribunal, have lately held a general meeting of the society, [and] sent forth an address to the nation....

It may be more advantageous to humanity to show them at first, that their opponents are neither mob nor rabble, but an indignant oppressed people, in whom is not yet entirely extinct the valour of their forefathers.

Your neighbourhood must severely feel the dreadful consequences of an iniquitous, depopulating, and ruinous war; but you are not the only sufferers. From various parts of the country we learn, that the war abroad has already spread desolation at home; yet such is the blindness of some folks, that they talk of it being continued for years. Peace we wish to all men; but to such friends destruction.

※　　　※　　　※

In Ireland,[5] as in England, the French Revolution aroused strong emotions, but the majority of Irishmen, in view of their long-standing religious and commercial connections with France, supported the revolution, and a Catholic, pro-French organisation, whose members called themselves the Defenders, was founded in 1790. On 14 July 1791 the Dublin Volunteers held a parade, and at the end of the year a radical society known as the United Irishmen of Dublin was founded. Within a matter of weeks similar societies sprang up all over the country.

A particularly significant development at this time was the inclusion of Catholics among the reformers. In Ireland, the principle of religious freedom was reinforced by expediency in recruiting the bulk of the population to the cause; there was, therefore, a powerful alliance between the Roman Catholics and the radicals. The Irish Parliament was passing legislation to relieve Catholics of many of their legal disabilities, but they were not satisfied, and a formidable Catholic convention with some 280 members representing the counties and the large urban areas met in Dublin in December 1792, and presented a petition to the King to demand further concessions.

In the meantime, radicals were pressing for parliamentary reform; new Volunteer corps were formed, and a convention representing the whole of Ulster was held at Dungannon in February 1792. There was also a plan to form an exceptionally large Volunteer corps in Dublin; it was to be a thousand strong, dressed in sansculottes[6] and green cockades, and buttons bearing a shamrock crowned with a cap of liberty. The Dublin Society of United Irishmen had been infiltrated by a spy, John Collins, who warned the government what was happening, and that it was planned to hold the first meeting of the corps on 9 December 1792; the Privy Council issued a proclamation, effectively banning the assembly and the corps did not meet, but its secretary, a surgeon called Archibald Hamilton Rowan, did parade through the streets in his green uniform with a mob crowding at his heels.

During the following week, there was a private meeting of the Society of United Irishmen and an Address was drawn up. On 16 December, over a hundred Volunteers met in a fencing school in Cope Street; Rowan was there, and another leader of the Society, James Napper Tandy, handing round papers to the people on the floor and to others in the gallery. At Rowan's trial, two witnesses were called to describe what happened in the fencing school, but in essence the case for the Crown was contained in the Address which was circulated: its basic proposition was a call to arms, to defy the proclamation, and to hold a convention supported by force of arms to secure peace and freedom. Rowan was arrested very soon afterwards, but released on bail; there was then a long delay before proceedings were commenced, in spite of his demand for a speedy trial.

In 1793, while Rowan availed himself of the opportunity of going to Scotland, the Irish government, fearing a repetition of the Dublin Convention of 1784 but in a much more dangerous climate, took measures to control the activities of the radical reformers. The Irish parliament passed the Convention Act on 16 August; this was the Act which received so many adverse comments in England and Scotland.

*   *   *

After his return from Scotland, Rowan was eventually put on trial in Dublin on 23 January 1794, on a charge of seditious libel, before the Earl of Clonmell CJ and two other Irish judges. He briefed Curran, who was the great forensic orator of the time in Ireland and who spoke for two hours or more, but the Earl expressed his firm opinion that the address was libellous in the extreme; the jury took the same view, and after a retirement of about ten minutes returned with a verdict of Guilty. Rowan was conveyed to the New Prison, attended by both the sheriffs, and a formidable array of horse and foot-guards. During the next few days, attempts were made to have the case re-opened and new evidence called, but he was ultimately sentenced to a fine of £500 and two years imprisonment.

The United Irishmen were now in decline, but the Defenders had become increasingly active; they were secret societies, mostly Catholic, and with extreme radical views and close links with France. They swore oaths to 'be true and faithful to the present United States of F. and I'; they administered a catechism to new members, including such questions as 'Are you conse-crated?' 'I am.' 'To what?' 'To the National Convention – to quell all nations – to dethrone all kings, and plant the Tree of Liberty on our Irish land.' 'Where did the cock crow when the world hear him?' 'In France.' Their password was 'Eliphismatis', and they had special signs to recognise each other: by putting their hands on top of their heads and pretending to yawn.

It might have been supposed that there would have been strong links between the Defenders and their contemporaries in England and Scotland, but this does not seem to have been the case;[7] the Defenders were swearing oaths of allegiance to the United States of France and Ireland; a United Republic of Great Britain and Ireland never seems to have been on anyone's agenda. There was, however, one link between Ireland and the London Corresponding Society in the person of William Lawler. He changed sides later, and gave evidence for the Crown when several of the Defenders were put on trial in the winter of 1795/96, and much of his history was prised out of him in cross-examination. He said he was a protestant by upbringing and had been apprenticed as a carver and gilder to Jack Robinson in College Green,

Dublin; after three years, Robinson accused him of theft, and gave him a whipping, so he left and went to England in 1791. There, he enlisted in the 29th Regiment of Foot, but deserted a month later and changed his name to Wright, and it was under that name that he joined the London Corresponding Society, where he knew Baxter who had asked him if he would go and drill at Turnstile, Holborn . He was probably in England for a couple of years, and on returning to Ireland he joined the Telegraphic and Philanthropic Society, which was supposed to be a literary society, but was probably a cloak for a collection of revolutionaries. It was then that he became a Defender.

CHAPTER 5

OVER THE BORDER

The Parliamentary representation of Scotland was if anything more deplorable than that of England;[1] on the other hand, the holding of Conventions was a well-recognised part of the Scotch constitution. The Convention of the Royal Burghs had been instituted as far back as the Sixteenth century, and in the early 1790s it met to recommend reform in the methods by which the burghs themselves were governed.

Throughout the 1780s petitions for reform were repeatedly presented to the House of Commons; in July 1792, the Lord Provost of Glasgow had presided over a meeting which demanded frequent elections and universal suffrage. Reforming societies were being established; of these, the Society of the Friends of the People in Edinburgh was probably the strongest.[2] This Society held a Convention in Edinburgh for a few day in December 1792 and about 170 delegates attended.[3] With a view to demonstrating their peaceful intentions, they pledged to expel anyone who was guilty of disturbing the peace, but when some of them went to subscribe their names on the roll of the newly formed Goldsmith Hall Loyalist Association, they were rejected when they signed themselves 'Friends of the People'. One delegate called on members to take an oath to 'live free or die', which was sworn by the whole assembly with hands raised and prolonged cheering (although the oath was later erased from the minutes). The convention then adjourned until October.

In August 1792, Hardy had written to Scotland, expressing the hope that the Scottish societies would enter into correspondence with the London Corresponding Society; the proposal seems to have lapsed, but was revived in May 1793, when Margarot and Hardy wrote to William Skirving, the Secretary of the Friends of the People, inviting them to unite their endeavours. Skirving was the son of a farmer; he had studied for the ministry at Edinburgh University but changed his mind and he too became a farmer. He was interested in the theory of agriculture and had once applied for the Chair of Agriculture at Edinburgh University, and had recently published a book called *A Husbandman's Assistant*.[4] On 25 May, he wrote to Hardy. It was a long letter, even by the standards of 1793, and included, for example, a forecast that when the tabernacles of oppression in the palaces of ambition are broken down, under the madness and folly of their supporters, we may then, without anarchy and all dangerous delay, erect at once our tabernacle of righteousness, and may the Lord himself be in it!

*   *   *

There was in those days no Scottish Office. The Lord Advocate was the representative of the Crown north of the Tweed; he was his own legal adviser and counsel; and in 1792 he was Robert Dundas, the nephew of Mr Secretary Dundas who had himself been Lord Advocate for eight years. It was the Lord Advocate who had to decide what to do.

Early in 1792, he prosecuted John Morton, James Anderson and Malcolm Craig for sedition; they had been in the canteen of Edinburgh Castle, giving seditious toasts – 'George the Third and last' was one of them – in the presence of the troops of the 37th Regiment of Foot; they were convicted, and sentenced to nine months imprisonment in the Tolbooth. Other men were prosecuted on similar charges and imprisoned for short terms.

The light sentences imposed suggest that until then the Scottish courts had taken a relatively relaxed view of these events; the case of Thomas Muir, who was also charged with sedition, was different. Muir was himself a member of the Faculty of Advocates; he had been born in Glasgow in 1765, and it is said that he was an infant prodigy who had gone to the University of Glasgow at the age of 10.[5] He had distributed copies of Paine's *Rights of Man*; he had been haranguing the people and had taken an active part in the convention of the Friends of the People. He had left Scotland and gone to France – he was later to tell the Court that he had gone there to rescue the king from his persecutors. He returned to Scotland on 16 May (so he was, presumably, in France for some weeks while the war was in progress), but, although he said that he wanted to be put on trial, it was not until 31 July that he was found and arrested. He wanted to brief Henry Erskine who many years later wrote a letter to the editor of the State Trials in which he explained that he had agreed to act, but only on condition that the conduct of the defence should be left entirely to him; Muir declined his assistance on these terms and pleaded his own cause.

The case was tried in the Court of Justiciary on 30 August, 1793. The president of this court was the Lord Justice General, but he rarely sat and the Lord Justice-Clerk was his deputy – and in 1793 the Lord Justice-Clerk was Robert Macqueen, Lord Braxfield, Scotland's counterpart to Judge Jefferies (see Figure 6).

Lord Braxfield had been born in 1722 and became the best feudal lawyer in Scotland – he had been counsel for the Crown in the forfeiture cases following the '45 rebellion; he had been elevated to the bench in 1776 and was appointed Lord Justice-Clerk in 1788. He was, wrote Lord Cockburn[6] in the following century, a profound practical lawyer, a powerful man, coarse, debauched and illiterate, who had probably never read a book except textbooks on the law and two or three works of indecency; he was utterly devoid of judicial

Figure 6. Robert Macqueen, Lord Braxfield, Lord Justice-Clerk of the Court of Justiciary: that 'formidable blacksmith' who presided over the trials of the 'Scottish martyrs'; by Sir Henry Raeburn. (By permission of the Scottish National Portrait Gallery.)

decorum and had no conception of principle in a political case except the duty to uphold the party which had appointed him. He had a hard head for drinking and thinking, and a tyrannical will – he was strong built and dark, with rough eyebrows, powerful eyes, threatening lips, and a low growling voice, like a formidable blacksmith; his accent and dialect were exaggerated Scotch. 'Bring me prisoners, and I'll find you law', he used to tell his friends when they were hesitating to prosecute.

In Muir's case, after the evidence had been concluded, Muir himself addressed the jury in a long speech. The Lord Justice-Clerk then summed up, and it was then that he made known his own political and constitutional theories, evidently based on the doctrine of 'no representation without taxation':

> Mr Muir might have known that no attention could be paid by Parliament to such a rabble. What right had they to representation? He could have told them that Parliament would never listen to their petition. How could they think of it? A Government in every country should be just like a corporation; and, in this country, it is made up of the landed interest, which alone has a right to be represented. As for the rabble, who have nothing but personal property, what hold has the nation on them? What security for the payment of taxes? They may pack up all their property on their backs, and leave the country in a twinkling of an eye. But landed property cannot be removed.

Muir was found guilty of sedition, and sentenced to 14 years' transportation to Botany Bay.

The method of selecting or 'picking' a jury in Edinburgh[7] in those days was for the sheriffs of the three Lothians to send a list of 45 names, selected at their discretion, to the Justiciary-Clerk (an officer appointed by the Lord Justice-Clerk) who in turn selected 45 to attend the trial; and the Lord Justice-Clerk then picked any 15 of these as he chose. There was virtually no provision for challenging a juror, so, in effect, the judge could select whom he wished and be sure of securing a verdict in advance. Nevertheless, Muir's jury was astonished at the sentence which had been imposed. They were thunderstruck, said Lord Cockburn, at the severity of the sentence, and they thought Muir's guilt was so trivial that a few weeks imprisonment would have been sufficient, and they resolved to prepare a petition to the court, and to meet next day to sign it. But when they met, one juror produced a letter he had received, threatening to assassinate him for his concurring in the verdict – on which the jury separated, considering it impossible for them to interfere. And about 35 years later, Lord Cockburn asked a surviving juror if he could account for his conduct, to which he replied simply, 'We were all mad'.

The outrageous conduct of Lord Braxfield, and his hold over the juries, became clearer as the cases went on. When the editor of the State Trials was preparing the transcripts about twenty years later, he was astonished at what he read; but when he went to Edinburgh he found that the different reports of the trials were all almost identical, and, after he had consulted some of counsel who were still alive and had been involved, he decided that the records were accurate.

A fortnight after the case of Muir, the Revd Thomas Fyshe Palmer was put on trial for sedition before Lord Abercromby in the Circuit Court of Justiciary at Perth. Fyshe Palmer had been brought up in England – Eton and Queen's College, Cambridge – but had lived and preached for many years at Montrose. He was charged with the publication and distribution of inflamatory documents attacking the government, and he too was found guilty and sentenced to seven years' transportation.

*   *   *

During the summer, and notwithstanding the fate which had befallen Muir
and Fyshe Palmer, Skirving was organising the next convention. On 2
October, he communicated his plans to the the London Corresponding
Society; Hardy replied on 5 October[8] and he noted in a postscript that
Skirving should not mention the Society in any further correspondence 'for it
was a thousand to one that I received that letter by post'; he said that he and
Margarot regarded the general convention as 'a very excellent measure', and
added that if the Society received an invitation to send a deputation, it would
be accepted with pleasure. Such an invitation, also dated 5 October, was in fact
already on its way and was read to an open-air meeting of the Society held on
24 October in a garden behind a house belonging to Thomas Briellat at
Hackney. There was a throng of people there, perhaps as many as 4000; some
were under the impression that Paine was going to plant a tree of liberty, some
that the Jacobins had landed, some that the Society was going 'to lower the
price of provisions'.[9] It was at this meeting that Margarot and Joseph Gerrald
were appointed delegates to the convention.

Gerrald had been born in the West Indies. After his father's death, he was
sent to England for his education at Dr Parr's school at Stanmore; young
Joseph was talented (he was his ablest pupil, Dr Parr once said, not excepting
even Richard Sheridan)[10] but was expelled for 'extreme indiscretion' and sent
home. He spent several years in the West Indies and later in Pennsylvania,
where he was qualified as a barrister, and on returning to England he wrote to
Dr Parr asking him to renew the friendship; Dr Parr agreed and they entered
into a correspondence with each other.

The London Corresponding Society gave their delegates written instructions not to depart from the original object of the Society, namely to obtain
annual parliaments and universal suffrage by rational and lawful means.

The Society for Constitutional Information were also in correspondence
with Edinburgh, and at a meeting on 28 October they too decided to send
delegates, and drew up a set of instructions for them, with provisions for
paying them 7 guineas each for travelling, and a further 3 guineas a week while
the convention was sitting. George Sinclair[11] and Henry Yorke were
appointed, but the latter refused to go unless he was paid all his expenses in
advance.

The convention met on 29 October, a fortnight after Marie Antoinette had
been executed in France. The list of delegates and a complete set of minutes,
together with reports of some of the proceedings reprinted from the
Edinburgh Gazeteer, appear in the State Trials in the case of *R.* v. *Skirving*.
The 153 delegates who attended were mostly from the lowlands: apart from
one delegate from Montrose, it is doubtful whether anyone came from further
north than Perth and Dundee; there would later be a delegate, Matthew
Brown, from Sheffield as well as from the two London societies. Some
gentlemen, including Samuel Brown from Virginia, were admitted as visitors.

The convention sat at Mason Lodge Room on four days, 29 October to 1
November, sitting from 10 a.m. to 4.30 p.m. and again from 6 to 10 p.m.

Skirving was the secretary and had minutes prepared for the beginning of each session. It seems that the authorities in Edinburgh were already on the alert, for it was reported, on the first day, that soldiers were under arms and that patrols were on the streets; but the session passed peacefully. Two members were appointed to dine each day with Muir, who was still in the Tolbooth, and when the turnkey objected, a formal protest was made to the Lord Provost, who said that as many members as wished could dine with the prisoner as long as the convention was in session. Various resolutions were debated and discussed; whenever a motion was carried unanimously, the delegates stood up, joined hands, and congratulated each other. Resolutions were passed against the slave trade, but the recurring theme throughout was the need for universal suffrage and annual parliaments. Funds were collected each evening; they usually amounted to £2 or £3.

After the convention dispersed, a general committee meeting was held on 6 November, primarily to receive Margarot, Gerrald and Sinclair, who had just arrived from London (Yorke had not come; he was now said to be ill). Margarot said that 500 constables had attended their meeting in Hackney in order to apprehend them: 'They had overcome that obstacle. But a journey of 400 miles is not a journey of a moment'. He hoped that recalling the delegates would strike terror into their enemies, and went on to say that the reforming societies in London were very numerous; there were 50,000 reformers in Sheffield and its environs, and 30 societies in Norwich. If a convention of England and Scotland could be called, it might represent 600,000–700,000 males, a majority of the adults in the country. The chairman thanked the new delegates, including Hamilton Rowan and a Mr Butler from Ireland, and arrangements were made for re-convening the convention on 19 November.

Throughout the previous proceedings, all delegates had been referred to as 'Mr' or some appropriate title; in the minutes of this committee they were, for the first time, referred to, as in France, as 'Citizen'.

The English delegates then took rooms at the Black Bull, at the head of Leith Walk (where Gerrald, it is said, held morning *levées* 'crowded with worshippers'),[12] and on 7 November, Sinclair wrote to his Society to report his arrival. After describing 'the extreme joy shown by the friends of liberty here on our appearance among them', he went on to complain of the severity of the sentences which had been inflicted upon Muir and Palmer; Muir was confined in a small room with a stone floor, and was permitted no more than two visitors at a time; 'all judicial proceedings here are summary, and all punishments are severe in the extreme; if a man is suspected, he is immediately apprehended, and undergoes a secret examination'; Rowan had been arrested in Muir's room, only two hours after his arrival, on a charge of seditious intention:

> Since even the intentions of men are here become matters of legal inquiry, and, in some degree, of punishment, and as the crown lawyers may attribute what intentions they please to the accused, it is not improbable that the delegates from London, notwithstanding our utmost caution, may be honoured by a visit from these worthy alguazils.[13] Be not, however, apprehensive about us; for, upon examination, I find the proceedings here something more mild than the inquisition.

He closed his letter by inquiring what had happened to his colleague, Yorke, and saying that it was absolutely necessary for him to be replaced.

When the convention reassembled on Tuesday 19 November, the minutes indicate that there was a very different atmosphere. The English delegates – Margarot, Gerrald, Sinclair, and, to a lesser extent, Matthew Brown – monopolised the proceedings from the start (a fact which the natives no doubt resented, for the daily financial collections dropped by half). Members now referred to each other regularly as Citizen. Immediately the session opened, Margarot proposed that a 'committee of regulations' should be set up to draw up rules of procedure, and thereafter committees sat every morning (following the system which was then operating in Paris). On the following day, Gerrald made a speech on the Glorious Revolution, and subsequently recommended that the convention should apply to the Almighty for divine aid; from then onwards meetings were always opened and closed with prayers. Brown expressed the hope that the next meeting of the convention would be held in England; Gerrald said that York had been mentioned as an appropriate venue, 'but I can assure you, that city is the seat of a proud aristocracy, the seat of an archbishop; however, I would not object to going there – the Saviour of the world was often found in the company of sinners'. On the Saturday, Sinclair proposed a motion that the convention be known as the British Convention of Delegates of the People, associated to obtain universal suffrage and annual parliaments: this was unanimously agreed.

Much business was transacted during the following week, and on Thursday 28 November the convention passed its most momentous resolution (hereafter referred to as the Resolution of 28 November). This appears to have been proposed by Alexander Callender and was subject to an amendment proposed by Sinclair, and

> after an excellent discussion...the convention was resumed, and the whole as amended being read over, the members stood upon their feet, and solemnly and unanimously, passed the resolutions, as follows:

A blank in the minutes followed, but the text of the Resolution was later found in Sinclair's papers, and read:

> That the first notice given for the introduction of a convention bill, or any bill of a similar tendency, to that passed in Ireland in the last session of parliament;
> Or any bill for the suspension of the Habeas Corpus act, or the act for preventing wrongous imprisonment, and against undue delays in trials in North Britain;
> Or in case of invasion;
> Or the admission of any foreign troops into Great Britain or Ireland – all or any of these calamitous circumstances shall be a signal to the different delegates, to repair to such place as the secret committee of this convention shall appoint, and the first seven members shall have power to declare the sittings permanent, and twenty-one shall constitute a convention, and proceed to business.

It is hardly necessary to say that considerable importance was attached to this Resolution in the subsequent trials, and both the prosecution and the court returned to it over and over again. As it was not incorporated into the minutes, questions arose as to whether it had ever in fact been passed; but several members of the convention who gave evidence were firmly of the opinion that some such resolution had been passed, that the word 'invasion' had been included, and that 'invasion' referred, and it could hardly mean anything else, to an invasion by the French. Sinclair evidently opposed the motion in its original form, but it was never known whether he disagreed with it, or whether, on the contrary, he agreed with it in principle but regarded it as too dangerous to have it recorded in writing.

The minutes then went on to record that Gerrald and Brown expressed their keen support for the motion, and that Margarot proposed that a secret committee should be set up at once to determine where a convention should meet; Margarot, Gerrald, Skirving and two others were nominated as members of the committee.

Friday 29 November was another significant day. For the first time, the minutes bore the date '1st Year of the British Convention', the clearest indication yet that the convention was following in the footsteps of France. This was also the day on which the Highlands were on the agenda, on a motion from Archibald Wright who had been brought up there; and he gave a graphic report of life there: the smallest trifle was made the subject of a dispute, and the unfortunate tenants, who could not afford a law suit, were driven from their homes;[14] in some areas, sheep had been drowned, and when the poor people went to complain to the lairds of their suffering, the reply was: 'Is there not water enough? Go and drown yourselves'. But the chief hardship was the forcible recruitment of soldiers:

> We have often heard of the bravery of the Highlanders, and their courage and gallantry has been acknowledged and admired in every quarter of the globe, but little did their admirers know, that these men, though prodigal of their blood in the day of battle, were not voluntary soldiers, that they were forcibly embodied and torn from the bosom of their families, with all the cruelty which can disgrace the African Slave Trade. I speak of this practice with the greater certainty, because I have been a sufferer by it. In my early years, I was marked out as a proper object for the army and I was fixed upon by the laird's son, who had got a commission for raising a certain number of men, and who was determined to *force* me to become a *volunteer*.

Wright had saved himself by flight, but others were confined or starved, or hunted like wild beasts in the hills, or seized in the supposed sanctuary of the church on Sundays:

> but nowhere can the poor Highlanders find asylum when the laird wants volunteers. Such are the practices publicly carried on in a part of Great Britain, which we are so frequently told, possesses the best of all possible constitutions, and is the most free and happy country in the world.

Several guineas were donated for enlightening the Highlands.

After this, there were signs that some members were beginning to lose interest. On 30 November, it was moved that letters should be sent to delegates who had gone home, ordering them to return to their posts; and

David Downie,[15] an elderly goldsmith from Bridge Street, moved that members who did not attend should be fined.

On Tuesday 3 December, the delegates made a strong attack on the English judiciary; this was reported in the *Gazeteer*, and when it came to the notice of the Lord Advocate, he decided to take action and had warrants prepared.[16] On the Wednesday, Margarot nade a speech about spies, in which he said that the convention was admitting spies under the name of strangers – 'I say they are welcome, and if the men by whom they are employed were to come here, they should be welcome also', for they could not deny that the convention was met for a legal and constitutional purpose. He added that he had heard rumours that it was intended to disperse the convention by force, and such dispersal should be regarded as a summons to every delegate to repair to the place appointed by the secret committee in cases of emergency; and a resolution to that effect was passed unanimously.

The next day, the chairman of the day, Citizen Paterson, informed the convention that Skirving, Margarot, Gerrald, and four Scotchmen had been arrested; Skirving had been released, but his papers had been seized. The chairman and several other members offered themselves as bail for 'such of their suffering brethren as might be in need of the same', but before they left the room, the Lord Provost and magistrates of the City came in and demanded to know whether the assembly was the British convention. A curious scene was then enacted. Yes, the chairman replied, it was a lawful meeting to consider the constitutional means for obtaining universal suffrage and annual elections. The Lord Provost ordered him to leave the chair and dissolve the meeting; the chairman replied that he had no power to dissolve the meeting, but he was prepared to leave the chair. Skirving now arrived and he intervened; he told Paterson that he could not leave the chair, and he told the Lord Provost that he had no power to dissolve the meeting. An argument then developed. The Lord Provost said they could meet in a private house, to which Skirving replied that that was a private house; Brown said that if the meeting was illegal, it must have been illegal from the outset and the Lord Provost had, therefore, been neglecting his duties in failing to disperse it previously.

Paterson left the chair, and Brown was unanimously elected to take his place. The Lord Provost said, 'I insist upon your immediate departure, otherwise I shall be under the disagreeable necessity of using force'; Brown said he would remain until compelled by force; the Lord Provost called in the constables. Skirving then devised a compromise, to the effect that if the Lord Provost appeared to put the chairman out of the chair, that would be treated as a token of force, and the meeting would be dismissed. A discussion ensued as to whether this was acceptable, until in the end the Lord Provost said, 'I will then act as chief constable', and stepped up and pulled Brown from the chair; at the bottom of the steps upon which the chair was raised, Brown told the Lord Provost (who, in the words of the *Edinburgh Gazeteer*, never lost sight of the behaviour and deportment of a gentleman) that he could not possibly wish to be attended on such an occasion by a more respectable chief constable than the Lord Provost of Edinburgh. To conclude this strange affair, a member stood on a table and moved that the meeting adjourn to Canongate Lodge, and off went the assembly, leaving the Lord Provost in possession of the premises.

A few minutes later, at 8 p.m., the convention reconvened in Canongate Lodge, with Brown again in the chair; it was unanimously resolved that the convention be instantly declared permanent – in imitation, perhaps of the Tennis Court Oath – and the chairman launched into a harangue about the 'dreadful and iniquitous alarm which had lately been raised of plots and conspiracies, which have not, nor ever had, the smallest existence, except in the fertile and wicked brains of those who fabricated these barefaced falsehoods', and much more in the same vein.

The convention met again at 5 p.m. the following evening. The other prisoners had now been released on bail. Margarot gave a dramatic account of his arrest and interrogation, and he was followed by Gerrald who was interrupted by the arrival of the sheriff substitute of the county, accompanied by the magistrates and constables of Edinburgh, whereupon Gerrald exclaimed: 'The rights of Britons are violated by the illegal interruption of our peaceful meeting.... I defy them to assign one reason against the lawfulness of our meeting. But if they thirst after our blood they may now gratify themselves; mine I shall see flow with pleasure, if with it flows the freedom of my country'. Margarot was now called to the chair and told the sheriff that the meeting was a lawful one, but the sheriff replied that he had orders to disperse them by force; Margarot requested that some mark of force should be shown before he left the chair, so the sheriff touched him by the hand; Margarot said, 'No, it must be a little more than that', so the sheriff took him by the arm, and gently pulled him out. Gerrald was then called to the chair, and delivered an extempore prayer while, apparently, everyone listened in silence; finally the same token of force was employed, and the meeting was adjourned.

The British Convention never met again.

                            *   *   *

While the convention was in session, the English representatives were in regular correspondence with London. One letter from Margarot and Gerrald, dated 4 November, was in Hardy's hands on the 7th, and he replied the following day, expressing his satisfaction at the 'great number and zeal of the friends of freedom in Scotland'. A week later, Hardy was giving an account of events in London, and went on to say that it was the general wish of his Society that they should stay as long as they were of use; 'but it wholly depends on the one thing necessary, *money*'. He and his friends had hit on an expedient. They had held a subscription, and when the box was opened, it was found to contain £13.4.5d (including nine bad shillings).

They also employed the talents of John Thelwall. Thelwall[17] had been born in 1764, the son of a silk-mercer; for a time he had worked in his parents' business, had been apprenticed to a tailor, and articled to an attorney; but his real interest was in literature, and he became a friend of many of the leading writers of the day. At about this time he was writing *The Peripatetic*, a love poem for the girl he had married in 1791, but much of it was devoted to his horror of the slave trade, his indignation at landowners who would evict the population of a whole village to enlarge their hunting grounds or open up a vista, and his hatred of social injustice. He also frequented the 'spouting-shops' which were attended by shoemakers, weavers, Quakers, law students and MPs; the entrance fee was 6d, which entitled one to a glass of porter or punch, and debates took place there with a great display of oratory. He was already well known to the authorities.

Thelwall delivered a course of lectures at the Beaufort Buildings, and the proceeds were put into the fund;[18] he had audiences of up to 700 and charged an entry fee of 6d a head. Groves, a government spy, attended and said that his oratory was hot and strong, and full of sarcasm, that he spoke with contempt of all branches of the legislature, and had called for a convention of the whole body of the people to remodel the government.[19] Hardy thought that the lectures would bring in a considerable revenue, and in the meantime he enclosed a draft for 12 guineas; but on 29 November, he said he was afraid that the draft must have miscarried, otherwise its receipt would have been acknowledged.

On 2 December, Margarot and Gerrald wrote jointly to Hardy, acknowledging the receipt of the letter and the money which had now arrived; Gerrald had been ill, but not so as to prevent him from fulfilling his duty; Sinclair, however, had been confined to his bed by a violent fever and sore throat – 'he is a valuable young man, and should he die, his loss would be severely felt'. They described the work of the convention and the arrangements for setting up a secret committee if the government attempted to suspend Habeas Corpus or to introduce a convention bill, or on 'the landing of foreign troops in Great Britain or Ireland', a point of some significance, since it confirmed, at least in part, the text of the Resolution of 28 November. Then they went on: 'Our time is so constantly employed that we find it absolutely impossible as yet to write to you more than once a week...; eighteen hours out of twenty-four are devoted to public business, and you may rest assured they are not misspent....' Sinclair, who evidently made a rapid recovery, was also busy writing to the Society for Constitutional Information.

After the dispersal of the convention, Margarot found time to write a much longer letter to his Society on 8 December. He said that 'supplies are now become more necessary than ever. Surely the pecuniary exertions of any individual in the society can never be compared to our endeavours', and added that he no longer dared to trust to the post and would send the papers in a parcel.[20] He then described how at 7 p.m. on the previous Thursday, the sheriff's officers and five other men had entered his and Gerrald's bedroom, arrested them, and seized their papers and a small trunk – the key of the latter had been forcibly taken from them – and the trunk opened and examined. How the sheriff and his myrmidons had dispersed the convention was also related. On 19 December, he wrote again:

It is impossible for us to find time to write to you as we ought; every instant we are interrupted, or rather the house is not free from visitors from early hours until twelve at night.... We have to acknowledge your last two letters; they came safe, but slow, delivered only five days after their date, where the delay originated we cannot tell – your first gave us a draft for twelve guineas; and your second enclosed a ten pound note, both very acceptable, but we are sorry to add that they do not cover our expenses.... *Vale et amor.*

CHAPTER 6

THE SCOTTISH MARTYRS

In England, anyone who spoke or wrote words which were designed to subvert the government or the constitution could be convicted of the criminal offence of seditious libel; in Scotland, there appears to have been no such crime, but 'sedition' was an offence defined in the textbooks of the time[1] as a commotion or rising – 'raising commotions or disturbances in the state' – more akin to the English common law offence of riot.

The Lord Advocate was faced with a difficulty. Many historians, I suspect, believe that the reformers were prosecuted for advocating universal suffrage; but in fact there could be, and was, no objection to holding meetings to petition Parliament, or to oppose measures while they were going through Parliament. Adopting the forms and practices of the National Convention of France during a time of war with that country could well have been regarded as treacherous; alternatively it could have been explained as folly, or, in the words of Eyre CJ in *R.* v. *Horne Tooke*, as 'mere mummery'. But no government can tolerate a situation in which an organisation within its borders plans to set up a secret committee to meet in the event of an invasion.

Under the old law of Scotland, this conduct might well have constituted treason,[2] and indeed throughout the trials it was constantly (and most improperly) asserted, by both the prosecution and the judges, that the 'panels' (as defendants were called in Scotland) would have been guilty of treason under the old Scottish law. However, immediately after the Union in 1707, the new United Kingdom Parliament passed an act which abrogated the old law, and laid down that the English Treason Act, 1351, with its much stricter definiton of the offence, was to apply to the whole country. The result was that there was no offence which catered for the situation, so the Lord Advocate fell back on the offence of sedition, which had never been designed for conduct of this type, and in spite of the fact that there had been no 'commotion' or 'disturbance'.

Skirving was put on trial on 6 January 1794. The indictment set out many of the papers which he had circulated and many of the resolutions which had been passed by the Convention. The Lord Advocate and the Solicitor-General for Scotland appeared for the Crown; Skirving was not represented, and alleged that counsel were refusing to act, a suggestion which was vigorously denied afterwards by Henry Erskine, the Dean of the Faculty of Advocates, both in open court and in a letter which he wrote many years later to the Editor of the State Trials.

The case commenced with an argument on relevancy, that is to say on the nature of the crime and whether it could be supported by the evidence set out in the indictment. Skirving said that sedition was such a vague term as to be meaningless, but the Court, which consisted of the Lord Justice-Clerk and four other judges, brushed his arguments aside; one judge simply asserted that the 'crime was well understood by everyone in this assembly'; another stated that the facts set out in the indictment 'amount in a most aggravated form to the crime of sedition'. Skirving also objected to all jurors who were members of the Goldsmiths Hall Association on the ground that they had prejudged him by striking his name off their society, but this objection was dismissed out of hand.

After the evidence had been called, Skirving addressed the jury for some two hours; his speech was a rational and logical defence in which he quoted lengthy passages from respectable writers such as the Earl of Buchan's *Political Essays*. The Lord Justice-Clerk summed up, late at night, for about 20 minutes; as to sedition, he said: 'I take [it] to be violating the peace and order of society; and it is attended with different degrees of aggravation, according to what is the object of it. When sedition has a tendency to overturn the constitution of a country, it borders upon high treason'. Skirving was found Guilty, and sentenced to fourteen years transportation.

❉   ❉   ❉

It was probably when Skirving was on trial that Margarot was temporarily released on bail. Lord Cockburn, then a boy of 15, was in an upstairs room of a house on the south side of the High Street, when he saw a crowd coming out of Parliament Close, following a little middle-aged man; he was put into a coach, and the people took off the horses. Henry Cockburn and several other boys ran down the stairs, and heard that it was Margarot, whose name was familiar to them, although they knew nothing of his story, except that he was one of the Friends of the People and was about to be sent to Botany Bay. However, a cry went up that he had been let off and some of the populace drew him in triumph to his lodgings in the Black Bull; Henry Cockburn ran alongside the carriage, and thought it excellent fun to give an occasional haul, for which he was afterwards scolded by the Lord Advocate as if he had committed some base immorality, although the boy's horror of the Friends of the People was equal to his own.

About a week later, Margarot came back to be tried, attended by a procession with banners, and a tree of liberty made up of poles in the form of a letter M, about 20 feet high and 10 feet wide. Two members of the convention were carrying the poles, and the little culprit walked in the centre, below a circular placard proclaiming liberty and equality: he was a little, dark creature, dressed in black, with silk stockings and white metal buttons, like everyone's idea of an impudent Frenchman.

Henry Cockburn was looking out of a window in the old Post Office at the northern end of the west side of North Bridge; the whole North Bridge, from the Tron church to the Register Office, was empty, but the Post Office and adjoining houses had been secretly filled with constables, and with sailors from a frigate, all armed with sticks and batons. When the tree emerged out of Leith Street at the north end of the bridge, the Provost and magistrates appeared, all robed, out of Tron church at the south end. The magistrates were in line across the street, with the Provost in the centre, and about a hundred men behind them. The two parties advanced towards each other till they met by the Post Office. The Provost stepped forward and ordered the procession to retire – and at that instant, the constables and sailors burst out of the houses, the tree was demolished and thrown over the bridge, the street was covered with those who had been knocked down, and Margarot was dragged into court.

Margarot's trial began a week after Skirving's. He, too, was not represented by counsel, but he raised certain matters of relevancy, and digressed to Pitt's resolution at the Thatched House:

> My Lords, it seems to have been in the year 1782 a very laudable and a very constitutional thing to assemble, to meet to consider of the grievances, and to plan a method by which they were to be redressed.

The Court repelled his arguments, and the case proceeded. There was a great deal of evidence about the secret committee and the prospects of a French invasion, and the adoption by the Convention of the French forms and practices – matters on which the Lord Advocate concentrated in his reply on behalf of the Crown, adding

> Who then is this Mr Margarot ?... He is a merchant, he tells us, in London; and the trade in which he is engaged, permits him, it would seem, to dedicate six weeks of his time to us, and to teach the people of Scotland how they are to obtain those blessings of law and liberty, to which they are told they are strangers.

It was during the course of this trial that Margarot raised the question of Mr Rochead's dinner party.

There was a story going round Edinburgh that the Lord Justice-Clerk had been at a dinner party at Mr Rochead's at Inverleith at about the time of Skirving's trial, and that he had said, with reference to Margarot, 'what should you think of giving him a hundred lashes together with Botany Bay?' and that when a lady said that the mob would never allow you to whip him, he replied that the mob would be better for losing a little blood. Margarot called the Lord Justice-Clerk to give evidence of this conversation, but the other judges ruled that it was irrelevant and that his lordship could not be forced to testify. According to Lord Cockburn, Mr Rochead did keep a luxurious table at his home at Inverleith, and held a dinner party there every Sunday; Lord Cockburn's father was a regular attender, and so were the Lord Advocate and the Lord Justice-Clerk. Rochead was a bachelor, but his mother acted as hostess, and ladies were present on these occasions. Lord Cockburn thought that it was very likely that the Lord Justice-Clerk had indeed made the remark attributed to him.

Margarot addressed the Court for four hours in a speech which ranged from the Spitalfields weavers to the prisons which Pitt was alleged to be building in London. When he concluded, the Lord Justice-Clerk described the speech as 'all sedition from beginning to end'. He too was found Guilty and sentenced to fourteen years transportation.

*   *   *

Charles Sinclair was the only panel who was prepared to accept Henry Erskine's condition and he briefed him on that basis; his case was adjourned from time to time and eventually the Lord Advocate 'deserted the diet', that is to say he abandoned the prosecution; why he did this is not really clear, but the most likely explanation is that Sinclair agreed to act as a spy. It was, however, while this case was in progress that the Lord Justice-Clerk gave a ruling on the meaning of the term 'sedition' which suggests that he was virtually making up the law as he went along:

> Sedition is no stationary crime. It is co-eval with the existence of society itself; it is cognisable by the common law of almost every state; indeed it is a crime which reason as well as law, must concur in reprobating and punishing.

*   *   *

There remained Joseph Gerrald. His trial was originally fixed for 8 January; however, in December he asked the Lord Advocate's permission to go home to settle up some family affairs. It is anomalous that, while the Crown was accusing Gerrald of a crime which was, in their eyes, one of the most heinous imaginable, its ministers in Scotland were prepared at the same time to allow him to travel freely about the country on bail – it may be, of course, that they hoped that he would not return and would no longer be their responsibility. Many English radicals were at that time leaving the country in order to emigrate to America, and Gerrald's friends, including Dr Parr, urged him not to return for his trial; but he was eager to become a martyr in the cause of freedom. Another of his friends, William Godwin, now busy writing *Caleb Williams,* wrote him a letter advising him how to conduct his defence.

The trial was now fixed for 27 January, and Gerrald set off from London on the 24th; however, he was caught in a snowstorm and failed to arrive in time. There were further delays while he briefed counsel, Gillies and Laing, and it was not until 10 March that the case commenced. It was only now, for the first time, that a determined attempt was made to show that the facts of the case could not possibly amount to sedition; the prosecution replied by asserting that the word 'commotion' could mean 'any illegal convocation of people... tending to disturb the peace and order of society' – 'a new law', said counsel for the defence, 'incapable of proof and unknown in law, is extorted by inference'. But the Court was adamant, one judge stating succinctly: 'I say it amounts to a seditious conspiracy to overturn the constitution by force and outrage if it cannot be done otherwise.' It was the opinions of the *judges*, not *the law*, against which Gerrald had to defend himself.

Other matters were raised at this stage. It was strenuously urged that sedition was not an offence for which a sentence of transportation could be imposed, since the powers of punishment under the relevant Scottish legislation were by 'fining, imprisonment or banishment', and that banishment from Scotland could not cover transportation to a particular destination. These arguments, however, carried no weight with the Court which ruled that either sedition was not covered by the legislation and so it could impose such punishment as it thought fit, or alternatively that banishment did cover transportation.

Gerrald also raised the issue of Mr Rochead's dinner party, this time as a preliminary objection on the ground that the Lord Justice-Clerk had prejudged the case and was disqualified from sitting. The Lord Justice-Clerk left the Court while the matter was being argued, and his deputy, Lord Henderland, took the chair. It was not an edifying scene. One judge observed: 'I do not think that this panel is well advised in making [this objection]; what could be his motive for making it I cannot perceive. He has the happiness of being tried before one of the ablest judges that ever sat in this court.... I can ascribe it to nothing but malevolence and desperation.' And another said:

> My lord, an objection of this kind, coming from any other man, I should consider as a very high insult to the dignity of this court; but coming from him, standing in the peculiar situation in which he now stands at the bar, charged with a crime of little less than treason, the insolence of his objection is swallowed up in the atrocity of his crime.

When Gerrald protested, Lord Henderland declared: 'Once for all, sir, I must inform you that you are not entitled to interrupt the judges.' Finally, another judge said that if Gerrald was convicted, even fourteen years transportation was too slight a punishment for an offence of such magnitude. The objection was then repelled, and the Lord Justice-Clerk returned into court.

Then there was the problem of the jurors. Gerrald first objected to William Creech, a bookseller, on the ground that he had said, in a private conversation, that he would condemn any member of the British Convention; their lordships repelled this objection, concluding with this astonishing statement from the Lord Justice-Clerk: 'As this objection is stated, I hope there is not a gentleman of the jury, or any man in this court, who has not expressed the same sentiment.' The panel next objected to William Rankin, a tailor, on the ground that he was a tailor to the King, and being in the pay of the Crown and in the habit of receiving favours from the Crown, he was not a proper person to act; but the Lord Justice-Clerk ruled: 'If it had been the King himself, I do not see that it could have been a valid objection'. This dictum drew from the Editor of the State Trials the laconic footnote: 'So in the original edition'.[3]

It was in this atmosphere that the case now proceeded. Although Gerrald had briefed counsel, he chose to make his own closing speech; and whereas

Margarot's had been in the nature of a political harangue, Gerrald's was a learned lecture. He spoke for three hours or more, and what he said could have filled a whole issue of a professional journal: he quoted from Tacitus, *de Germania*, and from Bishop Squire's book on the Anglo-Saxons, where it was said that the affairs of the country were conducted not only by the king and the witenagemot, but by the myclegemot, chosen by the people at large. Then, following Godwin's advice, he adopted a more philosophical approach, based on the premise that 'the great and distinguishing mark of man is reason', and quoted from the works of Cardinal Bellarmine, Algernon Sidney and Edmund Burke.

But Gerrald knew that no amount of antiquarian research or philosophical speculation could explain away the Resolution of 28 November; this had to be dealt with in a different way. During the course of cross-examination, his counsel had elicited from the witnesses that when Skirving, Margarot and Gerrald himself had been arrested, their papers had been put in a trunk which was locked and sealed, and that the trunk was later opened and the papers inventoried in their presence. However, Sinclair's papers, including the text of the Resolution, had been wrapped up and taken away in a towel. Gerrald contended that the text of the Resolution was a forgery which had been planted by the authorities in Sinclair's papers. It was a dangerous line of defence; no witness had ever made such a suggestion; recollections of the terms of the Resolution varied, but there was a wide measure of agreement that some such resolution had been passed, and that Sinclair had moved that it should be amended, so that it seemed likely that he would have taken it away.

Gerrald was suffering from a consuming cough, and at one stage he told the jury he was exhausted; but an eyewitness who was in court at the time said that his speech annihilated all the remembrance of all the eloquence that had ever been heard before in the walls of that building; he quietened the judges in spite of their interruptions, and produced a silence in which one might have heard a pin drop.

As usual, the summing-up was brief and brusque; and the Lord Justice-Clerk demolished Gerrald's allegations of dishonesty in no uncertain terms:

> Is it possible to suppose that these persons – all men of character – would do that, in order to convict an innocent man, for which they ought to be hanged, by extracting evidence and putting false evidence in its place?

Gerrald was found Guilty. It was while the court was discussing sentence that the Lord Justice-Clerk again demonstrated his political opinions, on the basis that anything can be justified in the interests of the safety of the state:

> I say '*salus populi suprema lex*', and it becomes us, let his intentions be as pure as they possibly can be, to remove that man from society, and to put it out of his power to disseminate these dangerous principles.

The formal sentence of fourteen years transportation was pronounced. Gerrald said nothing. Although only 30 years old, he was in poor health. He knew, and the judges must have known, that it was a death sentence. It was an unsavoury business: justice was manifestly seen not to be done.

❖   ❖   ❖

By 11 January, Hardy knew of Skirving's conviction, and sent copies of Margarot's indictment to the Society for Constitutional Information, together with a pamphlet on brewing, to encourage people to brew their own beer and so avoid paying duty on it. On 22 January, John Martin, the new chairman of the London Corresponding Society, wrote to 'Citizen Maurice Margarot' at the Tolbooth, where he was now being detained; he was a Scot himself, and he raised with Margarot the possibility of appealing against his conviction:

> Do you incline to try the writ of error?[4] What do the Scotch lawyers think of it? And what do you think of the legal knowledge of my countrymen? I firmly believe that the law is the only science of which they know nothing.... I am happy to find you in good spirits suffering the mild and just sentence of the law. You may remember that I told you to be thankful you were not hanged.... Mrs Martin desires me to say more for her than I have room. Were it not that you are safe enough, and all of us married, I would almost think she is in love....

Two days later, Margarot wrote to Hardy from the Tolbooth; the letters crossed in the post. One of the points he raised was the possible publication of his trial:

Figure 7. Maurice Margarot, engraved in response to his letter of 24 January 1794. "Did you not say that the Mob would be the better for losing a little Blood." (By permission of the Trustees of the British Museum.)

> If you publish my trial, it might be necessary to print my handsome figure in front, if so, Mrs Margarot can furnish you with a miniature, whence an engraving can be taken; if that is done, pray let the engraver put into my hand the paper, containing the questions to the Lord Justice-Clerk, and let the last of them be legible, viz. Did you not say, that the mob would be better for losing a little blood? (See Figure 7.)

He went on to describe conditions in the Tolbooth:

> We have had an additional padlock put upon our door and the captain of the Tolbooth is not entrusted with the keys at night, but delivers them to the magistrates, and calls for them again in the morning.

The letter ended by asking Hardy to remember him to Muir and Fyshe Palmer, who were already sailing south; they were put on board a hulk in the Thames off Woolwich, where Fyshe Palmer was visited by his friends, including Dr Priestley (shortly before he emigrated to America); from there they were taken to Portsmouth, and kept on board transports until a convoy was ready to depart.

Margarot followed in the early spring, and Hardy visited him on the *Surprize* Transport at Spithead on 7 March, as he reported in a letter to Citizen Buckle of Norwich on the 12th: 'He is in good health and high spirits.... I saw the captain; he appears to be a very good kind of man, and bears an excellent character'. He also said that he had seen a letter from Muir, informing him that 'the convoy has hoisted signal for sailing; and I am afraid, by this time, they are gone from Portsmouth; if so they were without many necessaries that were preparing for them.' Hardy also met Thomas Banks, the sculptor, on the *Surprize*; he was taking a cast from Muir's head, from which he later made a bust.

In the meantime, Margarot had written from Spithead to Norwich on 10 March; he acknowledged the receipt of £20 which Hardy had delivered and then he went on:

> This morning 10 ships of war have left Spithead for the Channel, and it is here reported that the Brest fleet is out; rumour, always magnifying things, says there are 70 sail of French at sea, if so, there must be a number of transports among them, and a descent may probably be the consequence.

The convoy did not sail as expected, and a fortnight later, on 28 March, the Society for Constitutional Information resolved that an address be sent to the five convicts commiserating with them for their suffering. Fyshe Palmer replied from the *Surprize* Transport on 16 April: he described how the jury which had tried him had been packed by the servants of the Crown, and said that the strongest objections were mere air; 'a majority of the fifteen condemns. If, therefore, ministry...can in three counties find only eight servile tools... the liberties, the lives of all Scotland are at their mercy'. Later in the month, Muir and Skirving wrote long letters to the Society for Constitutional Information; and there, for the moment, we must leave them, about to sail away to Botany Bay.

Hardy and Buckle were not the only ones to be concerned about the fate of the 'Scottish martyrs'. The conviction of Muir was raised in the House of

Lords by Lord Stanhope, but his motion was rejected by 49 to 1; Sheridan raised Fysshe Palmer's case in the Commons, but his motion was rejected by 104 to 34, and another motion on behalf of Muir was rejected by 171 to 32; finally Lord Lauderdale raised both cases in the Lords, but his motion was rejected without a division. It was during these debates that the Prime Minister openly gave his support to the Scotch judges; and when Secretary Dundas wrote to Lord Braxfield to tell him that the sentences which had been imposed were the subject of complaints in England, he wrote back with his advice that the royal mercy should not be extended to the convicts.[5]

As for Gerrald, he spent some time in Newgate, where Godwin visited him and gave him a copy of his thriller and spy story, *Caleb Williams*, advertised with some justification as 'the most wonderful and surprising history and miraculous adventures of Caleb Williams', and at the same time a denunciation of the way in which the establishment manipulated the administration of justice to do injustice to the innocent. He sailed to Australia in a later convoy.

CHAPTER 7

THE ROAD TO TREASON

I The Rights of Swine and the King's Head in a Basket

In England, in the meantime, the reforming societies were adopting a more strident tone. The New Year was ushered in by an address headed Rights of Swine, from Stockport, a town which had grown in size from 700 to more than 2000 houses in ten years.[1] It stated that thousands of honest and industrious people in Great Britain were literally starving to death for want of bread, war had ruined commerce and reduced wages, but rents and the price of provisions remained unabated. The poor calico weavers in the vicinity of Manchester were working for wages fifty and sixty per cent lower than two years previously; impudent nobles were advertising their 'Grand dinners' in the very face of the hungry poor, while widows and orphans were weeping, and often dying for want of bread. 'Awake! Arise! arm yourselves', the Address concluded, and 'claim, as your inalienable right, Universal Suffrage and Annual Parliaments.'

On 17 January, while Gerrald was on bail in England, there was a meeting of the Society for Constitutional Information at the Crown and Anchor. Horne Tooke was in the chair; Gerrald himself was present, and so were Sharp, Bonney, Sinclair, Kyd and Richter. It was resolved:

> That law ceases to be an object of obedience whenever it becomes an instrument of oppression;
> That we recall to mind, with the deepest satisfaction, the merited fate of the infamous Jefferys, once lord chief justice of England, who at the era of the glorious revolution, for the many iniquitous sentences which he had passed, was torn to pieces by a brave and injured people.
> That those who imitate his example, deserve his fate.

Horne Tooke then left the chair, and Gerrald took his place; further resolutions were passed, deploring the injustice committed in Scotland, and approving the conduct of the British Convention; and it was further resolved that copies of these resolutions should be printed and transmitted to Skirving 'now imprisoned under the colour of law in the Tolbooth of Edinburgh', and published in the papers.

On 20 January, the London Corresponding Society held its anniversary meeting at the Globe Tavern. Lynam, the spy, went to the Globe before the meeting began, but he found some of the members already assembled there in 'the one pair of stairs room',[2] and while they were talking there, the floor gave way 'and created a vast deal of confusion'. So they adjourned to a room on the next floor, where there was a gallery where the musicians played when the room was used for a dance; there the chairman, Martin, took his place, along with Richter and Thelwall; Hardy stood at the back. Ramsey, a shorthand writer from Edinburgh, reported on Margarot's trial; an address to the nation was carried. The meeting then adjourned to dinner, where Thelwall took the chair; there was a large company, 300 it was estimated, and Lynam had to eat in an adjoining room with a few others who could not get seats.

Earlier that afternoon, Thelwall had taken a document to James Davidson, a printer in Russell Place, Covent Garden, who printed 200 copies, and during the afternoon took them to the Globe; there, on the stairs, he met Hardy who asked him to take them away, so he went home but returned in time for dinner at 6 p.m.; during the meal, someone was sent to collect the papers and copies were passed round the table. Later on, he printed many more, a total of some 8000 between then and March, and Hardy paid for them.[3]

This document was an Address to the Nation, signed by Martin and Hardy as chairman and secretary.

> CITIZENS;– We find the nation involved in a war, by which, in the course of ONE campaign, immense numbers of our countrymen have been slaughtered;...
> To add to our affliction, we have reason to expect, that other taxes will soon be added to [those]...with which we are already overwhelmed; for the purpose of defraying the expenses which have been incurred...to re-establish the odious despotism of France....

The Address went on to attack corruption in government and in the administration of justice, and referred to chapter 14 of Magna Carta, which imposed restrictions on fines, and laid down that no fines should be assessed, except by a jury:

> But by the usurped power of the judges, in assessing Fines (and what Fines!!) in the cases of Misdemeanor; this glorious Right of the subject, of having fines assessed by the Jury (the only possible protection from slavery and the vilest oppression), is unjustly and infamously ravished from us.

The Address then set out the text of chapter 29 of Magna Carta, which prohibited imprisonment, except by the law of the land, and the denial, delay, or sale of justice, and then commented that the various methods by which the benefits of this provision were destroyed might induce people to suppose that the Great Charter had been repealed – the exorbitant expense of judicial proceedings and the dilatory practice of the courts shamefully contradicted the clause which forbade the denial, the delay, and the sale of justice.

The Address then turned to Scotland and the disruption of the British Convention:

their papers have been seized, and made use of as evidence against them, and many virtuous and meritorious individuals, have been as cruelly as unjustly for their various actions disgraced and destroyed by infamous and illegal sentences of transportation. And these unjust and wicked judgments have been executed with a rancour and malignity, never before known in this land; our respectable and beloved Fellow-citizens have been cast FETTERED into Dungeons amongst felons in the Hulks, to which they were not sentenced.

CITIZENS;–...Can you believe that those who send virtuous Irishmen and Scotchmen fettered with felons to Botany Bay, do not meditate and will not attempt to send us after them?... It is both our duty and our interest to stand or fall together. The Irish parliament and the Scotch judges, actuated by the same English influence, have brought us directly to the point.... We must now choose at once either liberty or slavery for ourselves and our posterity. Will you wait till BARRACKS are erected in every village, and till *subsidized* Hessians and Hanoverians are upon us?

You may ask, perhaps, by what means shall we seek redress?

We answer, that men in a state of civilized society are bound to seek redress of the grievances from the laws; as long as any redress can be obtained by the laws. But our common Master whom we serve...has taught us not to expect to gather grapes from thorns, nor figs from thistles. We must have our redress from our own laws and not from the laws of our plunderers, enemies, and oppressors.

THERE IS NO REDRESS FOR A NATION CIRCUMSTANCED AS WE ARE, BUT IN A FAIR, FREE, AND FULL REPRESENTATION OF THE PEOPLE.

The Address was followed by a Resolution to the effect that the general committee of the Society should meet daily during the ensuing session of Parliament and, at the first introduction of any bill for the landing of foreign troops in Britain, for suspending the Habeas Corpus Act, for proclaiming martial law, or for preventing the people from meeting in societies, it should summon a general convention of the people to take such measures into consideration.

It was at about this time that Hessian troops from the King's dominions in Germany were landed temporarily on the Isle of Wight and at Portsmouth, to prevent sickness on the transports and prior to their re-embarkation for service abroad; but it was widely believed that they were to be employed in England.

Shortly after the anniversary dinner, a committee meeting of the London Corresponding Society arranged for a hundred thousand copies of the Address to be printed and distributed, and for a series of toasts, drunk at the dinner, to be added at the end of the Address: these included The Rights of Man and Citizen Thomas Paine; The British Convention; Citizen William Skirving; Citizen Maurice Margarot, 'and may his *manly* and *patriotic* conduct be rewarded by the attachment of the people' (when this toast was proposed, Gerrald had stood up, and in 'a stream of inspired eloquence', had pronounced a eulogy on 'this truly valuable citizen', and wished that 'we might die the last of British Freemen than live the first of slaves'); Citizen Joseph Gerrald; The transactions at Toulon,[4] Citizen Hamilton Rowan, 'and may the authors of the *Convention-bill* find that they have committed a *bull*'; Citizens Muir and Palmer, 'Success to the arms of *Freedom* against whomsoever directed; and confusion to *despots* with whomsoever allied'; a speedy and honourable peace with the brave Republic of France; the starving manufacturers and neglected peasantry of Great Britain and Ireland; Citizen John Frost, 'and a speedy restoration of that health which he lost in the dungeons of Newgate'.[5]

On the following day, 24 January, Hardy sent some copies of the Address to the Society for Constitutional Information, and that night a resolution was passed at the Crown and Anchor 'that the London Corresponding Society have deserved well of their country', and ordered that 40,000 copies of the Address should be printed for circulation in England, Scotland and Ireland.

A meeting of the delegates of the London Corresponding Society met at No. 3 Compton Street on 30 January. Proposals were made to have meeting houses all over London; a secret committee was set up, including Baxter, Martin and Thelwall, to consider what measures were necessary, and to report to the general committee. It was probably immediately after this meeting that Hardy wrote, and had printed, a circular letter for distribution to the affiliated societies:

> Citizens! – The critical moment is arrived, and Britons must either assert with zeal and firmness their claims to liberty, or yield without resistance, to the chains that ministerial usurpation is forging for them.... We need not intimate to you, that notwithstanding the unparalleled audacity of a corrupt and overbearing faction, which at present tramples on the rights and liberties of the people, our meetings cannot in England be interrupted without the previous adoption of a convention-bill, a measure it is our duty to anticipate.... We must, however, be expeditious; Hessians and Austrians are already among us! and, if we tamely submit, a cloud of these armed barbarians may shortly be poured in upon us; let us form then another British Convention; we have a central situation in our view, which we believe would be most convenient for the whole island; but which we forbear to mention...till we have the answer of the societies with which we are in correspondence. Let us have your answer then, by the 20th at the farthest – earlier, if possible, whether you approve of the measure, and how many delegates you can send... – We remain yours, in civic affection, the London Corresponding Society.
>
> For the management of this business we have appointed a secret committee; you will judge how far it is necessary for you to do the same.

At another meeting the Society resolved to print 50,000 hand-bills of a speech by Lord Stanhope relating to foreign troops. In Norwich, a general meeting of delegates was held at Postle Cellar on 24 February and resolved, 'That one or more delegates should be sent to the next general convention, so soon as called for by our London correspondents.'

It was in the same month that Daniel Eaton, a printer, was prosecuted for publishing a pamphlet called *Politics for the People, or Hog's Wash* in the form of a fable about a farmyard, which was based on a lecture by Thelwall who, having been debarred from lecturing on politics, chose instead to talk about the love of freedom and of the fair sex; this he developed into a parable of King Chanticleer strutting about the farmyard:

> I had a fine majestic kind of animal, a game cock, a haughty sanguinary tyrant covered in blood and slaughter from his infancy, fond of foreign wars and domestic

rebellion...; now this haughty old tyrant would never let my farm-yard be quiet; for not content with devouring by far the greater part of the grain that was scattered for the morning and evening repast...the restless despot must be always picking and cuffing all the poor doves and pullets, and little defenceless chickens so that they could never eat the scanty remants, which his inordinate taxation left them, in peace and quietness;

and there were references to his spotted ermine breast, the fine gold trappings about his neck and shoulders, the flowing robe of plumage tucked up at his rump, and above all that fine ornamental thing about his head, his crown or coxcomb. The prosecution alleged that this could only refer to the King of England, and that was the question which the jury had to decide. Eaton was lucky: he was acquitted. He put up a sign of the Cock and Swine over his printing shop, and later a medal was struck in his honour, impressed with a design of a cock presiding over some pigs in a sty.

The last day of February was declared a General Fast Day by Royal Proclamation, and the London Corresponding Society demonstrated its views in a resolution:

> That the commanding a *General Fast*, for the purpose of imploring the Divine Father of *Mercy* and *Peace* to support and prosper us in the *horrid* act of deliberately *destroying* our fellow-creatures, is repugnant to the true spirit and principles of Christianity, where we are commanded to *pray* for our enemies....

On 27 March, Hardy wrote to the Society for Constitutional Information; he addressed them as Citizens, and asked them whether they agreed to the necessity of a 'speedy convention', to obtain in a constitutional method, a redress of their grievances which could only be effectually removed by a full and fair representation of the people of Great Britain. After signing himself, 'I am, fellow citizens (in my humble measure) a friend of the rights of man, T. Hardy', he appended resolutions – that

> Equal laws can never be expected, but by a full and fair representation of the people.... For this, we are ready to hazard everything; and never, but with our lives, will be relinguish an object which involves the happiness, or even the political existence of ourselves and posterity.
>
> It is the decided opinion of this Society, that...there ought to be *immediately* a CONVENTION of the PEOPLE, by delegates, deputed for that purpose, from the different societies of the *Friends of Freedom*, assembled in the various parts of this nation.

In another postscript, he added that a general meeting of the Society was to be held on Monday[6] 14 April, at a place to be notified by public advertisement. This letter was read at the Crown and Anchor on the following evening, and the secretary of the Society for Constitutional Information was ordered to reply that they heartily concurred with the London Corresponding Society.

The month concluded with the production of a document, some say prepared by Baxter several months previously, some say fabricated and planted by government spies, in the form of an advertisement for a play to be performed on All Fools Day:

For
The Benefit of JOHN BULL

At the
FEDERATION THEATRE, in EQUALITY SQUARE
On Thursday, the 1st April, 4971.
Will be performed,
A new and entertaining Farce, called
LA GUILLOTINE;
or
GEORGE'S HEAD IN A BASKET!
Dramatis Personae,
Numpy the Third, by Mr GWELP,[7]
(Being the last time of his appearing in that character)
Prince of Leeks, by Mr GWELP, junior
Duke of Dice, by Mr FREDDY,
(from Osnaburgh.)
Duke of Jordan, by Mr WILLIAM HENRY
FLOGGER (from the Creolian Theatre.)
Uncle Toby, by Mr RICHMOND.
Grand Inquisitor, Mr PENSIONER REEVES
Don Quixote, Knight of the Dagger,
By Mr EDMUND CALUMNY
And Chancellor of the Exchequer, by Mr BILLY TAXLIGHT
Municipal Officers, National Guards, &c.
By Citizens XOF, NADIREHS, YERG, ENIKSRE,
&c
Banditti, Assassins, Cut Throats, and Wholesale Dealers in Blood, by THE
EMPRESS OF RUFFIANS, the EMPEROR OF HARM-ANY, THING OF
PRUSSIA, PRINCE OF S. CASH-HELL, &c.
Between the Acts,
A new song, called "Twenty more, kill them!"
by BOBADIL BRUNSWICK
Tight Rope Dancing, from the Lamp-post,
By Messrs. CANTERBURY, YORK, DURHAM, &c.
In the course of the evening will be sung
in Full Chorus,
CA IRA.
AND
BOB SHAVE GREAT GEORGE OUR ——!
The whole to conclude with
A GRAND DECAPITATION
OF
PLACEMEN, PENSIONERS AND GERMAN LEECHES.
Admittance, Three-pence each Person.
Vive la Liberté! Vive la Republique!

II Sheffield blades

On the last day of February, the Fast Day, the Friends of Peace and Reform at Sheffield assembled in their thousands (according to a pamphlet which described the event) on a 'spacious plain near West Street, Backfields'; the meeting was opened with a prayer and a serious lecture, and a hymn was sung. William Camage was called to the chair, and a series of resolutions was put to the meeting – that war was a system of rapine and blood, unworthy of rational beings; that the present war, of kings combined against the people of France, was a war of the most diabolical kind; that when public fasts were ordered with the same breath which commands the shedding of vast oceans of human blood, they were solemn prostitutions of religion; that the landing of Hessian troops, 'a ferocious and unprincipled horde of butchers', had a suspicious and alarming appearance; that it was high time to be on guard against those armed monsters which might at any moment be let loose. Thanks were given to Muir, Palmer, Skirving and Margarot, and to Sheridan for his speeches in the cause of injured patriotism, and finally it was resolved that 'the people have no remedy for their grievances, but a REFORM IN PARLIAMENT – a measure which we determine never to relinquish, though we follow our brethren in the same glorious cause to *Botany Bay*'. After these resolutions had been passed unanimously, 'the meeting dissolved in that orderly and peaceable manner, which so eminently distinguishes the patriotic inhabitants of Sheffield.'

Cutlery had been manufactured in Sheffield since the Tudor period, and in recent years the industry had been developing rapidly.[8] Two factors contributing to this were the presence of high-quality sandstone from which grindstones were made, and the confluence of five fast-flowing streams which were ideal for turning the grindstones used by the cutlers and toolmakers; by the 1770s, there were more than 150 water-powered workshops within a five mile radius of the town centre. A watch-maker, Benjamin Huntsman, had had difficulty in making his components from the metal then in use, and he devised a new method of making steel; he melted it in crucibles and skimmed off the slag which floated to the surface, and then poured the liquid into moulds to solidify; this became known as crucible or cast steel, and it was of such good quality that it gave Sheffield pre-eminence in the manufacture of cutlery for many years.

Whatever opinion the people of Sheffield had of themselves, the presence there of enthusiastic reforming societies, composed largely of cutlers who made the best knives in the country, was a source of anxiety to the government; and this anxiety was increased a few weeks later when there was another meeting on Castle Hill. This was probably the largest and most formidable which had so far been held, and it was addressed by Henry Yorke; and evidence relating to the meeting was given both at the treason trials at the Old Bailey, and subsequently at York assizes when Yorke himself was charged with seditious conspiracy.

Yorke himself is an enigma. He was probably born in the West Indies, but he was brought up at Little Eaton near Derby; he usually called himself

Yorke, but sometimes Redhead, which was his father's name. In 1794 he was still only 21 or 22, yet he had a magic eloquence which would have been the envy of any advocate, politician or preacher twice his age, a gift which was demonstrated by the quite remarkable speech which he made in his own defence at York.

Yorke's name had occasionally cropped up before. He had been in Manchester in the spring of 1793 and is said to have arrived in the town with the 'apparatus of a kind of apostolic mission', addressed to the various assemblies in the neighbourhood;[9] he said he was visiting all the societies to find out how many men they could muster in the event of an invasion by the French, to add to the armies of France. He had said that he was expecting the French to land about 40 or 50 thousand men and he was collecting the names of those who could be best relied upon to find out how many could be brought into the field in such an emergency; and when he was present there was a sort of holiday or festival of sedition. On another occasion, he was said to have told some friends in Sheffield that he would go up to London with the people – an observation which was later taken to mean that he would lead an armed force to the capital. In the autumn he had been in London and was telling people that he was going to Belgium, and would be back by Christmas at the head of a French army; and he said that the King and Queen of France had got what they deserved.

William Broomhead, the secretary of the Sheffield Constitutional Society, was for a time under arrest, but he agreed to give evidence for the Crown and was called as a witness both at the Old Bailey and at York assizes. According to Yorke he was a wild and incoherent man, who had at one time asserted that he was pregnant and had had a miscarriage at three months;[10] but this is not the impression which comes through on the transcript, where he appears as a reluctant witness, treading delicately between his duty to tell the truth and his desire not to let down his friends, and displaying a dry sense of humour – having a 'trifling desultory, pleasing, irregular conversation' about a night-cat with his friends at Sheffield, he told the Old Bailey; and later, 'it is really painful to be pressed so much on both sides together, in London and here too', he said under cross-examination at York, 'I have had enough of it in London. I am sick of this.... I tell you, I won't be pinched.'

A committee meeting of the Sheffield Constitutional Society was held on 2 April; it was decided to hold an open-air meeting at Castle Hill on the following Monday, 7 April, and the agenda was discussed. One of the items was a petition to Parliament, but this was, according to Broomhead, a mere sham; the motion was not to be seconded and would be negatived, thus clearing the way for the main business, namely an address by Yorke under the guise of a petition to the King. Two days later, the meeting was advertised in the *Sheffield Register*, a paper published by Joseph Gale;

> The Friends of Justice, of Liberty, and of Humanity, in the town and neighbour-
> hood of Sheffield, are desired to meet on Monday next, at three o'clock in the
> afternoon, on the Castle Hill, Sheffield.

The advertisement listed the topics to be considered and concluded with a resolution that Citizen Yorke be requested to attend the meeting. At his trial, Yorke called evidence that he had no prior invitation to attend, but was present by chance and was called upon to speak on the spur of the moment; but this was contradicted by the evidence of William Frith, a surgeon who was then in practice in Sheffield. On the morning of 7 April, he was delivering a lady who told him that they must all be ready to go to the Castle Hill at two o'clock, for Henry Yorke was to make a very eloquent speech: 'Doctor, you will go, won't you?' she said. 'I have no intention of going', said the surgeon. 'He is certainly sent by heaven,' said the girl, 'to be the saviour of his country; and they talk of taking him up; but if they do, many a fine house will be burnt down, and many a head laid low by tomorrow.' She was married, and very pretty, the doctor added, when giving evidence, and she had gone on to say: 'If the child is born, it shall be christened Henry Yorke Rhodes' – and so it was.[11]

Intrigued by the conversation, the doctor decided to go to Castle Hill. He found there a wooden pulpit or tribune (when Broomhead was asked to describe it, he said, 'It was never christened; we never had a parson to it'), with Yorke standing beside it. Broomhead proposed the motion to petition Parliament, but it was not seconded and was therefore dropped; another witness described how Yorke came to the Hill, 'and immediately when it was known that Mr Yorke was without the ground, a great noise was made from all quarters – Mr Yorke, Mr Yorke in the chair!' and the crowds made an opening for him and he was pressed forward. Broomhead thought there were 5000 or 6000 people present, but another report put the figure at ten to twelve thousand, in spite of the fact that it had been raining hard until a few minutes before the meeting.

Dr Frith was called away to another confinement in the middle of Yorke's speech, but not before he had heard part of it; and other witnesses were called who had heard it all. The principal issue was whether the speech which was subsequently printed in a pamphlet by Gale was an accurate account of what Yorke actually said. Several witnesses called by the Crown said that the printed version was accurate. Witnesses called by the defence, on the other hand, asserted that the printed text was a travesty of the original. Some of the passages in the printed version were highly inflammatory:

> Fellow citizens, the day is at length arrived, when fanaticism and superstition, deprived of their tinsel trappings, and exposed, in their native ugliness, to the view of mankind, slink scowling back to the cave of obscurity; there, I hope, they will remain. The energy of Englishmen will no longer endure this strange uproar of injustice. I trust my countrymen...will demand the annihilation of corruption and abuses, and the restitution of the original rights of human nature.
>
> It must be granted, that this experience is important, because it teaches the suffering nations of the present day in what manner to prepare their combustible ingredients, and humanists in what manner to enkindle them, so as to produce with effect that grand political explosion, which, at the same time that it buries despotism, already convulsive and agonizing, in ruins, may raise up the people to the dignity and sublime grandeur of freedom.

Teach your children and your countrymen the sacred lessons of virtue, which are the foundations of all human polity.... When such a revolution of sentiment shall have dispersed the mists of prejudice, when, by the incessant thunderings of the press, the meanest cottager of our country shall be enlightened, and the sun of reason shall shine in its fullest meridian over us, then the commanding voice of the whole people shall recommend the 558 gentlemen of St Stephen's chapel to go about their business.[12]

And so on, for several pages; the publisher of the pamphlet conceded that, as the speech lasted more than an hour, it was impossible for him to give his readers a just account.

Dr Frith heard some other parts of the speech. At one stage, Yorke had said:

You behold before you, young as I am, about 22 years of age, a man who has been concerned in three revolutions already; who, though late, assisted the revolution in America; who so essentially contributed to that in Holland; who has materially assisted in that of France; and who will continue to cause revolutions all over the world.

There was also the question of arms. Dr Frith said that Yorke had declared that the people had a right, by the Bill of Rights, to arm themselves, and requested that they should do so. And both at the Old Bailey and later at York, Henry Hill, a cutler, said that he had made about 130 pikes at that time.

One witness was George Widdison, who was both a hairdresser and a turner. He had made some pike-shafts; he dressed Yorke's hair when he was in Sheffield and they used to discuss universal representation; he was a member of the Constitutional Society and Yorke attended meetings from time to time. He dressed Yorke's hair after the Castle Hill meeting, and Yorke asked him what people said of his speech, to which he replied guardedly that there were various opinions of it. William Camage told the Old Bailey that after the meeting, Yorke was drawn in triumph in a carriage by the people through the streets of the town.

What Yorke actually said will never be known; but Broomhead summed up his speech neatly, and probably came as near the truth as anyone is likely to get:

His manner of speaking may sometimes lead him to go farther than he ought.... He is peculiarly energetic, and at the same time very fiery, very warm, very strong; but at this meeting I do not know that he said anything that was detrimental to the constitution of England – not at this meeting.

All one does know for certain is that, a few days after the meeting, Gale the printer published a large number of pamphlets which contained his version of the Castle Hill meeting, couched in the most inflamatory terms. One was sent to 'Mr Felix Vaughan, esq. counsellor at law', and another to 'the honourable Charles Fox'; others were sent to Erskine and Wharton, and a boxful to Thomas Hardy. Broomhead believed that Yorke had written the printed version himself.

III Loyal Lambeth

On 2 April, George Sanderson, who kept the Bunch of Grapes[13] in Butcher Row by Temple Bar, and who was either a spy from the outset or became one later, went to a hatter called Skelmerdine in 'the borough'[14] in order to decide a bet. When he got there, he found a couple of dozen armed men and seven or eight racks of arms; it seemed to be the general topic of conversation among those present that parliamentary reform could not be achieved, except at the point of the bayonet. These men proved to belong to the Loyal Lambeth Association, an avowedly military organisation. Its constitution was dated 15 November 1793, and the preamble commenced with the words:

> Whereas the fear of invasion, and civil commotions, have alarmed several of the inhabitants of this parish and its vicinity, we have thought proper to form ourselves into a military association, to be distinguished by the name of the Loyal Lambeth Association;

and Article I laid down:

> This association shall consist of one captain, one lieutenant, one ensign, a serjeant-major, three corporals, sixty rank and file, two drummers and fifers.

Further articles declared that every member should pay 1/6d a week for the purchase of arms and accoutrements, and as no armourer was appointed they were to keep their own weapons clean, and they agreed to 'step forth in case of fire, tumults, commotions and riots in...the parish of St Mary's Lambeth'. Their uniform was to be 'a blue coat lapelled, scarlet collar, plain gilt buttons, white waistcoat, nankeen breeches, white stockings, half-black gaters, black stock, cocked hat and cockade'; swords, eppulets (*sic*), sashes and swordknots were to be purchased for the use of the officers. John Francklow was appointed Serjeant-Major, Treasurer and Secretary – as serjeant-major, he was responsible for training the members in the use of arms, as treasurer he was to receive subscriptions, and as secretary he was to keep the muster-roll. Francklow was a member of the London Corresponding Society, and when Sanderson asked if he could join the Association, he was allowed to do so only on condition that he also joined the Society; this was to be one of the principal items of evidence to show that the Society was an armed body, or at least had an armed branch.

Samuel Williams, a gun engraver, also had dealings with the Association. He too was a member of the London Corresponding Society, and when he ordered a pair of shoes from Hardy, he said that he dealt in guns; Hardy told him to bring a gun to his shop, which he did; later, he ordered a pair of boots, and Hardy placed an order for three more guns. On one occasion, Hardy gave him Francklow's card, and told him that he was raising an association and wanted someone to supply guns; so he went to No. 1 China Street, Lambeth, where Francklow lived, and supplied him with eleven muskets, with steel rammers and bayonets. He and Sanderson found men exercising there; they had stopped going to Shelmerdine because he was a hatter and changed his men frequently, and some of them might not be staunch to the cause, which was, said Sanderson when giving evidence at the trial, to obtain parliamentary reform at the point of the bayonet. Williams himself, and a taylor called Orr, who said that he had served in the French army, trained them there, and in a blacksmith's shed just by Tothill Fields Bridewell, in Westminster.

Thomas Spence was also involved. Spence had been born on the Quayside in Newcastle in June 1750, one of nineteen children, whose father sold hardware in a booth on the Sandhill; he was still in Newcastle, working as a clerk and later as a schoolteacher, in the 1770s. The Spence family were members of the Forster Street Meeting House which believed in common property, and in 1775 Thomas Spence read a paper to the local Philosophical Society in which he advocated the communalisation of all the land in the nation. This became known as Spence's Plan, and in 1792 he moved to London and set up a shop, which he called the Hive of Liberty, at No. 8 Little Turnstile, Holborn, where he sold saloop[15] and books, but particularly pamphlets of his Plan which he sold at $^1/_2$d a copy, and a $^1/_2$d periodical called *Pig's Meat or Lessons for the Swinish Multitude*. He was also interested in coins and had a series of punches cut with which to stamp slogans on them, such as 'Spence's Plan is Small Farms'; and he advertised his pamphlets by showering copper medals, like pennies, from his window.[16] Frederick Polydore Nodder, who had been appointed the King's botanical artist in 1788,[17] became a member of the Association at the same time as Sanderson, and he told the Privy Council that he went to the Hive of Liberty once and found men exercising in a two-pairs-of-stairs room over the shop – three men with a rusty musket and a broomstick, in candlelight and the curtains drawn across the windows.[18]

IV Chalk Farm and the Crown and Anchor

The London Corresponding Society was now preparing to hold a general meeting on 14 April. Early in April, that Society and the Society for Constitutional Information set up a joint committee; its members included Baxter and Thelwall, and Sharp, Joyce, Holcroft and Kyd. This committee recommended that a convention of the friends of liberty should be called to take into consideration the proper methods of obtaining a full and fair representation of the people; and this was embodied in a resolution of the Society for Constitutional Information on 11 April.

Hardy was also corresponding with the Friends of the People. On 4 April he wrote to Sheridan, their chairman, to ask them to help him to assemble a Convention of the Friends of Freedom, and reminded the Friends that 'some of our most virtuous brethren, whose only crime has been an imitation of Mr Pitt and his associates', had been sentenced to 14 years transportation, that attempts had been made to introduce foreign troops into the country and to embody foreigners into his majesty's service, that a train of spies was being maintained at the taxpayers' expense, and that riots, public disturbances and seditious assemblies had been excited by the enemies of reform. The Friends maintained their usual cautious attitude: in their reply a week later, whilst expressing alarm at the 'late extraordinary proceedings of Government', they said that Hardy's proposals would simply furnish the enemies of reform with the means of calumniating its advocates; they therefore declined to send delegates to the proposed Convention.

The principal witness of the meeting on 14 April was John Groves, the spy. The original intention had been to meet in a dancing-room in Store Street, Tottenham Court Road, and Groves and Thelwall went there together. But they found a notice stuck up saying that it was to be held at Chalk Farm,[19] so there they went. There was a man taking tickets at the gate, and the crowd was assembling on a trap-ball[20] green beside the long room. When they arrived, there was a clamour raised that spies were being let in (Groves himself joined in the cry) but Thelwall's response was that they should be admitted so that the minister would be able to judge their proceedings and numbers.

Before the meeting began, Groves found some men sitting in a kind of shed, eating bread and cheese and drinking porter; and several of them pulled out identical spring knives, or French knives as they were called, 'so that when the blade is out, unless you undo that spring, it cannot close'; and someone from Sheffield told him that they were made in a bungling manner, and that many better ones had been made in Sheffield.[21] It was these *couteaux secrets* to which the prosecution attached so much importance, and the defence so much ridicule, at the subsequent trial.

John Lovett, a hairdresser, presided on the steps by the long room, and the meeting commenced with the reading of Hardy's letter to the Friends of the People and their reply; the latter was received in silence, until some started hissing. Then a series of resolutions was put to the meeting by Richter:

That the society beheld with indignation the rapid advances of despotism in Britain and the violation of all those provisions of the Constitution intended to protect the people against the Prerogative;

Their abhorrence at the arbitrary proceedings of the Court of Justiciary in Scotland, where all the doctrines and practices of the Star Chamber, in the times of Charles the First, had been revived and aggravated;

That the proceedings of the British Convention at Edinburgh were such as to claim their approbation and applause;

That the conduct of citizens Margarot and Gerrald had inspired an enthusiasm of zeal and attachment which no time could obliterate, and no persecution remove;

That any attempt to violate those laws which were intended to secure Englishmen against the Tyranny of Courts and Ministers and the corruption of Judges ought to be considered as dissolving the social compact between the English nation and their Governors, and driving them to an appeal to that incontrovertible maxim of eternal justice, that the safety of the people is the supreme, and in cases of necessity, the only law;

That the arming and disciplining in this country of emigrants and foreigners, driven from their own country for their known attachment to an infamous despotism, was an outrageous attempt to overawe and intimidate

the free spirit of Britons, and to subjugate them to an army of mercenary cut-
throats, whose views and interest must of necessity be in direct opposition to·
those of the Nation;

That the unconstitutional project of raising money and troops by forced
benevolences brought Charles I to the block, and drove James II from the
throne; and consequently ministers who advised such measures ought to
consider whether they are not guilty of high treason.

There followed two further resolutions congratulating and thanking the Earl
of Stanhope for opposing the introduction of Hanoverian and Hessian
mercenaries; and finally:

> 10. That it is the firm conviction of this society, that a steady perseverance in the
> same bold and energetic sentiments, which have lately been avowed by the Friends
> of Freedom, cannot fail of crowning with ultimate triumph, the virtuous cause in
> which we are engaged; since whatever may be the interested opinion of *hereditary*
> senators, or *packed* majorities of *pretended* representatives, Truth and Liberty, in
> an age so enlightened as the present, must be Invincible and Omnipotent.

An address to Gerrald was then read; he was then serving an:

> *unprecedented* sentence: a sentence one of the most vindictive and cruel that has
> been pronounced since the days of that *most infamous* and *ever-to-be-detested*
> Court of Star Chamber, the enormous tyranny of which cost the first Charles his
> head.
> For us it is that you are suffering the sentence of transportation with felons, the
> vilest outcasts of society!... We wish you Health and Happiness; and be assured we
> never, *never* shall forget *your name, your Virtues*, nor your GREAT EXAMPLE.

Further resolutions were passed to convey the approbation of the Society to
Rowan, then imprisoned in Dublin, to Curran who had defended him, and to
the United Irishmen; to Skirving, Palmer and Muir, and to Gerrald's counsel;
and to Thomas Walker, who had just been acquitted at Lancaster.[22] Another
resolution was passed that 200,000 copies of the proceedings and resolutions
of the meeting be printed and published. All these resolutions appeared over
the names of the chairman, J. Lovett, and the secretary, T. Hardy; and there
was yet another resolution, over the signature of Hardy alone, 'That the
thanks of this meeting be given to the Chairman, for his manly and impartial
conduct this day.'

Thelwall made two or three speeches that day; Richter read the resolutions,
but Martin claimed to have written them and had said that they were very
warm ones, for he had put plenty of Cayenne in them and that there would be
very warm work. According to Groves, Hardy himself, who rarely spoke on
public occasions, uttered only four words during the proceedings – when
Richter paused in reading a resolution to make some observation, Hardy said,
'Read, sir, without comment'.

Yet more resolutions were prepared in draft: That all sovereign, legislative,
and judicial powers were the rights of the people; That the constitution of
England was held by the King, Lords, and Commons in trust, and they could

not alter or subvert it without committing treason against the nation; That the office of King of England was not instituted by the people as an office of profit and honour to the King, but that he was appointed as chief trustee and guardian of the constitution and rights of the people; That it was the duty of the king to preserve the constitution and the rights of the people against every encroachment, according to the text of the Coronation Oath; That the constitutional rights of the people had been violated, and that it was their duty to assemble and inquire into the innovations or infringements which had been made upon their rights;

> That this society do invite the people to meet in their respective neighbourhoods, to elect one or more person or persons as delegates to meet in a convention, to be held on the   day of   next, at such place as shall be appointed by the secret committee of the society...(and to transmit vouchers of their elections to the secretary at No.9 Piccadilly).
> That it is the right and the bounden duty of the people to punish all traitors against the nation, and that the following words are now not a part of the oath of allegiance; to wit, 'I declare that it is not lawful, upon any pretence whatever, to take arms against the king.'[23]

There is no evidence that these resolutions were put before the meeting, but the parliamentary committee which was set up to inquire into these matters attached considerable importance to them as demonstrating the state of mind of the draftsmen.

Groves thought that there were up to 3000 people at Chalk Farm, mostly out of curiosity, but including some 800 or 900 members of the London Corresponding Society. Afterwards, he and Thelwall went to have supper in their own division room in Compton Street. It was there, said Groves, that Thelwall took up a pint of porter which had been handed to him by a waiter, and blew off the head saying, 'this is the way I would have all kings served', or 'this is the way I would serve all kings'; and he added that a toast was given to the lantern or lamp-iron, at the end of Parliament Street, and someone called from the back of the room, 'the Treasury Bench'.

On the day after the Chalk Farm meeting, Edward Gosling, another spy, was invited to join the London Corresponding Society. At his first meeting, members were saying that they were determined to hold a convention, and that it would be necessary to protect it in the same manner as they had in France. On the following Monday, 21 April, he went to another meeting in the house of a jack-maker in Brick Lane, and several members agreed to visit one of their number, Dr Hodson, who was in Newgate. So they went there the next day, and Dr Hodson explained that the Society was dividing into smaller divisions to facilitate training in arms at each other's houses; a toast was given, 'The World a Republic or a Desert', and Dr Hodson said he hoped that a revolutionary tribunal would soon be established as he despised all others.

On 23 April, Gosling was at a meeting at the Hope in Northampton Street; as the meeting was breaking up, one member asked him if he had any arms, and when he said No, the other member said he had got a musket and it was necessary that they should all have arms as they might very soon be compelled to use them; and someone else said he had a pike. Two days later, he was in Hillier's house in Bishopsgate Street; a man called Wicksley or Hicksley was there, and said that he had received a letter from Sheffield with a drawing of some knives specially designed to be fixed on poles for cutting reins; these were to be used against the royal family, and if they could be secured, the army would have no one to look to, and would be glad to accept the additional pay they would be offered.

✻   ✻   ✻

A week after Chalk Farm, and a fortnight after Castle Hill, there was an open air meeting at Halifax. Broomhead described it in a letter to Thelwall: there had been friends there from Leeds, Wakefield, Huddersfield, Bradford, and the adjacent neighbourhood, and an arrangement had been made to hold a further meeting at Bristol to prepare for a general convention. The writer added that they were not in the least intimidated in Sheffield, and they could hold public meetings whenever they wanted. Later in the month, Hardy received a letter from Newcastle: after complaining that the local aristocrat magistracy were endeavouring to stop the genial and benign spirit of national liberty from spreading, the letter said that the societies in Newcastle were in great spirits while the British convention continued to act, but after its suppression a damp was cast on them; but they now wished to copy the example of the London Corresponding Society and asked their advice in stimulating their membership. The letter ended, 'Farewell, hoping the hydra of tyranny and imposition shall soon fall under the guillotine of truth and reason.' Hardy replied to this on 1 May, congratulating the society in Newcastle, and expressing the hope that

> ...the glorious reign of liberty and equality will ere long be established; and modern governments, with every appendage of wickedness and corruption, will flee, in time, from their genial influence, as beasts of prey to their dens of rapine and darkness from the rising sun.

On the same day, there was a letter sent from Bristol commending the plans of the London Corresponding Society to hold a general convention. And on that day too, there was a letter from Sheffield: after stating that 'the bare-faced aristocracy of the present administration' made it necessary for them to act against 'any attack they may command their newly-armed minions to make' on them, the writer, Richard Davison, went on to say that a plan had been made for the manufacture of pikes:

> The blades are made of steel, tempered and polished after an approved form. They may be fixed into any shafts (but *fir* ones are recommended) of the girt of the accompanying hoops at the top end, and about an inch more at the bottom.
> The blades and hoops...will be charged one shilling. Money to be sent with the orders.

There was a postscript:

To prevent post suspicion, direct to Mr Robert Moody, joiner, Cheney-square, Sheffield. Please to forward the inclosed.

The last remark referred to a letter in similar terms to be forwarded to the secretary of the Norwich Patriotic Society. At the trial of Hardy, the Crown laid much stress upon this letter from Sheffield, although there was some doubt as to whether he had ever read it, and no evidence at all that he had acted upon it.

*   *   *

Between 9 and 10 p.m. on 1 May, Hardy went to Groves's house in Crown Court, Covent Garden, with a ticket; it was priced 7/6d, but Hardy told Groves that there was nothing to pay;[24] it was for the annual dinner of the Society for Constitutional Information for the following evening. Groves went to the Crown and Anchor and found about twenty other members of the London Corresponding Society were present; about three hundred were there altogether, with John Wharton MP for Beverley in the chair. Just before the dinner started, said Groves at the trial, the Society received news of some public event; it was 'bad news for the country', but was welcomed with universal satisfaction and was carried eagerly round the room.[25] The band struck up *Ca ira* as soon as the company got into the room, and it was encored time after time; and they played other popular tunes – the Marseillois march, the Democrat, and the Carmagnol: 'I never heard such an universal din of approbation in the course of my life,' said Groves, 'it was nothing but a scene of clamour, for I do believe most people's hands smarted, and their ears ached.' Eighteen toasts were drunk: The Rights of Man; The Swine of England, the Rabble of Scotland and the Wretches of Ireland; May Despotism be Trodden under the Hoofs of the Swinish Multitude; The Armies Contending for Liberty; Lord Stanhope, which was amended, amidst thunderous applause, to Citizen Stanhope; the Chairman thanked the company, and proposed a toast to That Steady Friend of Liberty, John Horne Tooke; in reply, Horne Tooke hoped that it would be the last time his health should be drunk; his ambition was, that hereafter *his MEMORY should be given*.

The toasts and replies were recorded in the minutes, but according to Groves, Horne Tooke made another speech after dinner; he opened by saying that one out of fifty in that room might be considered a government spy, and to them he particularly wished to address himself – 'So I must confess I did attend', said Groves when giving evidence at the Old Bailey.

There were times when Horne Tooke tasted nothing but water for months on end; but since his term of imprisonment, there had been times when he drank immense quantities of alcohol: people used to say that he had drunk enough to float a 74-gun ship. On one occasion he had had a quarrel with James Boswell, who promised to make up the breach on condition that they both drank a bottle of wine between each toast at a dinner party; Horne Tooke agreed, but on condition that brandy was substituted for wine, and he soon left Boswell sprawling on the floor. On another occasion, in 1793, he had attended a meeting of Whigs at the London Tavern, and asked permission to address them. He stood on a table, and so many of his supporters and opponents crowded round that the table collapsed under their weight; but he still stood erect, holding a glass of wine steadily in his hand, and to the surprise of his audience, drank it off, and delivered his speech as if nothing unusual had occurred. Tonight, he begged the company to notice that he was not in a state of inebriation, for he had taken care to refrain from his glass for fear of being mistaken; he called Parliament a scoundrel sink of corruption, and the opposition a scoundrel sink of opposition; he said there was a junction between those two scoundrel parties to destroy the rights and liberties of the country, and to abuse (or amuse) (Groves was not sure which word he employed) that poor man, the King; and he started to speak of the hereditary nobility and 'that skip-jack Jenkinson'.[26] The whole speech was greeted with applause, and they sang The Free Constitution to the tune of God Save the King.

It is safe to assume that Groves, Lynam and Sanderson and the other government spies were keeping their employers well-informed as to what was happening.

V The French connection

Evidence now came to light of a new conspiracy. This involved three men: the Revd William Jackson, a priest of the Church of Ireland; William Stone, a coal merchant in London; and his brother Hurford Stone.

William Stone lived in a villa called Old Ford at Newington;[27] he was a partner in a firm of coal merchants, Messrs Lawrence & Co., of Rutland Place, Thames Street; it was evidently a substantial business, for he claimed that he gave employment to 10,000 tons of shipping, and contributed £50,000 annually to the customs. William's brother, John Hurford Stone, was in business in France, and liked to be regarded as the leader of the English community there; for a time, he was working closely with the French Assembly.

Hurford Stone wrote many letters to his brother, mostly long business letters, sometimes hastily, even incoherently written; sometimes words were illegible; sometimes he used shorthand symbols. Sometimes he wrote on political matters. On 30 April 1792, he said that he was on intimate terms with Mr François, a member of the Assembly and chairman of the Committee of Commerce; and that he had dined with the Mayor of Paris. On 2 October, 1792, '1 o'clock, Hall of the Convention', he wrote that 'This moment the news has arrived that the Prussians have raised their camp', and on 24 October, he explained how he had received the news so promptly – 'for I have access to the secretary's table, and the dispatches into the provinces thro' which you receive my letters'. He had evidently been to the battle front:

I was a whole week in returning home, which I did exactly through the very march of the enemy, and found the country in such a state of inconvenience, bad roads, broken bridges, &c. rather than devastation, that we could not move sometimes more than a post, which is five miles English, in three hours and half; but it was impossible to miss our way, for had we been blind our sense of smelling would have directed us, for the carcases of horses or men presented themselves literally at every step we took; in one day's journey, which did not consist of but between 20 and 30 miles, we counted, of horses only, at least 2000, and the arms and legs of men obtruded themselves whenever we took the trouble of looking into the ditches, where they lay but half buried.

There was talk of expeditions to Spain, Savoy, Nice, Sardinia, even Rome:

For there is no mischief of which these Marseillois are not capable; and their present whim is, to bring the pope and the cardinals prisoners to Paris – It was the Marseillois who executed the revolution of the 10th August; the Marseillois who have chiefly at their own expense made this expedition against Nice; it is these gentlemen who are going in search of the Pope.

On 1 February France declared war on England, and Hurford Stone scribbled a note to his brother on the following day:

Dear Brother; – I have only 3 minutes to write, by a gentleman who is departing for England. Yesterday we declared war against you in due form, with the general approbation and general regret: this was more than you expected, but the patience of the French was exhausted: and now the event is committed to the last resource – arms. Holland it is expected will be in our power in a very short time; and this will likely bring it with England to a short conclusion.

On 18 March, he wrote that there was a plan to send a force to the Cape of Good Hope and the West Indies, and then added:

At home a descent will be made on England, with a force that will be almost irresistible, but in what manner I have not yet learnt: I was applied to by General Dillon on the subject, but I declined any interference. You must be careful not to mention these circumstances, especially as coming from me.

A few days later, William Stone received another letter in which his brother warned him that there were plans to invade England in two places simultaneously, one as near to the metropolis as possible, the other in the north with a view to destroying the collieries. William Stone was now in a position of acute embarrassment and difficulty, and he decided to go to the Prime Minister in person; this he did, early in April, and followed the interview with a letter setting out what he knew of the enemy's plans and enclosing abstracts of his brother's letters (but omitting any reference to the letter of 2 February); Pitt replied on 16 April, returning the documents and adding:

I am obliged to you for having communicated such public information as you thought might be useful, and have nothing further to add on the subject of these papers. I am, sir, your obedient servant, W. Pitt.

There was then a gap in the correspondence between the two brothers – letters were probably being intercepted – until the autumn of 1793. When they resumed, they were mostly business letters: the sad plight of the starving English workmen; the difficulty of corresponding (he suggested sending letters to Mme Henvenne, rue Ferrenestriere, Liege) and of transferring money (bills of exchange should be sent to Sir Robert Barclay, bart., Aix-la-Chapelle). But there were regular political references as well. Hurford Stone was constantly advising his brother to sell Old Ford, the inference being that it would lie in the path of an invading enemy; and on Boxing Day 1793:

> What can you say to the continuance of the war, when you see the fate that attends you. You see that we are every way invincible; and of this the taking of Toulon will serve as an evidence for thousands of our countrymen perished there; but this is not a hundredth part of the evil that awaits you; the Vendee is crush'd entirely by this time,[28] and troops are gathering on the coasts. I wished you to dispose of your house. You now fully understand me [shorthand characters] must take place.... Yesterday was our Christmas-day also. Having the gout, I could not go out to partake of a dinner given by our countrymen the Williams's; but I had a few countrymen around me at home, where we drank all your healths, and success to the cause of liberty.

✻ ✻ ✻

The Revd William Jackson was a native of Ireland. He was for a time a priest in London, and it was while he was living in England that he became acquainted with the Duchess of Kingston; he was employed by her as her secretary, and some said that they had a more intimate relationship. The Duchess' attorney was John Cockayne, and the two came to know each other, and Jackson employed him in a professional capacity. He spent many years in England and was connected with the Royalty Theatre, and became heavily in debt. Subsequently, he went to France, and he resided there for a considerable time.

Early in 1794, Jackson was sent to England by the French government, to learn the state of affairs there and in Ireland, and he was given letters of introduction by Hurford Stone to his brother (who had aleady been warned of his impending arrival) and to Horne Tooke. He sailed from Hamburg to Hull in the *Elbe*; he reached England on 25 February, and went straight to London where he represented himself as an American businessman. He made himself known to William Stone, and arranged to communicate with him under the name of Thomas Popkins, Stone to be known as Enots.

Jackson stayed in the Buffaloe Tavern in Bloomsbury Square and he resumed his contact with Cockayne, who was then in practice in Lyons' Inn; he asked Cockayne to address letters for him, ostensibly on the ground that he did not wish his handwriting to be seen lest his creditors should find out that he was in London. Cockayne did so, until he began to realise that the letters might be of a treasonable nature, or at least might concern commercial dealing with France in prohibited goods.

It was an appalling situation for an attorney. Jackson was a friend and a client of long standing (and owed him £300 in fees); on the other hand, the letters were liable to interception in the post, and he was in danger of being compromised as a party to a treasonable conspiracy. Towards the end of

March, Jackson was preparing to go to Ireland, so Cockayne decided to take the best advice he could: he consulted the Prime Minister. Pitt advised him to travel with his client and to spy upon him. And so the pair of them set off for Ireland; they arrived on 1 April, and took lodgings at Hyde's Coffee House in Dame Street at the corner of Palace Row in Dublin.

Cockayne's hope that his client was simply concerned with commercial contraband was soon dissipated. Hospitable Irishmen invited Jackson and Cockayne to dine with them, and Jackson directed the conversation towards the attitude of the Irish people, and whether they would be prepared to rise in support of a French invasion. He was advised that the best person to inform him was Hamilton Rowan, now in the Dublin Newgate, whose brother-in-law was Benjamin Beresford, a business associate in France of Hurford Stone. A meeting between Jackson and Rowan was arranged, and the latter invited Jackson and Cockayne to breakfast in Newgate. Theobald Wolfe Tone, a barrister whose name was soon to become famous in Irish history, was also present at this meeting, and they decided to send an emissary to France to tell the French government that the Irish would rise and overthrow their oppressors if an invasion was launched. They asked Wolfe Tone to go, but he had a wife and three children, and business and professional commitments, and he declined the invitation.

In the meantime, 'Thomas Popkins' had, on 5 April, written to William Stone, referring apparently to certain business transactions – 'the price and nature of the articles being entirely changed' – which a contemporary reader would have little difficulty in recognising as a coded reference to the recent assassination of Danton in Paris; 'W. Enots' replied on 11 April, addressing his letter to John Cockayne. The Irish government had already been apprised of addresses to which Jackson was writing and were intercepting his correspondence. On 24 April, Jackson directed Cockayne to write a letter to M. Beresford, chez Bouchard & Co., Basle, Switzerland, asking him to apprise 'Mr Madgett', believed to be a reference to the French minister of marine, of 'the opinion of the first counsel in this kingdom relative to the family lawsuit', and advising him that he 'may therefore proceed for the recovery of his family fortune by hostile or pacific means as he and his friends think proper'. At the same time Jackson set out the results of his research in a letter in which he said that the population of Ireland could be divided into three sects: The established Church, numbering some 450,000, consisting of aristocrats who had in their hands the entire church patronage, the profits and honours of the country and much of the landed property, and who were the enemies of the French Revolution; the Dissenters, some 900,000, who were the most enlightened members of the community, steady republicans devoted to liberty, and enthusiastic supporters of the Revolution; and the great majority, some 3,150,000 Catholics, in the lowest degree of ignorance, and ready for any change because no change could make them worse off. The whole peasantry in Ireland, the most oppressed and wretched in Europe, were Catholics, and they were a bold and hardy race and would make excellent soldiers. In England, it was morally certain that all ranks would be united to oppose an invasion, but in Ireland, a conquered, oppressed and insulted country, the name of England was universally odious; the dissenters were enemies of the English by reason and reflection, the Catholics from a hatred of the English name. And then he went on:

In a word...there seems little doubt but an invasion in sufficient force would be supported by the people. There is scarce any army in the country, and the militia, the bulk of whom are Catholics, would to a moral certainty refuse to act, if they saw such a force as they could look to for support.

There were two copies of this document, one directed to go to M. Daudebuscaille at Amsterdam enclosed in another envelope addressed to Messrs Texier, Angely and Massac at Amsterdam, the other to M. Chapeaurouge at Hamburg; the envelopes were each marked with a large cross, which was a sign in those days that the letter was to be opened by the addressee in person, not by a clerk. These letters were intercepted by Isaac de Joncourt, the deputy constable of the post office in Dublin, on 24 April; and at 10 a.m. on 28 April, Oliver Carlton, acting under a warrant signed by the Earl of Clonmell, Chief Justice of the Court of King's Bench of Ireland, went to Hyde's Coffee House, and found Jackson in bed in a room up two pairs of stairs, and arrested him. Carlton also found several papers on a table beside the bed, and some more in a trunk.

The papers found in Jackson's room included Hurford Stone's letter, never delivered, to Horne Tooke, dated 'Paris, 25 Nivose Second Year of the Republic, One and Indivisible'. The letter begins 'My dear Friend,' and, although written in fairly general terms, it did contain various phrases which would have been highly prejudicial to Horne Tooke if it had been found among his papers:

And now my patriotic friend, let me offer you my warmest and most heartfelt congratulations on the immense prospect of public happiness which is opening before us; you are amongst the small number of those, who in the worst of times have never despaired of the cause of liberty, and you are the only one who when the name was but a barbarism amongst us, taught the great principles of sacred equality which we have so completely reduced to practice. I look forward...to the moment...when the various parties...of churchmen, nobles, priests and kings, shall sink into one undistinguished, mass of ruins, and nothing shall be seen or acknowledged but the people, the sacred voice of the people.

The writer then referred to a commission to a milliner which he had undertaken for the ladies (possibly a coded political message, but probably a genuine undertaking on behalf of Horne Tooke's daughters), and concluded:

God bless you, we shall meet under happier circumstances than our last, and drink a cool bottle of good Burgundy under the shade of our trees, an early day in the next summer.... Health and fraternity, J. H. Stone.

Another important document found in Jackson's room was the draft of a report on the state of affairs in England: There were no petitions against the war; men were ready to enlist; there was 'much quietness' in being impressed on the part of seamen; terror pervaded the friends of liberty; England had supported the first French Revolution, but not the second;

> if France were to invade England, every man would turn out from good will or fear, and the few who are discontented would be quelled with ease;... There could be but one line of conduct for Englishmen to pursue, should the country be invaded. – They must defend it.[29]

Accordingly, the writer advised the French government to adopt a more philanthropic language to pacify the English, to liberate all the English under arrest in France unless accused of crimes, restore them to their property and allow them to leave the country.

                              ✻   ✻   ✻

In the evening of 3 May, Thomas Maclean and Edward Lauzun, two of the King's Messengers,[30] went to William Stone's villa in Newington and arrested him; they were followed a few minutes later by John King, the private secretary to Secretary Dundas, and Joseph White, the treasury solicitor. King asked Stone if he had corresponded with Jackson under the names of Popkins and Enots, and Stone denied this; so a search was made, and soon a letter from Popkins was found in an escritoire; many other letters were found in drawers and little holes or places which were part of the writing-desk – Stone opened the drawers himself, and made no attempt to conceal them.

Also discovered were two more drafts of the report on the state of England, one in Stone's writing, the other in Jackson's writing with amendments by Stone; at Stone's trial, one of the principal issues which the jury had to decide was whether a person could be said to be giving aid and comfort to the enemy when he was warning him not to invade; but to the under-secretary of state and the treasury solicitor, sitting in the library at Old Ford that night and reading the letters from the drawers, this must have appeared as clear a case of adhering to the enemy as one could well imagine.

CHAPTER 8

THE ARRESTS

On 12 May 1794, at 6.30. in the morning, Mr Lauzun junior, the son of the King's Messenger, gave a thundering knock on the door of No. 9 Piccadilly, before the shop was opened; Hardy jumped out of bed, and went, half-dressed, to see what the matter was. When the door was opened, Lauzun rushed in, followed by John Gurnel, a King's Messenger, two Bow Street Runners (colloquially known as thief-takers), P. Macmanus and John Townsend, John King, and two or three other men. Lauzun seized Hardy and searched his pockets, where he found some letters and papers, and his pocket-book which contained two bills of exchange to the amount of £196. When Hardy asked by what authority he was being treated in this way, Lauzun showed him a paper, which he called a warrant for his apprehension on a charge of High Treason; but before he could read more than a few lines, Lauzun re-folded it and put it back in his pocket; Hardy had no chance to see who had signed it.

Lauzun rummaged through all the drawers, even those containing Mrs Hardy's clothes. He demanded the key of a bureau, and when he could not obtain it, he threatened to break the bureau, and tried to force it open with a poker. When Mrs Hardy begged him to desist, King called in a smith who was waiting outside and brought in a box full of pick-locks and skeleton keys. This man did his work very expeditiously; he opened the bureau and some trunks, and soon the party had four large silk handkerchiefs filled with papers, including many of Hardy's private letters. 'When they had ransacked every place in our bedroom that they thought fit,' said Hardy, 'then they went into the shop, expecting, no doubt, to find treason hatching among the boots and shoes.'[1] It so happened that Hardy had handed over the records of the London Corresponding Society to his assistant secretary, so these were not found. King then called for a hackney coach, into which Hardy and the four bundles of papers were put, accompanied by Townsend and Gurnel, and taken to the latter's home in King Street, at the corner of Charles Street, Westminster. The rest of the party stayed behind and collected nearly enough books and pamphlets to fill a corn sack. 'The feelings of poor Mrs Hardy', wrote her husband, 'may be easier imagined than described. In an advanced state of pregnancy, sitting in bed all the time, and unable to dress before so many unwelcome visitors, whom she could hardly consider in a better light than that of robbers'. According to one story, not mentioned by Hardy himself, when she protested at his arrest, one of the officers replied: 'I hope you will have the pleasure of seeing him hanged before your door'.[2]

*   *   *

For a year or two now, one of the government spies had attached himself to Horne Tooke and become a frequent visitor at Wimbledon. His host soon realised his intentions, but instead of dismissing him, he decided to hoist his enemies with their own petard. So he pretended to admit the spy into his complete confidence; he began to drop hints about the strength and enthusiasm of the popular party, magnifying their numbers, praising their unanimity, and commending their determination. Gradually, he proceeded to supply detailed information, and finally told the spy, under the most solemn promise of secrecy, that some of the Guards were won over, that an armed force was being organised, and that the country was on the verge of a revolution. Finally, he pretended to confess that he himself was the leader of a conspiracy, and he boasted, like Pompey of old, 'that he could raise legions merely by stamping on the ground with his foot'. And on the day on which Hardy was arrested, the government intercepted a letter which Jeremiah Joyce had written to Horne Tooke and which seemed to confirm their fears that an insurrection was imminent.

Few men in England, of whatever rank, had been so outspoken in their support for the French Revolution as the third Earl of Stanhope. He and the Prime Minister had long since been drifting apart. The Earl had removed the ornamental coronets from the gates at Chevening; he was openly being addressed as Citizen Stanhope; he had repeatedly attacked the government in the House of Lords – on the war against France,[3] on their support for the Scottish judiciary, and on the landing of Hessian and Hanoverian troops on the south coast. He had recently employed the Revd Jeremiah Joyce as a tutor to his sons, and the government was well aware that Joyce was taking an active part in the affairs of the London Corresponding Society. His letter to Horne Tooke was concise and to the point:

> Dear Citizen. This morning, at 6 o'clock, Citizen Hardy was taken away by order from the Secretary of State's office. They seized everything they could lay hands on. Query, is it possible to get ready by Thursday? Yours, J. Joyce.

When this letter was intercepted, ministers thought that a definite date had been fixed for an insurrection, and they determined to forestall it. All approaches to Horne Tooke's house were watched, and the following morning his carriage was followed into London. Soon after he had sat down to dinner with his doctor, Dr Pearson, in Spital Square, a detachment of soldiers was sent there, and during the afternoon a troop of light horse passed by the window where he was sitting. He was arrested, under a warrant from the Secretary of State, early in the morning of 16 May. He was perfectly at ease with his own fate, but he was concerned for his daughters and wrote a letter to a lady upon whom he could rely:

Whitehall, May 17 1794

Dear Madam

I take the liberty of requesting you to go to my house, at Wimbledon, for a short time, to accompany my poor girls in my absence. I am in custody, by order of the secretary of state, and cannot return. The gentleman who brings this note will accompany you this evening to Wimbledon. You will greatly oblige me by this act of kindness.

Your most obedient servant,

J. Horne Tooke.

John Thompson, described as a clerk in the public office in Lambeth Street, Whitechapel, and James Thornton, a clerk in the police office[4] in Marlborough Street, went to Wimbledon to search Horne Tooke's house, which they did in the presence of John Frost and Felix Vaughan to represent the accused. They read many of his papers – 'There are more papers in my house than a man could read in a year', he said at his trial.

∗ ∗ ∗

On the following day, early in the morning, John King and one of the King's messengers went to Chevening to arrest Joyce: 'He was just coming down to breakfast,' said Lady Hester many years later, 'when a single knock came at the door, and in bolted two officers with a warrant, and took him off without even my father's knowledge'. Joyce himself left a rather longer account of his arrest:

It was immediately rumoured that other persons would be favoured with domiciliary visits and that I must not expect to escape.... On Wednesday about 8 in the morning, while I was conversing with Lord Mahon and his two brothers, Mr King, Under-Secretary of State, and Mr Ross, one of his Majesty's messengers, were introduced to me as having some private business to communicate. When the young gentlemen had left the room, Mr Ross produced a warrant against me for 'Treasonable Practices', by which he was authorised to seize my person and all books and papers connected with the Society for Constitutional Information and the London Corresponding Society. He demanded my keys, and after having searched my pockets and bed-chamber, they selected from my drawers and bookcases whatever they pleased.

∗ ∗ ∗

In those times, as still today, a person accused of a serious crime appeared before the justices of the peace to hold a preliminary inquiry into the offence. In the case of suspected treason or other serious offences against the state, this inquiry was carried out by Privy Counsellors in their capacity of justices of the peace for the whole realm.[5] Hardy, who remained in the custody of Gurnel, where he was well treated, for over a fortnight, was interrogated on several occasions before the Privy Council, which included, according to his own account, the Prime Minister, Secretary Dundas, Lord Loughborough LC, the Attorney and Solicitor General, John Reeves 'of notorious memory', and others. White, the Treasury Solicitor, although not a Privy Counsellor, was also present, possibly to act as clerk to the Council.

The first interrogation took place at 11 a.m. on the day of Hardy's arrest. According to Hardy's own account, the Secretary of State asked him his name and occupation, to which he gave a ready reply; he was then asked many questions to which he could not reply, and many letters and papers were shown to him which he had never seen before and of which he knew nothing; but he readily acknowledged letters and papers which he had written and signed.

The examination was continued on the next day, Tuesday, and on the Wednesday, and then again on the following Monday when he was asked about guns, pikes and other warlike instruments. In his Memoirs he asserted:

> Of such instruments he knew nothing. It is impossible that so many societies as then existed, could be without some violent characters, among which might be included the Government spies; but whatever such unworthy persons may have hinted, in any of the numerous Societies, about arms, Hardy, and the real patriotic part of them, abhorred the very idea of having recourse to violence of any sort. All their efforts were directed to the recovery of the lost rights of themselves and of their fellow citizens – in fact to the attainment of Parliamentary Reform, by constitutional and peaceable means.

⁂

Joyce was taken to London and appeared before the Privy Council at 1 p.m. on the day of his arrest, and was examined for three-quarters of an hour; after stating that he lived with Lord Stanhope and had the care of his two elder sons, he refused to answer any questions about his political activities. He was then detained in Ross's custody, and on the following Monday was transferred to the Tower.[6]

Horne Tooke was also interrogated, but he was treated in a rather different manner from the others. Dundas informed him that the nature of the treasonable practices for which he had been arrested was that he was a leading member of the Societies which had been plotting to hold a Convention to supersede the established government, and that he was to be examined so as to have an opportunity of removing the suspicions which were entertained about him. He replied that if he received an assurance from any member of the Privy Council that there was any information on oath against him for a single act of treason, he would not ask the name of the informant and would answer any questions which might be put to him; when no such assurances were given, he refused to answer any further questions, and he too was conveyed to the Tower.[7]

⁂

Daniel Adams, the secretary of the Society for Constitutional Information, had been arrested at 8 a.m. on the same day as Hardy. The books and papers of the Society were found in his house in two trunks; he produced the keys and unlocked them himself, and later before the Privy Council he gave all the information he could.[8]

Lovett, Richter, Bonney and Thelwall were arrested on the following day. Thelwall was interrogated by the Privy Council, and left his own version of what occurred. He was called in and saw the Privy Council, including Lord Loughborough LC, Secretary Dundas and the Prime Minister 'chin deep' in the papers which lay scattered all over the table. The Attorney-General asked him his name, and he replied 'John'. The Attorney-General asked if his surname was spelt with two Ls at the end or one, and he replied,'With two – but it does not signify. You need not give yourself any trouble. I do not intend to answer any questions'. 'What does he say?' asked the Prime Minister darting round from the other side of the room and seating himself beside the Chancellor, who said, 'with silver softness, almost melting to a whisper', 'He does not mean to answer any questions'.'What is it? What is it?' asked the Prime Minister; and Thelwall turned his back on them and started to contemplate a water-colour on the wall. So they dismissed him. In later life, he used to say that he had felt near to committing treason by compassing and imagining the act of pulling a Privy Counsellor by the nose.[9]

Then they called in a young boy of 14, Henry Eaton, who had been living with Thelwall; but they did not get much change out of him either, for he started to harangue the Prime Minister and upbraided him for imposing exorbitant taxes on the people.[10] And when Thomas Spence was interrogated, he told the Privy Council that the plot for the reform of Parliament would go on, notwithstanding all the examination of witnesses and the seizure of papers.

*   *   *

The Government could have good reason to suppose that, in Scotland at least, the conviction and transportation of the principal members of the British Convention had put an end to any further trouble north of the border. They were mistaken.

At about midday on Thursday 15 May 1794, William Lockhart, the sheriff's clerk, and William Middleton, one of the sheriff's officers, accompanied by a locksmith, went to a house in North Bridge Close in Edinburgh where a merchant and dealer in spirits, Robert Watt, was residing; they had a warrant to search the house for fraudulent bankrupt goods which were believed to have been secreted there. They found the goods in a cellar. While they were carrying out their search, the locksmith opened a wardrobe, and Middleton noticed some spears there; he took one in his hand and showed it to Lockhart, who remarked that he thought it a dangerous instrument, and asked if there were any more; yes, said Middleton, and laid out a dozen on the carpet. They immediately obtained a warrant for Watt's arrest, although it was not until about twelve hours later that they returned and carried out a second search of the house; they found two more pikes and two battle-axes hidden in a closet; they also found a fount of type, and thinking it strange that a spirits dealer should have such apparatus in his home, they took it away and arranged for a printer to run off some copies. The document was addressed to the Scottish army, and was a blatant attempt to seduce the men from their duties.

The Lord Advocate was in London at the time, and when he heard the news, he was thunderstruck, for Robert Watt was an informer in whom he had complete confidence. He had set up in business in Edinburgh in 1786 and had decided to offer his services to Mr Secretary Dundas. He attended several meetings of the Friends of the People at Mather's Tavern, and in August 1792 he wrote to the Secretary of State to say that he was observing the activities of the societies in Scotland, and was astonished at their political sentiments – one gentleman had expressed the opinion that a king should be sacrificed to the nation once in every hundred years – and he offered to keep the Secretary of State informed as to their further proceedings. Dundas replied on 5 September: he said that he trusted that the number of evilly disposed persons was not great, but it was necessary to keep a watchful eye over them. During the autumn he was in Scotland, and he and his nephew, the Lord Advocate, and the sheriff made inquiries about Watt and decided that he was a man on whom they could rely. Watt met the Lord Advocate at his home, and kept providing him with useful information.

Two incidents, however, should have put him on his guard. On one occasion, Watt informed the Lord Advocate that a party of soldiers had been incited to mutiny; the troops in question were identified and brought to Edinburgh, where they were interviewed by the Lord Advocate and the Commander-in-Chief, and they completely denied everything that Watt had said. And then, in March 1793, Watt wrote to the Lord Advocate in London, telling him that he was in a position to obtain some valuable information but required £1000 to pay his informants. The Lord Advocate decided not to participate in this transaction, but later, on returning to Scotland, he did pay Watt £30 which Watt told him had been incurred as a debt to his informants.

Watt ceased to send information to the Lord Advocate while the Convention was sitting in the autumn of 1793. However, hardly had the Convention been dispersed, when a 'Committee of Union' was set up early in January 1794 to keep the objects of the societies alive: Watt was a member of this Committee. In addition, a 'Committee of Ways and Means' was set up to raise money; Watt was also a member of this, and the treasurer was David Downie.

On 10 March the Committee of Way and Means was meeting at Watt's house; Arthur M'Ewan, a weaver, and a Mr Bonthorne, a school-teacher, were there, together with Watt and Downie, when Watt produced from his pocket a paper which, in the words of M'Ewan:

> contained a plan to seize the lord justice clerk, the rest of the lords of session, and the lord provost; also to have a number of men placed at the Weigh-house, and a number at the Lucken-booths; to put a fire at the Excise-office, to draw the military from the Castle, and when they came down, those placed at the Weigh-house, with the others at the Lucken-booths, were to enclose them, at the same time numbers were to seize the different banks of this town, and to appoint commissioners to go and demand the cash of them...

After reading this remarkable document, Watt put it away in a press. At another meeting, Watt produced a copy of a proclamation which was, apparently, to be issued immediately after the attack on the Castle:

> to all farmers and dealers in corn, meal and hay, not to remove the same from their habitation under pain of death; and also for all gentlemen residing in the country not to leave their habitation above three miles under pain of death.

Coupled with this, there was an address to the King – To dismiss his ministers, to put an end to the present war, or to meet bad consequences.

There was at least some evidence to suggest that this wild scheme was not merely a fantasy. In March Watt approached Robert Orrock, a smith who lived at Dean and had been a delegate at the Convention and was now a member of the Committee of Union, and showed him a drawing of a pike and asked if he could make one. Orrock made a sample, and Watt then asked how many he could make in a week; Orrock said that he and his two men could make fifty, so Watt put in an order for two or three dozen, and the same number of cross-pikes or halberds. Watt said that there might be thousands wanted, and Orrock said that he could make thousands as well as fifty. Watt also said that if anyone inquired what he was making, he could say they were ornamental spikes to put on top of a gate.

While weapons were being prepared, John Fairley, a cabinet-maker, who had also been a member of the Convention, was appointed a Collector – to go round Scotland to collect money and sentiments: the money was required to pay off the debts of the Convention, to relieve suffering (Skirving's wife got 15/-), and to pay the delegates of the next convention; the 'sentiments' were the views of the people on universal suffrage and annual parliaments. He had a sister in service at Airth and he set out ostensibly to visit her, but took in Queensferry, Stirling, St Ninians, Kilsyth, Campsie, Glasgow, Paisley and Falkirk, and he took with him a circular letter from the Committee of Ways and Means to remind their fellow citizens of the melancholy state of affairs and of the cruel effects of the war.

In April, there was increasing violence in Edinburgh. On 9 April, Downie wrote a letter to a correspondent in Perth in which he described a riot which had taken place two days previously at the Theatre while a tragedy about Charles I was being performed: some aristocrats called for the band to play God Save the King, which was received with hisses from all over the house; so they played Maggie Lauder instead, to universal applause. The aristocrats then called in the troops from the Castle, and they set about the unarmed audience with their swords. He also reported that some of the Fencibles in the Frith had been turbulent and had fired balls at an armed boat which had been sent to overawe them. In a postscript he added:

> We are happy to have it in our power to assure you from our information from England, and different parts of Scotland, that the late persecutions, instead of retarding have accelerated the great cause of freedom.

Also on 9 April, Alexander Mitchell from Strathaven wrote to Hardy to tell him that the society there had united with others in Kilmarnock, Galston,

Newmilns and Dervill, had elected a delegate for the forthcoming national Convention, and had appointed a secret committee for carrying out their business.

The document which had been found in the fount of type in Watt's house was unsigned, but dated Dundee, April 12th 1794. It commenced with the words 'Friends and Brethren', but was clearly addressed to the troops who had been raised in Scotland and stated that it was with great pleasure that the writer had learned that they had refused to leave the country, contrary to the terms on which they had been engaged. The tone became more strident as the address went on; after rejoicing that his readers were now learning that they could not forcibly be compelled to take up arms and leave their families, the anonymous writer continued:

> When you are gone, where is their defence ? They may be either left without protection, or may soon see their country overrun by foreign troops, such as in time past have already shed the blood of your ancestors without provocation, and without remorse; and who would feel perhaps as little compunction in shedding yours.
>
> Prepared for every deed of horror, these foreign mercenaries may violate the chastity of your wives, your sisters, and your daughters, and when desire is satiated, cruelty may resume its place in their hearts, as experience has too well and too fatally shown, and friends, parents, children, brothers may be involved in one common slaughter.
>
> The cruel massacre of Glencoe cannot yet be forgotten; are there not amongst you, whose forefathers perished there? their hearts throbbing with kindness and hospitality were pierced with the daggers of their treacherous guests, and the feast, prepared by the hand of unsuspecting friendship, was closed with a scene of blood...
>
> The circumstances which might require you to quit your country have not yet taken place. – No invasion has yet happened, you cannot be compelled to go.

There is little evidence as to how many copies of this address were distributed, but one was certainly being circulated among Lord Hopetoun's Fencibles when they were in Dalkeith in the middle of May, on their way south to Liverpool.

                         *   *   *

On Monday 12 May, Mr Secretary Dundas presented to the House of Commons a message signed by the King to the effect that he had received information that certain societies had been planning to hold a Convention to subvert the Laws and Constitution, and that he had ordered their papers to be seized and laid before the House. On the following day, Tuesday, the House took the message into consideration, and it was resolved that a committee of secrecy should be set up to consider it; the committee was to consist of 21 members who were to be elected by ballot of all members. On the Wednesday, the Serjeant at Arms was ordered to go to all places frequented by members and summon them to take part in the ballot, and each member put a list of names into a glass. The lists were scrutinised and the names of the committee were read out; they included William Pitt, who was both Prime Minister and Chancellor of the Exchequer, both the Law Officers of England and the Lord Advocate, that 'skip-jack' Robert Jenkinson, and Edmund Burke.

The Committee produced an interim report on Friday 16 May. It contained many of the papers of the London Corresponding Society and the Society for Constitutional Information. The Committee concluded from these documents that the Societies were planning to hold a Convention similar to the National Convention of France, and to overthrow the Constitution; they added that measures had been taken to arm the members of the Societies.

A Bill to enable His Majesty to secure and detain such persons as he suspected of conspiring against his government was immediately introduced, read twice, and passed by a majority of 172 to 22. The Bill was then referred to a Committee of the whole House, where it was discussed until the early hours of Saturday morning; and it received its third reading at 3 p.m. that afternoon. On Monday, the Bill, along with the papers which had been seized, was transferred to the House of Lords, who passed it without amendment on Friday 23 May. It received the Royal Assent the same day.

Secretary Dundas received the news of Watt's arrest on 19 May, and wrote that same evening to the Committee to inform them that he had received information from Scotland that weapons had been found in Watt's house; he kept the House of Commons informed of additional evidence as it came in day by day from Edinburgh. About the same time, too, information was received from Sheffield that a large number of pikes were being manufactured and that 2 July had been fixed as the day for storming the town and the barracks; a warrant was issued on 20 May for the arrest of Broomhead and other members of the Sheffield Constitutional Society.[11]

The Committee submitted its Report on Friday 6 June. The Report occupies some 80 pages in the Journals of the House of Commons, including the text of many documents. It opened with an account of the evidence that the societies, and the London Corresponding Society in particular, were procuring arms; their information was that the question of arms was not discussed in the societies' open meetings, but in private after the meetings had ended. They reported that pikes and night-cats were being made in Sheffield; that the so-called Loyal Lambeth Association were exercising in the use of firearms; and that there were stories of 4000 pikes being manufactured in Scotland.

The Report then proceeded to give an account of the London Corresponding Society's relations with France, and of its outspoken opposition to the War. There were stories that the Society was planning to seduce members of the Army from their duty; that the Royal Family were to be seized; that the convicted delegates to the Scottish Convention were to be rescued from the transport in the Thames; that Newgate was to be attacked and the prisoners released; and that the Tower of London and Edinburgh Castle were to be seized.[12] The Committee stressed that the general tenor of the Society's publications was to inflame the minds of the people, and to encourage them to sedition and rebellion; every means of exciting discontent were employed, even by measures which might at first sight appear trivial – by play bills and seditious toasts, and by songs and tunes imported from France. The Report also traced the history of the Society since its foundation in 1792; it set out their correspondence with provincial societies and with France, and referred to the speeches of Barrère, Roland and St André – speeches which were delivered for the express purpose of accelerating the condemnation and execution of the French King.

The Report then traced the history of the Society for Constitutional Information, drawing attention to the fact that all the principal societies in the country had been regulated under its auspices, and had looked up to it for advice; stressing, in particular, its support for Paine's *Rights of Man* since the publication of that work in 1791.

From the beginning of 1793, the Committee reported, the correspondence of the Societies seemed to have been directed to the ostensible purpose of petitioning Parliament, but the Committee had formed the opinion that their real purpose was to assemble a representative body without any reference to Parliament and with the intention of arrogating to itself the whole legislative authority of the nation; the Committee's views were strengthened by the transactions of the Edinburgh Convention, which they reviewed in detail with particular reference to the resolution of 28 November 'which necessarily attracted the attention of the Law Officers of the Crown'.

The Report concluded with a review of the evidence which led them to believe that the Societies had abandoned their ostensible purpose of applying to Parliament and were intent on using some other means, by intimidation or force, to achieve their objective; and that they were using language which distinctly pointed to the use of open force, to obtain the redress of their grievances, not from Parliament or Government, but from themselves, and their own laws – and thereby to lead to the destruction of the monarchy and the House of Lords, and the entire destruction of the constitution:

> A proposition so extravagant may at first be difficult to be credited; but it appears to the Committee to be distinctly proved, from an examination of the principles themselves; from a consideration of the system as actually carried into effect in France, and proposed as a model by those who were the chief actors in these proceedings in this country; and, by repeated declarations or acts, which either directly or by necessary inference point to the destruction of hereditary monarchy, hereditary nobility, and every distinction of orders and ranks in society.

The Report then referred to a paper which had been printed by the London Corresponding Society after Hardy's arrest, in which it was openly asserted that it was their intention to call a Convention to supersede the House of Commons and admitted that some of their members had been training in the use of arms. And finally the Committee added that information had recently come to their knowledge that the ruling powers in France had been taking measures to ascertain, both in Great Britain and Ireland, the degree of co-operation and assistance which they might obtain in those countries.

The report was presented to the House of Commons by William Pitt in his capacity as Chancellor of the Exchequer.[13]

✢   ✢   ✢

While the Parliamentary inquiry was in progress, more arrests were made and interrogations continued before the Privy Council. There was Stewart Kyd, the barrister and author of a *Treatise on the Law of Corporations*, the first volume of which had been published a few months earlier; pressure was brought to bear upon him to give evidence for the Crown, but he resisted and was sent to the Tower where he completed the second volume of his book and dedicated it to Horne Tooke. There was William Sharp, the finest engraver of his age, who was a link between the Society for Constitutional Information and the Royal Academy; he was at the time at work on a portrait of the Polish hero, General Kosciusko, and when he became exasperated at the interrogation he pulled a subscription list out of his pocket and passed it across the table to Pitt and Dundas for their signatures – at this they all burst into laughter, and the list was passed round the Council. Subsequently, Sharp was prevailed upon to give evidence for the Crown.[14] Thomas Banks, the sculptor, was another member of the Society for Constitutional Information; the Crown decided not to proceed against him and he was released. John Richter, described as a manservant, was not yet 25, and he grew hot and flustered and asked for a glass of water: Dundas asked him if he was alarmed, and he said 'No', but the Solicitor-General said they had noticed that his voice had failed him. But he parried all the questions which were put to him. John Pearce was an articled clerk and an assistant secretary of the London Corresponding Society; he said he had always believed that the Society had nothing in view but Parliamentary reform, and if he had thought that they had deviated from that, he would not have assented to it. John Bonney asked to be committed for trial, so that the question of his guilt or innocence could be settled once and for all by a court of law. Jeremiah Joyce said that he would answer no questions until he was protected by counsel. John Baxter, a silversmith, was described by one witness as a mean-looking man of about 40, with a sallow complexion, thin faced, with black hair in a queue, wearing a dark brown coat and a black snuff waistcoat; when it was pointed out to him that the members of the London Corresponding Society seemed to be persons of very inferior station in life, without any property, and yet they 'voluntarily took great pains for reforming the State, as if what they thought or did could have any influence with the Nation', he replied that, whatever they were, they were persons who thought that they had a good right to their opinions on public matters. Thomas Wardle and Matthew Moore, of whom little is known, were also arrested; a man called Richard Hodgson disappeared, the only one of those charged with treason to do so.[15] Henry Yorke also tried to flee the country but was arrested at Hull on 16 June; when he was interrogated by the Privy Council, he was told that he was suspected of adhering to the enemy – although there was in fact a warrant out against him, issued by the French Committee of General Security, because he had opposed a petition by expatriate English that France should declare war on England.[16]

CHAPTER 9

RIVALS IN LAW

The leaders of the principal reforming societies were now under arrest; the law was to take its course; and the law was to become personalized in a contest between the two greatest advocates of the time: Sir John Scott, the Geordie[1] Attorney-General – he retained his Northumbrian 'burr' until the end of his life, said his biographer, Lord Campbell, who knew him well – the son of a Newcastle[2] hoastman; and Thomas Erskine, sailor and soldier, the champion of liberty, in whose veins flowed the blood of the royal House of Scotland. Neither of them had, originally, been educated for the law, and in both cases they came to the head of their profession as the result of prodigious industry added to a strange series of coincidences – although to the readers of most history books they appear simply as disembodied names.

I Jack Scott and Bessy

The earliest information concerning the Scott family relates to one William Scott of Sandgate, who is said to have been clerk to a 'fitter' (or a 'fiddler' as they were sometimes called in Northumbria), the person who conveyed coals overland from the mine to the barges, and then along the Tyne to Newcastle or Shields where they were loaded into the deep-sea ships for export. Sandgate, an old street by the waterside, had long been connected with this trade. The barges were also known as 'keels' and both they and Sandgate are commemorated in the song:

> As I came thro' Sandgate, thro' Sandgate, thro' Sandgate,
> As I came thro' Sandgate, I heard a lassie sing,
> Weel may the keel row, the keel row, the keel row,
> Weel may the keel row, that my laddie's in.

William Scott became a 'hoastman', the owner of a keel; his son, also William, inherited his father's keel and in 1724 was admitted into the Hoastmen's Company, which was highly regarded. He also acquired a public house near the Quay for supplying his own boatmen with liquor. Later he expanded his business into marine insurance.

William Scott junior lived in Love Lane, a narrow alley, known in Newcastle as a 'chare', with his first wife until she died in 1734. In 1740 he married Jane Atkinson, who came from Heworth, a village in County Durham just across the river from Newcastle – a fact which was to have a significant influence on the future history of the English legal profession. Jane had thirteen children: two girls were born in the early 1740s, and then, in the autumn of 1745, she was pregnant again. On 17 September, Edinburgh had surrendered to the Jacobite rebels and it was believed that the Pretender would march south along the Great North Road: Newcastle was directly in his way. Cannons were set up on the City walls, and preparations were made for a siege. Love Lane, although near the Quay, was within the walls, but Jane decided that it would be safer to have her baby in the country, so she went to her parents' home at Heworth where she gave birth to twins, another William and Barbara. After the Pretender had retreated to Scotland, she returned to Love Lane. It was there that she gave birth to her second son, Henry, followed, some years later, on 4 June 1751, by John; he, also, had a twin sister, Jane, but she died in infancy.

The Scott brothers went to the Royal Newcastle Grammar School; this had fallen into disrepute, but the Revd Hugh Moises had recently been appointed headmaster and was raising its reputation so that for a time it was to become the Eton or Westminster of the northern counties. Its fame even reached the Palace: one contemporary of the Scott brothers was Cuthbert Collingwood who went into the Navy and took command of the fleet after Admiral Nelson's death; the King, on reading his account of the Battle of Trafalgar, expressed surprise that a naval officer could write such an excellent despatch, and then suddenly added: 'I forgot that he was educated under Moises'. Moises steeped his students in Latin and Greek; he made them practise English composition; he paid particular attention to their religious instruction, and led them to church every Sunday. Master and boys remembered each other with mutual affection and esteem – despite the floggings which he gave them.

While he was at school, John, or Jack as he was usually called, was seriously injured. He fell backwards against a desk with such force that he was rendered unconscious. For some time he was at death's door, and he retained an indentation near the crown of his head for the rest of his life.

In addition to the Grammar School, there was the dancing school, which may be best remembered in John Scott's own words:

I believe no shoe-maker ever helped to put on more ladies' shoes than I have done. At the dancing-school, the young ladies always brought their dancing shoes with them, and we deemed it a proper piece of etiquette to assist the pretty girls in putting them on. In those days, girls of the best families wore white stockings only on the Sundays, and one week day which was a sort of public day; on the other days, they wore blue Doncaster woollen stockings with white tags. We used, when we were at the Head School, early on the Sunday mornings, to steal flowers from the gardens in the neighbourhood of the Forth,[3] and then we presented them to our sweethearts. Oh, those were happy days – we were always in love then.

At Christmas, William Scott senior gave a supper and dance at Love Lane for all his keelmen, and John danced the horn-pipes for them. It is probable that the three boys would have gone into the family business, too – as indeed Henry did – and their names would have disappeared from history, but for the accident of William's birth in County Durham. This rendered him eligible for a scholarship at Corpus Christi College, Oxford, and as there was a vacancy, his father sent him off and he passed the scholarship in the spring of 1761 (he was still only 15); subsequently, he became a Fellow of University College, and, before he was 20, a college tutor.

William recommended that John too should go to Oxford; so in May 1766, aged 14, he set off on the Newcastle stage-coach; it was called a fly, because it travelled to London in three or four days and nights, but, said John later, 'there was no such velocity as to endanger overturning or other mischief'. On the panel of the coach were painted the words *sat cito, si sat bene* – quick enough if done well; and he used to say that he always kept this motto in mind for the rest of his life.

John was matriculated as a member of the University, and became a commoner of University College under the tuition of his brother. When he returned home for the long vacation, he was sent back to school, where Moises used to tease him: 'Now, let us hear what the Oxonian will tell us; that is what the Oxonian has to say, is it?'

There is little record of John Scott's life at Oxford, which in those days was chiefly celebrated for hard drinking and punning, the latter often conducted in Latin or Greek. The examination was a farce; he was asked two questions:

'What is the Hebrew for the place of a skull?'
'Golgotha.'
'Who founded University College?'
'Alfred.'
'Very well, sir,' said the examiner, 'you are competent for your degree.'

He also won the Earl of Lichfield's essay prize on The Advantages and Disadvantages of Foreign Travel, an ironic topic for one who, save for his one quick dash to Scotland, never set foot off English soil. The prize gave considerable pleasure to Moises who, on receiving the news, said to the senior boys 'See what John Scott has done'; and often in later years, when congratulating some boy on an achievement, he would say, 'Well done, very well done; but I have had lads who would have done better – the Scotts would have done better than that'.

At this stage in his career, John was assuming that, after a year or two as a fellow at Oxford, he would enter the Church, and he envisaged spending the rest of his life as a country parson. It was, perhaps, in contemplation of such a future that he happened, sometime in 1771, to attend a service in the church at Sedgefield, about seven miles south-east of Durham. Also attending the service was a beautiful 16-year old girl. On making inquiries, he discovered that she was Elizabeth Surtees, the daughter of Aubone Surtees, a banker who lived at Sandhill in Newcastle: about the only girl in town who had not been to the dancing-school and with whose feet he was not familiar. She was staying at Sedgefield with her aunt, and he arranged to stay at a local inn for a few days. It was a case of love at first sight, and before the end of the week they were secretly engaged.

The Surtees were an aristocratic family, and bankers did not mix socially with coal-fitters, especially one who ran a public house for his keelmen. And they had other plans for their beautiful daughter. There was Sir Walter Blackett MP, 'the king of Newcastle', 70 and an heirless widower; he lent Bessy a horse and they used to go riding together. He went to London and died there, but she continued to ride his horse, chaperoned by a man-servant; John used to bribe him with an occasional half-crown so that he could meet her. There was Mr Spearman, a young man with considerable property in County Durham; he proposed to Bessy in a letter delivered by a servant; the servant was detained for a few minutes while she wrote her reply. There was Mr Errington, a wealthy gentleman from Northumberland, who made a proposal to Aubone Surtees for Elizabeth and was likewise rejected.

John and Bessy used to go to the weekly dances which he described in his old age:

> At the Assembly Rooms in Newcastle there were two rooms and a stair-head between them, so we always danced down the large room, across the stair-head, and into the other room. Then you know, that was convenient, for the small room was a snug one to flirt in.

The affair was now the talk of the town. The Scott family regretted the entanglement, but as Elizabeth was so charming and her family so respectable they would not forbid a marriage. The Surtees family, on the other hand, were implacably hostile to the friendship, and in 1772 they sent Elizabeth to her mother's brother, Henry Stephenson, who had a splendid mansion in Hyde Park; the family hoped that she would be noticed by the Duchess of Northumberland and introduced by her into London society. At the same time, they ordered that she should have nothing more to do with John Scott. The old hoastman was badly hurt, but told his son to think no more of Miss Surtees.

Undeterred, John pursued his fiancée to London, where the Duchess of Northumberland would take her by the arm and introduce her to her guests as 'my Newcastle beauty'; he found her in Hyde Park and on several occasions when she was walking there with a chaperone he contrived to speak to her, and they renewed their pledges to each other. She stayed in London throughout the summer, and we have a portrait of her at that time from a relative:

> Her figure was slight and of middle size; her hair, of the deepest brown, streamed in rich ringlets over her neck. From her mother she had inherited features of exquisite regularity, as well as a strongly marked character, and a warm temper.

Elizabeth returned to Newcastle and her parents now made arrangements for her marriage – to whom, is not recorded – and told her peremptorily that she must comply with their wishes. However, she managed to meet John. There are two versions of what then happened. According to Twiss, Elizabeth 'made up her mind to a decisive measure'; according to Lord Campbell, when she had told John of the pressure which was being brought upon her, he proposed that she should run away with him, and she blushed and consented.

The Surtees lived in a large building, part of a row of houses called Sandhill; the ground floor was occupied by the shop and warehouse of a clothier; there was no communication between the shop and the house, but John had a young friend who was apprenticed to the clothier. Wednesday 18 November was chosen as the night for the elopement as William Surtees, Elizabeth's brother and another school-friend of John, and the member of the household most likely to intercept the flight and lead the pursuit, was away visiting some friends. James had concealed a ladder in his master's shop, and John placed it against the most westerly window of the first floor, and down it the future Countess of Eldon – she was just 18 at the time – descended into the arms of her lover (see Figure 8).

Until 1753, it had been possible for a young couple to get married within the hour; for any promises *de praesenti* or *de futura*, for the present or for the future, spoken in the presence of a clergyman, constituted a binding contract of marriage which the parties could later be compelled to repeat *in facie ecclesiae*, in the presence of the congregation; but in 1753 Parliament passed an Act to ban these 'clandestine' marriages, and laid down the procedural requirements which form the basis of marriage ceremonies in the Church of England to this day. In Scotland, however, it remained much easier to achieve a precipitous marriage.[4] So the young couple, in a post-chaise which was waiting for them, set out for the north, travelling through the night via Morpeth, and crossing the border at Coldstream, and then on to Blackshields near Fala on the way to Edinburgh. Why they proceded so far is not clear; but the marriage ceremony was performed by the Revd J. Buchanan according to the ceremonies of the Church of England so it seems likely that John Scott was acquainted with him and had made arrangements in advance.

Immediately after the ceremony, they set out again for home, intending to spend the wedding-night at Morpeth. On arriving there, however, they found that a fair was in progress (which they had not noticed when they were passing through the town in the dark on the previous night) and that all the inns were full; but on learning of their predicament, the landlord and landlady of the Queen's Head gave up their own room to the newly-married couple.

We have no record of what happened at Sandhill when the Surtees learnt that their daughter had gone; but we do know what happened at Love Lane. John had confided his intentions to Jane, another sister who had been named after his mother and his twin. Barbara knew nothing about it, but when the two girls went to bed that night, Jane burst into tears; Barbara could not tell what the matter was, until at last Jane said 'Oh Babby, Jack has run away with Bessy Surtees to Scotland to be married – what will father say?' There was no sleep for either of them, and they cried all night; but in the morning they bathed their tears in cold water, composed themselves as best they could, and

Figure 8. An early nineteenth-century drawing of the family home of the Surtees in Newcastle. Bessy Surtees eloped from the left-hand window of the first floor. (By permission of the Newcastle City Art Galleries and Libraries.)

went downstairs. There was a letter from Jack lying there for their father which he read and put in his pocket, but never said a word about it. Moises heard the news on the same day, and rushed into school exclaiming, 'Jack Scott has run off with Bess Surtees! The poor lad is undone!'

In Morpeth, the exhilaration of the escape had been succeeded by exhaustion and despondency; the third day of the marriage was the worst,

Bessy used to say: 'Our funds were exhausted; we had not a home to go to, and we knew not whether our friends would ever speak to us again.' It was while she was in this frame of mind, sitting in the window of the Queen's Head, that she saw a fine large wolf-dog walking along the pavement; she recognised it as Loup, the Scott family dog, and it was followed by Henry. John had written a contrite letter to his father, and Henry had been despatched as an emissary, with an invitation to the young couple to come and live in Love Lane.

The Surtees, on the other hand, remained implacable. Bessy's mother was so affected that she remained in bed for several days, fluctuating between sorrow and anger; nor was she pleased to receive a letter from her sister-in-law, Mrs Henry Stephenson, who wrote: 'Mr and Mrs John Scott cannot be received in Park Lane, as our own family consists only of a daughter with a very pretty face and a very good fortune, before whom it would be imprudent to present a sanction to elopements.' Bessy's father refused to speak to William Scott and rebuffed him when the latter tried to break the ice.

John's own future was, of course, in the melting pot, but his father wrote to William at Oxford for his advice, and he replied that John should be sent back to his college, wife and all, and that he would do what he could for them. John's own plans at this time were to return to Oxford and be ordained, and if a living became vacant within a year, he would accept it; but now, for the first time, it seems, he began to look to the Bar as an alternative career.

Some time during the winter Bessy wrote to her father, who replied with a letter of forgiveness and sent her brother John to deliver it. Soon afterwards the newly-weds left Love Lane and went to live at Sandhill, and on 19 January they were re-married at the parish church of St Nicholas in Newcastle. A chaise was waiting for them at the church door, and immediately after the ceremony, they set out for Oxford.

*   *   *

II Tom Erskine, sailor and soldier

The Erskines, the Earls of Mar, had played a long and honourable part in the history of Scotland. Thomas, the first Lord Erskine, had married the granddaughter of James I of Scotland, and thereafter, for five generations, his family acquired an almost hereditary right to have the custody of the heir to the throne during his minority. The family was closely involved with Mary Queen of Scots and the education of James VI, the 6th Earl of Mar being the young King's regent. The son of the 7th Earl married the heiress to the Earldom of Buchan, and had a new title conferred upon him as the 6th Earl of Buchan. This was the title by which the family now became known, and about a century later Thomas Erskine's father, the 10th Earl, was born.

'It was the general opinion', wrote Ferguson, 'that though Henry David, the tenth Earl, was a man of infinite good-nature and pleasing manners, his abilities were not much above the average'. But he displayed a rare discrimination in his choice of a bride, Agnes Steuart of Goodtrees, the daughter of Sir James Steuart, Solicitor-General of Scotland. She was described by Lord Campbell as 'a woman of extraordinary intellect, which had been highly cultivated, and she was equally remarkable for eminent piety and for peculiar skill in housewifery'; and she studied mathematics under Sir Isaac Newton's friend, Colin Maclaurin, who was Professor of Mathematics at Edinburgh.

The Buchans had a country house at Uphall, and a town house at the head of Gray's Close, High Street, Edinburgh. They had three sons: the eldest had the courtesy title of Lord Cardross; the second was Henry; and Thomas, who was born on 10 January 1750, was the third. The Countess herself taught them to read, and instructed them in the Presbyterian faith; and the house was frequented by the eloquent divines of Edinburgh, the leaders of Parliament House,[5] and members of noble families who came to partake of 'a social dish of tea'.

In 1762, the family left Edinburgh and went to St Andrews, at that time consisting of one principal street with decaying houses on either side, with an old plastered church wall where Henry and Thomas used to play at fives; nevertheless, it was a University town with two colleges, about 100 students, and some reputable professors. At St Andrews, Tom was at school and in the same class with Lord Campbell's father, who described him as 'of quick parts and retentive memory, rather idly inclined, but capable of great application – full of fun and frolic – and ever the favourite of his masters and playmates'. He learnt Latin there, and was carefully taught to compose in English, and started to read many books; and he attended one session of the Mathematical and Natural Philosophy classes at the University.

By the time he was 13, Tom was giving serious consideration to his future career. He would have liked to be trained for a learned profession, but his parents could not afford this: Lord Cardross was now at Leyden University and Henry was being trained for the Scottish Bar; they could think of nothing better than to send Tom to sea as a midshipman. Tom objected to this, for reasons which he set out in a letter to his aunt, Lady Steuart, on 4 November, 1763:

> I am extremely glad that you approve of my not going to sea. I shall tell my reasons for it.
>
> In the first place...I could have no opportunity of improving my learning, whereas in the army the regiment is often quartered in places where I might have all advantages.... My second objection is, that I would be obliged to keep company with a most abandoned set of people that would corrupt my morals; whereas in the army, though they be bad enough, yet I should have the advantage of choosing my company when I pleased, without being constrained to any particular set; and thirdly, I think my constitution would not agree with it, as I am very subject to rheumatic pains.

Lord Campbell attributed these pains to gout, of which both his parents afterwards died; but the problem disappeared, and Erskine enjoyed remarkably good health throughout the rest of his life.

However, the family could not afford to purchase a commission in the army, so the original plan of sending Tom to sea was resumed, and it was arranged that he should be put under Sir David Lindsay, an experienced captain, in command of the *Tartar*; Sir David, on the recommendation of his uncle, Lord Mansfield, a friend of the Buchans, promised to be kind to the 'young middy'. And so Tom, with his blue jacket, cocked hat, and sword, and now just 14 years old, embarked at Leith in March 1764; he never again set foot on Scotch soil until he returned as a Peer of the Realm, a Knight of the Thistle, and the greatest forensic orator that Britain had ever produced.

Like Samuel Smollett, Erskine was posted to the West Indies, but it was a time of peace, and he missed the sort of episodes, such as the disastrous attack on Cartagena, which are described in *Roderick Random*. In those days, young officers were taught little except to smoke tobacco, drink flip, and eat salmagundy;[6] but Erskine, while never neglecting his professional duties, often contrived to escape from the midshipmen's quarters to some quiet corner of the ship where he read the books which he had brought with him, picking up some new volume at every port of call. He took a deep interest in everything he saw, and joined in the dances of the negro slaves; and he became a warm admirer of the English seamen.

He kept writing letters home. His parents had now gone to live at Walcot, near Bath, and his father received one letter from Tom before he left Spithead, in which he said that he was very well, that he had never been sick, had been at the top-mast head, and everyone had been very kind to him. In a letter to Lord Cardross from Kingston, Jamaica, in July 1764, he said that he liked the West Indies, and had never had an hour of sickness; he was studying botany with the Physician General to the militia and was drawing all the curious plants which he saw; and he had sent a 'land turtle' to his mother to walk about her garden at Walcot. The following year, writing from Pensacola in September 1765, he described how he had been struck by lightning: he had been standing near the mizzen-mast when he was knocked down by the lightning, which struck his arm, giving him intense pain; when he recovered from the shock, he went below deck, and had his arm chafed with spirits. Then they heard a noise like all the guns of the ship exploding at once; this shock of lightning destroyed the masts, tearing them in a million pieces, large splinters flew round the ship, and the sails were blown to pieces.

Sir Richard Lindsay was replaced by Commodore Jackson, who appointed Erskine an acting lieutenant, and in this capacity he sailed back to England in 1768, confidently expecting that his promotion would be confirmed. However, when the *Tartar* reached Portsmouth, the ship was paid off and he was told at the Admiralty that he could not yet have a lieutenant's commission, and there was no saying when his turn might come. He declared he would never go to sea again as a midshipman, after having served as a lieutenant.

Tom was still only 18 and he would have preferred to go to Oxford or Cambridge, but, although his father had just died, his inheritance was insufficient for this purpose; it did, however, suffice to purchase a commission in the army, and he became an ensign in the 'Royals' or 'First Regiment of Foot'.

He was described at that time as a good-looking young man, and while his regiment was stationed in Yorkshire an accentric relative, Mrs Mure, his cousin's wife, invited him to Harrogate and dressed him up as a woman and successfully passed him off for a whole day as a female friend. In Berwick, he 'fell in fancy'[7] with the girls and wrote poems in their honour; and in April 1770, he married Frances Moore, the daughter of Daniel Moore, MP for Marlow.

The Royals were now posted to Minorca, which was at that time a British Crown colony, and for two years Erskine and his wife were confined to the island. He spent the time on a course of English literature, studying Milton, Shakespeare, Dryden and Pope. He also deputised for the regimental chaplain when he was on leave and delivered sermons with great solemnity from the drum-head.

The regiment was in England again in 1772, and Erskine had six months' leave. It was at this period that he began to associate with Dr Johnson, Sir Joshua Reynolds, Dr Burney and other celebrated wits of the day. Boswell records meeting him:

> On Monday, April 6, I dined with Dr Johnson at Sir Alexander Macdonald's, where was a young officer in the regimentals of the Scots Royals, who talked with vivacity, fluency and precision, so uncommon that he attracted particular attention. He proved to be the Honourable Thomas Erskine, youngest brother to the Earl of Buchan, who has since risen into such brilliant reputation at the Bar in Westminster Hall.

It was at about this time that Erskine wrote a pamphlet called *Observations on the Prevailing Abuses in the British Army*. It was couched in strong language verging on mutiny; he condemned the whole system of purchasing commissions under which young men treated a tour through Italy and a commission in the Army as the finishing touches to their education, and rose over the heads of experienced officers who had no money to buy promotion.

By now, Erskine was the senior ensign in the regiment and was promoted to a lieutenancy; but he was dissatisfied with his mode of life – and he was again moving from one country town to another, he could ill afford the expense of keeping his wife and children in barracks or lodgings, and he had no money to buy a further commission. It was, moreover, a rare period in which England was not at war, and there was no prospect of active service.

It so happened that, in August 1774, Lord Mansfield CJ was holding assizes at Maidstone[8] where the regiment was quartered, and Erskine went into Court in full uniform; the judge asked who he was, and on learning that he was the younger son of the Earl of Buchan and had been at sea with his own nephew, he invited him to sit beside him on the bench and explained what was going on. A case of some importance was in progress, in which counsel were supposed to be displaying great eloquence; but Erskine thought that he could have made a better speech than any of them. It was then that the thought struck him that it might not be too late to be called to the Bar. That evening, Lord Mansfield invited him to dinner; when Erskine told him of his plan to change his profession, his Lordship was by no means discouraging, but advised him to consult his family.

He wrote to his mother, who strongly advised him to quit the Army for the law: 'Tom must go to the Bar and become Lord Chancellor', she said, perhaps on this occasion. Henry, now an advocate of the Scottish Bar, warned him of the thorny and uphill path on which he was entering, but neither he nor his elder brother, the Earl, opposed him.

In those days, the Inns of Court required a student to have his name on the books for five years before he could be called to the Bar, but the period was reduced to three years in the case of graduates of Oxford and Cambridge. It was arranged, therefore, that Erskine should join an Inn and be matriculated at Cambridge, and keep his academic and law terms simultaneously. He was admitted as a student of Lincoln's Inn in April 1775 (the fee in those days was £3.3.4d); as he was still on leave from the Army, he caused a sensation in hall by appearing with a student's black gown over the scarlet uniform of the Royals. In January 1776, he became a gentleman commoner of Trinity College, Cambridge, where he resided to keep his terms; as he was entitled to a degree without examination he took no part in the work of the University, but he did continue his study of English literature and composition. He raised some cash by the sale of his lieutenancy in September 1775, and soon afterwards became a pupil of Francis Buller and then, following Buller's appointment to the bench, of George Wood. He also took part in debates in the Robin Hood, Coachmakers' Hall, and other 'spouting shops'.

Erskine was at this time in dire financial straits; he had his wife and an increasing family to maintain besides his expenses at Cambridge and Lincoln's Inn; there were stories that he was shabbily dressed and ate cow-heel and tripe, but he retained his optimism, and his difficulties only stimulated him to greater exertions.

As a fellow-commoner, Erskine was entitled to graduate after two years, and he took his degree in 1778 and was called to the Bar on 3 July of the same year.

III Law and politics

The lives and careers of these two men now began to converge. As a married man, John Scott had a 'year of grace' in which he was allowed to remain a fellow of his college, although he could not continue permanently in that capacity. So he began to study the law, and became a member of Middle Temple on 28 January 1773.

At that time the Principal of New Inn Hall and Vinerian Professor of Law at Oxford was Sir Robert Chambers (another Newcastle man); he had just been appointed a judge in the East Indies, but it had been arranged that he should retain his appointments during his absence, and perform them through a deputy. He chose Scott, simply to read the lectures written by his superior.

The very first lecture, which was sent to him to read *immediately* to the students, was on an Act of 1557, Of Young Men Running away with Maidens: 'Fancy me reading that', Scott used to say, 'with about 140 boys and young men all giggling at the professor. Such a tittering audience no one ever heard'.

Scott soon gave up all hope of obtaining a college living, and on the anniversary of his marriage in Scotland he resigned his fellowship. His first son was born a few weeks later, but for some time afterwards Bessy was in poor health, and more than nine years were to pass before they had any more children.

Scott now redoubled his efforts to train himself for his profession. He used to rise at 4 a.m., took little exercise, ate abstemious meals, and sat up studying late at night with a towel round his head. Blackstone's *Commentaries* had just been published, but they had not yet become the standard textbook, and in those days the advice given to students was to read Coke on Littleton,[9] read it a second time, read it a third time, and then sit down and make an abstract of it. Bessy sat up with him, watching him with silent affection and moving about on tip-toe so as not to disturb his train of thought. His health suffered as a result of his studies. During the general election of 1774 he went home to Newcastle, where he took up his freedom as a hoastman's son, and exercised his right to vote. On the way back to Oxford, he stopped late at night at the Hen and Chickens in Birmingham, where he used to stay when he was an undergraduate; the landlady gave him a hot supper, but he looked so ill that she felt sure she would never see him again.

Scott was now about to be called to the Bar, so in the summer of 1775 he and Bessy left Oxford, and moved to a small house in Cursitor Street, near Chancery Lane. He called this his 'first perch; and many a time have I run down from Cursitor Street to Fleet Market to buy sixpenn'orth of sprats for our supper'. He began to attend the Courts, and sat in the students' box in the Court of King's Bench, where Lord Mansfield presided. At this time, Scott's intention was to settle in Newcastle as a provincial counsel and to specialise in conveyancing. In those days, Roman Catholics were not eligible to be called to the Bar, but they practised in chambers and most conveyancing work was in their hands; and Scott was fortunate enough to have been taken on as a pupil by one of these Catholic conveyancers, Mr Duane, who let him have the run of his chambers for six months without a fee. Here he worked day and night, building up a gigantic collection of precedents, and examining all the papers that went through chambers; he always attributed his later success at the Chancery Bar to the kindness of Mr Duane.

Scott was called to the Bar on 9 February 1776. He went on the Northern Circuit in the summer; he had some problems in acquiring equipment, but eventually hired a horse for himself, and borrowed another for a young lad who was to act as his clerk and ride behind him with the saddle-bags. When he approached the assize town, he looked back and there was no sign of his clerk; after riding back several miles, he found the lad crying by the roadside, the horse some distance away, and the saddle-bags even further off, and it was only with some difficulty that he effected their reunion. Through the influence of his father-in-law, he received a general retainer from Newcastle Corporation. His own father had died in the autumn, and he now made arrangements to return home, but at the last moment he changed his mind, and decided to stay in London and specialise in Chancery. He left Cursitor Street and moved to a small house in Carey Street near Lincoln's Inn, and in 1780 he first made his reputation as a chancery lawyer in a complicated case[10] arising out of a will: the parties were minded to settle out of court, but Scott took a point which had passed unnoticed, and argued it before the Master of the Rolls and, on appeal, before the Lord Chancellor who ruled in his favour.

*   *   *

Shortly after he had been called to the bar, Thomas Erskine was spending the day with some friends, and they were walking across Spitalfields when they came to a wide ditch. Erskine leapt across it, but slipped and sprained his ankle; he was carried home where he found awaiting him an invitation to dinner that same day – an invitation of which he would have known nothing but for his fall. By the evening, his ankle was better, and he went to the dinner.

Also at the dinner, although not known to Erskine, was Captain Baillie, Lieutenant Governor of Greenwich Hospital, a home for naval pensioners. Captain Baillie had discovered abuses by which those who were entitled to the services of the Hospital were being defrauded, and in vain had petitioned the Directors, the Governors, and the Lords of the Admiralty, for an inquiry and redress. Subsequently he had published a pamphlet setting out the facts, and casting serious reflections upon Lord Sandwich, the First Lord of the Admiralty, who had, for electioneering purposes, placed many landsmen in the Hospital. This led to the Captain being suspended from duty by the Board of Admiralty, and several inferior officers, prompted by the First Lord, applied to the Court of King's Bench for leave to commence proceedings for criminal libel against him. At the dinner Erskine, not realising that Captain Baillie was present, attacked the conduct of Lord Sandwich with great indignation; and the Captain, learning that Erskine was a young lawyer who had also been a sailor, decided to brief him as one of his counsel.

On the following day, Erskine was sitting in chambers, wondering whether all his labours and sacrifices had been in vain, when there was a knock on his door and a slip of paper was put in his hand on which was written:

King's Bench
The King v. Baillie
Retainer for the Defendant
One Guinea

The coin was put into his hand, and for years he kept it as a souvenir.

Erskine seems to have thought that he had been retained as the sole counsel in the case, but when the brief was delivered, he found to his dismay that he was fifth after Bearcroft, Peckham, Murphy and Hargrave, and he despaired of being heard after so many senior members of the profession. At a consultation, however, when his leaders were urging Captain Baillie to settle the claim, Erskine openly disagreed, whereupon the Captain hugged him and cried, 'You are the man for me'.

The case was heard before Mansfield CJ in the afternoon of 23 November; leading counsel argued the case at length, and Hargrave, who was suffering from a strangury – an inability to pass water – was obliged to interrupt his own speech several times to leave the Court, with the result that it was almost dark when he concluded, and Mansfield CJ adjourned the case until the following day. Had it been otherwise, Erskine would have addressed the Court in the evening, and it is doubtful whether anyone would have paid much attention to him.

When the Court sat next morning, Westminster Hall was crowded, and it was expected that the Solicitor-General, who was appearing on behalf of the Crown, would obtain the order for which he was applying. It was then that Erskine stood up to conclude the case for the defence. Everyone agreed that it was a remarkable, if not unique, maiden speech. After discussing the merits of the case, he launched into an attack upon the First Lord himself; Mansfield CJ interrupted him to point out that Lord Sandwich was not a party to the proceedings – 'he was not before the Court'; to which Erskine retorted, 'I know that he is not before the Court, but for that very reason I will bring him before the Court.... I will *drag* him to light, who is the dark mover behind this scene of iniquity'; and so he went on in defence of his client and in his attack upon the Admiralty.

It was an astonishing debut; he had persisted in his attack upon one of the leading statesmen of the day, in the face of being called to order by a judge whose word had been law in Westminster Hall above a quarter of a century. The Court ruled in favour of the defence. As Erskine left the Hall, he received congratulations from all sides. Briefs started to flock in: in later years he used to say that he received 65 before he had even left the Hall, but this seems improbable, especially as he had by then forgotten the names of counsel who were leading him; but he always remembered poor Hargrave, and blessed God for his providential strangury.

Erskine now joined the Home Circuit, riding on a pony, Jack, before he could afford a more expensive means of transport; but within a matter of weeks he was engaged in another *cause célèbre*, arising out of the court-martial of Admiral Lord Keppel,[11] who was accused of failing to engage the enemy in an action off Brest in 1778. The case was similar to that of Admiral Byng, who had been court-martialled, convicted and executed in 1756. Barristers had no right of audience before the Court, but the accused was allowed to sit by counsel and receive their advice. Keppel briefed Dunning and Lee, who in turn recommended Erskine on the grounds of his ability and his knowledge of the Navy.

The Court was convened on *Britannia* in Portsmouth harbour, but after the formalities had been concluded the hearing was transferred to the Governor's house and lasted thirteen days spread over five weeks; the speech for the defence was probably drafted by Erskine, and Admiral Jervis sat up all night writing out the final copy for Keppel to use. Keppel was acquitted by an unanimous verdict, the Court affirming that, far from having sullied the honour of the Navy, he had acted as became a brave, judicious and experienced officer.

*   *   *

At the time of the Gordon Riots, the Temple was fortified, and Scott and Erskine went there for safety; Scott took Bessy with him, and on the way her hat was lost and her clothes were torn. After the riots, Lord George Gordon was prosecuted for treason, and his trial gave Erskine his first opportunity to display his skill before a jury. The case was tried before Mansfield CJ and other judges; and Lloyd Kenyon was briefed for the defence, with Erskine as his junior. Kenyon had had little experience of criminal law, and had no talent for public speaking. In those days it was the practice for junior counsel for the defence to address the jury immediately after his leader and before the evidence for the defence was heard, but Erskine successfully applied to the Court for permission to postpone his speech until the evidence had been completed. It was after midnight when he rose, and he succeeded at once in revitalising the interest of the tired jurors – 'they seemed all to be inspired', wrote Lord Campbell, 'with a new etherial existence'; he succeeded in inculcating in the jury the belief that the acquittal of his client was a foregone conclusion, and so, after the Solicitor-General's reply and despite a hostile summing-up from the presiding judge, the defendant was found Not Guilty at 5.15 in the morning.

In the same year Scott was offered the recordership of Newcastle, but his friends urged him to stay in London, and he joined the Chancery Bar (although he still continued to go round the Northern Circuit).

Three years later, the Duke of Portland became Prime Minister and he invited Scott, who by now had a flourishing practice, to take silk, which was a rarity and a great distinction in those days. On the Wednesday of the week in question, he agreed to do so and was informed that he was to be sworn in on the Saturday; hardly had this been arranged, when he learnt that Erskine, who was junior to him at the Bar and had indeed been in practice for only five years, had also been recommended for silk by Lord Mansfield, and was to be sworn in on the Friday and would thus gain seniority over him. Scott immediately wrote to the Commissioner of the Great Seal to tell him that he would not consent to promotion accompanied by any waiver of his rank, and eventually the letters patent, dated 4 June, his thirty-second birthday, creating him a King's Counsel, were so worded that he retained precedence.

It was nearly ten years since the birth of their first child, but that summer Bessy was pregnant again, and a daughter, named Elizabeth after her mother, was born in November.

It was at about the same time that both Scott and Erskine were elected to Parliament. The member for Weobly, a pocket borough in Herefordshire, had just died, and the seat was offered to Scott on behalf of the Tory party; he accepted the offer and went there. On inquiring what to do, he was told to go first to the house which contained the prettiest girl in the place and give her a kiss, which he willingly did; a very old man told him that as he was a lawyer he ought to make a speech, so he stood on a heap of stones and addressed his constituents. The election was not entirely unopposed, for Lord Surrey, a reforming peer like Earl Stanhope and the Duke of Richmond, was the candidate for Hereford at the same election, and rode into the city on a cider cask, telling his audience that Mr Scott, a gentleman from Newcastle and totally unknown to the people of Weobly, was to be elected there by the influence of a nobleman. But elected he was, and on the following day he wrote from Lincoln's Inn to his brother Henry to tell him that, as a Member of the House of Commons, he had the 'right to frank',[12] but in case the Post Office was not yet aware that he had been elected, he would seal the letter with the usual 4d postage.

Fox and the leaders of the Whig party were anxious to secure Erskine's services in Parliament, and they promised that he would be appointed a law officer of the Crown if they formed a ministry. As he had been in the Navy, Portsmouth seemed to be a suitable constituency, and the sitting member was prevailed upon to apply for the Chiltern Hundreds; Erskine succeeded him, and took his place in the House in the autumn.

Parliament met on 11 November, and both Scott and Erskine chose to make their maiden speeches a few days later on Fox's India Bill;[13] Scott's speech was long and ambitious, but a 'singular display of pedantic pleasantry', as it was described in the *Law Magazine*, and it was not well received in the House. Erskine made an 'excellent speech',[14] and was subsequently congratulated by the Duke of Portland for his work on behalf of the party and the nation.

Parliament was dissolved in March and another general election was held. Scott was re-elected and took part regularly in the business of the House, earning the respect of Fox who said:

> None but a fool or a madman would hold the learned profession in contempt. He had a very high respect for it, and for the learned gentleman in particular whose great abilities and high character entitled him to the respect of every man.

Erskine lost his seat and his political career was in abeyance for seven years. However, he remained in close contact with the Whigs, and became a member of the entourage of the Prince of Wales. The Prince was spending much of his time at Brighton: there was cricket on the lawn in front of the Pavilion, and dinners afterwards in a marquée; songs accompanied by the Prince himself on the cello; and the conversation of some of the most eloquent men of the time – Fox and Sheridan, Erskine himself, and his Irish counterpart, Curran.

Both men's professional careers continued unabated. Scott was acquiring a busy practice at the Chancery Bar, but he was also one of the Circuit leaders, and spent much of his time in the northern counties. On one occasion, Bearcroft, a London barrister, came to Carlisle in a salmon fishery case with a special fee of 300 guineas;[15] Scott and his colleagues agreed to conduct the case entirely in the Cumberland dialect, which was unintelligible to Bearcroft. The jury were astonished that Bearcroft could not understand what they all understood so well, so they inferred that he must have a rotten case, and brought in a verdict for Scott's client.

Erskine was by now the undisputed leader of the Common Law Bar. When Lord Mansfield retired in 1788, it was Erskine who wrote a farewell letter to him on behalf of those who had practised in his court. His name appears as counsel in almost every other case which was heard in the Court of King's Bench, on a wide variety of topics. He used to say that in 28 years in practice at the Bar, he never lost a single day through ill-health; he often used to rise at 5 a.m. to prepare his cases before going into Court, and went into conference accompanied by his Newfoundland dog Aldeborontephosscornio, or Phoss[16] for short, who was trained to sit on a chair with his paws on the table, and with a wig on his head and bands round his neck to impersonate a judge.

On the resignation of Lord Mansfield promotions followed, and Scott was appointed Solicitor-General. He attended the King, who proposed to knight him there and then, evidently to his surprise, for it was not at that time customary to confer a knighthood on the Solicitor-General. He went on Circuit that summer for the last time, and on his return to London he immediately became involved in a major constitutional crisis. The King was taken ill and appeared to have become insane.[17] Parliament had been prorogued, and there was no-one who could properly reconvene the two Houses; but they met in December to try to decide what to do. Erskine was now attorney-general to the Prince of Wales, and argued that, in the case of the monarch's incapacity, the heir apparent automatically assumed all the prerogatives of the Crown; and it was agreed that if the Prince should become Regent, Erskine would become Attorney-General. The view of the Law Officers and of the Government was that it was entirely a matter for Parliament to decide what course to take, and when to appoint a Regent, but while the question was under consideration, the King recovered and the controversy lapsed. The King sent for Sir John to thank him for his support during his illness; the friendship between the two men continued for many years until the King eventually became permanently incapacitated.

After the regency crisis, the remainder of Sir John's term as Solicitor-General was relatively quiet, in spite of the clouds gathering across the Channel. At the general election of 1790, he was again returned for Weobly, and was joined in the House of Commons by his brother William as the member for Downton. William had been the Camden Professor of Law at Oxford from 1773 to 1785; he had been called to the Bar in 1780, and with his family background in shipping he had specialised in Admiralty matters, and had been appointed Advocate-General[18] and knighted in 1788.

After a further gap of some eight years, Bessy was pregnant again; the child was born in Newcastle on 23 September. Bessy returned south in October, and on her way she wrote to Henry's wife:

> I must say I have one of the best husbands in the world, for I have received four-and-twenty letters since I left Newcastle; every stage I come to, I am presented with two, three, or four. In one I received yesterday, he says that whatever business come in the way that may, 'a hint from you, that you wish me to come to you, will bring me immediately'.

The baby only survived a few months, and died in April following inoculation for smallpox.[19]

Shortly before he became Solicitor-General, Sir John had been appointed Chancellor of the County Palatine of Durham, and in the summer of 1792 he took the opportunity to purchase the manor of Eldon, a village in the county, together with some 1300 acres of land. For many years he re-invested the rent in the estate and improved its plantations.

*   *   *

Erskine visited Paris in 1790 and was favourably impressed with the progress of the Revolution. He returned a 'violent democrat', wrote Romilly in a letter to a friend; 'he has a coat made of the uniform of the Jacobins,[20] with buttons bearing the inscription *Vivre libre ou mourir*, and he says he intends to wear it in the House of Commons' – to which he had again been elected that same year. There he attacked the policy of seeking to oppose Jacobinism by new penal laws – it was better to conciliate the people, he said, to meet their complaints and to redress their grievances by granting them a fair representation in Parliament.

By the following year, when war was becoming increasingly probable, he addressed the House as one who had held a commission in the armed forces and he warned of the evils to be encountered by our troops:

> The life of a modern soldier is ill represented by modern fiction. War has means of destruction more formidable than the cannon or the sword. Of the thousands and tens of thousands who perished in the late contests with France and Spain a very small part ever felt the stroke of an enemy; the rest languished in tents and ships, amidst damps and putrefaction – pale, torpid, spiritless, and helpless – gasping and groaning, unpitied among men, made obdurate by long continuance of hopeless misery – and were at last whelmed into pits, or heaved into the ocean, without notice, without remembrance. Thus, by incommodious encampments and unwholesome stations, where courage is useless and enterprise impracticable, fleets are silently dispeopled and armies sluggishly melt away.

In spite of his political commitments, Erskine's professional career continued unabated. His income in 1791 reached £10,000, more by 1600 guineas than anyone had previously earned at the Bar. He bought at this time a villa called Evergreen Hill,[21] near Caen Wood at Hampstead (see Figure 9), near Mansfield CJ's country home and 40 minutes drive from London. He now had eight children, whom he described in a letter to his elder brother on Christmas Day 1791 – there was Fanny, a woman now, short but excessively well made; poor Bessy, who had suffered a misfortune from 'the ill madness of a quack inoculating' – a head and shoulders taller than Fanny, but the best girl in the world with a most astonishing genius for drawing; David, whose features had been thickened by natural smallpox but whose countenance was remarkably animated and intelligent; Margaret, whose hair darkened to auburn with eyebrows of the same colour and eyes a fine blue – a genius for music; Mary ('I am sure you could not see her without laughing') with dark

Figure 9. Evergreen Hill, Hampstead: a nineteenth-century drawing of Thomas Erskine's home: he had a tunnel dug under the road to his garden. (By permission of the Camden Local Studies Library.)

hair, red cheeks and thick form – as shrewd as Satan, the greatest gossip, but most affectionate and good-tempered; Henry David, nearly six, quick and merry, and remarkably good-tempered; Tom, aged four, round-faced, red-cheeked, made like a man of forty; and Esme Stewart, with small bright eyes, immensely long eyebrows and eyelashes an inch long.

Mrs Mure has left us a description of Erskine himself at this time:

> I saw Thom. and his family pretty often, and had he not been *so very daft about Thom. Paine* and such like, he is a charming, entertaining creature, and by much the happiest man in London; and he thinks he is right, and can make himself believe everybody he takes to all right.... He himself is the best-looked [*sic*] young-like creature I ever saw.

It was Paine who brought Erskine's political and professional lives into conflict and led to a double catastrophe which would have ruined many men's careers. When the Attorney-General instituted criminal proceedings against Paine, the latter sent a retainer to Erskine, who accepted it without hesitation. Others opposed his decision, and he related that when he was walking home across Hampstead Heath one November evening, he met Alexander Wedderburn, Lord Loughborough, walking in the opposite direction. His Lordship had been Attorney-General for a couple of years, and then, since 1780, Chief Justice of the Court of Common Pleas; but he was intent on becoming Lord Chancellor and had kept his finger in the political pie. On meeting Erskine he said, with unusual solemnity, 'I was seeking you, for I have something important to communicate to you.' 'Erskine', he began again, after a portentous pause, 'you must not take Paine's brief.' 'But I have been retained, and I will take it, by God', he replied. And he insisted on doing so.

Erskine's obstinacy in refusing to return the brief was much condemned, and he was told that if he defended Paine he would lose his office as Attorney-General to the Prince. And when the case came on for trial at the end of 1792, it was a professional disaster; Erskine spoke for more than three hours in support of the liberty of the press and the right to investigate the truth, but when he concluded his speech, the jury immediately insisted on returning a verdict of Guilty, without waiting for the Attorney-General to reply or for the judge to sum up. The crowd, on the other hand, received him with acclamations, and took the horses from his coach and drew him from Cheapside to Serjeant's Inn.

The Prince had already warned Erskine that his decision to act had displeased the King and that he should explain his conduct, which he did in a letter written to His Majesty himself: after expressing his sincere attachment to his person and to the constitution of the kingdom, he took the liberty to claim that it was an invaluable part of that very constitution that the subject should have the unquestionable right of making his defence by any counsel of his choice, unless previously retained by the Crown. A few days later, Erskine received a letter from the Prince, expressing his deepest regret in feeling himself obliged to receive his resignation, which was accordingly sent. However, the Prince later came to see his friend's conduct in its true light, and made the most handsome reparation, by conferring upon him the office of Chancellor to the Prince of Wales, which had been dormant since Lord Bacon had held it in the reign of James I.

᎒   ᎒   ᎒

Early in 1793, at the time when France declared war on England, Lord Loughborough fulfilled his ambition of becoming Lord Chancellor; Sir James Eyre succeeded him in the Court of Common Pleas. Sir Archibald Macdonald was appointed Chief Baron of the Court of Exchequer, and Sir John Scott replaced him as Attorney-General. So, at the age of 40, Scott became the senior legal adviser to the Crown and responsible for dealing with the problems, and the almost unprecedented perils, which flowed from the French Revolution. One of his first tasks was to draw up the Traitorous Correspondence Bill to sever dealings with the French, to which Erskine responded by saying that nothing had occurred which justified endangering freedom except that a false alarm had been propagated to strengthen the hands of government and weaken public liberty. But Erskine was out of step with the times and a proposal for parliamentary reform which he supported was roundly defeated.

IV Dress rehearsal

While he was in England in the autumn of 1792, John Frost had dined with members of a society for the Encouragement of Agriculture in a room above the Percy Coffee House. On his way out after the meal – he had been drinking but there was some doubt as to the extent to which he was under the influence of alcohol – he had to pass through the Coffee House, where there was a friend of his, Mathew Yatman; they had served together as commissioners for watching and lighting the street where they lived. Yatman asked Frost, 'Well, how do they go in France?' to which Frost replied in a loud voice, 'I am for equality and no king.' 'What!' said Yatman, 'No king in this country?' 'No king', repeated Frost – 'as loud as he could holla', according to Yatman, when later describing the incident in court. A stranger now joined in and asked Frost what he meant, and he repeated what he had said; another stranger, Colonel Bullock, decided that these words were treasonable, wrote down a note of the incident, and referred the matter to Macdonald A.-G., who decided to prosecute. An indictment for seditious libel was prepared, but Frost went abroad again and the trial was postponed.

By the time Frost returned, Macdonald had been replaced by Sir John Scott. Erskine was briefed for the defence. They had, previously, practised in different courts, and this may have been the first occasion on which they appeared against each other. The new Attorney-General seemed rather embarrassed about the whole business; he tried to bolster the case for the prosecution by referring to the unstable times in which the words had been spoken, but virtually told the jury that it would be proper for them to acquit. The evidence was over in a matter of minutes, but Erskine spoke for nearly two hours, concluding with a suggestion that the Attorney-General should waive his right to reply. Perhaps this was an unwise suggestion and one which nettled his opponent who now made a much stronger attack upon the defendant. Frost was found Guilty and sentenced to six months in Newgate, during which time he was to stand in the pillory at Charing Cross for one hour. Standing in the pillory was in itself a dangerous penalty: men had died there when stoned by the mob.[22] But in Frost's case, when his time came the people demolished the pillory and released the prisoner, who walked back to Newgate, arm in arm with Horne Tooke.[23]

*   *   *

During the summer of 1793, a story was being circulated that Thomas Walker of Manchester had damned the King and said that he would cut off his head as readily as he would tear a piece of paper, and that he was training men in the use of arms to assist the French if there was an invasion, or to support a revolt in Scotland or Ireland. There could be no doubt that if these stories were true he was guilty of treason, and a warrant was issued for his arrest by the Revd John Griffiths who was both a Justice of the Peace and a chaplain of the Collegiate Church at Manchester.[24]

Walker was in London when he heard about these rumours, and he wrote three letters to Secretary Dundas, demanding to know more about them, and inviting the Secretary of State to arrest him; but he received no reply. At the same time, Richard Walker, Thomas's brother, and his solicitor, William Seddon, accosted Griffiths, and spoke to him in a public house in the churchyard in Manchester; but Griffiths's answers were evasive and they made no progress.

It now began to emerge that Griffiths was acting on information supplied by a man called Thomas Dunn, and that Thomas Walker was not the only person involved. A paper-stainer called William Paul was arrested and kept in gaol for several weeks; James Cheetham, a hatter, was arrested and kept in gaol; Oliver Pearsall, a weaver, had been working in Manchester during 1792, but had gone home to Kidderminster where he was kidnapped and taken back to Manchester where Griffiths and Dunn attempted, without success, to induce him to give evidence against Thomas Walker. Griffiths had more success with a labourer called Benjamin Booth who was accused by Dunn of saying that he would guillotine the King, so he was arrested and kept in custody for a week, and subjected to threats and temptations to confirm Dunn's evidence against Thomas Walker, and warned that he would be hanged if he did not comply. Eventually he agreed, but as he did not know what Dunn's evidence was, the two were put together so that Dunn could tell him; Booth was subsequently prosecuted on a charge of damning the King, and convicted on the sole evidence of Dunn.

The charge of treason against Thomas Walker was dropped, but he was prosecuted for seditious conspiracy, before Heath J., at Lancaster Assizes on 2 April 1794. The Crown clearly regarded the case as one of great importance, and the Treasury Solicitor briefed John Law, in his capacity as attorney-general of the County Palatine of Lancaster, and four junior counsel; the defendant briefed Erskine, Serjeant Cockell, and three junior counsel, including Felix Vaughan. Joseph Gurney, the shorthand writer, went to Lancaster, so we have a full account of the trial.

Dunn was the principal witness for the Crown, although the government knew that he was a drunkard and were doubtful whether he would be believed.[25] Dunn said that he had been to Thomas Walker's house on many occasions, and had seen men practising the use of arms there; the defendant had told him that he expected 50,000 Frenchmen to land, and had said that the King had 'seventeen millions of money' in the bank at Vienna – 'damn him, and all kings', he had said, and had taken a piece of paper and torn it, and said he would as soon take the King's head off; and at one meeting, after the death of the King of France, they had all rejoiced.

In his cross-examination, Erskine asked Dunn if he had gone to the defendant and begged his pardon for having wronged him and for having sworn falsely against him, which Dunn denied. In his address to the jury, Erskine described the working of the constitution, and explained how desirable it was that it should be reformed, whilst at the same time how essential it was that the ranks and orders of society should be preserved ('I have the honour to be allied to his majesty in blood, and my family has been for centuries what is now called the aristocracy of the country'). Then he went on to describe the acrimonious sectarian differences which had arisen in Manchester; some societies were advocating reform, whilst the Church and King Club was set up to protect the monarchy; on 12 December 1792, this Club had paraded through the town, collected a mob, and attacked Mr Walker's warehouse; it was only then that he had collected some weapons from his home at Barlow near Preston, and when the mob returned he had fired them over their heads; and the mob returned no more, and he had taken the weapons back home.

It would be today, and no doubt was then, most improper for counsel to give evidence as to what he himself had seen, but Erskine could get away with it. He described how the weapons had been locked up in a bedchamber at Barlow, where he saw 'the mighty armoury' consisting of six little swivel guns, which had been painted and put on blocks to look like cannon, and given as toys to Master Walker, a ten-year old boy. He went next, 'under the protection of the master-general of this ordinance (Mr Walker's chamber-maid) to visit the rest of this formidable array of death', and found a little mushroom from which, when it was pressed, a bayonet sprung out, like a Jack-in-a-box; three or four rusty guns, and a bayonet and a broadsword covered in dust.

The defence then called witnesses who described the attack on the defendant's warehouse, and denied Dunn's evidence of the talk of sedition or rebellion; some of the defendant's servants from Barlow (including the 'master-general of the ordinance') gave evidence that they been to Manchester but had never seen soldiers exercising there; and George Duckworth, a solicitor, said that he had measured the warehouse to see if troops could be exercised there, and found it so low that if he had tried to shoulder arms, his bayonet would have stuck in the ceiling.

After that, William Seddon was called, and he gave evidence of a very different nature; he had been at Barlow with the two Walker brothers when Dunn arrived and said he had sworn falsely against Thomas Walker, and he threw himself down on his knees and begged for forgiveness. So Dunn was recalled, and Heath J. asked him if this was true, to which Dunn replied, 'I went there when I was intoxicated, the same as I am now'. The judge asked him how long he had been intoxicated, and Law asked him if Seddon's evidence was true, and Erskine asked him where he had been to dinner, and

Serjeant Cockell said that he had been told to stay in Court – they were all talking at once, and in the end the judge said that Dunn was so drunk that it was impossible to examine him. Then Duckworth was recalled and confirmed Seddon's account; and Law intervened to say that he could not expect one witness alone to stand against the testimony of all the others. 'You act very properly, Mr Law', said the judge, and the jury immediately brought in a verdict of Not Guilty. The judge added, uncharitably, 'I hope, Mr Walker, that this will be an admonition to you to keep better company in future', to which Walker, speaking for the first time, replied: 'I have been in no bad company, my lord, except that of the wretch who stands behind me.'

Dunn was committed on a charge of perjury; he was convicted the following autumn and sentenced to two years imprisonment and to stand once in the pillory. It is generally agreed that he was a government spy; on failing to find adequate information, he had become an *agent provocateur* and, finally, had fabricated evidence.

*   *   *

It was summer now, and the two leading advocates of the day were preparing for the greatest forensic contest which had ever taken place in an English court.

CHAPTER 10

THE TOWER

Terrible things were happening in France that year. Sanson, the public executioner, had become so skilled in operating the national razor that he could execute convicts at the rate of nearly two a minute; and Fouquier-Tinville, the public prosecutor, had devised a procedure for accelerating the supply of victims – when a case was slowing down, or the defence seemed to be swaying the jury, he would ask the jury 'if they had heard enough to be illuminated'; they usually had, and brought in a verdict of Guilty. On 10 June, a law was passed to enable juries to pronounce sentence without any evidence except their own internal conviction of the prisoner's guilt; whole lists were condemned without any ceremony but that of reading their names, and prisoners were not allowed to speak in their own defence.[1]

Elsewhere, massacres were occurring on a far greater scale. Lyons had been in rebellion and had been forced to capitulate in the autumn of 1793; hundreds of its citizens had been executed, hundreds more were shot in the Plaine des Brotteaux. In the Vendée, thousands were slaughtered, and when the national razor could not kill them fast enough, the national bath was used instead – priests, and men and women, were tied together naked in 'republican marriages', herded into barges, taken into the Loire, and drowned.[2]

In England, according to Adolphus, there were those who were prepared to forgive any excesses, any atrocities which were occurring in that unhappy land:

> While prisons for state offenders were multiplied in Paris, and thousands incarcerated in all parts of the republic, they stigmatized the prisons, to which persons charged with high treason were consigned, as Bastilles; while the levy-en-masse, the requisition and the maximum, deprived all men in France of every claim to liberty and property, they extolled those measures, but poured forth furious denunciations against the means by which the army and navy of England were recruited; while the streets of Paris were defiled with the daily bloodshed of men, women, and children, sent to death for undefined crimes, these acts were regarded as mere necessary means for the support of a free government.

*   *   *

Horne Tooke had been arrested on 16 May, and was conveyed to the Tower three days later. It was then that he started to keep a diary which contains a detailed account of the time which he spent in custody. He was visited by Felix Vaughan, who was allowed to spend half an hour with him, but always in the presence of Mr Kinghorn, the gaoler, or a warder; and by the order of the Privy Council he was supplied with pens, ink and paper, tea and sugar, lozenges for his cough, his close stool,[3] and shirts, stocks, stockings and handkerchiefs, and an allowance of 13/4d a week from the government. Two warders were always in his room, night and day, and a sentinel at the door.

On 29 May, Hardy and the other prisoners were committed to the Tower. Hardy was confined in a small room over the western gate; Thelwall, worried about financial problems and his wife's health, and spending his time writing on Nature and Freedom and Mankind, was in the next room; Horne Tooke was below. No one was permitted to see Hardy except by the written authority of those who had committed him, but after some days Mrs Hardy obtained permission and was allowed to visit her husband twice a week, but not to remain with him more than two hours, and always in the presence of the Gaoler or one of the Warders who were ordered to prevent any private conversation if it was inaudible – if the Hardys started to whisper, they were told to speak up so that they could be heard.

Conditions were, however, soon relaxed, and on 1 June Horne Tooke was allowed twice to walk on the leads, attended by two warders with bayonets fixed – once while his room was swept and once when his bed was being made. Far away, on the same day, Admiral Lord Howe encountered the French fleet in the Atlantic, and won the battle which subsequently became known as 'the Glorious First of June'. When the news reached London on 11 June, there was an illumination – it was the custom in those days to celebrate such occasions by placing lights in the windows – and a patriotic crowd took to the streets. When the crowd reached No. 9 Piccadilly, they began to attack the windows with stones and brick-bats, although they were also lit up as in the adjoining houses. They soon smashed the windows, and then attempted to break down the shop door – swearing that they would either pull down the house or burn it. The unfortunate Mrs Hardy was inside, with no one to protect her except an old woman who was acting as a nurse, and she was terrified at these threats and assaults. She called to the neighbours who lived at the back of the house,[4] and they were equally alarmed for her safety and advised her to make her way through a small back window on the ground floor, which she attempted to do. However, 'being very large round the waist' – she was now some six months pregnant – she stuck fast in the window and her friends had to pull her through by main force, and she was badly bruised in the process.

Earl Stanhope's London home in Mansfield Street was also attacked on the same night; Lady Hester said that he had to escape over the roof. Both Hardy and the Earl believed that the authorities had turned a blind eye to the outrages, or even encouraged them.

Horne Tooke was now receiving presents of garden produce – gooseberries, pease, strawberries – from his daughters, which he distributed to the other prisoners; snuff from Vaughan; and a selection of newspapers, where he read that Parliament had empowered the King to secure and detain such persons as he should suspect of conspiring against him and his government, and where he also found himself described as 'a hoary traitor' and 'the ringleader of a gang of conspirators, who had been employed to destroy our glorious constitution in church and state'.

The days of Horne Tooke's imprisonment were marked by small incidents recorded in his diary. One day he saw a man standing under his window with a pea-cart drawn by an ass, and the ass began to bray and the man started to belabour it until the soldiers interfered and told him to allow his ass to bray without being molested. He saw Kyd and Bonney across the leads, and they bowed to each other; one hot June day, Horne Tooke was taking snuff at his window when Kyd walked by, accompanied by a warder, and asked him for some snuff, so he screwed some up in a piece of paper and threw it down; then the warder said he would like to drink a glass with him and it transpired that it was his birthday, so Horne Tooke tied a bottle to a piece of string and lowered it, and the warder found a glass and drank his health. On the following day, Kinghorn came up to Horne Tooke on the leads and reprimanded him for talking to the warder.

Horne Tooke was now permitted visits from his medical advisers, Dr Pearson and Mr Cline. His long-standing medical problem was aggravated by his imprisonment, but he retained his sense of humour; one day when he heard his doctors refer to the neck of the organ affected,[5] he said cheerfully, 'I am much obliged to you for your kind care in respect of that particular part, and I will thank you to extend it to another *neck* no less valuable and no less in jeopardy.' It was Mr Cline who brought the unpleasant news that Frost had made some improper approach to Horne Tooke's maid at Wimbledon; the maid had left and had been replaced, and Frost was denied further admittance to the house.

On 14 July Horne Tooke read a report in the press that, on the previous day, Pitt had dined with Dundas at Wimbledon: 'the air no doubt blew fresher for them', he wrote, 'from the consideration that his next door neighbour was sent to spend his summer a close prisoner in the tower'. The following week, he happened to look out of his window to watch a boat on the river, when some people on the wharf saw him and they all pulled off their hats to him, three times; he bowed in reply, and withdrew from the window.

                              *   *   *

In July, the Prime Minister established a coalition government; the Duke of Portland and other leading Whigs (but excluding Fox and a few of his supporters) entered the Ministry; the Duke became Home Secretary, replacing Dundas who became Secretary of State for War.

In August, there was rioting in London.[6] There was a crimping-house in a court near Charing Cross, where the girls – 'the gallows-bitches' – worked in collusion with the recruiting serjeants and the press-gang; on 15 August, a young man threw himself from a window, up three pairs of stairs, from this house and was killed on the spot. A few days later, a crowd collected and demolished the house and stoned the picket guard which was called to protect it, and the crowd destroyed the White Horse and other crimping-houses in Holborn, Clerkenwell and Shoreditch. The Lord Mayor read the proclamation prescribed by the Riot Act[7] and called out the troops. On 21 August Horne Tooke saw some 300 men marched out of the Tower to go on patrol, and Dr Pearson told him that no less than nine large concourses of people had gathered on the crimp account, and they had been throwing bricks, tiles and jugs from the tops of houses on the troops. On the same day, Dr Pearson also brought a message of respect and affection for Horne Tooke from his old friend and enemy, John Wilkes; and on the next day, he received a dozen bottles of fine madeira and a dozen bottles of old Hock from a friend called Mrs Tuffin.

*   *   *

Mrs Hardy's health now began to decline rapidly, but she did her best to appear as cheerful as possible, and continued to visit her husband as often as she was permitted until 27 August. On that day, she left her husband at 2 p.m., in as good spirits as was possible for someone in her situation. Later that day she went into labour, and was delivered of a dead child; Hardy attributed its death to the violent compression which its mother had suffered while crawling through the window. She herself now felt her death approaching, and said that she believed it was entirely due to what she had suffered in her own mind and body on account of the imprisonment of her husband. A few hours before she died she started to write a letter:

> My Dear Hardy,
>   This comes with my tenderest affection for you. You are never out of my thoughts, sleeping or waking. Oh, to think what companions you have with you! None that you can converse with either on temporal or spiritual matters; but I hope the Spirit of God is both with you and me, and I pray that he may give us grace to look up to Christ. There all the good is that we can either hope or wish for, if we have but faith and patience, although we are but poor sinful mortals. My dear, you have it not in

and there the letter broke off.

Hardy found it impossible to describe the state of his own mind when he heard the news of his wife's death the following morning. On Saturday 30 August, Horne Tooke made a brief entry in his diary: 'By Governour's permission, Mr Cline visited Mr Hardy whose wife died on Thursday morning last'. For ten or twelve days Hardy remained in his room; at length, however, Horne Tooke managed to persuade him to walk out and meet his friends, to relieve his spirits and to enable him to meet with more fortitude the tremendous trial which was awaiting them; for by now there were reports in the press that they were indeed going to be put on trial for high treason.

On 17 September, Horne Tooke recorded: 'Intelligence of a Special Commission with a variety of particular circumstances, all satisfying me that there is a deep conspiracy for deliberate murder'; and he claimed that he was at a loss to know what he was accused of, and was confident that he had not committed any offence which could be construed into treason by the law of England; and he began to wonder whether it was intended to cut him off by an act of attainder passed expressly for the purpose. His nephew John Wildman was permitted to visit him and help him prepare his papers, and from time to time he would rise from the table where the documents were spread out, commenting contemptuously 'on the weakness as well as the wickedness of his enemies', and exclaiming that he wished 'they had given him something to defend, for he could not give serious attention to such ridiculous imputations as these'. When, however, he received a collection of papers of the London Corresponding Society he was able to guess at the nature of the charge to be brought against him, and to realise that he was going to be tried according to the ordinary processes of law – although rather disappointed that he was to be treated as a common criminal.

It was in September that information relating to a new conspiracy came to the knowledge of the govenment. Robert Ward, a barrister and novelist, met some members of the London Corresponding Society, and learnt of a plot to assassinate the King. For this purpose, they had approached some brass founders for the manufacture of a tube three feet long, and a maker of mathematical instruments to devise some means of operating it with compressed air for the purpose of discharging a poisoned dart at His Majesty.[8] Ward reported what he had heard to the Prime Minister and towards the end of the month some of the men involved were arrested (on 29 September, Horne Tooke wrote in his diary: 'Rumours in papers of a Plot to assassinate the King. The *villains* have timed this well, to destroy whom they please'). No proceedings were taken at the time, and to many the whole episode appeared to have been a farce; but it was hardly a matter which could be treated lightly by the authorities.

*   *   *

It is the duty of the Law Officers of the Crown to investigate allegations of criminal offences and, if they think that a crime has been committed, to institute criminal proceedings. Both Houses of Parliament had expressed the opinion that there was a traitorous conspiracy in the country; and, following the interrogations in the Privy Council, those of the judges who were Privy Counsellors – the Judicial Committee of the Privy Council, as we should say today – had expressed the opinion that the parties were guilty of treason.[9]

High treason has always been regarded as the most serious crime known to the law, involving a breach of the fundamental duty which all subjects owe to their sovereign.[10] It still carries the death penalty, which in those days was to be put into effect in the most barbarous manner. In ancient times treason had been an ill-defined offence, which was left to the discretion of the judges, who used their power to invent many 'constructive treasons', by raising offences into treason which were never intended to be so. It was to put an end to this problem that Parliament passed the Treason Act 1351.[11]

The editor of the 1730 edition of the State Trials expressed his views of the importance of the Act as follows:[12]

This is a charge of a general nature, and therefore more difficult to make a defence to...; the Crown is more nearly concerned, by reason whereof the Prisoner has a more powerful adversary to contend with; this is the fatal engine so often employed by corrupt and wicked ministers against the noblest and bravest patriots, whose laudable opposition to their pernicious schemes those ministers are very ready to construe into Treason and Rebellion against the Prince, thereby confounding their own and the Prince's interest together, as if the one could not be opposed without the other. Our ancestors therefore thought this a case wherein the subject needed more than ordinary assistance...; they took care to particularise the several species of treason by an express law; and to guard against all forced constructions and innuendoes, it was by the same law farther provided that all Treason should be proved by some manifest plain act or deed.

It is hard to suppose that the Law Officers of the Crown would embark on a prosecution for treason without giving the matter the most serious consideration.

The principal heads of treason specified were: (i) compassing the death of the King; (ii) intercourse with the Queen or the wife of the heir to the throne; (iii) levying war against the King; and (iv) adhering to the King's enemies. Most criminal offences consist of two principal ingredients, the factual element, known technically as the *actus reus*, and the *mens rea*, the mental intention to commit the crime. It will be readily apparent that the offence of 'compassing the death of the King' consists of a mental element only, but as a state of mind can only be manifested by overt acts, the Court required proof of such acts and a body of case law grew up as to what could, or could not, be alleged as an overt act. Thus, in the case of the regicides who had plotted the execution of Charles I, the actual execution was pleaded as an overt act of compassing his death; likewise, a conspiracy to kill the King and the provision of weapons for that purpose. The levying of war against the King is an act of treason in its own right, but it is also an overt act of compassing his death – a plan to levy war against him, while insufficient to constitute an offence under the third head, may be an overt act under the first head. The imprisonment of the King, or even a plan to imprison him, is an overt act on the ground that 'there is generally but a short interval between the prisons and the graves of monarchs',[13] as had so recently been demonstrated in France by the imprisonment and execution of Louis XVI. And a decision of the Twelve Judges a century earlier was positive authority for the proposition that a plot to depose the King was also an overt act on the same ground.[14] It was the overt acts which the prosecution had to prove, and to which the accused had to direct his defence; and it was the function of the jury to decide whether any overt acts had been committed. Beyond that, there was a difference of opinion: some said that proof of an overt act was conclusive against the accused and left the jury with no option but to convict; but many authorities took the view, which indeed seems to be embodied in the words of the Act itself, that even if the jury decided that an overt act had been committed, it was still a matter for them to decide whether an intention that the King should die could be imputed to the accused.

In spite of the views which had been expressed both in Parliament and in the Privy Council, the Attorney-General was widely criticised, both at the time and in later years, for deciding to prosecute for treason rather than for seditious libel or conspiracy.[15] Whatever problems there may have been over the offence of sedition under Scottish law, there was no doubt that, in England, any words spoken or written which were designed to bring the government into disrepute constituted a seditious libel;[16] and where more than one person joined in the libel, it amounted to a seditious conspiracy. This, as has been seen, was the instrument which the government regularly employed in their attempts to silence men like Paine. Furthermore, it is, in general, a principle of our law that a person accused of one offence may be convicted of a less serious offence.[17] In the case of treason and seditious conspiracy there was, however, a problem which did not escape the notice of the Attorney-General, although it has been overlooked by his critics: for it was a good defence to a charge of seditious conspiracy to show that the accused should have been indicted for treason, as the Attorney-General himself said in his own memoirs:

> I could not but be aware what blame would have been thrown upon the Law Officers of the Crown if [the prisoners] had been indicted for Misdemesmor and the evidence had proved a Case of High Treason, which proved would have entitled them to an Acquittal for the Misdemesmor, and then the country would not have tolerated, and ought not to have tolerated that, after such an Acquittal, their lives should have been put in jeopardy by another Indictment for High Treason.[18]

Furthermore, he regarded it as more important for the public interest that the whole of the defendants' transactions should be made known to the public than that they should be convicted. If he had prosecuted for certain selected documents or topics, he could no doubt have secured a conviction on the lesser charge,[19] but the full scope of the defendants' schemes would not have become known to the public.

And so, early in September, a definite decision was reached to prosecute for treason, and on 10 September a Special Commission of oyer and terminer was issued under the Great Seal to inquire of certain high treasons within the County of Middlesex. Sir James Eyre, Chief Justice of the Court of Common Pleas, was appointed to preside over the Commission.

The next stage of the proceedings was to submit the evidence to a grand jury. Since ancient times, evidence of any indictable offence was placed before a grand jury of up to 23 members, whose function it was to decide if there was a 'true bill of indictment' against an accused person; as the years went by, the functions of examining magistrates came to supersede those of the grand juries, although it was not until the 1930s that the latter were abolished.

On Thursday 2 October, the Special Commission was opened in the Sessions house in Clerkenwell, otherwise known as Hicks's Hall; a panel of 21 grand jurors was sworn in, and received a charge from Sir James Eyre. In his charge,[20] the judge outlined the law and told the jury that 'Jurors and judges ought to feel an extraordinary anxiety that prosecutions of this nature should proceed upon solid grounds'; he explained that Parliament had declared that a traitorous conspiracy existed in England to overthrow the constitution, upon which it became the duty of the Crown to institute proceedings, but it was for them, the jurors, to hear the evidence and to form their own judgment upon it. He then went on to explain that the principal evidence which they would hear would relate to the proposal for calling a convention, and that there were three possible ways of looking at this. First, that the proposal was a mere pretext to 'cover deeper designs', the most traitorous purposes being hidden under the veil. Secondly, that the proposal was genuinely to obtain a reform in Parliament: could 'an association for the reform of Parliament work itself up into the crime of high treason?' to which question the answer was 'yes', if bad men found their way into such associations and used their innocent aims 'as a stalking horse for their purposes of a very different complexion'; if the purpose was to obtain a reform of Parliament without the authority of Parliament – a reform that would amount to an attempt to overthrow the constitution, to introduce anarchy, to bring the King to the scaffold – then that too would be treason. If, on the other hand, the plan was simply to obtain a reform of Parliament through parliamentary means, then that was not treasonable. If they thought, the judge concluded, that the purpose of the convention was to overawe Parliament and to compel them to change laws for re-modelling the House of Commons, perhaps it would be fitting – as this was 'a new and doubtful case' and merited a full inquiry as to whether it would or would not amount to treason – to find 'true bills'. On 6 October, they brought in true bills against all the accused (including Thomas Holcroft who was not under arrest) except John Lovett, who was then released.

Very soon after Eyre CJ had delivered his charge, a pamphlet was published in the *Morning Chronicle* called *Cursory Strictures on the Charge delivered by Lord Chief Justice Eyre to the Grand Jury, October 2, 1794*. This document is usually regarded as having been written by William Godwin, although the editor of the State Trials attributed it 'on sufficient authority to the late Mr Felix Vaughan'.[21] It is ironic that, almost alone out of the mass of documents spawned by this case, the 'Strictures' remain well-known to some modern readers; it was a travesty of what the Lord Chief Justice had said and does not, in my opinion, merit any of the esteem which it has received over the years.[22]

One man who was indicted, although he was not under arrest, was Thomas Holcroft. Holcroft had had a varied career: for some years, his father had travelled the country, and Thomas had gone with him, a starving tinker's boy; then he had been a stable lad in Newmarket, before going on to the stage; in later life he had become a prolific novelist, playwright, and translator.[23] He had been a member, and a regular attender, of the Society for Constitutional Information. On the afternoon of 6 October, a friend came to tell him that he had just come from Hicks's Hall where he had heard the indictment read and it included Holcroft's name; he advised immediate flight, but Holcroft was determined to face his accusers, so next morning he went to the Hall where Eyre CJ was still sitting, and said that he had come to surrender himself to the Court. Eyre CJ then said, 'If I understand you rightly, you admit that you are the person standing indicted in the name of Thomas Holcroft', to which he replied that he could not so affirm as he had heard it only from reports. The judge said that he could only accept Holcroft's surrender on the supposition that he was the person indicted; Holcroft said that he had only come as Thomas Holcroft of Newman Street in the County of Middlesex, and the judge said that it was impossible for him to know whether he was the person named in the indictment. The Solicitor-General was present, and he now intervened and said that he believed Holcroft to be the right person, and moved that he be committed. Eyre CJ said he did not know how many persons there might be called Thomas Holcroft. There was a consultation between the Solicitor-General and Joseph White, the Treasury Solicitor, and eventually the Solicitor-General again moved that he be committed, and he was taken into custody. After a further delay while a warrant was made out, he was taken to Newgate.

The trial was now fixed to commence on 27 October, and on 13 October the Treasury Solicitor came to the Tower and served copies of the indictment upon the prisoners there, together with the lists of 207 witnesses and 228 jurors, upon which Horne Tooke commented in his diary: '207 + 228 = 435. To inquire after 43½ per day; out of 228 jurors I see 11 honest men.'

The prisoners and their advisers had been able to ascertain pretty well what evidence the witnesses were going to give, but there was one name on the list which they could not account for. This was Jane Partridge, described simply as the daughter of an apothecary in Nottingham.[24] A few days after the indictment had been delivered, a strange incident occurred. Mr Kinghorn and a warder came to Hardy's room, and asked him to go to the Governor's, where a gentleman wished to speak to him. Hardy inquired who it was, and Kinghorn replied that he did not know, except that it was something to do with subpoenas. Hardy went to the Governor's house on the parade and was shown into the dining-room where one of the Treasury Solicitor's clerks was sitting alone; he stood up and said, 'Mr Hardy, Mr White omitted to inform you, when he delivered the indictment, that your solicitor, by applying to the Crown office, may have subpoenas for your witnesses without any expense to you.' Hardy made a low bow, said, 'Very well', and went out to return to his room. On the way, he met Mr Gibson, his own solicitor, and told him what had happened, and Gibson was obviously puzzled because he had already received a letter from the Treasury Solicitor to the same effect. While they were talking together, the other Treasury Solicitor's clerk, with a woman on his arm, came close to them, and the woman stared very hard at Hardy; the couple walked on a few paces, and then returned and stared as before. Hardy then recollected having seen the same couple standing opposite the Governor's door, watching him as he came out. The mystery deepened when, a few minutes after Hardy had returned to his room, the clerk who had been in the dining-room came to Thelwall's room with the same message for him; why had there been such a parade about Hardy going to the Governor's, yet the same massage was delivered to Thelwall in his own room?

The woman, it transpired, was Jane Partridge, and by a stroke of good fortune that same evening she was having tea with a party of young ladies, among whom there happened to be a sister of Thomas Wardle, one of the defendants; and she told the party that she had travelled with a man in a stage coach from Nottingham to London two years previously, and that he had said to her that he would no more mind cutting off the King's head than shaving himself. She had been taken to the Tower to identify Hardy as this man. As soon as Miss Wardle heard this, she went to a friend of Hardy, who in turn went to the Tower to tell Hardy; and his friends found witnesses who could prove that Hardy had never been out of London for a whole year both before and after the time she was going to swear to. And there the matter rested until the time of the trial.

❖   ❖   ❖

When London was a walled City, prisoners had been kept in Newgate and other gates in the walls; by the Fifteenth century, the accommodation was no longer adequate and the Corporation built a new gaol at Newgate, with the proceeds of the estate of Richard Whittington which he had left for works of charity for the good of his soul. A room in this new prison was employed as a court, and it became known as the Old Bailey from the name of the street on which it stood. During the 1770s, a new prison, incorporating a new court, was built; much of the structure was demolished in the Gordon Riots, but the work was resumed and completed, and remained there until the present century, when Newgate was finally demolished and the Central Criminal Court was built on the site.[25]

Near the end of October, the prisoners were moved from the Tower to Newgate; Horne Tooke left this account of the transfer in his diary:

> Thursday, Oct. 23. Erskine and Gibbs are to dine with me & settle & arrange for my trial *tomorrow*. They are to come at ½ past 3. Mr Cline came, and at nine of night, whilst Mr Cline & my nephew were with me, Kinghorn the jailer, came to lock me up, as usual. Mr Cline and my nephew were preparing to depart, Kinghorn gave me the Governour's compliments & informed me that the sheriff would take me tomorrow at eight in the morning to convey me to Newgate. Short notice for a removal, especially with my infirmity.

> Friday, Oct. 24, 1794. I rose at four, because of my infirmity that I might be ready at eight for the Sheriff. I packed up my papers in a trunk.... Half past six o'clock – Kinghorn tells me that I am to walk through the tower on foot & there to be delivered to the Sheriff. I desired my compliments to the Governour...and to represent to him, that it is wet above and below, that my gouty feet compel me to wear thin shoes, being unable to bend a strong sole or strong upper leather; that it would be cruel just at this moment to make me catch cold, and thus carry me a *dumb* man to my trial; that there is chance enough of that in the sudden change of my bed and apartments; & therefore to request that I may go in a coach to the Gate of the tower; and that if it is necesaary that I should be delivered on foot, that I may descend there & be so delivered. I expect the Governour's answer. He permitted me coach. We are paraded, with great attendance, slowly throᵸ St Paul's Churchyard to Newgate. Thus I lose my consultation with Erskine and Gibbs. Sheriffs very civil.

A curious incident occurred on Horne Tooke's arrival at Newgate. Keeper Kirby refused to receive him, for no warrant had been brought for the purpose; and so, while the prisoner sat in the Keeper's parlour in front of a blazing fire, his nephew, John Wildman, returned to the Tower and applied to the appropriate officer for the necessary authority to detain him; and as the clerk was absent, there was a further delay until eventually John took up a pen and in his own hand drew up the order for the commitment of his uncle. Having then obtained the official signature, he returned to Newgate, and the supposed traitor was transferred to a cell which had all the characteristics of a dungeon – although it was above ground, the water trickled down the walls, the floor had just been washed, and the bed-clothes were so damp that they steamed when artificial heat was applied to them. Such were the comforts reserved for a man who had attained nearly sixty years of age, was oppressed by misfortunes, overwhelmed by disease, and doomed to stand on trial for his life.

CHAPTER 11

THE TRIALS OF WATT AND DOWNIE

While the law officers of England were making up their minds as to what to do with all the men they had arrested, the Lord Advocate had decided to prosecute Watt and Downie for treason. It has already been seen that in 1707 Parliament laid down that the English Treason Act of 1351 should apply to Scotland. English law was made to apply to procedure as well as to the substantive law. A Special Commission was appointed by proclamation;[1] a grand jury was empanelled on 14 August, and received a charge from Ilay Campbell, the Lord President of the College of Justice; they found a true bill. And at the commencement of the trial, as in England, the accused were allowed to challenge up to 35 jurors.

The trial of Watt was held on 3 September before the Lord President, the Lord Chief Baron, the Lord Justice-Clerk, and four other judges. The Crown was represented by the Lord Advocate, the Solicitor-General, Mr Anstruther, and another Mr Dundas; the defence by Robert Hamilton and William Erskine. The Lord Advocate had been subpoenaed as a witness for the defence, which may explain why, although present in Court, he played a relatively minor role in the opening stages of the case, and it was Mr Anstruther who addressed the jury. Mr Anstruther explained the law properly, although his references to the great English writers and judges – Hale, Foster, Holt, Hawkins – sounded hollow north of the border; he set out the overt acts relied on, and the evidence, concentrating on the paper circulated to the Fencibles and Watt's scheme to seize Edinburgh Castle, and the manufacture of arms.

The evidence lasted throughout the day. There were the minutes of the Edinburgh convention; a member of the London Corresponding Society described its operations and particularly the Chalk Farm meeting; the Globe Tavern and Chalk Farm resolutions were put before the Court on the ground that Watt was a party to the scheme to hold a convention; Lockhart and Middleton described how they had found the pikes and the fount of type in Watt's house, and the other weapons in Orrock's smiddy. A copy of the address to the Fencibles was produced, and troops from the Earl of Hopetoun's regiment were called to say that they had read it. M'Ewan and Bonthorne described the occasion when Watt had produced his plan for seizing Edinburgh Castle, and Fairley described his peregrinations to collect money and sentiments. Orrock and Brown described their manufacture of pikes and halberds (Orrock was examined by Mr Dundas, who for some reason kept addressing him by his Christian name as if he was a personal friend: 'Now Robert, recollect yourself...').

After the close of the case for the Crown, the defence produced the correspondence which had passed between Watt and Secretary Dundas, and then called the Lord Advocate; it must be most unusual, if not unique, for the principal law officer of the Crown to go into the witness box on behalf of a defendant in a criminal case, but he agreed to do so and described his relationship with the accused.

Hamilton then addressed the jury and poured scorn on his client's 'rhodomontade scheme, if it ever existed, of seizing the Castle. Could there be a more ridiculous absurdity than supposing the possibility of such an attempt!' The sheriff, he said, after the most thorough search, had only managed to find 46 or 47 pikes, and

> I have only been able to discover seven men that are alleged to have borne any chief part in this conspiracy.... Gentlemen, you have seen before you this day those seven conspirators, and it does not strike me that they bear any resemblance to those heroes of antiquity which we read of in romance, and who might, perhaps, in days of yore, have been able to accomplish such a wonderful adventure; yet these seven champions were to perform wonders; they were to use forty-seven pikes, and with these they were to take the Castle of Edinburgh; with these forty-seven pikes they were to way-lay all the soldiers who were to be marched out for fear of some fire at the excise-office; then these seven men are to secure the banks, and with these forty-seven pikes are to lay hold of the whole government of this country.

When the Lord Advocate replied on behalf of the Crown he drew attention to his own peculiar situation regarding this man 'to whom I once looked with a favourable eye, and on whom my duty, as a servant of the crown and the public, led me to bestow confidence': and he told the jury that if it was their opinion, either that the scheme was a wild, absurd rhodomontade, formed in frenzy, conceived in madness, and never seriously intended to be carried into execution; or that the part played in it by Watt was merely to detect and divulge it, then they should return a verdict in his favour.

The Lord President had maintained a firm control over the case throughout; apart from asking a couple of innocuous questions, the Lord Justice-Clerk had contributed nothing to the proceedings. The record does not mention the time of day, but it must have been past midnight when the Lord President started to sum up, but he did so concisely, clearly and impartially; he stated the law accurately, and made it clear that, 'if these acts...have been proved against the prisoner, it will then be necessary for you, to deliberate upon the effect of such proof'; and he told the jury that if they were in doubt, they would naturally be inclined to the merciful side. The jury was evidently in no doubt; after retiring for ten minutes, they found Watt Guilty.

No tears were shed for Watt. I know of no petitions or resolutions to condemn the verdict, no motions in the House of Lords to set it aside. If his schemes were genuine, then he double-crossed the Lord Advocate and the Secretary of State; if he was acting as an agent provocateur, he was leading his friends into a scheme of treason for their ruin and his advantage. At first sight, the most likely explanation, as his counsel tried to convince the jury, was that the whole plot was the production of a disordered mind. Yet in his own declaration, which was drawn up in the last days of his life and witnessed like a testament by the Revd Dr George Baird, principal of the University of Edinburgh, and the Revd T.S. Jones, one of the ministers of Lady Glenorchie's Chapel, Watt maintained that he had genuinely changed his mind in favour of reform, and had joined the Committees of Union and Ways and Means to co-operate with the Friends of the People in achieving their objectives; and he gave a much more detailed and comprehensive account of the conspiracy than had emerged at the trial.

According to this version, in which he gave an account of his childhood – he had been influenced by religion when he was very young, he said, to such an extent that, in the space of two hours, he would be three or four times at prayer, drowned in penitential tears – and described how he had first approached the Lord Advocate, he had sent emissaries to many parts of Scotland, and was planning similar missions to England and Ireland. The first rising was to be made simultaneously in Edinburgh, London, and Dublin; while every town throughout the kingdoms was to be ready to act at the first notice which they received. In Edinburgh, four or five thousand men were to be assembled at the Gaelic Chapel, head of the West Bow, Tolbooth, or head of the High Street and when the soldiers came out of the Castle, they were to be surrounded; the magistrates, lords of justiciary, commander-in-chief, and many others were to be apprehended and detained till the mind of the ensuing convention was known; there was no intention to put any to death, but if found guilty of oppression and injustice to the patriots, they would share a similar fate with them – namely transportation.

The soldiers were to be induced to leave the Castle by means of a letter, signed by the lord provost or commander-in-chief, who would by then have been in custody, ordering the commandant to send a company, without any ammunition, to a fire that was to be kindled in St Andrew's Square. The company would be secured and disarmed; the other troops were to be drawn out by means of fires kindled in other quarters of the city; but in case they could not be drawn out of the Castle, they were to be starved into surrender. The public offices, banks and the post office were to be secured to cut off communications between those who were hostile to the patriots.

It was expected that all this would be accomplished in Edinburgh, London, and Dublin by about six or seven o'clock in the morning, and couriers would then be dispatched throughout the whole nation; proclamations would be issued to the landholders and officers under government not to go more than three miles from their dwelling-places, under pain of death; to farmers, not to conceal or export any grain; to ship-masters, not to carry any person coast-ways; to recruiting officers to deliver up their commissions and men to persons to be nominated, under the same penalty. An Address would be made to the King, consisting of a long catalogue of abuses, and requesting him to dismiss his present ministers and dissolve Parliament, and to replace them by men in whom the people could confide. His motives, said Watt, were 'the good of society; and not robbery or murder'; but he went on to concede:

> Yet, on reflection, I perceive that I erred in taking such an active part, without maturely weighing the probable consequences. Bloodshed and rapine might have ensued.

It is difficult to believe that these plans really existed outside Watt's imagination; the government's information services were such that if a rebellion had been planned on the scale described, it must have come to their notice and the evidence would have been placed before the Court.

✻   ✻   ✻

Downie was put on trial on Friday 5 September. The Court was similarly constituted, save that the Lord Justice-Clerk was absent. The prisoner was represented by Cullen and two junior advocates. The case proceeded, after an opening address from the Lord Advocate, along the same lines as the previous one. The evidence against Downie was, however, much weaker: it was Watt who had produced the scheme for seizing the Castle, Downie simply listened in silence; no pikes were found in Downie's house when it was searched – his maid-servant said she saw a pike once when she went to dust the dining-room, but it disappeared, and she heard Mrs Downie call it a 'dividing-knife',[2] but the girl was evidently puzzled – 'I had never seen such a large dividing-knife', she said. There was, on the other hand, some evidence to connect Downie with the circulation of the Address to the Fencibles.

Cullen opened his address by telling the jury that he felt under 'very great perplexity': he felt particularly distressed because this was a trial upon the law of another country, with which he had little acquaintance. But he had done his work well. The Erskine brothers might have spoken at greater length, but he made the law abundantly clear:

> The statute itself was written in French, and the words are *'compasser ou ymaginer la mort nostre seigneur le roy'*. It is perhaps singular...that the life of every British subject prosecuted by the crown for treason should continue to depend upon the critical construction of two obsolete French words.

Two more centuries have passed since then, and Cullen's comments remain as true today as they were in 1794.

His attack upon the evidence was in scathing terms; referring to John Fairley, he said:

> This great man is sent out as their missionary, and he travels on foot to Stirling, to Glasgow, to Paisley, and a variety of other towns, in order, as it is said, to form that combination which was to carry into effect this great enterprise, of seizing the judges, the castle, the banks, and the other public offices in the city, and to overwhelm King, Lords and Commons in one common ruin.

And what was the recompense given to this confidential minister, this negociator, who was sent through the land, in order to achieve such mighty things? Why, gentlemen, you have it in evidence, that it was no more than fifteen shillings sterling! Surely the cheapest embassy of which diplomatic history can furnish an example....

And he concluded:

I trust you will be satisfied that no crime has been proved, of so deep a dye as can entitle you to take away the life of this poor old man at your bar; and that you will therefore return a verdict, finding him not guilty of the crime charged.

Anstruther replied for the Crown, and the Lord President summed up. The jury retired at about 3.30 a.m. on the Saturday morning, and half an hour later brought in a verdict of Guilty, adding a rider: 'Upon account of certain circumstances, we desire to recommend the prisoner to mercy'.

The Court re-convened at midday on Saturday, and the Lord President addressed the two convicted prisoners, exhorting them to 'make the best use of your time, and to apply for assistance to those who can assist you in such important meditations'. He then pronounced sentence:

The Court doth adjudge, that you, and each of you, be drawn upon a hurdle to the place of execution; that you there be hanged by the neck, but not until you are dead; and that being alive, you, and each of you, be cut down, and your bowels taken out, and burnt before your face. That each of your heads be severed from your bodies; and your bodies divided into four parts; and that your heads and quarters be disposed of as the king shall think fit: and so the Lord have mercy upon your souls.

This is the sentence of the law; and I give farther notice to you, and to each of you, that this sentence will be carried into execution upon Wednesday the 15th October next, between the hours of twelve at noon, and four in the afternoon, in terms of a precept to that effect, which will be delivered to the sheriff; this notice I give you by order of the Court.

The reporter records that the two men received this dreadful sentence with much firmness and composure, and they were immediately conducted to the Castle.

Downie received a pardon[3] from the King. Watt hoped that he too would be reprieved, but when, in mid-October, he realised that this would not be forthcoming, he wrote his Declaration to which reference has already been made; this was completed at about 8 p.m. on Tuesday 14 October and sent in a sealed cover addressed to James Clerk, the sheriff depute, along with a covering letter requesting him to give a parcel of other papers to the Revd Messrs Baird and Jones, and his watch and clothes and other effects to Mr James Stalker, at Mr Wilson's, the baker in Cross Causeway, to whom he owed some money.

On the following afternoon, according to the account from the New Annual Register, reprinted in the State Trials:

About half-past one o'clock, the two junior magistrates, with white rods in their hands, white gloves, &c, the Rev. Principal Baird, and a number of constables, attended by the town officers, and the city guard lining the streets, walked in procession from the council chamber to the east end of Castle-hill, when a message was sent to the sheriff in the Castle, that they were waiting to receive the prisoner, Robert Watt. He was immediately placed in a hurdle, with his back to the horse, and the executioner, with a large axe in his hand, took his seat opposite to him at the farther end of the hurdle.

The procession then set out from the Castle, the sheriffs walking in front, with white rods in their hands, white gloves, &c; a number of country constables surrounding the hurdle, and the military keeping off the crowd. In this manner they proceeded till they joined the magistrates, when the military returned to the Castle, and then the procession was conducted in the following order:- The city constables; town officers bare-headed; bailie Lothian, and bailie Dalrymple; Rev. Principal Baird; Mr Sheriff Clerk, and Mr Sheriff Davidson; a number of country constables; the hurdle painted black, and drawn by a white horse; a number of country constables. The city guard lined the streets to keep off the crowd.

When they had reached the Tolbooth door, the prisoner was taken from the hurdle, and conducted into the prison, where a considerable time was spent in devotional exercises. The prisoner then came out upon the platform, attended by the magistrates, the sheriffs, Principal Baird, &c. Some time was then spent in prayer and singing psalms; after which the prisoner mounted the drop-board, and was launched into eternity.

When the body was taken down, it was stretched upon a table, and the executioner, with two blows of the axe, severed off the head, which was received into a basket, and then held up to the multitude, while the executioner called aloud 'This is the head of a traitor, and so perish all traitors'.

The report concluded by saying that that part of the sentence which related to being quartered, &c., had been previously remitted.

CHAPTER 12

THE TRIAL OF THOMAS HARDY: THE CASE FOR THE CROWN

At 1 p.m. on Saturday 25 October, the Lord Mayor of London took his seat on the bench at the Old Bailey (see Figure 10), accompanied by Eyre CJ, Macdonald CB, Hotham B., Grose and Buller JJ, and six aldermen of the City of London. The Keeper of Newgate, Mr Kirby, was ordered to bring the nine prisoners to the bar.[1]

At counsel's table were the Attorney-General, Sir John Scott; the Solicitor-General, Sir John Mitford; and six other barristers to represent the Crown – Serjeant Adair and Messrs Bearcroft, Bower, Law, Garrow and Wood: 'Never was such a host of Crown lawyers employed against any person tried for High Treason', wrote Hardy, 'and they certainly did justice to their employers, for they strained every nerve, in order to criminate their intended victim'. John Gurney, the son of the shorthand writer, represented the defence. The Court asked Gurney whether the other defence counsel were present, and Gurney replied that he was expecting Mr Erskine, Mr Gibbs and Mr Vaughan; the court condescended to wait a few minutes.

The window behind the dock had been opened to let in some air, and Horne Tooke took advantage of this to open the case for the defence: 'My lord, I beg leave to represent to the Court, that we have just come out of a very confined and close hole, and the windows now opened at our backs, expose us to so much cold air, that our health, particularly my own, will be considerably endangered, and most probably we shall lose our voices before we leave the place. I shall, therefore, request of the Court to be dismissed as soon as their convenience will permit.' Eyre CJ replied: 'If you are prepared to plead, sir, you may be dismissed almost immediately. We were waiting for your counsel, that you might have the benefit of their assistance.'

Horne Tooke said that he was prevented from saying anything about the indictment, because they had not had the ten clear days allowed by Act of Parliament; by the change of custody they had lost a whole day and had not had an opportunity to confer with counsel. Erskine and Gibbs had arranged to dine with him on Friday but he had been removed at eight o'clock that morning; it was perfectly impossible for him to consult his counsel, as all his papers which he had arranged in the Tower were thrown into disorder. 'Your lordship,' he concluded, 'who never was a prisoner, can have but a very

Figure 10. The Old Bailey in Session (c. 1800). Note the position of counsels' table below the bench; the dock with the mirror above the prisoner's head: and the desks, presumably for the shorthand writers, opposite the witness box. (Rowland and Pugin.) (By permission of the Museum of London.)

imperfect idea of the change of custody.' Eyre CJ said that the Court was inclined to make every allowance that could be expected, and was willing to await the arrival of counsel, and Horne Tooke continued: 'Rather than catch cold, I should choose to plead at present. I ask no indulgence, but desire substantial justice'. Then he went on: 'I am, however, ready to plead, though deprived of the advantage of my papers, and the benefit of advice. We have been six months in close confinement, without being able yet to imagine what was the nature of the charges to be brought against us, nor have we been able to discover it from the indictment found against us.'

Thelwall then took up the story and said that he also had been deprived of his papers which he had collected in the Tower. When he was removed from the Tower, the sheriffs would not allow him time to take them with him; they promised that he would have them sent, but when he had an opportunity of sending for them through a friend he was refused, and was told that they could not send what he wanted.

Shelton, the Clerk of the Arraigns, then proceeded to read the indictment. It set out the charge which was alleged, namely that the defendants had compassed the King's death. There followed, at great length, a list of the overt acts on which the Crown relied: planning to hold a convention to subvert the duly established government and to depose the King; publishing documents to encourage the people to send delegates to the convention for the same purpose; the provision of arms for the purpose of resisting the King in the lawful exercise of his powers; conspiring to levy war against the King. The prisoners were then in turn asked the usual questions, starting with Hardy:

'Guilty or not guilty?'
'Not guilty.'
'How will you be tried?'
'By God and my country.'

This was the routine formula for claiming trial by jury.

The questions were then put to Horne Tooke:

'Guilty or not guilty?'
'Not guilty.'

Then, on being asked how he would be tried, the record says 'he eyed the Court for some seconds with an air of significancy, which few men are so well able to assume, and, shaking his head, emphatically answered – "*I WOULD be tried by God and my country. But*" – and the sentence was left unfinished.

After the other prisoners had been arraigned and pleaded in the usual way, Eyre CJ said: 'Tooke having complained of the coldness of the air, may withdraw.' Horne Tooke then withdrew. Bonney complained that he had been wrongly described in the indictment, but waived any objection and pleaded that he was not guilty. Thelwall also complained of an error in the indictment, but despised the idea of availing himself of any paltry subterfuge.

'I feel perfectly convinced', he said, 'that when the long expected day shall come, no *honest* jury can say otherwise than I do now – Not guilty.'

Bonney then made a speech concerning his accommodation, to the effect that he would not have complained if he had been arraigned for any known and certain treason, murder, or felony, but as, even if the facts charged were proved, there would still be doubt as to the law:

> I trust I do not make an improper request when I solicit your lordships, that we may be allowed as many of the little comforts and conveniences of life (to which we have been accustomed) as may be consistent with the security of our persons. Your lordships, I am sure will agree with me, that a situation in which a man can neither sleep by night, nor cast his eye on a ray of comfort by day, is not much adapted to prepare his mind for so important a trial as mine – and yet, my lords, such is my situation. I beg to be understood not to intend the smallest insinuation against the sheriffs; their language and their countenances, when they visited me yesterday in my cell, sufficiently convinced me of the concern they felt at not being able to afford me better accommodation. My request, therefore, to your lordships is, that we may be remanded to the custody of the governor of the Tower, where we have been treated, for two and twenty weeks, with the greatest humanity and attention.

Richter and Baxter also complained of the want of accommodation in Newgate, and the Lord President replied that he could only refer them to the discretion and humanity of the sheriffs.

The Attorney-General then spoke for the first time, to say that the prisoners had signified their desire to be tried separately, and he moved that Hardy be tried first. Erskine, who had come into court with Gibbs and Vaughan while the indictment was being read, apologised for their absence. He understood that Horne Tooke had explained his problems, and he confided in the discretion and humanity of the Court that they would not proceed to trial until Tuesday next at the soonest, so as to allow time for consultation with his clients.

The Attorney-General said that the prisoners had known in advance that they were to be arraigned that day; but as the great object which he had in view was that a jury of the country should decide whether or not the charges against them were well or ill-founded, he was ready to assent to the delay which had been proposed, and had no objection if the trial of Hardy should stand over till Tuesday. And so it was agreed.

✻   ✻   ✻

As arranged, the Court reconvened at 7 a.m. on Tuesday and Thomas Hardy was set to the Bar (see Figure 11).

The Sheriffs had summoned 238 jurors. Some were not freeholders and were therefore ineligible to sit on a jury in a case of treason. Some were challenged by the defendant, some by the Crown.[2] When Adam Steinmetz was called, the Attorney-General asked him if he was a natural subject; he said he was, and he was sworn. Eventually, the following were empanelled:

Thomas Buck, esq. from Acton;
Thomas Wood, esq., coal merchant, from Hanging Hill, Ealing;
William Fraser, esq. from Queen Square, Bloomsbury;
Adam Steinmetz, biscuit-maker, from Limehouse;
Newell Connop, distiller, from Shadwell;
John Mercer, mealman, from Uxbridge;
Thomas Sayer, esq., distiller, from Bow;
Richard Carter, esq. from Paddington Street, St Mary-le-bone;
Nathaniel Stonard, brewer. from Bromley;
Joseph Nichol, gentleman farmer, from Wilsden;
John Charrington, esq., brewer, from Mile End;
Joseph Ainslie, esq., coal merchant, from Broad Street, St George's in the East.

Figure 11. Thomas Hardy, presumably in the dock at the Old Bailey. (From the Mansell Collection.)

The swearing in of the jury and the reading of the indictment must have lasted about an hour.[3] Sir John Scott then addressed the Court; he spoke for nine hours. After some initial remarks concerning Parliament's decision to pass the Act for detaining persons suspected of treasonable activities, he went on to deliver a learned lecture on the basic principles of our constitutional law. It was the King's function to enact laws by and with the advice and consent of Parliament, to execute the laws which had been enacted, and to convene in Parliament those whom he was bound to convene – and, by the terms of the Coronation Oath itself, 'to govern the people of this country according to the statutes in Parliament agreed upon, and the laws and customs of the same...'; any attempt to induce him to govern in some other manner, it was his duty to resist – even at the hazard of his life. It followed, therefore, that any attempt to induce him to govern otherwise than in accordance with his constitutional duties amounted to an attempt upon his life.

He passed on from there to the law of treason and explained how the Treason Act 1351 had come to be passed. As he has been accused over the years of trying to extend the law to its utmost limits, by developing the doctrine of constructive treason, in order to secure the conviction of the reformers, it is right to record that he expressly adopted the passage in Lord Hale's *History of the Pleas of the Crown*, Ch. 11, in which this most learned judge had pointed out:

> first, how necessary it was that there should be some fixed and settled boundary for the great crime of treason...; secondly, how dangerous it is to depart from the letter of that statute, and to multiply and enhance crimes into treason by ambiguity and general words...; and thirdly, how dangerous it is by construction and analogy to make treasons, where the letter of the law has not done so, for such a method admits of no limits or bounds, but runs as far as the wit and invention of accusers, and the odiousness and detestation of persons accused, will carry men.

And he went on to disavow any charge of constructive treason, or of any cumulative or analogous treason. It was his contention that the defendant was guilty of treason as specified in the statute – he had embarked upon a course of conduct which was likely to lead to the death of the King. The overt acts, by which the defendant's intention was to be proved, involved a scheme to hold a national convention with the purpose of subverting the legislature and the government, and deposing the King; the publication of documents to the same effect; the provision of arms and a conspiracy to make war for the same purpose – all these, as history and particularly recent events in France had shown, were actions likely to lead to the King's death. He reminded the jury of the Gordon Riots:

> It is within the memory of most of us living, that a few thousand men in St George's-fields, combined in one purpose, reduced this metropolis to a state of anarchy, a state in which no government existed. If any man had been asked, a fortnight before the event to which I am now alluding, Is it possible for four or five thousand men to assemble in St George's-fields, and to rob and plunder every body they choose in London and ten miles round? That would have been thought utterly impossible – but yet it happened – why? because a combination of the few will subdue the many, who are not combined, with great facility.

The Attorney-General then described all that had happened in the last five years – that societies had combined to subvert the government; that the convention which was to have met could have had no other object except to follow the example of the National Convention of France and to take over the functions of King and Parliament. He emphasised the correspondence which the societies had had with France, and he read extracts from their addresses and resolutions – 'their opinions are conveyed in the terms *no king, no parliament*'. When the idea of a convention was first mooted in 1792 or even in 1793, its object might have been to petition for reform, but by 1794 it had become abundantly clear that it was to be a convention of delegates, elected by themselves: it would be for the jury to decide whether that convention was simply to petition Parliament, or was to absorb all the powers of government and to create its own legislature.

This led to the Scottish Convention, in relation to which the Attorney-General declared that if 'certain persons...had been tried for high treason, they would have had no right to complain.' After explaining how the events in Scotland were part of a general conspiracy, and therefore admissible as evidence against the defendant, he showed how the Scottish Convention had adopted the forms and procedures of the National Convention of France; he analysed the Resolution of 28 November clause by clause; when he came to the reference to an invasion, he reminded the jury of the letters from France in which the writers had promised their arms, bayonets and pikes in the service of England; and when Margarot, in a letter to Hardy, had said, 'letters convey very imperfectly, and with no great degree of safety, what we might wish to inform each other of', the Attorney-General said:

> Now what do you think it is that they do not inform him of in this letter? They do not inform him... *that the convention was to meet in case of invasion* – that was a secret which durst not be trusted to correspondence by letter, and...they consider it of such a nature, that they determine not to insert it even in their own minutes.

The Attorney-General then drew attention to the resolutions and toasts made by the London Corresponding Society on 20 January 1794. The resolutions provided for the calling of a general convention in circumstances almost identical to those set out in the Scottish Resolution of 28 November, although the case of invasion was omitted; the toasts were calculated to inflame their minds, and included 'Success to the Armies of Freedom' – and this was during the war, he added. And always he came back to the basic proposition, that the convention was to be a 'convention of the people...to take upon itself the power of the people...claiming all civil and political authority'.

Occasionally, there were lighter moments. 'It will appear from the written evidence', said the Attorney-General at one stage, no doubt with a sidelong glance across counsel's table, 'that a gentleman of the name, I think, of Felix Vaughan, was appointed a delegate upon the 30th April...'; and when he read the letter from the Society of the Friends of Liberty and Equality of Laon, containing the reference to 'the gift which you have presented to the warriors of France', he interjected sarcastically that 'they had sent some shoes, and were at that time thinking of giving them some more'. But to the prisoner sitting in the dock, it appeared that Sir John Scott was resolutely and relentlessly seeking his destruction; and the final, and what he no doubt expected to be the most devastating part of his case, he reserved for the last few minutes:

> You will not be surprised to find pikes in the hands of these men and their associates – to find muskets in the hands of these men and their associates. Do not, gentlemen, let us be misled by the great doctrine of the Bill of Rights, that every man has a right to arms for his own protection – he has without question a right to convenient arms for his own defence; but the point before a jury will be, for what purpose had he the arms? If he attempts to say that he had them for his own defence – if he had them in fact for a worse purpose, the attempt to colour the fact makes the fact more criminal.

They had been manufacturing pikes in Sheffield; they had manufactured iron instruments called night-cats which were to disable horses; they were manufacturing muskets for military societies in Lambeth and Holborn; they drilled with them.

He admitted that the Government had been employing spies:

> I say, if, with these projects going on in the country, a secretary of state, or any other person in the executive government, had hesitated a moment to procure information, these parties might have been able to put into execution the projects they were meditating, and he would have been answerable for it.

Finally, he asked the jury to do their duty:

> on behalf of the public which is due to yourselves, to the public, to your posterity and theirs. But on the other hand, if, after hearing this case fully stated, and attempted to be fully proved, you should be of opinion that it is not proved, or you should be finally of opinion that the offence is not made out according to the *hallowed* interpretation of the statute of Edward 3rd; I say then...God send the prisoner a safe deliverance!

*   *   *

It was already evening, and the candles in the old Bailey were alight, when Sir John Scott concluded his speech and the Crown began to call their evidence. Almost immediately, they ran into difficulty. It was essential to the case that Hardy's handwriting, and his signature to the documents which were being put in evidence, should be proved, and the Crown called Alexander Grant, a member of the London Corresponding Society, for this purpose. But he could not swear to it; he agreed that the documents which were shown to him were in the defendant's writing, but he could not take his oath on it. On this rather unsatisfactory basis, the prosecution proceeded to place the documents before the Court.

King's Messengers were called – Thomas Maclean, Edward Lauzun, John Gurnell. They produced the papers which had been seized in Hardy's house and in the house of Daniel Adams; as the papers were shown to him one by one, Grant said he believed they were in Hardy's handwriting. There were various letters and papers: the resolutions of the London Corresponding Society of 24 May and its Address to the Nation of 6 August 1792; letters to Edinburgh, Manchester, Stockport and Norwich, and to the Society for Constitutional Information and the Friends of the People, and replies to Hardy – all through the evening, Mr Shelton, the clerk of arraigns, was reading out the papers to the Court.

Erskine hardly spoke a word during the evening, but towards midnight he intervened to ask whether the prosecution were likely to conclude their case

> within a time that human nature is equal to pay attention to it.... I confess, that for one, I do not feel myself at all fatigued, and am extremely ready to go on and to remain here any length of time which my duty to the prisoner can possibly require; but if the evidence on the part of the crown should go on to such an extent as that it would be impossible either for your lordships or the jury to give any farther attention (and your lordships and the jury are but men), then the prisoner's defence could not possibly be heard.... I would ask my learned friends, whether they can finish their evidence tonight?

Eyre CJ asked, 'What is your own judgment as to the course we ought to pursue: Mr Attorney-General, have you nearly concluded your evidence?' The Attorney-General's reply was concise and to the point: 'Not half.' Eyre CJ then said that there were two issues to consider: first, whether a criminal case had to be concluded in a single sitting or could be adjourned; and, if the latter, whether the jury could be allowed to separate. He said that it was a general rule that there was to be no adjournment until the jury gave their verdict and that he would not depart from it except in a case of extreme necessity. He referred to such precedents as existed, and went on to add:

> I made some inquiry as to what might be done (the subject, you see, was not totally out of my thoughts)...and the sheriffs...did promise that they would endeavour to accommodate the jury in this house;

and Mr Sheriff Eamer said: 'My colleague and I have made the best provision the place will admit; we have prepared a room and beds.' Then Eyre CJ said:

> It is a distressing thing to put the jury into these circumstances...but it is better than sitting up for three days and two nights, which, for anything I can see, must be the case. I am very ready to take my share of the fatigue, but my apprehension is, that the cause cannot be so effectually tried as it would be if the Court and jury had the refreshment of food and rest.

Erskine intervened to say, 'It is impossible to figure to one's self a more delicate situation than that which we hold who stand as counsel for a person who is upon trial for his life'; but he added that he was sure that his client would accept the word of the jurors that they would not be approached by anyone if they went home. One juror, Richard Carter, said that he lived at Marylebone and was rather an invalid, but he would prefer to go home, and several others agreed. Hotham B. pointed out that the judges could go home, but nevertheless he thought that the jury should not be allowed to separate.

Eyre CJ then asked: 'Do you think you are able to go on all night? if you do go on all night we shall make but a certain progress, and I am afraid we shall be in no condition to pursue our business tomorrow.' Buller J. said that he understood that the sheriff had beds prepared for all the jury, and Sheriff Eamer repeated that beds and 'mattrasses'[4] had been prepared.

Finally, Eyre CJ reached his decision: the case could be adjourned, but the jury must stay together; and bailiffs were sworn to attend them. It was now a quarter past 12 o'clock on Wednesday morning; the case was adjourned until 8 a.m.

✻   ✻   ✻

It was the usual, although not admittedly the invariable practice, for a case of treason to be tried before the Chief Justice of the Court of King's Bench, so Kenyon CJ would apparently have had a prior claim to be the president of the Special Commission which had been appointed to try this case. Why was it, then, that the appointment was given to Sir James Eyre, Chief Justice of the Court of Common Pleas? Who was responsible for the decision?

It is ironic that of all the men who played a leading part in this drama, least is known about the presiding judge.[5] His family is thought to have originated in Wiltshire, and his great-grandfather, a surgeon, had been mayor of Salisbury in 1685; three members of the family had been judges in the previous century – Sir Giles, Sir Robert and Sir Samuel. His father is believed to have been a vicar at Wells in Somerset, and it was probably in Wells that James was born in 1733. He was educated at Winchester and St John's College, Oxford, and was called to the Bar by Gray's Inn in 1755. Shortly afterwards, he purchased the place of one of the four Common Pleaders to the City of London, in which capacity he practised in the Lord Mayor's and Sheriff's Court.

In 1761 the Recorder of London, Sir William Morton, who was growing old, applied to the Court of Aldermen for leave to appoint a deputy. The natural choice for the post was the Common Serjeant, Mr Nugent, but the two men had quarrelled so James Eyre was appointed instead. He carried out his duties so satisfactorily that, on the Recorder's death in 1763, he was appointed to succeed him. The office was of great respectability and wealth, and entitled the holder to a silk gown and precedence next after the Serjeants-at-Law; he is said to have acquired a considerable practice at the bar, although his name is hard to find in the Reports except in *Wilkes* v. *Wood* where the reporter said that he 'shone extremely'.

It has already been noted that he twice came into conflict with Horne Tooke whilst he was Recorder, the latter occasion leading directly to his elevation to the bench as a Baron of the Court of Exchequer in 1772; he was a member of the court which imposed sentence upon Horne Tooke following his conviction for seditious libel in 1777. Ten years later he became Chief Baron, and early in 1793, when Lord Loughborough fulfilled his ambition of becoming Lord Chancellor, he was promoted to the post of Chief Justice of the Court of Common Pleas.

It is known that the King took a personal interest in judicial appointments – according to Brougham he devoted too much of his time to matters of detail

when he should have been concerned with 'the nobler branches of information connected with state affairs';[6] so it is likely that he was personally
concerned in reaching a decision as to the composition of the Commission, in
consultation with the Privy Council and with the Lord Chancellor in
particular.

According to Lord Campbell, in his *Lives of the Chief Justices*, the original
plan was that the trial should be before Lord Kenyon in the Court of King's
Bench; 'but some apprehension was entertained of his intemperance of
manner,[7] and they were arraigned at the Old Bailey before that quiet and safe
judge, Chief Justice Eyre'. This, however, does not seem to me to be an
adequate explanation. Lord Campbell does not appear to have known that
Kenyon and Horne Tooke had been students together, and Kenyon may well
have made it clear that he would not put himself in a position in which he
might have to sentence his old friend to death; or it may be that those who
knew Kenyon did not think that he had the force of personality or stamina to
conduct such a case as this – as was indeed demonstrated when he presided
over the trial of William Stone two years later.

❖   ❖   ❖

Throughout the Wednesday, the Crown continued to place before the Court
a great mass of documentary evidence. There were the minutes of the Scottish
Convention – Erskine objected to these, but the Crown argued that Skirving
was, as it were, an agent of the defendant and acting on his behalf: they were
read. There were papers printed at the request of Thelwall without the
knowledge of the defendant; again Erskine objected, but the Crown argued
that every step in the conspiracy was evidence of the conspiracy and therefore
admissible against any member of the conspiracy, and Eyre CJ ruled in favour
of the Crown.

Later in the morning, the Crown wished to produce a letter written by
Martin to Margarot on 22 January 1794, in which Martin had written.

> A woman, moved and seduced by the instigations of the devil, and traitorously
> intending, &c, did, in St James's Park, take off her patten and threw it with all her
> force at his majesty, whereby the glass of the stage-coach was broken, and his
> majesty put in fear;

As it was one of the very few items of evidence which the jury might regard as
displaying some degree of personal animosity against the King, the Crown
were very anxious to put it in evidence; Erskine and Gibbs asserted that a
private letter passing between two other persons could not possibly be
evidence against their client. It was one of the most important issues of law to
be raised during the whole trial, and it was argued for two hours. The
Solicitor-General reviewed what had happened in the cases of Lord Stafford
in 1640 and Lord Lovat in 1747; Bearcroft asserted that in a trial for any kind
of conspiracy, once if was established that the prisoner had conspired with
others, then the acts of those others were admissible against him. He was

interrupted in mid-sentence by Erskine, and a discussion ensued between him, Eyre CJ and Serjeant Adair, until Bearcroft came back into the discussion:

> I had received this interruption with the greatest patience, because it is made by a counsel for a man now trying for his life; if it had been made in any other place, and in a civil cause, I could not have forborne instantly to express my astonishment at the gross irregularity of the interruption.

Both Bower and Law added their arguments on behalf of the Crown, and eventually Erskine replied; after commenting on the fact that they were now towards the middle of the second day of the trial, he said:

> My lord, this is no trifling matter, I stand here for the life of an innocent man, and I stand here for the law and constitution of England, and I will suffer nothing to be done while I stand here that is not consonant to both.

He went on to point out that if the arguments of the Crown were valid, thousands of His Majesty's subjects might be brought to trial – everyone who had been a member of the Society for Constitutional Information or the London Corresponding Society, and anything written by any member of either of these societies would be evidence against all of them.

Eyre CJ gave judgment for the Crown and Macdonald CB followed: 'This is a paper which is addressed by one of several conspirators to another of those conspirators.... It is an act by one of the conspirators, which in order to show the nature and tendency of that conspiracy may be read as against any other.' Hotham B. agreed, and so did Buller J., who had been Erskine's master in the law; Grose J. also agreed: 'I am of opinion this evidence must be received for the purpose of showing that there was a conspiracy, and of what nature that conspiracy was.' Eyre CJ directed: 'Then now you will read it.'

It was a decision of paramount importance for the future conduct of the case.[8] From this point onwards, the Crown was not restricted to calling evidence relating to documents which Hardy had written, or were found in his possession, or to words which were spoken in his presence; they could now range over the whole field of the alleged conspiracy, and call evidence on matters of which the defendant had no knowledge, over which he had had no control, and to which he had never given his consent or approbation.

The case proceeded. There was evidence of the correspondence with Scotland and with the provincial societies; there were the minutes of the Society for Constitutional Information; Thomas Paine's letter to the People of France was read, and extracts from *The Rights of Man*; Joel Barlow's letter to the National Convention of France was read, and Hardy's Address to the French people. This was the day when the correspondence with the President of the National Assembly and the French provincial societies was read, and Frost's account of his journey to Paris. It was also the day when William Huskisson[9] gave evidence: he had been residing with the British Ambassador in Paris in the summer of 1792 and he gave an eye-witness account of some of the events of 10 August. Huskisson also acted as the translator of the French papers which were distributed by the French-speaking Swiss, Joseph Deboffe.

Late at night, the Crown was calling evidence of the anniversary dinner of the Society for Constitutional Information on 2 May 1794; the minutes were read, and Garrow added: 'There follow several songs, which are stated to have been sung at the dinner. I do not desire them to be read, but have not the smallest objection to their being read, if Mr Erskine wishes it'; to which Erskine replied, 'I am not particularly anxious for a song at the present moment.' The songs were not read.

It was now past midnight. The jury stated that they could not have the necessary refreshment of sleep in the Sessions House, as there was only one room and nothing but 'mattrasses' to lie on, and they had not had their clothes off for more than forty hours. The Court was informed that there was accommodation with beds available for them at the Hum-mums, an hotel in Convent Garden; and so, with counsel's consent, and accompanied by the under-sheriff and four officers, they were taken there by coach.

*   *   *

Readers may wonder whether the transcript of the shorthand note of the trial, as printed in the State Trials, can be regarded as an accurate record. Even if we assume that the judges on the bench and counsel at the bar could retain command of the case, that the jurors could maintain their attention from early in the morning until late at night, was it possible for Joseph Gurney[10] to keep up his skills hour after hour?

The answer is, I believe, that the record is accurate. No one, as far as I know, has ever claimed that it was not accurate, and many writers since 1794 have quoted from it. After R. v. Hadfield in 1800, Erskine wrote to the editor of the State Trials to tell him that there were many blunders in Gurney's report of that case, but he added that he was then getting very old, the inference being that he had been more reliable in his younger days. We know, moreover, that Gurney did not work alone. It was Joseph's father, Thomas Gurney (1705–70) who was the first official shorthand writer at the Old Bailey;[11] he had taken up shorthand as a hobby when he was a boy of 16, and received his official appointment sometime in the middle of the century. Joseph (1744–1815) assisted his father and succeeded to his office in 1790; he in turn was assisted by his son, John. As we have already seen, John was by now a barrister, and was briefed as an additional counsel for the defence by both Hardy and Horne Tooke. As he took no active part in either case it is reasonable to deduce that he was engaged in taking a note, and indeed it is known that it was John who took the note of the Solicitor-General's opening speech in R. v. Horne Tooke.

There is another item of evidence which may be taken into account. In the case of Horne Tooke, the editor of the State Trials employed two shorthand notes, one by Gurney and another by Blanchard, and compared the two, noting any discrepancies between them – there were remarkably few, and most of those were of minor significance. I think, therefore, that one can safely say that, within the ordinary limits of human fallibility, Gurney's notes are an accurate, verbatim record of what was said.

*   *   *

The jury were allowed a little extra time that morning: the Court sat at 11 a.m.

The Crown dealt with the history of the London Corresponding Society; its constitution was produced and read. Then came the witnesses from Sheffield; about half a dozen men from Sheffield had been arrested, and they had agreed to give evidence for the Crown, but they were still in custody, at the house of Mrs Mary Parkinson,[12] in Little Charles Street, Westminster. They were called to give evidence relating to the manufacture of arms. It was at this point that the case for the Crown began to crumble, even in examination-in-chief. In answer to Law, one witness, William Camage, said that they had been making pikes, but only to defend themselves against illegal attacks; another, Henry Hill, a cutler, had made a pike-blade like a bayonet and shown it to Henry Yorke – 'there were some young girls in the room that he was very fond of, he took it in his hand and pretended to give it a push at one of them'. Law never had much luck with military matters: earlier that summer he had been portraying Thomas Walker drilling his men in a room where the bayonets would have stuck in the ceiling; and many years later, in the invasion scare of 1805 when he enrolled in one of the Inns of Court Regiments, he was the awkward member of the company, who never could tell his left foot from his right.

Garrow had no more success with night-cats. When he was examining William Broomhead, he asked if he had ever heard anything of night-cats; Broomhead replied that he had seen a model of one, but it was only like the plaything of a child.

> 'Now we will have an account of the manner in which children play in Sheffield, what sort of an instrument was it?'
> 'A little instrument standing up with a point about an inch high.'
> 'It had four points?'
> 'It was in a ball, was it not?' asked a juror.
> 'No.'
> Garrow asked: 'It had four cross points?...So that if you threw it down it always presented a point.'
> 'It did.'

In answer to further questions, the witness described how, if thrown on the floor, the night-cat always had one point sticking up, and Garrow asked whether he had ever heard any conversation about it being used against cavalry.

> 'I do not recollect any conversation about its use but a mere trifling, desultory, pleasing, irregular conversation with one another.'

Garrow also called Robert Moody, a joiner, to give evidence on the same issue. He had seen a lead model of a night-cat, lying in the window of

Camage's shop – he had never heard of any being made from the model. But he had made shafts for pikes – six or eight, perhaps; one of these was brought into Court to be exhibited, and it stood in a corner for the rest of the trial. If there had been evidence of the manufacture of weapons on any significant scale, that would, of course, have been a factor of great weight; in the event, this evidence only served to bring ridicule upon the prosecution and outweighed the relatively more serious evidence of arms and drilling by Francklow and the Loyal Lambeth Association, and in particular the evidence of Samuel Williams (who was also in custody), who described the connection between the Association and Hardy.

Some of the evidence called by the prosecution on the Thursday was, however, much more convincing. The jury heard an account, not challenged at this trial, of Yorke's speech at the Castle Hill meeting; and there was the programme for the Farce called La Guillotine, or George's Head in a Basket.

During the early stages of the trial there had been little cross-examination: most of the evidence was documentary, and a matter for comment therefore, rather than to be challenged; and some of the early witnesses were favourable to the defence – both Erskine and Gibbs cross-examined the Sheffield contingent at some length, but only to confirm that they had been arming in order to defend themselves. Then, on the Thursday afternoon, Henry Alexander gave evidence. He was a linen-draper from Fleet Street, and he said that he had joined the London Corresponding Society on 5 November 1793, and that Yorke had been there and had told him that he was going to Belgium to head the French army, and should be back by Christmas – they would be ripe for revolution by Christmas, and he (Yorke) hoped to see Mr Pitt's and the King's heads on Temple Bar. After Yorke's speech, he said, they all got up and shook hands with him. But Alexander did not remain a member of the London Corresponding Society, and he went to Mr Dundas's office.

Erskine's cross-examination started on a low key, requesting the witness to repeat the evidence which he had already given; then suddenly the atmosphere changed:

'You became a member, because you wished to propagate their opinions and doctrines?'
'Not at all,' the witness replied.
'Then in plain English you went there as a spy, did you not?'
'When I went, I did not know what it was.'
'When you became a member, did you not become a member for the purpose of informing?'
'After I knew what they were I did...'
'Are you acquainted with Mr Dunn of Manchester?'
'No.'
'I should have thought you were?'
There was no answer, and Eyre CJ asked: 'Why do you not answer the question?'
'I do not understand the question', said Alexander.

'I am sorry for it', said Erskine, 'I believe you are the only one in Court who does not.'

Erskine pressed on; he established that the witness had lost his business: 'So you gave up your employment voluntarily, because you were wanted here at the Old Bailey, for half an hour?'

'Yes, for no other reason.'

Erskine investigated his private life; the witness said that he had worked for Mr Smith in Cheapside, but had left him to go and live in the country with an aunt near Salisbury, and then with another aunt in Old Bedlam.

'What did you leave Smith for?'

'We had some words.'

'Had some words – what might the words be, think you?'

'I do not know, I am sure, exactly now...'

'You have an amazing good memory: you have repeated a whole speech a man made at a meeting, but you cannot remember the few words that passed between you and your master...'

Eventually Eyre CJ intervened: 'Give him fair play.'

'He has certainly had fair play – I wish we had as fair play', said Erskine, 'but that is not addressed to the Court.'

'But whom do you mean?' asked the Attorney-General.

'I say the prisoner has a right to fair play', replied Erskine.

'But you said it was not said to the Court', said Garrow, to which Erskine replied firmly: 'But I am not to be called to order by the bar.'

So, having silenced his opponents, he returned to the case.

Then there was John Edwards, a silversmith, who produced the programme of La Guillotine, with Erskine interrupting to say that it had been fabricated by the spies who supported the prosecution.

'You shall not say that till you prove it', said the Attorney-General.

'I shall prove it.'[13] said Erskine.

'Till you prove that, you ought not to say it', said the Attorney-General, 'it is a charge that ought not to be made.'

Eyre CJ intervened: 'If there is any point between you which should be heard, the appeal, to be sure, must be made to the Court.'

'I wish to God it was', said Garrow, 'we should save much time and trouble.'

'A little indulgence, on both sides', said the presiding judge, 'would save much time and trouble.'

Under cross-examination, Edwards admitted making a pike, but it was for his own use, not against the Government. He also said that he had been at one meeting of the London Corresponding Society and they were reading Mr Pitt's and the Duke of Richmond's address at the Thatched House Tavern, upon which Eyre CJ asked whether the meeting was more or less legal on that account, and Erskine responded that he wished it to be understood that he was no advocate for the conscience of the Duke or of Mr Pitt.

> 'It is certainly true', said Eyre CJ, 'but this is rather too grave an occasion for such an observation.'
> 'It is not a proper occasion for this frippery', said the Attorney-General.
> 'I say that is not a proper expression', said Erskine.
> 'I will repeat it', said the Attorney-General.
> Eyre CJ said, 'The gentlemen I hope will recollect that they are upon a solemn trial.'
> 'I think it is really hard upon me upon this solemn trial', said Erskine, 'that I should be eternally assailed by these gentlemen, when I have the arduous task of extracting the truth from these witnesses.'
> 'If any person were disposed...to give you any interruption, it would be my duty to preserve order', said Eyre CJ, 'but it is impossible the cause can go on, unless the gentlemen at the bar will a little understand one another, and by mutual forbearance, assist one another.'
> 'As far as came from me, I am sorry for it', apologised the Attorney-General.

So Erskine went on to extract from the witness an admission that Hardy had never made any proposition for the use of pikes or other arms, that he was not a man of a turbulent disposition, and that he had no reason to believe that Hardy had ever been acquainted with the programme for La Guillotine.

There followed George Sanderson who had gone to exercise to Spence's house in Holborn, and at a blacksmith's shed by Tothil Fields Bridewell; and he said that a member of the London Corresponding Society had announced the 'good news' of the defeat of the British army, and that he had heard with pleasure that one of the King's messengers had been killed. At the end of his examination-in-chief, he said that one member of the Society had observed that, if he discovered a spy among them, he would blow his brains out. So Erskine began his cross-examination:

> 'So a member said, he would not care for blowing any spy's brains out?'
> 'Yes.'
> 'Were you not a little afraid when you heard that?'
> 'I was.'
> 'Oh! you were a spy, were you?'
> 'I was.'

And then, when he had been cross-examined on a memorandum which he held in his hand and asked for a particular date, Sanderson said:

> 'I think it was the 21st.'
> 'None of your thinking, when you have the paper in your hands....What date have you taken, good Mr Spy?'
> 'I do not think, upon such an occasion, being a spy is any disgrace.'

Eyre CJ intervened: 'These observations are more proper when you come to address the jury.'

The Attorney-General lent his support to the judge: 'Really that is not a proper way to examine witnesses.'

'I am sure I shall always pay that attention to the Court which is due from me', said Erskine, 'but I am not to be told by the Attorney-General, how I am to examine a witness.'

'I thought you had not heard his lordship', said the Attorney-General.

'I am much obliged to his lordship for the admonition he gave me', said Erskine; 'I heard his lordship and I heard you, which I should not have heard.'

Late in the evening, Edward Gosling was giving evidence; he was a clerk to William Wickham, one of the justices in the police office in Lambeth Street, Whitechapel, and at the outset of his evidence he said he had been recommended by a magistrate to become a member of the London Corresponding Society. He described meetings of the Society, and the plot to seize the royal family: Baxter, said Gosling, had said that for his part he did not wish the King or any of his family to lose their lives, but he thought they might go to Hanover – 'it must be expected that some blood must be shed; some particular persons had offered such insults to the people, that human nature could not be overlooked'.

Erskine started his cross-examination by asking him his Christian name, and went through his various employments: he had been a writer to Mr Colquhoun, a magistrate; he had kept a broker's shop; he had been a dealer in naval stores – but he denied he had lived by smuggling and cheating the King; he had been a hairdresser for seven years, working under the name of Douglas in Petty France;... Did he know a Mrs Coleman?

'I do not', he said.

'Look across to the jury', said Erskine.

'I do not know a Mrs Coleman now'.

Yes, he admitted, he had known a Mrs Coleman, she had rented a shop of him, she had died in his house and he had buried her; yes, he wrote her will, and she left her money to one Burroughs and one James Leech – Leech was a son of his wife's; no, the will was not drawn up by an attorney – no complaint was ever made that he had forged the will.

'Will you swear positively, you never have been charged with it; a man that is charged with a capital felony cannot forget it?'

'I do not recollect that ever I was.'

'Good God ! Do you mean to swear that you do not remember whether you were charged with a capital felony or not?'

'I do not know that I ever was.'

'Will you swear that no such charge was brought against you?'

'I can swear no farther than, that to the best of my knowledge, it never was.'

Eyre CJ intervened to point out that, even if a charge had been brought, it might not have come to the witness's knowledge, so Erskine dropped that line of cross-examination and turned to a different topic. Yes, said the witness, he knew a cheesemonger called Cox; he had dealt in cheese, butter and hams.

'I thought you were a hair-dresser; what! do you deal in hams?'
'My wife kept a shop of that sort; I dressed hair....I purchased hams of him, and in some there were great holes filled up with mortar and stones.'

The significance of Mr Cox's hams never became clear, for Erskine reverted to Gosling's earlier career as a dealer in naval stores, accusing him of stealing copper and cheating the King, and informing on others who were purloining material – 'merely hints to prevent pilfering', Gosling said, 'No person was accused upon that information, nor did I receive any reward for it...'

Garrow, in re-examination, did his best to salvage the reputation of the witness: no suit was ever instituted to dispute the legality of Mrs Coleman's will, no prosecution for forging it, nor any complaint against him; it was a fair and honest transaction.

It was now past half-past one o'clock on the Friday morning; the Court adjourned and the jurors rode away in their carriages to the Hum-mums.

*   *   *

By the eighteenth century, criminal trials were conducted in much the same way as they are today. The jury was sworn in; counsel for the prosecution addressed the jury; witnesses were examined in-chief ('original examination' it was called in those days) and cross-examined; counsel addressed the jury; and the judge summed up. Minor differences appear on the transcript: there was the useful system of having two witnesses giving evidence simultaneously, one to produce documents, the other to prove them ('I believe that is Mr Hardy's handwriting', said Alexander Grant, over and over again as the papers were shown to him); counsel were much readier to interpose questions when their opponents were examining a witness than they would today; and jurors played a more active role – it is quite common to find a juror intervening to ask a witness a question.

There was, however, one fundamental difference between contemporary and modern procedure. In those days, the defence had no advance knowledge (other than the indictment and a list of the names of witnesses) of the case for the prosecution. Arguments on the admissibility of evidence could not be prepared in advance; they had to be raised impromptu as and when the issues arose; and they were, apparently, always heard in the presence of the jury. (On one occasion, a song was read; subsequently it was ruled inadmissible, and it was solemnly erased from the record.)

*   *   *

The Court sat at 9 a.m. on Friday 31 October. John Groves,[14] described in the list of witnesses simply as a gentleman, was in the witness box most of the morning and at the outset Law, for the Crown, put it to him that he was spying on the London Corresponding Society:

'You became a member for the purpose of discovering their proceedings?'
'I was desired by a particular gentleman to go there for that purpose....'

He gave his account of the Chalk Farm meeting, and produced the letters and resolutions which had been read there; he described what Thelwall had said about the King, and the toast to the lamp-iron at the end of Parliament Street. And then there were the knives. In answer to Law, the witness described how he had found the men eating cheese with their *couteaux secrets*, and someone had said that they were bread-and-cheese knives, and 'upon that observation', said Groves, 'there was a smile'. Groves had asked where he could get one, and had been sent to Thomas Green, a hairdresser and perfumer in Orange Street, Leicester Fields. He went there and Green told him he had two or three hundred, and also told him 'to speak very low, for the parlour door was open which was adjoining the shop, and he smiled and said, for my wife is a damned aristocrat'.

Groves then went on to describe the Society for Constitutional Information's dinner where Horne Tooke made his speech in which he had begged the audience to note that he was not inebriated and called Parliament a scoundrel sink of corruption.

Groves was cross-examined by Gibbs, who managed to ascertain, after several evasive answers, that the witness was an Old Bailey solicitor. Gibbs asked him who had sent him to join the London Corresponding Society, but he declined to answer unless he was directed to do so by the Court. There followed a short discussion on the law: John Law said that the channels of communication must be protected; Gibbs said that he would not press the matter further, and Eyre CJ thought it was not proper. So the cross-examination continued.

'You have been giving an account of some conversation that passed there; cannot you recollect who the persons were that had that conversation?'
'No, I do not know.'
'A gentleman used to practise at the Old Bailey, and meaning to give evidence afterwards...did not think it material to learn by whom these conversations were held?'

Eyre CJ interrupted him, pointing out that questions should not be accompanied by comments: 'The business of a cross-examination is to ask to all sorts of facts, to probe a witness as closely as you can; but it is not the object of a cross-examination, to introduce that kind of periphrasis as you have just done.'

Gibbs sent for Erskine who was having a rest in the parlour, and he returned into Court and there was a discussion as to the extent to which leading questions could be put to a witness in cross-examination. Eyre CJ apologised for having intervened, but the rule was that the examination should be limited to ascertaining facts, and observations on those facts should form part of the defence. So cross-examination proceeded, and there was a laugh at the French knives, and at Green calling his wife a damned aristocrat.

Gurnell was called again to produce a parody of the Vicar of Bray;

Why should we vainly waste our time
    Repeating our oppressions?
Come rouse to arms, tis now the time
    To punish past transgressions.

Erskine pointed out to the jury that it had been sent to Hardy in a letter 'by somebody or other'. John Thomson was called for the sole purpose of producing a pike, with a blade two feet two inches long, found in the possession of Mr Hillier. William Camage was recalled to say he had visited Margarot in the Tolbooth and saw him using a spring knife: 'Was it concealed?' he was asked in cross-examination; 'No, it was laid for him to get his dinner with – it was a curious knife and Margarot had showed it to him on the table'. Erskine asked him if he was a cutler – 'No, he was an ink-stand maker'.

Then George Lynam was called; he was described simply as an ironmonger from Walbrook. He had joined the London Corresponding Society in October 1792; it was never really determined whether he had joined the Society out of genuine interest and decided to become an informer later, or whether he was employed as a spy from the start, but he certainly kept a detailed record of what the Society had been doing. In June 1793, he fell under suspicion, but on appearing before a jury of his fellow-members, he was acquitted, and resumed his activities. He was in the witness-box for six or seven hours on that last day of October: he gave an account of all that the Society had been doing over a period of many months.

Erskine began his cross-examination by saying that he had little to trouble the witness about, but started to ask some probing questions concerning his business affairs: he had been an ironmonger originally, said Lynam, but more recently in the commission line, attending in the coffee houses to take orders from the captains and mates of the East India Line. 'I should think you have hardly leisure to concern yourself with those sort of transactions, have you?' asked Erskine, but the matter was not pursued. So Erskine turned to another topic and asked him when he first communicated to a magistrate that he was inquiring into the affairs of the Society; Lynam replied that he had consulted a friend and was reporting to him. Erskine pressed him to say who it was, and Lynam said:

'If I am by your lordship's direction to answer this question, I certainly will.'
'I think you may say that it was or was not to a magistrate?' said Eyre CJ.
'It was not to a magistrate', said the witness.
'Then to whom was it?' asked Erskine.

The Attorney-General objected. Erskine said that he was entitled to know the name of the person so that he could call him as a witness to say whether or not the reports had been made. Eyre CJ intervened to say that there was a rule that those persons who were the channel by means of which crimes were detected should not be unnecessarily disclosed. The Attorney-General said that when he had practised in the Court of Exchequer, this sort of problem occurred every day: 'A witness says, "I had information that the defendant had committed an offence against the revenue laws...." What is the principle upon which the Court says, you shall never ask where he got that information?' It might be essential to have an answer to this question to test the credibility of the witness, but the Court proceeded upon the great principles of general justice: 'It says that individuals must suffer inconveniences, rather than great public mischief should be incurred...if men's names are mentioned...; great crimes will be passed over without any information being offered about them, or without persons taking that part which is always a disagreeable part to take.'

Erskine said that the proof of innocence was as important in the administration of justice as the punishment of crimes, and the Attorney-General agreed: 'Most surely'. Erskine went on to ask how it would be possible for him to establish that the evidence of the witness was all an invention and a fabrication without knowing the name of the person to whom the communication was made: 'I submit he must state the name of the person to whom he communicated.... I will then ask, when did you tell him? at what place? who was present? Then I ask that person, is it true?' The Attorney-General replied that it might be a hard rule, but he had his duty to perform as the public prosecutor – 'It has become a settled rule that private mischief gives way to public convenience...; great numbers of persons in the world would not choose to have their names mentioned on such occasions; and with respect to that feeling, call it fear, or imprudent reserve, it is a substantial principle in law, that a man should not have his name disclosed'.

The whole Court gave judgment. It was now late on Friday evening; their lordships had already sat through four exhausting days; there was no prior warning that the issue was to be raised; the judgments were all delivered *ex tempore* – yet they have survived for two centuries as the leading authorities on this point of law.[15] Eyre CJ started by saying that when 'we run into very nice distinctions upon a principle, we get into difficulties from whence I never know how to disentangle myself or relieve my mind'; then he went on to say that channels of discovery should not be disclosed, and that all persons in that position are to be protected from discovery. Macdonald CB, in a dissenting judgment, agreed with the general rule – 'There is no rule more sacred' – but thought that there was a distinction between an informer and a friend whom the witness had consulted. Hotham B. affirmed that public justice demanded, in many cases, that sort of secrecy without which government could not be carried on, and that he could see no distinction between a friend and an informer. Buller J. re-stated the principle, but seemed to think that the person consulted was a private friend not the discoverer: his, therefore, was at least in part, a dissenting judgment. And so the final decision rested with Grose J:

I therefore, however unwilling I am...in a case where life is at stake to shut the door of evidence, yet where a point of great constitutional law, that which is to affect the public justice of the kingdom is in question, I must decide upon it as my conviction tells me is right.... He appearing to be essentially the informer, I think, according to the rule of law, the question ought not to be put.

So the question was not put, but Erskine still tried to find out more about the witness's friend:[16]

'Was it a man or a woman?'
'That I cannot answer', said Lynam.
'Not whether it was a man or a woman?'
'Certainly not', said Eyre CJ, and brought the matter to an end.

After Lynam, John Coates was called: he had been an apprentice of Francklow and described his master exercising his men. Erskine asked him a few deadly questions:

'How did your master dress himself?'
'I saw him with his regimentals on.'
'Had he a blue coat with a red cape, white waistcoat and breeches, and a cockade in his hat?'
'Yes.'
'The cartouche boxes were lying upon the cutting-out table, openly in the place?'
'Yes.'
'Your master walked out publicly in the street with his uniform?'
'I have seen him with them on.'

Then they called Thomas Green the perfumer to give his version of the *couteaux secrets*; the Attorney-General himself took the witness. Green told the Court that he had always dealt in cutlery, as was customary for perfumery shops, and he had got three dozen of these knives from Scofield & Co. at Sheffield – their riders came to town and went about the shops to show samples. He bought his shoes from Mr Hardy, and he had given him a package of six or seven knives; the defendant had bought one, and the others were returned; they were on sale in other shops in the Strand and about town. Again, Erskine's cross-examination was deadly:

'If this is worth pursuing, I would ask you whether you have one of these knives here?'
'Yes, I have one in my pocket – Here it is.'
'Is this all?'
'Yes; I have had one of the kind seven years, and used it in my business.'
'And you sometimes cut a bit of meat with it?'
'Yes, and cheese or anything.'
'You had no intention to cut throats with it, I hope?'

'Never.'

'How many of these knives have you now?' interrupted the Attorney-General.

'I have twenty left out of three dozen....'

'I think there is hardly a cutler's shop in town', continued Erskine, 'that has not such knives?'

'Very few that are anything of a cutler's shop....'

'It is a very useful knife; and I will buy one of them next time I see you.'

Erskine then went on to ask him if he had ever called his wife a damned aristocrat: 'I will make oath', replied Green, 'that I did not make use of such an expression as that. I swear I said no such thing; these knives all lay open in my shop, so far from hiding them from my wife, or from any man in the parish, that they lay openly in the show-glass, and in the window for sale.'

Finally, at about midnight, they called evidence from Scotland, of the Scottish Convention, and of Watt's schemes. Erskine objected to this evidence, and the Attorney-General spent about twenty minutes reading letters to explain the link between Hardy and the Scottish conspirators; Erskine said he was so tired that he was having difficulty in following the argument, but then conceded the point. And lastly, after the Court had resumed on the following day, William Lockhart described how he had found twelve pike-blades, a couple of battle-axes and a pole in Watt's house. James Clerk, the sheriff of Edinburgh, was the last witness, and he screwed one of the battle-axes on to the pole and then unscrewed it and replaced it with a pike-blade. Neither of these witnesses were cross-examined.

*   *   *

But one witness never came. Jane Partridge was sitting in the Crown witnesses' waiting-room; twice she was called, and each time she fainted. So the Attorney-General decided to dispense with her evidence. Hardy always believed that it was her intention to perjure herself; but in those days many people were going around saying how they would like to decapitate the King, so her story was almost certainly a case of mistaken identity.

CHAPTER 13

THE TRIAL OF THOMAS HARDY: THE CASE FOR THE DEFENCE

At about 1 p.m. on the morning of Saturday 1 November, just as the Court was about to adjourn, Erskine addressed the bench; it was the fourth day, he pointed out, that he and Gibbs had stood in a very anxious situation – there had been a voluminous body of written evidence, not all of it printed, and copies of some of it had not yet reached him; yet two days had been spent in hearing oral evidence, and he and Gibbs had been constantly engaged in Court. He himself, he went on, had been extremely ill – nothing less than a case of this magnitude would have brought him to Court – he had not got home until between two and three o'clock in the morning, and had been in Court again at nine. He therefore asked the Court for some indulgence to enable him to prepare his defence.

A discussion between Erskine and Eyre CJ then ensued. The judge appreciated Erskine's problems, but at the same time he had the jury to consider – 'we have a jury who have been thrown into the most arduous service that ever I saw a jury engaged in; they have borne it in a manner which does them infinite honour'; he regarded it as his duty to conclude the case as expeditiously as possible. Erskine pointed out that the Attorney-General ('I am sure I think as highly as it is possible of the ability of the Attorney-General and of the manner in which he has performed his duty') had spent nine hours in opening his case, and his client 'most unquestionably may expect an equal time', and he needed to arrange his papers and prepare his defence. The Attorney-General said that he thought that the remaining witnesses would take about forty minutes; so Erskine suggested that the Court should sit at midday, and he would be ready to start his defence at one o'clock. Eyre CJ responded that he felt so much for the jury that he could not think of it and suggested adjourning until 11 a.m.; then one of the jurors intervened: 'My lord, we are extremely willing to allow Mr Erskine another hour, if your lordship thinks proper.' And so, it being then after half-past one, the Court adjourned until midday.

As arranged, Erskine started to address the jury at about 1 p.m. on the Saturday afternoon and he spoke for seven hours (see Figure 12). He opened his speech by thanking the Court and the jury for allowing him a few hours

Figure 12. Engraving of Thomas Erskine by Cruickshank, published at No. 3 Piccadilly, on 13 December 1794. (By permission of the Trustees of the British Museum.)

retirement 'to arrange a little in my mind that immense matter' which he was now to lay before them, and implored God himself

> that he will fill your minds with the spirit of justice and of truth; so that you may be able to find your way through the labyrinth of matter laid before you, a labyrinth in which no man's life was ever before involved, in the annals of British trials, nor indeed in the whole history of human justice or injustice.

After these preliminary observations, he addressed the jury on the law for the space of two hours, as if he was arguing the issue on an appeal to the House of

Lords. He covered every aspect of the law of treason. He analysed the wording of the Act, and in particular the word 'compassing'; at common law, compassing a person's death had been a separate crime, and its meaning was well-known, covering such offences as assault with intent to murder. When this ceased to be an offence at common law, Parliament retained it as a special protection for the King, and it meant *precisely* to bring about the death of the King – and over and over again throughout his speech, he reiterated that the crime with which the accused was charged was that of compassing the King's death, and nothing short of proving that that was his intention would suffice to secure his conviction:

> The question must return at last to what YOU and YOU ONLY can resolve – *is he guilty of that base detestable intention to destroy the King?*... If you can say this upon the evidence, it is your duty to say so, and you may, with a tranquil conscience, return to your families; though by your judgment the unhappy object of it must return no more to his. – Alas! Gentlemen, what do I say? HE has no family to return to; – the affectionate partner of his life has already fallen a victim to the surprise and horror which attended the scene now transacting.

He dealt with the law relating to overt acts, explaining that they were simply the evidence from which the traitorous design and intention might, or might not, be inferred. He started to review 'the most prominent cases' – the case of Sir John Freind, accused of a plot to restore the Protestant Pretender to the throne, and the case of Lord George Gordon, in which he himself had played such a prominent part – but found that he could proceed no further with them for fear of consuming his strength in the preliminary part of the case.

So he turned to the facts, and the proposal to hold a convention which was modelled on that of the Duke of Richmond and 'hundreds of the most eminent men in the kingdom'; he discussed the conventions which had been held in Scotland and Ireland; the government, he said, knew full well that Colonel Sharman had been supporting a convention in Ireland, at the head of ten thousand men in arms, without any commission from the King, any more than poor Francklow had, for regimenting fifty. He read long passages from Burke and Locke and discussed the rights of man. Then he declared:

> Gentlemen...I am utterly astonished, on looking at the clock, to find how long I have been speaking; and that, agitated and distressed as I am, I have yet strength enough left for the remainder of my duty.

It was well into the evening before he started to deal in detail with the evidence. He concentrated on the Scottish convention, pouring scorn on any suggestion that it was anything other than a peaceful meeting, assembled to petition Parliament ('I concluded that there had been raised', he said, 'in the first session of this parliament, £15, from which indeed you must deduct two bad shillings'); he described the way in which it had been dispersed, and associated himself with the attacks on the courts of Scotland (but he omitted any reference to the Resolution of 28 November, although it had been put in evidence to the Court).

It was, however, in the final hour of his speech that Erskine really came into his own. The Crown had painted a picture, he said, of an armed rebellion, and all the evidence on this score was turned to ridicule. He reminded the jury that Green, a witness called by the Crown, had himself told the Court that his knives lay constantly in his open shop-window where cutlers exposed their ware to public view. As for pikes, there was a joke going round that when the government agent who was looking for pikes eventually found one, he was transported with delight and enthusiasm, and hung over the rusty instrument with all the raptures of a fond mother, who embraces her first-born infant, and *thanks her God for all her travail past*. In Sheffield, they made pikes – three dozen – to protect themselves against illegal attacks upon their homes. And something had been said about guns, and the Crown had referred to Francklow who had collected forty people by public advertisement, and who himself attended the Globe tavern publicly in his uniform, whilst the cartouche boxes of these secret conspirators lay publicly upon his shop-board, exposed to the view of his customers and neighbours.

If Erskine had heaped ridicule upon the evidence of armed force, he turned his ferocity upon the governmant spies. He quoted a passage from Burke, who had written that under a system of mercenary informers, 'The tables and beds are surrounded with snares. All the means given by Providence to make life safe and comfortable, are perverted into instruments of terror and torment.' He reminded the jury of the first of this tribe, Mr Alexander, who could not in half an hour even tell where he lived or why he had left his master – 'You saw how he dealt with it, and how he stood stammering, – confused, – disconcerted, – and confounded.' Mr Groves, an Old Bailey solicitor, had been called to give respectability to the suggestion that this miserable, solitary knife was the engine which was to destroy the constitution, and he alleged that Groves had carried his system of spying to such a pitch as to continue it even after Hardy's arrest, by insinuating himself into the committee preparing his defence, so that he might disclose to the Crown the evidence by which he meant to defend his life.[1]

Erskine now turned his last attack upon the Crown, who had brought in evidence against Hardy the activities of one Watt, a ruffian and a scoundrel, whose very existence was unknown to Hardy:

> How is a man to defend himself against such implications of guilt? – Which of us all would be safe, standing at the bar of God or man, if he were even to answer for all his *own* expressions, without taking upon him the crimes and rashnesses of *others*.

It was now eight o'clock.

> I am sinking under fatigue and weakness. – I am at this moment scarcely able to stand up whilst I am speaking to you, deprived as I have been, for nights together, of everything that deserves the name of rest, repose, or comfort;

He reminded the jury again of the basic principle of the law of treason – did they believe that Hardy had been compassing the King's death? He reminded them of the fearful precedents to be found:

If the state trials in bad times are to be searched for precedents, what murders may you not commit.... You might have convicted without any evidence, for many have been so convicted, and in this manner murdered.

And then finally, he referred to a witness whom he intended to call, Mr Francis, a Member of Parliament, who had proposed an inquiry into the seditious practices which were said to be in progress; Mr Hardy offered himself voluntarily to come forward, proffered a sight of all his papers, which were afterwards seized, and tendered every possible assistance to give satisfaction to the laws of his country, if found to be offended:

> I will show likewise his character to be religious, temperate, humane, and moderate, and his uniform conduct all that can belong to a good subject, and an honest man – When you have heard the evidence, it will beyond all doubt confirm you in coming to the conclusion which, at such great length (for which I beg your pardon), I have been endeavouring to support.

Major Cartwright was in Court that night, and said that Erskine's voice was reduced to a whisper; he was quite hoarse, and was leaning for support on the table; but so intense was the stillness that his faintest words were heard in every corner of the Court. When he sat down everyone started to applaud; the scene was described by the Editor of his speeches, in a passage reprinted in the State Trials:

> An irresistible acclamation pervaded the Court, and to an immense distance round. The streets were seemingly filled with the whole of the inhabitants of London, and the passages were so thronged that it was impossible for the judges to get to their carriages. Mr Erskine went out and addressed the multitude, desiring them to confide in the justice of their country; reminding them that the only security of Englishmen was under the inestimable laws of England, and that any attempt to overawe or bias them, would not only be an affront to public justice, but would endanger the lives of the accused. He then besought them to retire, and in a few minutes there was scarcely a person to be seen near the court. No spectacle could be more interesting and affecting.

*   *   *

Gibbs examined the witnesses for the defence that Saturday night. Mr Goddard was the first – Florimond Goddard – who had been a member of the London Corresponding Society for two years, and said Hardy was a friend to order, and desired, particularly when members went to a private house, that no one would even bring a stick with them. Francis Dowling had been a member of the Society, and said that Hardy was a peaceable, orderly and pious man. Alexander Wills was another member; he said that the intentions of the Society towards the King were full of respect, honour and fidelity; he had only got to know Hardy because he had made him a pair of boots, they were very excellent and cheap. Archibald Hunter and Alexander Fraser were members; they had never heard of any plan to attack the government by force of arms.

William Barclay was a shoemaker who had known Hardy for fifteen years; Hardy had been his foreman for seven years; he was as quiet a man as could be. The Revd Thomas Oliver was a dissenting minister: he had met Hardy about four years ago when they were both sheltering in a house from a shower of rain; he became friendly with him, and used to call at his shop at No. 9 Piccadilly and they talked on religious and sometimes political matters. He had gone to the house in May, and was informed by his wife that he had been arrested – she was in a great deal of trouble and very ill and frightened: 'She is dead since?' asked Gibbs, 'Yes', he replied.

Daniel Stuart was the secretary of the Friends of the People; he did not always agree with Hardy's views, but said he was a very simple man, very inoffensive, the last man, he should have thought, who would have been guilty of violence.

John Carr had known Hardy for twenty years: he was a sober, peaceable, worthy man. John Stevenson had known him when he was working for Mr Barclay – he was peaceable and mild, and 'as to moral character, I know no man that goes beyond him'. Alexander Gregg was a bookbinder who had known Hardy for seven years, and William Henderson was a dealer in eggs who had known him for twenty years: they too had the same opinion of him; as had the Revd James Stevens, who was the minister of Hardy's congregation and had known him since he came to London.

Peter Macbean was a shoemaker who had known Hardy for seventeen years; Alexander Gordon was another shoemaker who had known him for twenty years. John Bogue was a cabinet-maker, Matthew Dickey a Scotch factor, and James Hardy (no relation) a grocer from Smithfield; they had all known the prisoner for many years and he had always been sober and industrious and honest.

Both Goddard and Wills were subjected to long cross-examinations, mostly about the Globe Tavern and Chalk Farm meetings; they had been there, but everything was quite peaceful, they said, even though some songs were sung. It was while Goddard was being cross-examined that the Attorney-General accused Felix Vaughan of prompting the witness; Vaughan had been sitting at counsel's table next to Erskine and Gibbs throughout the trial; he had been advising them, but denied the Attorney-General's accusation; Eyre CJ said that he could remain where he was provided he acted correctly and did not speak so loudly that the witness could hear. It was while Wills was being cross-examined by Bower that he agreed that he had contributed to a subscription for William Carter, a bill-sticker – he could not remember how much – a shilling, or half-a-crown, or a guinea or five guineas; Bower repeatedly challenged him on this until Eyre CJ intervened

> You have brought yourself into a scrape, only for the sake of a flourish. When you are upon your oath, if you wish only to speak plain English, you would be under no difficulty; there is a great difference between a shilling and a guinea and five guineas.... It was certainly absurd in the witness not to recollect that he was upon his oath, and to talk in that rhodomontade way. I dare say he meant to speak the truth.

And when the Attorney-General asked the Revd Thomas Oliver whether he had discussed *The Rights of Man* with Hardy, the witness replied firmly that he had no time to meddle with those matters – he was always ready to visit the sick and the poor, 'but I have four sermons to preach in a week, and as I make them myself, I have very little spare time'.

After that, cross-examination became more and more perfunctory and as the night wore on it virtually ceased. During the course of his speech, Erskine had impressed upon the jury that, before they could convict Hardy, they must be convinced beyond all reasonable doubt – was this, perhaps, the first recorded use of this famous phrase? – of his criminal intention; when the Court rose at 12.20 on that Sunday morning, he and Gibbs must have been fairly confident that they had gone a long way towards proving his innocence.

✻   ✻   ✻

There had never been a case like this before. Practically all criminal trials in those days were completed in single sitting, even if the Court had to sit into the early hours of the morning: this one lasted nine days.

During the trial, Hardy was confined in Newgate, in the inner prison, and every morning he had to pass through the yard in which the felons were allowed to walk. They were heavily ironed with fetters; they lined up in two ranks as he strode past – he was at that time a tall, thin man – and gave him their good wishes and congratulated him on his good spirits. Every morning, when he passed Stewart Kyd's cell, they shook hands through the iron grating; on the third day, he said cheerfully, 'Now Kyd, this day, death or liberty'; but he was mistaken, 'for his persecutors', to use his own words, 'protracted the struggle as long as they had any hopes of success'. Various others were confined on the State side of the prison for publishing seditious libels, 'or, in other words, for publishing the truth'. They too crowded to the gate as he passed by every morning on his way to the Court, anxious to shake hands with him and express their good wishes. And every evening,[2] Thelwall watched him march back, tired but undaunted, into the prison.

On the Sunday, he and Kyd were walking in the yard when Keeper Kirby asked them if they would like to see the condemned cell – the 'condemned hole', Moll Flanders had called it when she was under sentence of death a century earlier and waiting for her name to appear on the 'dead warrant', although she had been sufficiently successful in her 'trade' to be able to pay for a dirty little chamber to herself. The poor unfortunate condemned prisoners were walking about in a small yard opposite the doors of their dwellings, and consequently the cells themselves were empty. Hardy did not record what conversation took place, or what remarks he made about those horrible places; but the execution of Watt had taken place in Edinburgh a fortnight earlier, and Hardy himself was on trial for his life. The sight was not very pleasing to a man in his situation, he wrote, when it was uncertain whether he might not be lodged in one of those cells himself in two or three days time; and from thence through the debtor's door to the platform where public executions took place;[3] opposite the door was the Magpie and Stump, whose landlord charged up to £50 for a window seat on hanging days.[4]

❖   ❖   ❖

On the morning of Monday 3 November, the Court sat at 8 a.m. Erskine first called John King, the Under-Secretary of State, to prove that Davison's letter about pikes had been found unopened among Hardy's papers.

He then called a series of witnesses from Sheffield: Hardy's solicitors must have arranged for these men to stay in London throughout the trial. There was David Martin, an engraver; Edward Oakes, a plater; William Dewes, a razor-maker; and Edward Smith, a cutler. They gave evidence about the events in Sheffield: their objects had been peaceful, they said; they had armed themselves in self-defence, they had never had any design to attack the government – if they had wanted to, said Smith, they could have furnished ten-thousand pikes in one day; they had intended to adopt the Duke of Richmond's plan for the reform of Parliament. There were references to the Castle Hill meeting – 'I take it for granted that every now and then a hot spirit might show itself?' asked Erskine at one point, at which Eyre CJ interjected, 'Do not take anything for granted when you are examining a witness'. There were lengthy cross-examinations about Castle Hill and correspondence with London; the Friends of the People were mentioned, so Daniel Stuart, their secretary, was recalled. He read out the Society's declaration of 11 April 1792, calling for the restoration of freedom of elections and a more equal representation in Parliament, and a list of signatories – Charles Grey, Esq. MP; Thomas Maitland MP; when he came to 'Hon. Thomas Erskine MP', Erskine interjected, 'Meaning me, gentlemen'; and a few names further on, 'John Scott, Esq. MP', the Attorney-General said, 'That is not me, gentlemen'. Erskine added, 'This gentleman is not John Scott, Esq., but Sir John Scott; they are both very good men, gentlemen.' Other documents were read, including one addressed to Samuel Ashton, Esq., and there was a discussion as to why a currier or tanner had been addressed as Esquire.

Altogether, the evidence that morning seemed to be of little relevance to the case until Garrow stood up to cross-examine Edward Smith, who had been asked about parliamentary reform, and the manufacture of arms for self-defence. He introduced his cross-examination by an astonishing announcement:

> I shall not trouble you with the questions the gentleman has repeated several times, whether you are a traitor, and ought to be hanged; I shall not ask you whether you have been guilty of high treason or not....

Then he asked a series of questions about the use of arms; he asked about the Duke of Richmond's plan:

> 'Have the goodness to inform a very ignorant man, which I profess myself to be, about all these things; what was this plan of the Duke of Richmond's and Mr Pitt's?'
> 'I understood equal representation in parliament', said the witness, 'and without it the people would not, as I understood the matter, have their rights.'

'What did you take Mr Pitt's plan for a more equal representation to be?'
'For every man to have his voice.'
'That you took to be Mr Pitt's plan?'
'Yes.'
'So much for the accuracy of your information'.

Then he went on to cross-examine the witness about *The Rights of Man*; he was a cutler, so he would have a cheap copy:

'You know every cutler in Sheffield had one; you had a cheap copy, had you?'
'I have seen one of the others.'
'I dare say you have seen the best edition; have you one of the cheap copies?'
'I have seen both.'
'I am sorry to be so troublesome, but I must have an answer'.

And so it went on; and having established that Smith had read *The Rights of Man*, he proceeded to cross-examine him on its contents: Did he not understand the book to be a specific for getting rid of kings everywhere? Did he not understand that Paine's works were written to inculcate a notion that the monarchy was destructive of all civilised states, and they could not too soon get rid of all kings? And on, and on; while the unfortunate, floundering witness struggled to find answers that would not incriminate him. And surprisingly, there was no attempt, either by the judge or by counsel, to come to his rescue. There had been nothing like it throughout the entire trial. In later life, Garrow was to acquire a practice that surpassed even Erskine's, and a reputation for 'tact';[5] it was not demonstrated on this occasion. At the end, Erskine asked only one question, concerning the Castle Hill meeting, in re-examination before calling his next witness:

> I next propose to read this letter from his grace the duke of Richmond to colonel Sharman; it has been stated by one or two of the witnesses; but if it is thought more regular, I will call the duke himself; I believe his grace is in attendance.

The Duke was sworn and Erskine referred to the letter; the Duke said that he knew that the printed edition of his letter had been mutilated and he could not say whether the pamphlet which the Sheffield witnesses had referred to was accurate, so he handed Erskine a copy of the original; Eyre CJ invited the Duke to sit down and the letter was read. It was dated 15 August 1783, and set out in detail various schemes for the reform of Parliament and repeatedly recommended universal representation. After it had been read, Law said that he had been checking it against the Sheffield copy, and the two were identical except for a couple of printing errors.

Erskine then re-called Daniel Stuart for the second time and said that he had one question to ask which he could not, with propriety, have asked him before – had he ever heard Hardy state what his plan of reform was? Stuart replied:

'Yes, I have; he always stated it to be the duke of Richmond's plan, universal suffrage and annual parliaments.'

'Was that said to you publicly, or in the privacy of confidence?'

'It was said publicly; and he sold me some copies of the duke of Richmond's letter.'

The Attorney-General interrupted: 'I really must object to this sort of examination.'

'Then I will now defend this question', said Erskine; 'I am persuaded your lordships will not refuse to the unfortunate man at the bar, that evidence which has been received for every prisoner under similar circumstances, from the earliest times of our history to the present moment. I am sorry to consume the time of the court, but if I am called upon I will repeat to your lordships, *verbatim*, from the State Trials, various questions upon similar occasions, put by different prisoners by consent of all the judges, all the attorney-generals, and solicitor-generals, and counsel for the Crown. I only wish to know whether the question is objected to or not.'

'It is.'

And so, on that Monday afternoon, for two hours or more, the Court debated the last major legal issue which arose in this momentous case – namely, whether the defence could call evidence to demonstrate the innocent intention of the accused. It appears clear to me that the issue was deliberately raised by Erskine as a trap into which the prosecution fell; he must have planned in advance what he was going to say and had scoured the State Trials for precedents ('I saw this question brewing some days since', he said at one point, 'and therefore prepared myself for it') while the prosecution was taken off guard; and it was an opportunity to draw the attention of the jury to a line of earlier cases of treason, all so different from the one which they were trying.

The point was neatly summarised by Gibbs when he spoke in support of Erskine about an hour later:

> Now if the Crown may give evidence of the whole of a man's life, for the purpose of explaining an indifferent act, and giving it a criminal complexion, surely it follows, upon the principle of administering equal justice, that whatever has been said upon the same subject, tending to prove a different intention, an innocent intention, it should be competent to him to give in evidence....

And he added that in cases of homicide it was the constant practice to receive evidence of statements of the prisoner of his good will towards the deceased in order to explain the fatal blow and to determine whether the crime was murder or manslaughter.

In the meantime, Erskine had reviewed a whole series of cases. He said that in *R. v. Gordon* he himself had asked various questions – for example, had the witness ever heard Lord Gordon make use of any expression which showed any disloyal or unconstitutional intention? – all without any objection.

There was the case of Lord Russell, who had been charged with planning to raise a rebellion and seize the King's guards; he had called witnesses to speak of his affection towards the government and his hatred of risings. There was the case of Rosewell, a dissenting minister, indicted for preaching a treasonable sermon, and tried by none other than Jefferies CJ himself; he was allowed to call members of his congregation to prove that he had frequently preached in favour of a Kingly government:

> Am I not from these authorities to be allowed to produce the same sort of evidence in support of this poor shoemaker, which the greatest men in the country have ever had an opportunity of doing without the smallest doubt...? And certainly it is fair evidence; a man is not a republican on Monday, a monarchy man on Tuesday, and a republican again on Wednesday, his sentiments do not change in a moment....

There was the case of Henry Cornish, charged with conspiring with Lord Russell and the Duke of Monmouth to levy war; witnesses gave evidence that they thought he was loyal and that he often drank the King's health. And Francis Francia, charged with corresponding with the Pretender – a witness was asked, 'What do you know of the prisoner's behaviour?' and he replied, 'It was a great surprise to me when I heard that he was taken up, for he used often to drink a health to King George.'

The Attorney-General admitted that he had not foreseen that such evidence would be offered and had not considered it, so instead he started to criticise Erskine: 'I wish my learned friend would at once decline talking of the difference between a poor shoemaker and men of higher rank, or that he would state the facts upon which he thinks it fit to hold such language', and he warned the defence that if that sort of evidence was let in on behalf of Hardy, it might let in other evidence against other prisoners who were to be tried later.

The Solicitor-General added his arguments. He pointed out that things are frequently passed over without objection which ought to be objected to, especially on the part of the Crown who are constantly accused of pressing prisoners too far: 'that sort of odium being constantly attempted to be thrown upon every crown prosecution; those who are employed by the crown are always extremely anxious not to raise objections, where they do not think that the general necessity of public justice requires that they should be raised...'. He then went on to argue that the illustrations given by Erskine had occurred during cross-examination, but Erskine interrupted to say that they were all from original examinations. The Solicitor-General got deeper into trouble:

> 'Would it be permitted upon a trial for murder, for instance, to give in evidence, that the prisoner said he would not commit a murder; and yet as far as I have any conception of this, as stated by my learned friend, it was simply that evidence; and therefore I think it must have been upon a cross-examination.'
> 'I tell you it was not.'
> 'Then I do not understand it.'
> 'I see you do not.'

The amicable relationship which had existed between counsel was fractured, and the Solicitor-General turned to address Erskine:

'The manner, sir, in which you have thought proper to conduct yourself towards me, in the course of this trial has been such as reflects upon my character. I will not submit to any man for knowledge of law; I am not used to talk of myself, but I will not be taught by you or any other person, propriety of conduct either in a civil or criminal case; I believe, I know my duty in both as well as you do; and I trust that I shall discharge it'.

Bower seems to have had time to look up the authorities which had been cited, and tried to deal with them one by one, and concluded with the proposition that the evidence which Erskine now wished to produce was no more admissible than would be a statement by a prisoner that he did not intend to commit a murder when he was in the act of committing one.

Eyre CJ intimated to Erskine that the Court would allow the question to be put, but Erskine had not finished, and insisted on his right to reply. But he was chiefly concerned to retaliate upon the Solicitor-General, and displayed his grave displeasure at his opponent's failure to accept his word that all his illustrations had been taken from original examination, not cross-examination – and he criticised the Attorney-General for complaining about his reference to the prisoner as a poor shoemaker. Finally, he returned to the point by saying that the question was designed to show that Hardy's object was to bring about the Duke of Richmond's object by the Duke of Richmond's means: 'If the court will put that question', he concluded, 'I have done'.

Eyre CJ ruled: 'You may put the question exactly as you propose; I confess I wished by interposing to avoid all discussion, because I consider what we are doing, and whom we have at the bar, and in that box, who are suffering by every moment's delay in such a cause as this.' 'I am sure the jury will excuse it', said Erskine, 'I meant to set myself right at this bar; this is a very public place'. Then, turning to Stuart, who was still in the witness-box, he asked him if he had ever heard from Hardy what his objects were, and Stuart replied that Hardy had told him that he always adhered to the Duke of Richmond's plan, and had said that that plan would be accepted in the end. That was the end of the matter. The Attorney-General, not amused it seems safe to say, commented: 'If this had been stated at first to be the question meant to be asked, I do not see what possible objection I could have had to it.'

Erskine now called Richard Sheridan. Sheridan is chiefly remembered today as the author of *The Rivals* and *The School for Scandal*; he had written these when he was a young man, back in the 1770s, subsequently becoming the manager of the Drury Lane Theatre, and getting deeply into debt. In 1780 he had been elected to the House of Commons, and three years later was appointed secretary to the Treasury; during the next decade, he was a leading exponent of Parliamentary reform. He gave evidence that early in 1793 he proposed that a committee should be set up to inquire into the societies which were supposed to be promoting sedition and treason; he invited Hardy to see him, and Hardy had told him that the information obtained by the government was accurate, and that the places mentioned as their meeting places were correct, but that the objects of the society were no other than parliamentary reform according to the Duke of Richmond's plan; he had also said his Society no longer met in public houses as the landlords refused to have them, and so they were meeting in private houses and he was quite prepared to let Sheridan have a list of these houses which could then be made available to the House of Commons; Hardy had also offered to let him see all his papers and books.

The next witness was Philip Francis. Early in 1793, he said, he had made a speech in the House of Commons, advocating reform, and Hardy had written to thank him and said that he wanted to have the thanks of his Society printed, so the witness had visited Hardy in his shop and told him that he was satisfied with their thanks, but declined to have the letter printed. In May of the same year, Hardy and Margarot had visited him and asked him to present a petition to Parliament; the witness said that he was satisfied with the petition itself, but utterly averse to the prayer annexed to it, which was for the granting of universal representation. Francis said that he found Hardy a 'most remarkably reasonable, quiet man', both then and when he visited him in his shop; both he and Margarot were 'very ready' in maintaining their arguments, and he expressed his surprise that men of their rank in life should have the command of such arguments, but they had said they were only following the opinions of the Duke of Richmond.

The final witness was the Rt. Hon. the Earl of Lauderdale. Erskine explained why he had decided to call him: one of the Scottish societies had invited him to be their delegate at the Scottish convention – 'It would therefore be very unreasonable to suppose that their intention was to destroy the honours of the nobleman to whom this letter was addressed.' In evidence, the Earl agreed that he had received such an invitation from the Friends of the People in Portsburgh, but had declined it. However, he had met Skirving on several occasions: he had never met a better or more humane man; the plan of the members of the Convention was to obtain universal suffrage and annual parliaments, and there was nothing to suggest that that was to be accomplished by force and violence. In cross-examination, there was some discussion as to whether the Earl's opinion of Skirving might have changed if he had seen his letter written to Hardy in July 1793, and the letter was read; but it was agreed that this was a matter for the jury. Then Erskine said: 'My lords, I have now closed the defence of Mr Hardy.'

It was not quite the end of the evidence, as the Attorney-General had a letter written by Samuel Ashton to the secretary of the Society for Constitutional Information; it had been inadvertently dated 26 May 1797 and had been overlooked; it was read.

                              ✳   ✳   ✳

Vicary ('Vinegar') Gibbs was the son of a surgeon in Exeter, named, maybe, after Sir Thomas Vicary, the great Tudor surgeon and author of a famous medical textbook. Vicary Gibbs had been at Eton and King's College, Cambridge; he was a little fellow, five feet four inches tall, embittered and ill-humoured, which, it is said, accounted for his nickname.[6] He began to address the jury late that Monday afternoon, and he had barely started – 'May it please your lordships, Gentlemen of the jury' – when he fainted. In 1916, Sjt Sullivan collapsed half way through his final speech on behalf of Sir Roger Casement, and in that case the Court adjourned until the following morning, when junior counsel, Artemus Jones, continued where his leader had left off. However, Gibbs recovered in a few minutes, and continued to address the jury for about four hours.

He explained the anxiety which he felt upon this occasion, but he would, if he could, do his duty to the miserable man at the bar. He felt himself incapable of comprehending the vast mass of evidence which the Crown had produced:

> It took the Attorney-General nine hours merely to open this case, a length of speech unheard of; the annals of this kingdom do not afford an instance of a prosecution founded on so many complicated facts, drawn out of such a tangled web, that less than a speech of nine hours could not render it intelligible to the jury.

Towards the end, he apologised for not reviewing the documentary evidence in its entirety: 'I have but one excuse for not doing it, which is, that to the reach of my ability, the thing was impossible; though I have had the accidental leisure of a Sunday to look into the papers...I found it, at last, absolutely impossible.'

Gibbs dealt with the law. He concentrated particularly on the case of Lord Russell and the Rye House plot, which was a scheme to raise an insurrection against Charles II and to imprison him and murder him. How different this was from the case against Hardy, who was accused of conspiring to hold a convention; in order to bring home the charge against him, the Crown would have to prove either that a convention could not be called except for treasonable purposes, or that this convention was to be called to procure the deposition, and thereby the death, of the King. He commented on the evidence that the defendant supported the doctrines of the French Revolution – 'Do you think that that shoemaker understands French? Do you think that that shoemaker ever read the *Moniteur*?' – before embarking upon the principle theme of the defence, which was that he had called the convention to follow the principles of the Duke of Richmond:

> It cannot be said that a man...holding such a rank in the state as the noble duke...meant...to invite the people to take up arms against the government, and to enforce that which would otherwise be denied them.

Nor could the Crown argue that this was simply a pretext for some different intention, for the defendant had never been without a spy at his elbow for two years; was it possible, that if he had conceived a design of carrying the project of the convention by force, that some unguarded word would not have fallen from him, indicating such an intention, and have been passed on to the government?

He dealt with the question of arms with a combination of common sense and ridicule. It was a matter of common knowledge that Dr Priestley's house in Birmingham had been attacked and burnt down; Thomas Walker's house in Manchester had been attacked; the house of the Mayor of Nottingham had been attacked – the latter had taken up arms to defend himself, and two of the rioters had been killed, and the jury had found it was justifiable homicide. And so the men of Sheffield had provided themselves with arms to defend themselves – and now it was being alleged that they were arming to resist the whole united military of the kingdom with three dozen pikes, an order for 60 muskets, and less than half-a-dozen French knives.

He turned to deal with the spies – 'that infamous set of men...who, having no means of supporting themselves, endeavour to procure a livelihood by insinuating themselves into the secrets of others, and discovering them to the government', and showed their evidence to be unreliable if not perjured. This led in turn to Watt, who had been employed as a spy and had then embarked on treasonable practices; and the only connexion between Hardy and Watt was that Watt was a member of the Scottish convention, with which Hardy had been in correspondence.

At the end of his speech Gibbs stressed the evidence of Sheridan and Francis, and of Hardy's friends and neighbours and the minister of his congregation, all of whom had given evidence of his peaceable disposition and respectable character, and finally:

> It is not proved, that...he ever dropped a single expression, from which it can be collected, that he meant to use force; if he did not mean to use force, he must be acquitted of the charge now brought against him. That he did not, I think this evidence goes fully to prove; and, therefore, I trust in God that you will give him your verdict of acquittal.

Eyre CJ then asked, 'Mr Hardy, the counsel whom you have had assigned to you at your own request, have hitherto conducted your defence, examined your witnesses, and each of them addressed himself to the jury on your behalf: you are also at full liberty to speak for yourself, if you wish to do so; and if you do, this is the proper time for you to be heard.'[7]

> 'My lord, I am perfectly satisfied with the defence my counsel have made for me; and I apprehend there is no need of my saying any more.'
> 'And you do not wish to add anything?'
> 'No, my lord'.

These were the only words spoken by the prisoner throughout the trial.

＊   ＊   ＊

At this time, the Attorney-General had chambers at No. 11 Serle's Court, otherwise known as The New Square, Lincoln's Inn (see Figure 13), and was living at Powis Place. Sir John Scott has himself described[8] how, every evening throughout the trial, when he left Court, a signal was given that he was coming, and for a general hissing and hooting of the Attorney-General; this continued all along the Old Bailey, and all the way down Ludgate Hill and by Fleet Market. One night, there was a strange man standing by counsel's table; as Sir John was about to leave the building, Garrow said to him, 'Mr Attorney,

Figure 13. New Square, Lincoln's Inn, from W. Herbert's *Antiquities of the Inns of Court and Chancery*, 1804. Sir John Scott's chambers, No. 11, are just off the right of the picture. (From a private collection.)

do not pass that tall man at the end of the table'; the man had a suspicious appearance and for some time had been standing at the door with his hat pulled down over his face.

'Why not pass him?' asked Law.
'He has been here', replied Garrow, 'during the whole trial, with his eyes constantly fixed on the Attorney-General.'
'I will pass him', said Law.
'And so will I', added Sir John.

Other counsel, and others around, opposed him and told him that there was a mob collecting, and they did not think that the Attorney-General's life was safe; but he answered: 'I tell you, gentlemen, I will not stay here; for happen what may, the King's Attorney-General must not show a white feather.' Then, in his own words,

> I went and left them, but I will not say that I did not give a little look over my shoulder, at the man with the slouched hat, as I passed him; however, he did me no harm, and I proceeded for some time unmolested. The mob kept thickening around me, till I came to Fleet Street, one of the worst parts of London that I had to pass through, and the cries began to be rather threatening. 'Down with him' – 'Now is the time, lads' – 'Do for him', and various others, horrible enough. So I stood up, and spoke as loud as I could – 'You may do for me if you like, but remember there will be another Attorney-General before eight o'clock tomorrow morning; the King will not allow the trials to be stopped.' Upon this, one man shouted out, 'Say you so? you are right to tell us. Let's give him three cheers, lads.' And they actually cheered me, and I got safe to my own door. When I was waiting to be let in, I felt a little queerish at seeing close to me the identical man with the slouched hat; and I believe I gave him one or two rather suspicious looks, for he came forward and said, 'Sir John, you need not be afraid of me; every night since these trials commenced, I have seen you safe home, and I will continue to do so until they are over. Good evening, sir.' I had never seen the man before. I afterwards found out who he was (I had some trouble in doing so, for he did not make himself known,) and I took care he should feel my gratitude.

Many years later, the *Law Magazine* explained that the stranger's interest in the Attorney-General's safety was accounted for because he had done a great kindness to his father. Erskine, on the other hand, was extremely popular, and

> was received with universal Plaudits, and there was nothing to disturb his Enjoyment of this Contrast, or to soften my mortification, save that, on one Evening, the Multitude, which thought proper to take his Horses from his Carriage to take him home, had among them such a Fancy for a Patriots horses, as not to return them, but to keep them for their one Use and benefit.

CHAPTER 14

NOVEMBER THE FIFTH

Sir John Mitford, the Solicitor-General, who replied on behalf of the Crown, had spent most of his professional career in Chancery; he had written a *Treatise on the Pleadings in the Court of Chancery by English Bill* which Sir John Scott later described as 'a wonderful effort to collect what is to be deduced from authorities speaking so little what is clear'.[1] He opened his speech late in the evening of Monday 3 November, with some flattering remarks about his opponents:

> The prisoner, I am sure, has been most ably defended; and if the defence is unequal to the purpose, it is because his case is indefensible, and not because full justice has not been done to him.

Then he went on to allege that the proposition that the accused had simply been following the views of the Duke of Richmond was a fraud and a deception, 'always professing one thing and really meaning another'.

At an early stage in his speech, he dealt with the manufacture of arms at Sheffield; yes, he admitted, they had been lawfully made for self-defence – but once they had arms to hand, they might have used them offensively. Linking Smith's boast that the men of Sheffield could have manufactured 10,000 pikes in a day with Broomhead's evidence that Yorke had told him that he would march to London, he said:

> A body of ten thousand men, with pikes, thus led, might have been like the Marseillois you have so often heard of, who have acted at Paris, in a manner not of the most agreeable to humanity...

And so, for a few seconds that Monday night, Henry Yorke, the lad from Little Eaton, was portrayed as a latter-day Cromwell and the captain-general of this new rebellion. This proposition seems to have escaped the notice of historians, but it soon came to the knowledge of Yorke who was now in custody in York Castle, across the 'Eye of York' from Clifford's Tower where Robert Aske, the leader of another rebellion, had been hanged in chains.[2]

The Solicitor-General turned to deal with the law. He was, he said, at a loss to understand Erskine's observations on the term 'compassing', although these were abundantly plain. He recounted various treasonable conspiracies in English history (schemes which did not bear the slightest resemblance to the one now under consideration) to prove that a plan to depose or imprison the King was deemed to constitute compassing his death. He referred to the rebellion of the Earl of Essex, which was a plan to seize Queen Elizabeth by force. He described how the wife of Edward II came to this country to deliver it from evil counsellors – and within a matter of months the King was cruelly murdered; and how Henry Bolingbroke landed at Ravensburg with 26 men, but he was soon joined by a large body of people, and Richard II was deposed and put to death. The Solicitor-General was, however, on rather stronger ground when he said that of those persons who formed the convention in France and deposed the King, few had any design upon his life, but they lost control of their own acts and the consequence was the death of the King.

Turning to another aspect of the law, he said that any measures designed to depose the King, or to dissolve the government, or despoil him of his royal authority, must tend to lead to the King's death, and therefore constituted compassing his death; the deposition of the King was such a serious matter, that had it not been covered by the Act of 1351, Parliament would have covered it by later legislation, but had not done so.[3]

Towards midnight, the Solicitor-General started to deal with the addresses of the Societies to the French National Assembly '(which, by-the-by, neither of the counsel for the prisoner at the bar took any notice of whatever, though they appeared very important papers, for the purpose of showing the intention of these people)', but shortly afterwards Eyre CJ called a halt to the day's proceedings: 'I think we had better adjourn; as it will be impossible for any human powers to sustain it if we do not.' At 12.25 a.m. the Court adjourned until 8 a.m.

For more than four hours on the Tuesday morning, the Solicitor-General reviewed the evidence. There were the communications with France, after the King had been deposed and while his life was under discussion. There were the addresses to the National Convention, addressed to the Servants of a Sovereign People, describing the destruction of the monarchy as a glorious victory; and the answer from them to the 'Generous Republicans' and assuring them of military assistance from France. There was the letter from Norwich, asking whether it was the intention of the London Corresponding Society to 'rip up monarchy by its roots'; and the reply (originally addressed 'Gentlemen', but the word crossed out and replaced by 'Fellow Citizens'), in which no attempt had been made to disassociate themselves from this suggestion. There was evidence that the London Corresponding Society proposed to hold a convention to insist on representation in government, which in turn would have led to the destruction of the monarchy and the establishment of a republic. There was the Scottish Convention, whose character changed so radically after the delegates from London had arrived: the jury would be entitled to infer that Hardy must have known of, and given his approval to, the resolution of 28 November. There were the Globe Tavern resolutions of 20 January 1794 – 'We must have redress from our own laws, and not from the laws of our plunderers, enemies and oppressors'; 'Gentle-men', said the Solicitor-General, after quoting this passage, 'my learned friend called upon us to show clear and plain declarations. Can anything be more clear and more plain?' Furthermore, if the evidence of this and similar transactions from spies was wrong, the defence could have called, but did not call, innumerable witnesses to contradict them – not even Felix Vaughan, an officer of the Court, who had been sitting in Court throughout the trial.

By mid-day, the Solicitor-General was exhausted: 'I could wish, also', he said, 'if I had strength for the purpose, to say something to you upon the subject of Chalk Farm; but I am really unable to do it.' And so he concluded:

> You, gentlemen, are to give your verdict, according to the truth of the evidence laid before you. – If that should enable you to give a verdict of acquittal, I have no doubt that you will give it with joy. – If it should compel you to give a contrary verdict; bitter though the cup may be, you may not pass it from you. You have a solemn duty to perform; you must tax your own feelings; you must perform it. I have had a duty which I have found not only difficult to fulfil, but painful to my own feelings. I have endeavoured to discharge it faithfully. Having done so, I will now trouble you no longer.

* * *

For many days now, from early in the morning until late into the night, Sir James Eyre had presided over this unprecedented trial. He had retained a firm grasp on all that was going on; apart from giving judgment on certain matters of law, his brethren on the bench hardly uttered a word throughout the proceedings. He was trying not only a capital charge, a relatively common occurrence for an assize judge in those days, but one which went to the very roots of the constitution and the safety of the state. He had before him, in Sir John Scott and Thomas Erskine, two of the strongest personalities and two of the foremost advocates of that or any other time, but he kept them under firm control. His concentration, it seems, never for one moment relaxed; he was always ready to intervene with some shrewd question, or to take the sting out of an argument, or give a ruling on a point of law. And all the time he treated counsel and witnesses with constant courtesy, whilst showing as much concern for the welfare of the jury as was possible in the circumstances.

As far as I am aware, Sir James kept no diary, wrote no letters to his friends, but we can be fairly sure what was going on in his mind during those first few days of November. The English judiciary had not, in the past, covered itself in glory when trying cases of treason. There was the loathsome Popham CJ who had conspired with Sir Edward Coke A.G. to secure the conviction of Sir Walter Raleigh. There was the monstrous Jefferies CJ, who presided over the trial of Algernon Sidney, of whose guilt, according to Macaulay,[4] no legal evidence could be procured, and who was beheaded in defiance of law and justice; and who had secured the conviction of the unfortunate Alice Lisle, a widow of 70, for harbouring a rebel after the Monmouth rebellion. Even Holt CJ – when Lord Preston was on trial, one of the overt acts alleged against him was that he had hired a boat for treasonable purposes; he protested repeatedly that this could not be an overt act, but Holt CJ dismissed his protests out of hand and refused his application for leave to instruct counsel to argue the law. We may be sure that Eyre CJ was familiar with all these precedents and was determined to set new standards.

✳ ✳ ✳

When the Solicitor-General completed his address to the jury sometime on the Tuesday afternoon, Eyre CJ said: 'We are at the seventh day of this trial; and it comes to me now to sum up this great and momentous case'; he asked if it was expected that the whole of the written evidence should be read to the jury. The Attorney-General said that he was quite prepared to leave it to the discretion of the judge; Erskine agreed, adding, 'Mr Hardy desires me to state his confidence in the justice of the Court, and to express his acquiescence in the mode your lordship proposes'.

The judge then addressed the jury for the rest of that day. He summarised the oral evidence which had been given to the Court, and it is immediately apparent that his own notes were almost as full as the shorthand writer's. He repeated what the witnesses had said in original examination and cross-examination; interposing, from time to time, his own comments – thus on Alexander's evidence of Yorke's proposal to go to Belgium and return by Christmas at the head of the French, he observed:

> You see the substance of it is, he gives an account of a very extravagant conversation held by this Yorke, at the meeting; what you will make of it, is for you to judge.

He was quite prepared to tell the Duke of Richmond how to behave:

> To be sure it is a lesson to men of high rank and consequence in the community, how they commit [their opinions] to the press...; by which means they find their way into the hands of persons too often unequal to the task of examining and discussing such topics, and they become by that means the source of infinite mischief to the community – and if this is the general history of this plan of reform, it is, I say, a lesson that I think men of rank and property ought never to forget.

He had the 'Guillotine' paper read, which he condemned as a most infamous and scandalous paper, but left it for the jury to decide whether it was connected in any way with the defendant. When he came to deal with the evidence of the spies, he pointed out that it was the duty of the magistrates to watch over the public peace and if there was anything going on by which the public peace of the country might be affected, it was their duty to bring them to light; and although the credit of these witnesses had been attacked, they had never been contradicted, except only that there was a conflict of evidence between Groves and Green as to what the latter had said about his wife.

He concluded his review of the case for the Crown by referring to the resolution contained in the paper which had been prepared for the Chalk Farm meeting – 'that the following words are now not part of the oath of allegiance; to wit "I declare that it is not lawful, upon any pretence whatever, to take arms against the King"; ... A more dangerous and treasonable paper, one has hardly ever seen', said the judge, '[but] I have to remark, that there is no evidence which directly brings it home to the prisoner.'

Late at night, the judge spent about an hour summarising, in equal detail, the evidence for the defence, until 11.30 p.m. when he told the jury that he would be unable to conclude the case that night and would adjourn until the morning.

✻   ✻   ✻

November the fifth, 1794: for many years, 5 November had been celebrated for two special events – the failure of the attempt to blow up Parliament in 1605, and the landing of William of Orange at Torbay in 1688. Now, a new anniversary was to be created.

The Court sat for the last time at 9 a.m. that morning, and Eyre CJ resumed his summing up. He thanked and congratulated the jury for attending to the case with such patience, and then turned to deal with the law, and sad it is to relate that this judge, who had conducted the whole case so impeccably, now went astray on this vitally important issue: his direction to the jury on the law was cursory, brief, and, in the view of at least two learned writers, plainly wrong.[5] All the arguments of counsel, on both sides, were summarily dismissed in a couple of paragraphs. 'There is, I think, no possible chance of our being entangled in any difficulties in point of law', he began; the overt act charged was a conspiracy to depose the King and subvert the monarchy, and he who conspired to depose the King, compassed and imagined his death. The conspiracy to depose the King was evidence of compassing his death and was conclusive in its nature – so conclusive that it became a presumption of law, which admitted of no contradiction. In other words, the overt act became, in effect, the treason and that was the end of the matter. This was contrary to Pemberton CJ's direction to the jury in the case of Lord Russell, it was contrary to the arguments advanced, so cogently and at such length, by Erskine; and indeed to the arguments of the Law Officers of the Crown. Eyre CJ should have directed the jury, first to decide if the prisoner had committed any of the overt acts alleged against him, and, if so, if they were satisfied that an intention that the King should die could be attributed to him. On the other hand, Eyre CJ's direction on the standard of proof was unexceptionable: 'The proof ought to be clear and convincing;...it may consist of a train of circumstances such as shall leave no doubt in your minds.'

Then the judge commenced a review of the whole case, and demonstrated that he had a total grasp of all that had been going on in the Old Bailey for the preceding week:

> Gentlemen, I have employed a part of that time since the Court broke up, which it was necessary enough for me to have devoted to sleep, in endeavouring to take such a review of the evidence in this cause, as might enable me to lay the questions of fact ... before you, that you might see where the matter hinged.... I do not know whether I shall succeed, or not, but I do hope I shall be able to point out to you the

leading features of this case, in a way that may be of some use to you in forming your judgment.

He said that it should be conceded on behalf of the prisoner, that he had set out originally upon the Duke of Richmond's plan for reforming Parliament. The question before the Court was whether the prisoner had changed his original plan and embarked on a criminal pursuit of another object; and among the great mass of evidence, there were some passages which were evidence of such a change of plan; but he added:

> I would observe, once for all, that in a case of this nature, much stress ought not to be laid on particular expressions. God forbid that men's lives should depend on nice interpretations and constructions of words ...; but sometimes expressions are too strong, sometimes transactions too explicit, to admit of any doubt as to their real interpretation and meaning.

There were the addresses to France, which went out of their way to express their zeal in the cause of Republicanism. And there were the replies from France, expressing hopes that felicitations might soon be extended to a National Assembly here. And it was significant that, so far from disassociating themselves from these matters, the Societies, of which the prisoner was a member of both and the secretary of one, had disseminated the republican views of Paine and Barlow, at great expense, all over the country. On the other hand, there was no evidence that Barrère's speech, coming to England in the *Moniteur*, had ever been translated into English, so that it was extremely probable that Hardy had no knowledge of Barrère's views.

Then there was the correspondence with Scotland. There was the strange letter from Skirving with the reference to erecting 'at once a tabernacle of righteousness, and may the lord himself be in it'. 'What', asked the judge, 'does this mysterious man mean? What is the tabernacle of righteousness to be erected without anarchy or delay?' Were the prosecution right in believing that Skirving was referring to an imminent revolution? It was Hardy's Society which appointed Margarot and Gerrald to act as delegates at the Convention; the Convention adopted the forms and usages of the National Convention of France; it assumed the date of the First Year of the British Convention; and after it had been dispersed Hardy embarked on a new scheme, a plan for a British Convention to be held in England which was the central issue of the present inquiry. It was for the jury to judge whether its object was the peaceable object which was insisted on for the prisoner; whether a reform of the House of Commons was really the bottom of the whole; or whether its object must have been to alter the constitution of our government, to obtain full representation of the people, but not in the House of Commons.

One would have supposed, Eyre CJ went on, that if their intention had been as they professed, they would have taken care to guard their language, instead, they published the Globe Tavern address; it was for the jury to decide whether that paper was to be understood as a manifesto to excite the people to overturn the government.

Then came the Chalk Farm meeting, where resolutions were passed which seemed calculated to prepare the minds of the people for a violent crisis, upon which a National Convention once assembled would immediately act. The resolutions were read once more, and Eyre CJ went on:

> Gentlemen, one cannot hear this paper read, without feeling astonishment that men could be so blinded by enthusiasm ... as not to see that ... the sword of the law was hanging over their heads by a single thread .... According to these resolutions, it was a probable case 'that they would soon be in a state where the great social compact would be actually dissolved, and that it would be necessary to appeal to that principle, that incontrovertible maxim of eternal justice, that the safety of the people was the supreme, and in cases of necessity, the only law', which admits but of one interpretation. If the social compact is dissolved, there is an end of the government ...; another government must be framed; this is therefore expressly encouraging the people to look out for the moment to arrive when another government was to be framed, to be created on the ruins of the present establishment.

On the other hand, although there was a rumour that some individuals had planned a personal attack upon the King, that was not brought home to the prisoner; and although there was some evidence that the Convention was to be protected by force of arms, 'I should have thought', said the judge, 'no great reliance was to be had upon it'.

Eyre CJ spoke for more than three hours that day. As he drew to a close, he urged the jury to consider everything that could be said on the part of the prisoner; but when all had been said about his peaceable and orderly character and the simplicity of his manners, the fact remained that he was the secretary of one of these societies and an active member of both and

> Though men declare upon their oaths that they are peaceable and orderly... yet, if they are found to be engaged in measures which imply directly the contrary, it does go very strongly to the credit of their testimony; for in that case, their testimony is 'Protestatio contra factum'.

And he concluded:

> Gentlemen, upon the whole of this ... evidence before you, you have now to exercise your judgments.... Every verdict ought to be the jury's own and ought to proceed on clear grounds of fact – It ought to do so in a case of this nature more particularly, if possible, because one great object of this prosecution must be that the country may be satisfied, that they may see the public justice of it has taken its fair course, and that you, the jury, have well and truly tried and true deliverance made between the king and the prisoner at the bar, according to the law of the land and the oath which you have taken.

Finally, the judge turned to the public:

> I am very sorry to have occasion to remark, that during the course of this trial the dignity of a court of justice has but too often been violated by improper behaviour both within and without doors; what it is men can mean by such conduct who do not wish at once to dissolve all government and the bonds of all society, I cannot imagine. – I trust I shall hear no more of this. You may now withdraw, gentlemen, and consider your verdict.

A member of the jury asked if they could take a copy of the indictment with them, and this was granted; and the judge remembered something else: 'Gentlemen, I must apprize you, that after you have withdrawn there can be no refreshment given to you. – Do you wish to take any moderate refreshment before you withdraw?' 'My lord, we thank you', replied a juror, 'we shall not have occasion for any.' They retired at 12.30 p.m.

*   *   *

The next three hours is a blank page in our history: we do not even know whether Hardy stayed in the dock in the court-room or was taken down to the cells; we can be sure, however, that he was accompanied by a turnkey – probably by Keeper Kirby himself.

Outside, in London and the country, children were building bonfires as they always did on 5 November; there was always a massive fire in Lincoln's Inn Fields (200 cartloads of fuel were sometimes assembled there, it has been said) and the butchers had another in Clare Market.[6] In the streets around the Old Bailey a great crowd was gathered; at the request of the Lord Mayor, troops were being deployed in the neighbourhood to protect the judges and the jurors should the need arise.[7]

Inside the building, in the parlour, counsel were waiting, as counsel have always waited, and as counsel will always wait, as long as criminals commit crimes and there are juries to try them – waiting and passing the time with tales of other trials, at Appleby and Durham, Lewes and Guildford. Capital offences were common in those days, and young barristers learnt their trade on 'the rope-walk', defending highwaymen and pickpockets on two-guinea dock-briefs. But this case was different. The name of Thomas Hardy was already linked with some of the most famous in our history: the Earl of Essex, Sir Christopher Blount, Sir Walter Raleigh; the Monmouth rebels and the Jacobites; or, as he himself put it, Hampden, Russell and Sidney.

Counsel had done their best, but the omens were not good. Only a few months before, Gibbs had been back home to defend the Revd William Winterbotham, a dissenting minister who had preached a sermon in Plymouth two years previously to the very day. Winterbotham was tried for seditious libel at Exeter assizes, and, according to Sjt Rooke for the Crown, he had said that he approved of the French Revolution and that a similar revolution was needed in England, and that he had attacked the constitution, the government and the King, although witnesses for the defence denied that he had ever spoken as alleged. The case was tried before Perryn B.; it was he who had taken a firm line to secure the conviction of the rioters who had destroyed Dr Priestley's house, and he now took a firm line on behalf of Dr Winterbotham and virtually directed the jury to acquit – but they ignored what he said and found the defendant Guilty. The following day Winterbotham was tried for another sermon, and again there was a conflict of evidence as to what he had said. Yet again Perryn B. advised an acquittal; but again he was convicted, so he was fined £200 and sent to prison for four years. And now the Crown were planning more arrests – 800 it was said, and 300 warrants were already made out and signed, ready to be executed.

At 3.35 p.m. the jury returned. Sir John Scott said that he would never forget the scene. Hardy was set to the bar for the last time. Mr Shelton, the Clerk of the Arraigns, who had spent so much time reading out the documents during the past week, called the names of the jurors, and then said:

> 'Thomas Hardy, hold up your hand – Gentlemen of the jury, look upon the prisoner – How say you, is Thomas Hardy guilty of the high treason whereof he stands indicted, or not guilty?'
> 'Not Guilty.' said the foreman.
> 'Did he fly for it?'[8]
> 'Not that we know of.'

Then Hardy himself spoke: 'My fellow countrymen I return you my thanks.' He was immediately discharged, and Eyre CJ closed the proceedings:

> Gentlemen of the jury; I ought to take the first opportunity, after this laborious attendance, very sincerely to thank you for the readiness with which you have sacrificed so much of your personal convenience, and with which you have undergone the fatigue of this trial.

In Hardy's own words, recorded in his Memoirs,

> Hardy was pronounced Not Guilty, by the unanimous voice of as a respectable jury as was ever empanelled. A jury which, with unremitting patience, underwent a fatigue and confinement unparalleled in the annals of our courts of justice. A jury, on whose awful voice depended the liberties of eleven million of their fellow citizens. A jury, whose integrity established on a firm basis the first and most important pillar of the English constitution – The Trial by Jury, which had been greatly on the decline, and much tampered with, for some time before, and thereby entitled themselves to the grateful acknowledgements and applause, both of the present and future generations.

As soon as the foreman of the jury pronounced the words Not Guilty, the Old Bailey was rent with loud shouts of applause. The vast crowd which was waiting anxiously outside heard the joyful sound, and

> like an electric shock, or the rapidity of lightning, the glad tidings spread through the whole town, and were conveyed much quicker than the regular post could travel, to the most distant parts of the island, where all ranks of people were anxiously awaiting the result of the trial.

When the cheering had died down in the Court, Mr Keeper Kirby advised Hardy to go through the prison to the debtor's door, where a coach was ready to take him to his sister and brother-in-law, the Walnes, who were living in Lancaster Court, in the Strand, for he had no house of his own to go to, and no family to welcome him home. He went to the coach as privately as possible and drove down Snow Hill, but he was seen and the crowd diverted the coach and drove it along Fleet Market; when they came to the end of Fleet Street, the crowd was very great, although it was 'a bleak rainy afternoon in the gloomy month of November'. Here they stopped the coach and took out the horses, and drew it along Fleet Street, the Strand, Pall Mall, St James's Street, Piccadilly, the Haymarket, and back to Lancaster Court. During the procession, the people frequently stopped and shouted at particular places, such as Charing Cross, Carlton House, and St James's Palace; at No. 9 Piccadilly, they stopped a few minutes in solemn silence. Hardy alighted at Lancaster Court, and addressed the crowd from a window in a short speech, after which they gave three cheers and quietly dispersed, leaving him to enjoy the evening with the Walnes, the Revds Dr Bogue and James Steven and a few special friends.

According to an obituary notice published in *The Times* of 17 October 1832[9] (although Hardy does not mention this himself in his Memoirs), the first use he made of his liberty was to go to St Martin's Churchyard where his wife and still-born child were buried together; on approaching the grave, he immediately fell and embraced the cold earth, and was lost in an agony of grief; it was with difficulty that he could be removed, and such was the effect upon him that for a considerable time there were fears for his own life.

Within a week of the end of the trial, Hardy wrote an Address which was published in the newspapers – 'With a heart overflowing with gratitude, I now sit down to the most pleasing task which I have experienced in the course of my life', it began. He thanked Mr Erskine and Mr Gibbs:

> Any words in my power to use, would fall far short of expressing what they TRULY DESERVE and what I REALLY FEEL they deserve; [but] ... every defect in my powers of expression to do them justice, is abundantly compensated by the force and eloquence of their own respective exertions, and their transcendent talents and integrity cannot fail to stand recorded, not only on the minds of the present race, but will receive additional lustre in every progressive movement their names shall make through the progress of time.

After thanking the public and his jury, he concluded by saying that it was his intention to go back into business as soon as he could find a suitable situation for a shop.

CHAPTER 15

THE TRIAL OF JOHN HORNE TOOKE: THE CASE FOR THE CROWN

John Horne Tooke was set to the bar of the Old Bailey at 8 a.m. on Monday 17 November. The Special Commission was again presided over by Eyre CJ, but Lawrence J. replaced Buller J. The Hon. Spencer Perceval had been added as junior counsel to the team of prosecutors; Erskine and Gibbs represented the prisoner, who had also briefed Dampier, Vaughan and Gurney, instructed by Messrs George and Romaine, William Clarkson, solicitors, of Essex Street.

While in custody awaiting trial, Horne Tooke had composed a speech which he had intended to deliver at the opening of the proceedings. It began with an attack on the presiding judge and on the government; he accused Eyre CJ, 'who have before your view the pension and peerage of your predecessor in office',[1] of having given a charge on 'a new and doubtful case' to a 'panel of jurors carefully picked out and selected' by the sheriff. Everything that had happened to him proved the necessity for a speedy reform in the representation of the people in Parliament, for until that took place

> there never shall be wanting *legal* butchers, with their proper instruments in their hands – *new* and *doubtful* cases – ready to explore and rake out pensions and peerages for themselves from the mangled entrails of their dying fellow-creatures...

This speech was never delivered. Following Hardy's acquittal, Horne Tooke decided to adopt a more conciliatory attitude; immediately he had been placed in the dock, he opened the proceedings as follows:

> My lord, I desire, as necessary for the purpose of my defence, that I may quit the situation in which I at present stand, and be placed near to those counsel which the Court have assigned to me for my assistance in my defence.

'That is an indulgence', said Eyre CJ, 'which I have hardly ever known given to any person in your position.' Horne Tooke replied:

> I am perfectly aware that it is unusual, but I beg your lordship to observe, that everything in the course of these proceedings is likewise unusual. I beg your lordship to consider, that the proceedings upon the last trial will fill, as I am well-informed by the short-hand writer, sixteen hundred close printed octavo pages. That trial lasted nine days, eight days trial, and one day between. The nature of the

indictment is such, that it has been impossible for me to instruct my counsel; they cannot know the passages of my life; and, from what I have seen of the last trial, the whole passage of my life, and those which are not passages of my life, but are only imputed to me, will be brought before you: how is it possible for my counsel to know those particular facts which are known only to myself? If there ever was a case where indulgence was fit to be granted it is this; yet your lordship will forgive me for saying, that I claim this as my right of law and do not ask it as an indulgence.

Horne Tooke asserted that the word *indulgence* was one which his lordship should never use, and that he was quite prepared to argue his rights with the Law Officers; then he continued:

My lord, it is not for a small stake that I stand here – it is to deprive me of my life, to beggar my family, to make my name and memory infamous to all posterity; so deep a stake as may very well overset my understanding; it is very well known that the best gamesters, when the stake is too deep for them, play the worst; I hope that will not be my case; and I hope and trust, if your lordship permits me to sit by my counsel, that I shall prevent a great waste of time to the jury, your lordship, and myself; for, I am certain, I shall make it impossible for the prosecutor to make any case against me that shall call upon me for my defence. I come here from a very close custody of a whole summer, and a whole autumn; I have not, any more than your lordship, many summers or many autumns to spare; that custody has been attended with many degrading and many humiliating circumstances, and some inhuman circumstances, at my age, and with my infirmities; it has, in some measure, impaired the health and strength of my body; I come to you but half a man; your lordship will expect a whole defence, and I do not doubt but that I shall give you a whole defence, provided you furnish me with the necessary means of doing it.

Further discussion took place between Horne Tooke and the judge, and it began to look as if they had reached a deadlock; the defendant was clearly refusing to accept as a favour that which he claimed to be his by right, whilst Eyre CJ thought that if it came to making a ruling on the law, he would be bound to turn the application down; however, he managed to find a compromise and suggested that he would grant Horne Tooke's request, not as an indulgence ('You have taught the Court not to use the word *indulgence*'), but on the ground of his ill-health. After further discussion, this proved acceptable to all concerned, and the defendant was allowed to take his place with counsel in the inner bar.

*   *   *

At that time, the dock at the Old Bailey was surmounted by a structure like a door frame with a mirror at the top, so that everyone could watch the prisoner's slightest movement; there the prisoner stood – defendants were not normally allowed to sit down – many yards from his advocate, with the back of the witness towards him, and with only an indirect view of the jury.[2] By securing himself a seat at counsel's table, Horne Tooke had won a significant first round in the contest. He had, moreover, and more importantly, established himself from the outset as the dominating personality in the proceedings: it was he who took the leading part in the cross-examination of witnesses called by the Crown, and in the examination of witnesses, including the Prime Minister, called in his defence; he raised and argued many points of law, usually introducing long and verbose speeches with the observation that he was trying to save the time of the Court – one can almost hear Eyre CJ sighing between the lines of the transcript, but he always listened courteously and patiently. At times, he even seemed to be taking over the conduct of the case for the Crown: many were the occasions when the prosecution found themselves in difficulty in proving the prisoner's handwriting, and he intervened to admit it. He was evidently beginning to enjoy himself, and was always ready to inject some frivolous and irrelevant anecdote into the proceedings.

Now that the preliminary issue had been satisfactorily resolved, the next stage was to empanel the jury. The sheriffs had summoned the same jurors, many of whom were challenged by the Crown or the defence. Thomas Rhodes, a cowkeeper, asked to be discharged because he suffered from a pain in the head whenever he was in a confined space, and swore on oath that he had such a headache that he would be incapable of recollecting anything: he was discharged. John Leader, gentleman, said he had a violent cold; he was excused for the present, but told not to go away. Adam Steinmetz applied to be discharged: 'My lord, I had the pleasure of attending here the last jury, I found myself very ill. I am not capable of continuing, I am sure, on this trial'; to which the Court replied, 'I am sorry you ask to be excused, because I do not wonder that duty was so heavy as to affect the health of any gentleman; it is impossible that you should be pressed, if you decline; the Court will excuse you undoubtedly, if you ask it.' Thomas Sayer said that he had served on the previous jury and had been ill ever since; he, and all the others who had served, were excused. James Keen told the Court: 'I am one of the collectors of the king's taxes, and it is just the time for finishing up the books, and I do not know what the consequences may be if I should be obliged to serve.'

> 'The only consequence will be that you may finish them afterwards', said Eyre CJ.
> Erskine said: 'I do not wish to disappoint the revenue; I challenge him.'

By the time the Clerk of Arraigns had gone through the entire list, only nine jurors had been sworn in. He then called over the defaulters – those who had failed to answer on the first occasion – and Henry Purrier appeared, but stated bluntly: 'My health will not permit me to serve on this jury'. A lengthy argument then ensued as to the rights of the defence to challenge jurors in general and this juror in particular – they had already exhausted their right to challenge 35 jurors. Purrier intervened to say that he had laboured under a complaint for some time, and could not have stayed in Court at the time of Hardy's trial for five minutes, otherwise he would have been carried out with a suspension of his faculties; he repeated on oath that he would be incapable of going through the fatigue of the trial, and he was discharged.

Horne Tooke then embarked on a lengthy argument. He contended that the Crown had no right to challenge jurors at all without showing cause;[3]

coupled with this argument was the risk that those jurors who had been excused on the ground of ill-health might, nevertheless, be compelled to serve, and might be incapable of properly fulfilling their functions:

> My lords, I have been in this case, and I dare swear that your lordships have, and the jury too – that when I have intended to travel a long accustomed road to my own house, some sudden distraction of the thought had made me inattentive to the passage; when I have come to myself, and my attention has returned, I have observed that there were not those objects, the house, the gate, the style or the gap I have been accustomed to see, and instantly I have recollected that I must be out of my road; then I have stopped and gone back, because the accustomed succession of objects did not occur. The same things happen upon these proceedings; see where we are; nine days upon a trial – the jury pass and return day after day without clean shirts, unshaved – the judges quitting the Court, and returning again and again – a question put upon what shall be done, in this strange and unknown case, for the jury – no question put what shall be done for the judge. An English jury, fairly and impartially taken, I have always believed to be incorruptible, and as little likely to be tampered with, as any judge whatever; the judge is compelled to stay as well as the jury; if the jury go unshaved and unshirted, so must the judge; it is true, that when the jury retire from the Court somebody goes with them as keeper; the judge is likewise upon the bench, and the eyes of every person in Court are his keepers.

He went on until Eyre CJ intervened: 'I do not see to what this address goes.' Horne Tooke endeavoured to explain: if the Crown were permitted to challenge anyone they wished without showing cause, a situation would arise where the panel would be exhausted, and in default the ill and infirm would be called upon to serve. Eyre CJ again interrupted and said he could see no cause for complaint in the way in which the Crown had acted. Eventually, the Attorney-General stood up to say that, whilst he had acted properly, he waived his objections to all the persons he had challenged. Thus Horne Tooke had now notched up two tactical victories before the trial had even started.

The panel of jurors eventually sworn in were:

> James Haygarth, esquire and builder, from Southampton Place.
> Thomas Harrison, cowkeeper, from Gray's Inn Lane.
> Edward Hale, gentleman, from Highgate.
> Thomas Draine, brewer, from Limehouse.
> Matthew Whiting, sugar refiner, from Shadwell.
> Norrison Coverdale, rope-maker, from Limehouse.
> Robert Mairis, gentleman, from Great Turnstile, Holborn.
> William Cooke, gentleman, from New Ormond Street.
> Charles Pratt, miller, from Tottenham.
> Matthias Dupont, gentleman, from Chace-side, Enfield.
> William Harwood, esquire, from Hanwell.
> Henry Bullock, brewer, from Colnbrook.

The case for the prosecution was opened by the Solicitor-General. Compared with the Attorney-General's speech in the previous case, his was relatively short; it lasted about three hours. His version of the charge against Horne Tooke was that the Society for Constitutional Information and the London Corresponding Society were embarking upon a scheme similar to that which had been successfully accomplished by the Jacobin Clubs in France. He stressed that the Societies had given their support to the revolution of 10 August 1792, and had congratulated the French in outspoken terms.

When the Solicitor-General was dealing with the relationship between the Society for Constitutional Information and the Scottish Convention, Horne Tooke interrupted him to ask if he pledged to prove all that he stated, and Eyre CJ said: 'Failing in the proof takes off, certainly, as far as that goes, the whole of it.' The Solicitor-General said that he was referring to a resolution of the Society for Constitutional Information, and was merely making an observation upon it.

> 'I understand the Solicitor-General to state that these resolutions were drawn up under the prisoner's directions....' said the prisoner. The Solicitor-General replied: 'At the meeting where these resolutions were come to, Mr Tooke appears by the books to have been *in the chair;* whether he actually drew up the resolutions is another matter, but *he was in the chair.* I meant merely to say, that Mr Tooke is a man who understands (unquestionably infinitely better than I can profess to do) the critical meaning of words, and their application in the clearest and plainest sense.'

Horne Tooke's professional reputation was employed against him later in the same speech. After referring to the plan to hold a National Convention, the Solicitor-General said that it was impossible that a man of his abilities and character should represent himself as a man deceived or deluded. He might say that he had no conception of obtaining reform by any other means than the lawfully constituted legislature, but men frequently professed that which they did not mean. Several of the members of that National Convention of France spoke with the greatest reverence for monarchy, until the time came when they thought they could overturn it.

> And we have a memorable instance that the greatest of traitors may profess attachment in the moment of the deepest treason. We know that the vilest traitor professed his loyalty whilst he was contemplating an act of the meanest treachery, and in the completion of that act cried, 'Hail Master!' and kissed him. But does it follow that because a man holds the language of loyalty, that he is therefore loyal? It certainly does not follow.

The Solicitor-General made it plain that he was in deadly earnest to secure a conviction, but not many minutes elapsed after he had concluded his speech before the prisoner had injected a different atmosphere into the proceedings.

The prosecution called Thomas Maclean to prove the seizure of Daniel Adam's papers, followed by William Woodfall, the printer, to prove the prisoner's handwriting; he could say no more than he thought he could recognise it. Horne Tooke rose to cross-examine:

> 'Are you sure you have seen me write?'
> 'Yes.'
> 'How long ago?'

'Some years ago; I believe full seventeen; the period is a memorable one; I allude to the circumstance of an advertisement for a subscription for the widows, orphans, and aged parents of the Americans who lost their lives at the battle of Lexington.'

'That was in 1775, nineteen years ago?'

'You are perfectly right; it was nineteen years ago.'

'I know the time for I was prosecuted for it.'

The witness then described how the prisoner's handwriting had been proved in the earlier case, and Horne Tooke said: 'The handwriting may be fairly admitted. I think I could give the prosecutor a great deal more than he has charged me with....If the gentlemen will be so good as to show me anything which I wrote, I will save them the time and trouble of calling witnesses to prove it – I will admit it.'

Eyre CJ intervened to say that he did not think that the prisoner should be called upon to acknowledge whether or not a paper was in his handwriting.

'I offer it freely and willingly,' said the prisoner.

'I see you do, but I should not feel very comfortable if it happened that you admitted, without proof, some paper of which more was made afterwards than you at the time were aware of, or thought there could be.'

'I protest, before God', said Horne Tooke, 'that I have never done an action, never written a sentence, never uttered a syllable in public or private, I have never entertained a thought of any important political nature which ... I have the smallest hesitation now to admit. I choose my life and character should go together. I wish to admit all I have ever said, done, or written, to save time.'

'I should prefer that the evidence should take its course in the ordinary way', ruled the judge.

Hardly had this point been disposed of, when Horne Tooke was taking another of an entirely different nature. The prosecution read an entry from a minute book in which the defendant's name appeared.

'Is the insertion of my name in that book evidence of my being present at the time?'

'It is certainly evidence to go to the jury of your being present', said the judge.

'My name being found in any book! that will be the most extraordinary evidence I have ever heard of; the bulk of the trash that is to be found in that book I never saw or heard of before; but that every time my name is to be found in the book, that that is to be evidence that I was present is a most extraordinary proposition...; if the secretary were here he would prove that names of persons were entered in that book who were there only at the beginning, or perhaps not at all; or if they were there, heard something or nothing that passed.... A society is nobody; the first six letters of the alphabet meet tonight, and vote black – another six meet tomorrow night, and vote white...'

Eyre CJ said that the prosecution would have to show that he gave credit to the entries by some conduct of his own. Horne Tooke then embarked on a long argument about how he had better things to do than read minute books going back over a period of thirty years, and said,

> 'I hope I am forgiven for saying so much about it.'
> 'A person in your situation is heard with attention', replied Eyre CJ, 'whether it makes directly to the point or not.... It is difficult to say what is or not evidence in itself, because it all depends upon the chain and connexion it has – if there are two or three links in the chain, they must go to one first and then to another, and see whether they amount to evidence.'
> 'I beg your pardon, my lord, but is not a chain composed of links? and may I not disjoin each link, and do not I then destroy the chain?'
> 'I rather think not, till the links be put together and form the chain.'

Erskine had been sitting silent during this discussion, but he now intervened; it was a lengthy speech, and hardly calculated to clear the air, but the gist of it was that it would be wrong to allow evidence to go before the jury, and possibly prejudice them, if it was later proved to be irrelevant and inadmissible.

Eyre CJ's ruling was not one of his best:

> We are entangled in a little puzzle about this species of evidence. If the question is, Whether it is now to be read? I think the objection is good. If the question is whether it is evidence admissible not yet to be read, but to be read, or not, as other evidence shall bring the matter of it sufficiently home to the prisoner? Then the objection is ill-founded...

Bower intervened:

> 'The parts wrote by Mr Tooke himself must be evidence.'
> 'Certainly', said the judge, 'but I do not apprehend that goes to this entry.'
> 'Mr Horne Tooke said he was a member of the Constitutional Society', said Garrow, to which the defendant responded:
> 'Mr Garrow must not slide in upon us any thing that has not yet been decided.'

Garrow regarded this observation as an affront to his professional reputation and rose to justify himself, and at the same time to defend himself from the misrepresentations as to his conduct of the case which, he said, were appearing day by day in the press; he had met Horne Tooke on previous occasions; he had no personal animosity against him, and was only doing his duty.

Horne Tooke apologised to Garrow, but took the opportunity to say that, all the time he had been in custody, he had been the subject of calumnies in the papers, paid for by the ministry, who had charged him with guilt and facts which were absolutely false. In conclusion, he said: 'There is abuse even printed on earthenware[4] as well as sermons, books, songs, and newspapers, full (sic), at which I might be angry as well as that gentleman – I am sure I meant him no wrong; he never did me any; nor did I mean him any disgrace; and if it will do any good to his character, let it be said in the papers tomorrow, that I humbly beg his pardon.' 'Mr Tooke has carried his apology much farther than I wished', said Garrow.

'I have permitted this explanation to go to its full length', said Eyre CJ, 'I hope, on all sides, there may be no occasion for any discussion of this sort again; it is very unpleasant. If everybody were to state their complaints of the calumny of newspapers, we might put an end to this trial, and listen to nothing else.'

The case then proceeded along more regular lines. The prosecution called Daniel Adams, for ten years the secretary of the Society for Constitutional Information, to produce its books. He was cross-examined by Horne Tooke with a view to establishing that the Society had never been involved in anything more harmful than parliamentary reform, and that in any event he attended the dinner at 4 p.m. and went home early in the evening: 'Do you know', he asked the witness, 'his gardener goes to bed at 9 o'clock, and gets up to work in the morning at 4 o'clock? Do you know Mr Tooke desired to get home very early? and frequently went away when the society met?'

It was during this cross-examination that the two men had a conversation about the finances of the Society for Constitutional Information:

'Was the Society very rich?' asked Horne Tooke.
'Never.'
'What sum of money do you think all the subscriptions together might amount to in a year?'
'About £60.'
'How much of that went for the regular expenses of the Society, the secretary, the room, paper, pens, ink, messengers and so forth?'
'At that time about £50.'
'Then there were about £10 a year left to overturn the government with.... I ask this question only to show the riches of the Society; how capable they were to overturn the great weight of government.'

At the conclusion of this conversation, Horne Tooke said to the bench: 'My lords, I am ashamed to have taken up so much time in this examination, but I thought it might rather shorten than delay.' It was not the end for Adams: he was now re-examined by the Attorney-General about a particular meeting.

'Who appears to have been in the chair that night?'
'It appears that Mr Tooke was in the chair', said the witness.
'Do you mean to say that I was in the chair when these resolutions passed?' asked Horne Tooke.
'No; I do not mean to say that.'
'That is breaking in upon my examination', said the Attorney-General.
'It was wrong; I ought not to have done it.'

The Crown called Thomas Chapman who was a friend of Thomas Paine, and had printed and published *The Rights of Man*. He was cross-examined by

Horne Tooke, who induced him to admit that there were certain passages in The Bible which were indecent:

> 'But you would not choose to read that part to your wife and daughter?'
> 'No, I should not appropriate those parts particularly.'
> 'You have been called to prove Mr Paine's books, and out of a great deal, small portions of it have been read; and so you might read certain parts of the bible –'
> Eyre CJ intervened: 'That is not a proper subject to examine the witness to, it is observation on the evidence...'
> '...If I have done wrong, I beg your lordship's pardon.'
> 'I only wished to set you right, without speaking with any asperity.'
> 'I have been but forty years a student;' said Horne Tooke, 'when I shall come to be called to the bar I hope I shall know better.'

John Thompson and James Thornton, two king's messengers and clerks to the public office at Whitechapel and Marlborough Street, were called to produce papers found in the defendant's home at Wimbledon (see Figure 14), including a copy of the Address in honour of the French Revolution. Horne Tooke asked:

> 'I do not know what papers may have been taken from my house; but are letters written to me to be produced as evidence against me?'
> Eyre CJ replied: 'All papers found in the possession of a man are, *prima facie*, evidence against him, if the contents of them have application to the subject under consideration.'

Figure 14. Horne Tooke's residence. Chester House, Wimbledon, drawn by William Porden in 1810. (By permission of the Wimbledon Society.)

'The reason for my asking it is, I am very much afraid that, besides treason, I may be charged with blasphemy.'

'You are not tried for that.'

'It is notorious that I do not answer common letters of civility, but I have received and kept many curious letters. I have received some letters from a man whose name is *Oliver Verall*, and he endeavoured to prove to me that he was God the Father, Son, and Holy Ghost. (I kept the letters out of curiosity, and it is probable they may be produced against me.) He proved it from the Old Testament; in the first place he was God the Father, because God is *O Veral*; that is, God over all. He proved he was God the Son, from the New Testament – verily, verily, I am he; that is *Veral I, Veral I,* I am he.[5] Now, if these letters, written to me, which I, from curiosity have preserved, but upon which I have taken no step, and to which I have given no answer, are produced against me, I do not know what may become of me.'

'If you can treat all the letters that have been found upon you with as much success as you have these letters of your correspondent', said the judge, 'you will have no great reason for apprehension, even if that letter should be brought against you.'

It was late on the Monday evening by now. There was a rambling discussion as to the admissibility of a letter which had been found in the possession of Adams; and then Eyre CJ interrupted: 'We are now come to a time of night, and the case is in such a stage, as I think makes it absolutely necessary for the Court now to come to some resolution as to its further proceedings'. He said that he had carefully considered the subject of adjournment, and went on:

What if any of the jury should be so totally disabled, in consequence of the fatigue and want of necessary refreshment, that they cannot proceed, that they might even die before they could pronounce their verdict! We have had an intimation that two hundred hours were spent in the discussion of the last case of this sort; I know what it was to sustain the fatigue of eight days' attendance, with the small intervals of rest that we had. My own case is a small consideration, because my individual loss would have been exceedingly well supplied by my lord and my brothers; but what if, instead of my being destroyed, it had happened that one of the jury had been! the consequence would have been, the prisoner must have had all this trial to undergo again, after all the evidence had been closed; and after all those evils would necessarily have arisen, which it was the object of refusing an adjournment to guard against.

So he came to the conclusion that it was for the Court to take the responsibility, without asking for the consent of either party, to direct an adjournment.

Then the defendant joined in:

'In order to meet your lordship here today at 8 o'clock, I was compelled to get up between three and four; and that will be my case every day. I labour under a very painful infirmity,[6] and I must be up four or five hours before I can come here.'

'What can we do for you?' asked Eyre CJ.
'If I go from hence, and have to attend very early, I shall have no time for sleep.'
'What I proposed was to meet at nine in the morning', suggested the judge, 'and to sit till nine at night punctually, with an interval of one quarter of an hour only to take refreshment.'[7]
'I will do the utmost in my power'.
'We shall not press you, Mr Tooke, if your infirmities shall require our waiting a little for you.'
'I will endeavour not to suffer your lordships to wait'.

It was now 10.30.p.m., and the Court adjourned until 9 o'clock the following morning.

÷   ÷   ÷

The Court sat at 9 a.m. on Tuesday 18 November. Thomas Maclean was in the witness box most of the day: he produced voluminous minutes, documents, resolutions, letters, proclamations, extracts from books, and communications with Scotland. Over and over again the question arose as to whether notes or signatures were in Horne Tooke's handwriting, and over and over again he interposed to admit that they were. At one point an account book was produced, and Eyre CJ asked what it was; Gibbs said that it was Adams's private account book, and Horne Tooke interrupted to say, 'I beg pardon, we confess the payment of our debts', and Erskine, in one of his very few contributions that day, added, 'Mr Tooke admits they paid their debts; I wish everybody could admit as much.'
    At one stage of the proceedings John Thompson was recalled to prove that a particular letter had been found in Horne Tooke's house, and this led to a further detailed cross-examination by the defendant in which the witness admitted that he had had no warrant to seize papers and could not tell how many had been taken – 'There were more papers in my house than a man could read in a year', the defendant interjected. On another occasion there was an altercation between the defendant and the Attorney-General as to how the latter proposed to prove a particular piece of evidence, which concluded with Horne Tooke saying, 'I hope I have not hinted or insinuated the smallest idea, when I think you have mis-stated anything, but that it is the effect of error, and nothing else'; to which the Attorney-General replied, 'I am always obliged to you when you correct me'.
    The day's hearing concluded with the reading of Margarot's letter from Spithead to Norwich, and the Court rose at 9 p.m.
    It was the twenty-second anniversary of the Attorney-General's elopement; Bessy was now pregnant again.

÷   ÷   ÷

Maclean was in the witness box again on the following morning: more letters were read, more entries from the books of the Society for Constitutional Information. That was the day when Alexander Grant was called to identify Hardy's handwriting; as in the previous case, he was reluctant to do so, and declined to swear that it was his, upon which Horne Tooke commented: 'It will be very difficult for him to abide by his opinion; for he has said both ways; that he did believe it to be similar, and that he did not; but we do not object; I have no objection to Mr Attorney-General's discrediting his own evidence, but I have no objection to admit this as evidence, and to the papers being put in.' But Eyre CJ said: 'I cannot do that; I must see that what is admitted is evidence to which no objection occurs to me.'

A few minutes later, the prosecution produced a rough draft of a series of resolutions which contained interlineations in what was thought to be Horne Tooke's writing; the defendant asked leave to explain what this paper was about.

'I should be very sorry to interrupt –' said the Attorney-General.
'This is observation upon the evidence', said the judge.
'Your lordship will see it is not observation –' said the defendant.
'It gives me great pain to interpose', added the Attorney-General, 'but that cannot be permitted to come from a gentleman because he takes an active part in his own cause, which should shut the mouth of counsel.'

Gibbs, for the first time showing some signs of the exasperation which he and Erskine must have felt for their client, said, 'As to the gentleman himself taking a part in this cause, it is utterly impossible for any counsel to possess himself of this cause.'

After an exchange of courtesies between the Attorney-General and Gibbs, Horne Tooke continued, unabashed, to explain that there were two methods of erasing words from a draft, one by striking your pen through the word you mean to erase, the other by encircling it with a line. A discussion then ensued between the defendant, the presiding judge, and the Attorney-General as to the propriety of commenting on words which were crossed out or encircled; the defendant maintained that he merely did it to save time, Eyre CJ objecting to the observation but commenting that it was fair and probably well-founded, and the Attorney-General adding that he would have his own comments to make at a later time.

This was virtually the end of the evidence called by the Crown; there were a couple of witnesses from Sheffield, but the prosecution made no serious attempt to resurrect the allegations that an armed insurrection had been planned.

And then, almost at the very end, the Crown called William Sharp. Why he was called, it is hard to know; he had for a time been under arrest, although in the end no charge was brought against him; he was a long-standing friend of the defendant; he had no significant evidence to give for the prosecution, save to say that he was a member of the Society for Constitutional Information, and had been proposed by Horne Tooke to be a member of the committee of co-operation with the London Corresponding Society. But as a witness for the defence, he was a godsend; the defendant did not need his forty years as a student to know how to deal with him, and in as many minutes the case for the Crown was falling apart.

'Mr Sharp', said Horne Tooke, 'the gentlemen who have called you have as good an opinion of you as I have. It is said that I nominated you to some delegation; did you think that I did it because I had a good opinion of you?' 'Yes.' Yes, went on the witness, he had often been to the defendant's house; he had taught his daughters to engrave. Yes, he knew the defendant had a horse in his stable; yes, he recollected him riding out on it – once in two years. How was the defendant employed? 'Generally in your garden; and when indoors, you was employed in looking over your old books, I suppose for your great work, and writing, and playing at whist.' Having established his good character, Horne Tooke then proceeded to turn the tables on the Crown by securing the production of that vital piece of evidence which they had at one time supposed to be the cornerstone of their case: Joyce's letter of 12 May.

'Can you recollect on the 15th May, the day before I was arrested, where you dined?' asked the defendant. 'Yes, in Spital-square', replied Sharp. Yes, he went on, there was a conversation about a letter which had been intercepted; yes, the letter alluded to the Red Book – there were to be extracts made from the Red Book of the sinecures and pensions which Mr Pitt and his family received from the public; Joyce had told the witness, on the day Hardy was taken up, that he had sent a letter to the defendant, asking him to be ready at Spitalfields on Thursday next with the extracts. Yes, the interception of the letter had been a topic of conversation and laughter at the dinner – the letter which contained the horrible plot of taking a list of sinecures and pensions enjoyed by Mr Pitt and his family.

> 'I ask these questions, because I believe it was for this plot that I was apprehended the next day; if the intercepted letter is in court, have I a right to ask for its production?'
> 'If there is a letter which is in the hands of the officers of the crown that appears to you to be necessary for your defence', said Eyre CJ, 'to be sure you may call upon them to produce it...'
> '... I am informed, from pretty good authority, that a letter was intercepted, which should have come by the post to me, on the Wednesday previous to my apprehension; that it was produced before the Privy Council, and made the subject of very serious examination; that great alarm, and great apprehension, were entertained from the particular wording of that letter..'

The Crown had some green boxes on the table, in which they kept their papers – Erskine was to say later that he would liked to have had the rummaging of those boxes – and they produced the letter from one of them and it was shown to the witness. Here, however, the defendant hit a snag: Sharp was unable to identify the handwriting on the letter, and unable, therefore, to prove it. However, as the defendant was passing on to another topic, Law said, 'Mr Tooke, you may have the letter read now, if it is to answer any purpose.' It was read.

Horne Tooke then went on: 'Do you know, by conversation with Mr Joyce, what it was that I was to be ready with by Thursday?'
'The extracts from the Red Book, of the emoluments that Mr Pitt and his family derived from the public.'
'Who was to make those extracts?' asked the judge.
'Mr Tooke was to make the extracts', said the witness.

The witness then went on to agree that, while dining in Spital Square, he had seen some light horse pass the window.

'Was it understood, or had you any reason to suppose, that these light horse were sent in consequence of this letter, containing this horrid treason?'
'I understood so, that the army was out.'

The cross-examination continued. The witness agreed that the defendant did not go frequently to London, but preferred to stay at home; he had been a guest of the defendant's Sunday dinners – all the conversation was open and public; he had never heard the defendant suggest any attack upon the establishment in the country; he was only advocating a reform of the House of Commons. Then suddenly, and without any explanation, the defendant changed the subject:

'Did you ever hear of such a society as the Lumber Troop?'
'I have.'
'Were you a member of it?'
'Never.'
'Did you ever hear that the first of their regulations is, that every member of that society has permission to knock down any bailiff, watchman, or constable he pleases?'
'No, I never did.'
'I did not mean to raise a laugh, my lord, I only meant to show the danger these gentlemen run.'

The Solicitor-General intervened to say that he had not objected to a great deal of this examination. 'A great deal of it, though not strictly correct, certainly goes materially to the defence', said the judge.
There was no re-examination; and so the case for the Crown was closed.

CHAPTER 16

THE TRIAL OF JOHN HORNE TOOKE: THE CASE FOR THE DEFENCE

A fortnight earlier, Erskine had established his reputation as the greatest advocate Great Britain had ever known, to rank with the Demosthenes from ancient Athens and Cicero from Rome; he had received the applause of London and the acclaim of the nation. Now for three days he had been consistently up-staged by his own client; he had hardly spoken a word to argue points of law; he had hardly asked a single question in cross-examination (the two witnesses from Sheffield had been cross-examined by Gibbs while he was out of court). That Wednesday afternoon, some workmen were carrying out repairs to the Old Bailey, and when Erskine stood up to address the jury they were making such a noise that he had scarcely completed his opening sentence when he had to break off until the clatter had stopped; he re-opened his speech with the words: 'Gentlemen, I am much too used to public life to be at all disconcerted by any of these little accidents.'

Erskine's speech lasted some five hours; and once on his feet, he regained his skill and eloquence. He summarised neatly the standard of proof required in a criminal case: 'It is the glory of the English law, that it requires, even in the commonest case...the utmost precision of charge, and a proof correspondingly high; hitting the bird in the very eye.' He referred sarcastically to all the documents which the Crown had produced: 'We have heard a great many of them read, and they will be a lesson to me never again to destroy old newspapers as useless wrappings, but to treasure them as precious *manuscripts* for the discovery of plots and secrets of conspirators'; and then passing on to the Crown's abandonment of their evidence of plans for an armed insurrection:

> But has such proof been given in the present trial? It has not been attempted – the abortive evidence of arms has been abandoned – even the solitary pike, that formerly glared rebellious from the corner of the Court, no longer makes its appearance; and the knives have retired to their ancient office of carving. Happy was it, indeed, for me, that they were ever produced; for so perfectly common were they throughout England, and so notoriously in use for the most ordinary purposes, that public justice and benevolence, shocked at the perversion of truth in the evidence concerning them, kept pouring them in upon me from all quarters. The box before me is half full of them; and if all other trades should fail me, I might set up a cutler's shop in consequence of this cause.

It must not be supposed, however, that the defence was conducted entirely in a light-hearted manner:

> Yet this gentleman, greatly advanced in years, and declining in his health, who was shut up *at this time, and long before,* within the compass of his house and garden at Wimbledon,...is nevertheless gravely considered to be the master-string...the planner of a revolution in the government, and the active head of an armed rebellion against its authority. Gentlemen, is this a proposition to be submitted to the judgment of honest and enlightened men, upon a trial of life and death? Why, there is nothing in the Arabian Nights Entertainments, or in the Tales of the Fairies, which is not dull matter of fact compared with it.

Erskine reviewed the law, and the cases of Lord Strafford and Lord Russell and Algernon Sidney – who were all convicted and executed on evidence far stronger than anything alleged against Horne Tooke, but whose convictions were subsequently reversed by Parliament. He made it abundantly clear that, even if the conduct of the other conspirators constituted treason, the defendant had either been absent from their meetings, or had disagreed with their proposals: 'There is not only no evidence upon which reasonable men might deliberate between a verdict of Guilty or Not guilty, but, literally, NO EVIDENCE AT ALL.'

Erskine, however, was not simply defending Horne Tooke. At the outset of his speech, he declared that he was pursuing his duty as an advocate on behalf of others who were waiting to be tried, 'and of the whole people of this land'; and in the penultimate paragraph of his speech, he said:

> Gentlemen, I cannot conclude without observing that the conduct of this abused and unfortunate gentleman, throughout the whole of the trial, has certainly entitled him to admiration and respect; I had undoubtedly prepared myself to conduct his cause in a manner totally different from that which I have pursued; it was my purpose to have selected those parts of the evidence only by which he was affected, and, by a minute attention to the particular entries, to have separated him from the rest. By such a course I could have steered his vessel safely out of the storm, and brought her, without damage, into a harbour of safety, while the other unfortunate prisoners were left to ride out this awful tempest. But he insisted on holding out a rope to save the innocent from danger – he would not suffer his defence to be put upon the footing which discretion would have suggested. On the contrary, though not implicated himself in the alleged conspiracy, he has charged me to waste and destroy my strength to prove that no such guilt can be brought home to others. I rejoice in having been made the humble instrument of so much good – my heart was never so much in a cause.[1]

So it was that he reviewed the whole history of the Society for Constitutional Information; the proposals for the reform of Parliament put forward by the Pitts and the Duke of Richmond; the convention which had met in the Guildhall in 1780; the conduct of the Society of Friends of the people, of which he, Erskine, was himself a member; the views of Edmund Burke in support of the American colonists. It was for holding views like this that Horne Tooke was in the dock, and his fellow prisoners were awaiting trial in their cells in Newgate.

As the evening wore on, Erskine became more and more exhausted – or so he said: 'Gentlemen, though I feel myself very much exhausted, I have strength enough left just to touch upon these matters in their order', he said, when dealing with the reformers' relationship with France. He asked Gibbs to read out a letter which Horne Tooke had written to Lord Ashburton on the subject of Parliamentary reform in 1782; and finally he closed his speech with these words:

> You may see that I am tearing myself to pieces by exertions beyond my powers – I have neither voice nor strength to proceed farther – I do not, indeed, desire to conciliate your favour, nor to captivate your judgments by elocution in the close of my discourse; – but I conclude this cause, as I concluded the former, by imploring you that you may be enlightened by that Power which can alone unerringly direct the human mind in the pursuit of truth and justice.

It was nearly nine o'clock, and the Court adjourned.

✻   ✻   ✻

Thursday, 20 November was the day of the defence: the day when some of the most distinguished men who have ever set foot in the Old Bailey came into the witness box to give evidence on behalf of an alleged traitor.

Erskine had addressed the jury; he had not made a submission to the Court that in law his client had no case to answer. The evidence for the Crown was such that he presumably would have made such a submission if that had been a standard procedure then as it is today;[2] Horne Tooke, however, was not to be frustrated by lack of precedent.

Erskine had just called the first witness for the defence, Major Cartwright, and had asked him five questions, when Horne Tooke intervened. On the previous day, his interruptions had been verbose and sometimes incoherent to the point of being unintelligible (unless one accepts the view of his biographer, who says that 'he contrived his questions in so able and artful a manner, as to conceal their drift, not only from the witness, but even from the bench and bar', thereby succeeding, by induction, to elicit the truth and produce a chain of facts eminently useful for his defence); this morning, however, he was precise, clear and to the point: having said that he had prepared a mass of evidence to place before the Court, he submitted:

> If the Court, the prosecutor, and the jury, should think it not necessary for me to go on, with that body of evidence which I meant to produce, I shall then be very well contented not to produce it.

Eyre CJ seemed nonplussed by this application, and said that it was a matter for the prosecutor, not for the Court; to which Horne Tooke replied that he was perfectly satisfied with his lordship's answer: 'but my address is, in fact, to the prosecutor, though I apply to your lordship'.

The Attorney-General said that it was his impression that the case for the prosecution had received no answer: 'I, therefore, desire that Mr Tooke will understand me as meaning to state to the jury, that I have proved the case upon the indictment'. So Erskine said: 'Then we will go into the whole case.'

Major Cartwright was then examined by Erskine and Horne Tooke, cross-examined by the Attorney-General, re-examined by Horne Tooke, and called again later for further examination by Horne Tooke; and the gist of his evidence was that the opinions of the defendant, whom he had known intimately for 16 years, had been constant throughout: a firm, inflexible friend to a reform of the House of Commons, but at the same time one who maintained that the royal and aristocratic branches of the constitution were excellent: 'If I had conceived that there was any man in that society acting the part of a conspirator, to overturn the government, I should have thought it my duty, not only to have opposed him, but to have removed him, if possible'.

The Duke of Richmond also gave evidence that day, and while he was in the witness box the Court became involved in an important point of law. The defence wished to call evidence, and in particular to produce documents, dating back ten years or more, to show the defendant's unswerving loyalty to the Crown. The Attorney-General objected that such evidence was irrelevant: 'What I wish to know is, upon what principle the works of a gentleman, in a former part of his life, are evidence in such a cause as this'. Horne Tooke explained: the very indictment itself alleged that he had published 'divers books, pamphlets, letters, declarations and writings' – he did not know how many came under the word *divers*: 'it is so loose that all the libraries in Europe might have been brought in evidence against me'. Erskine joined in: he must have been speaking for half an hour. Gibbs explained that common justice, common reason, and common honesty required that the defendant should be permitted to give in evidence those passages of his life which he believed would contradict the principles which the prosecution imputed to him, and he referred to cases – including one in which Jefferies himself had been involved – in which similar evidence had been admitted.

In reply, the Attorney-General said that he was not prepared to waive the right of the Crown in favour of the prisoner: it was preferable that there should be a ruling on the issue from the Court which should form a precedent, rather than that the evidence should be admitted merely by consent. He reviewed the case and much of the evidence, and went on, displaying for the first time some signs of tetchiness: 'I say again, I hope to conduct myself, throughout these causes, with temper, because I know it is my duty to do so'. He objected to this evidence on the ground that it was not relevant to the charge; just as, if the writer of a textbook on criminal law was accused of robbery, it would be irrelevant to show that he had condemned robbery in his book.

> I have no personal interest about this cause, but great interest committed to my care, which I have reason enough, God knows, to wish committed to any other, but I must, holding this office, take care that the justice of the country, be satisfied, and I have no further desire upon it.

Eyre CJ, in giving judgment, first set out the basic principle of the law, as it was then and still is:

Nothing is so clear as that all declarations which a prisoner makes against himself, are, by the law of England, evidence against him, upon this presumption, that no man would be supposed to make a declaration against himself, unless it were true, and that, on the contrary, the declarations which he makes for himself are not evidence for him, because there the presumption is the other way.

But, he went on, evidence as to general good character was always admissible, and in a case such as this, where the Crown was leading evidence to show that the defendant was engaged in a conspiracy for a particular purpose, he was entitled to call evidence to rebut it, if appropriate, in the form of statements demonstrating a contrary intention. The Attorney-General commented:

It is hardly consistent with the respect I owe to your lordship to say what my opinion on the subject is, but I am perfectly satisfied with your lordship's opinion.

Not long afterwards, Horne Tooke was involved in another legal argument. Major Cartwright had been recalled, and the defendant handed him a piece of paper, explaining that it was a document, signed by the witness, showing the disposition and objects of various members of the societies to which they both belonged. Eyre CJ stopped him, pointing out that Major Cartwright's state of mind was immaterial. Horne Tooke replied that, throughout the trial, evidence of the state of mind of other persons had been produced to show what his own state of mind was supposed to be:

The prosecutors have driven us to such sort of evidence, as any man, who ever had attended to the proceedings of a court of justice, would have blushed to have beheld in any other case.

They had all got entangled up, he said, because in compassing the King's death, the intention is the crime, the overt act only the proof; in all other cases, the act was the crime, but here it was the intention that was the crime. Professional men, he said, were expert in those branches of their professions where they regularly earned their livelihood, but they very rarely considered problems which did not normally arise; and he went on to describe, by analogy, how he, as a grammarian, had occasion to study the organs of speech, and had consulted the best anatomist of the day, who confessed he knew nothing of those organs – no disease being there, they were never called in to have a fee. He then went on to add:

I am sure that all the conduct I have received from your lordship and the prosecutor has been such as totally to change the temper of my mind, with which I first came into this Court; and I shall never be able to express the gratitude I have to acknowledge for it.

They argued the issue backwards and forwards:

'Whatever other people have done, neither constitutes your guilt nor your innocence...' said Eyre CJ.
'...I cannot help feeling that the jury would not very willingly pick out a single traitor from the country to make an example of', said the defendant.

'I cannot tell how that may be, but I must go by the rules of evidence', said the judge.

This seemed to be going on interminably, until Erskine intervened and changed the subject by telling the Court that he proposed to call Mr Fox.

The Right Honourable Charles James Fox: according to the Revd George Croly, his entrance into the House of Commons was lounging or stately as might be appropriate, but always good-humoured, and he always had some pleasantry to exchange with everybody; and he had plenty of friends in the Old Bailey that day. Erskine examined him himself, and he agreed that he had seen Horne Tooke at the Thatched House in 1785,[3] after one of Pitt's proposals for Parliamentary reform; they had all signified their approval to Pitt's plan. He was cross-examined by the Attorney-General and explained that the plan was for boroughs to sell to the public their right to return members to Parliament.

Philip Francis was called: he had drawn up a plan for Parliamentary reform, and had consulted Horne Tooke who was a neighbour of his – he regarded him as one of the most learned men in the country.

His Grace the Duke of Richmond was called again; Horne Tooke put it to him that he had drawn up his own plan for Parliamentary reform and had submitted it to his Grace; but the Duke had no recollection of the occasion.

The Right Honourable William Pitt, First Lord of the Treasury and Chancellor of the Exchequer. He was 35, but he had already held the office of Prime Minister for eleven years; when entering the House, his countenance used to be that of a man who felt that he was coming into his high place of business, advancing with a quick, firm step, looking neither to right nor left, favouring no one with a glance or nod.

Horne Tooke handed him a letter: 'I beg Mr Pitt to say whether that is his handwriting'. The Prime Minister replied, 'It is.' Eyre CJ asked what it was, and there followed what must be one of the strangest episodes in our legal history: the Prime Minister was standing silent in the witness box; Erskine sat silent at counsel's table; while the defendant and the judge conversed with each other in order to try to discover some method of admitting the letter in evidence (with the defendant taking the opportunity to assert yet again that his sole and invariable plan was Parliamentary reform along the lines advocated by the Prime Minister twelve years earlier). Eventually Erskine joined in: 'Never having seen the letter which my client holds in his hand, it was, for every reason, better that he should take this part of the examination himself'; but he thought that his client's intention was to fix the date of the meeting which had been described by the Duke of Richmond. There was a further discussion between the judge, Erskine, and Horne Tooke, with the Duke joining in; the Prime Minister still stood silent. At last, Eyre CJ asked the defendant directly:

'Whom is the letter to?'
'It is a letter written by Mr Pitt on the subject of Parliamentary reform.'
'To whom?'

'I do not know that....'

There was further argument, and ultimately the defendant turned to the Prime Minister:

'I beg Mr Pitt to say, if he can recollect, to whom the letter was sent?'
'I am not able to recollect the name and the person; I can only judge by the contents of the letter, what description of person it might have been directed to, probably to some person who acted as a chairman of a Westminster committee.... At this distance of time, really I have no recollection who the individual was.'

A discussion then followed between Horne Tooke and the Prime Minister as to who had been present at the Thatched House in 1782; the Prime Minister did not remember, but he did recollect that the general sense of the meeting was that petitions for reform should be presented to Parliament.

'I suppose I may now have that letter read?' inquired the defendant.
'No', said Eyre CJ, 'you are not at all forwarded for reading that letter.'
'Then I hope I may have it back again.'
'Certainly', said the judge.
'I did intend to ask the right honourable gentleman many other questions', said the defendant, 'but certainly the laugh of the Court prevents me being serious; therefore I will ask him no more.'

The Attorney-General started to cross-examine the Prime Minister and asked if the meeting in 1782 was designed to bring about a convention of the people; when the Prime Minister said it was not, Horne Tooke immediately intervened: 'Were we not a convention?... What was that meeting but a convention of delegates from different towns and counties throughout England?' The Prime Minister could not recollect; and in answer to a question from the judge, his final reply was, 'I cannot state exactly how that meeting was composed'.

Sheridan was the next witness; he was examined, cross-examined and re-examined about various meetings which he and the defendant had attended over the years; towards the end, the Prime Minister, who had remained in Court, interjected to say he did remember a meeting at the Duke of Richmond's, where there were delegates from county meetings, cities and towns.

Then the Earl of Stanhope gave evidence: he said that he had been in the chair at a public meeting held on 14 July 1790, to celebrate the fall of the Bastille; the defendant had made a speech, and was hissed and hooted because he said that the timbers of the constitution were sound, and proposed a resolution that we did not need a revolution in this country. (It was while Earl Stanhope was being examined by Erskine that the Attorney-General's patience temporarily snapped: Eyre CJ had intervened to ask the witness if the defendant was present at a particular meeting, to which he replied that he was not certain, but that he himself was there. 'That is nothing to the purpose', the Attorney-General interrupted, 'your lordship ought to know the rules of evidence better – be so good as to inform us of any thing that passed at the meetings where Mr Tooke was [present].')

The Revd Christopher Wyvill was called: but he had only met the defendant once, and never since 1785. John Macnamara was a founding member of the Constitional Club: they used to meet at the Thatched House, or next door in Willis' rooms; members used to wear a uniform – a blue coat and an orange cape, and buttons impressed with the words King and Constitution; Pitt and Dundas, Lord Campbell and Mr Speaker Addington were members; he knew Horne Tooke well – 'I have never met any public or private character who I conceived understood the government or constitution of this country better than the prisoner at the bar'; but he did not know what the prisoner had been doing since 1789 as he had been travelling in Europe. William Fielding, a barrister, was the next witness: he had worn the blue-and-orange, and so had Lord Frederick Campbell, the Lord Clerk Register of Scotland, and Earl Camden; at one meeting in Willis' rooms, 1200 members, including Horne Tooke, rose up and joined hand in hand as a mark of approbation to Fielding and his speech of loyalty to the King – but these events had taken place in 1788; the witness had had little contact with the defendant since then.

Henry Beaufoy was called, supposedly a friend of the defendant, but a reluctant witness; he could remember nothing. 'This gentleman's remembrance requires so much *flapping*, that I must beg leave just to wake it once more', said the defendant at one stage, interrupting the Attorney-General's cross-examination; but to no avail, the witness could remember nothing. Next was Thomas Symonds, a student barrister, and a personal friend of the defendant; while he was in the witness box, there was a discussion in Court as to the significance of the term 'convention', and the witness vigorously asserted that the defendant had always rejected the idea of universal suffrage; he knew several of the other alleged conspirators, and they were quite incapable of entering into a conspiracy to subvert the government.

Lieutenant-Colonel John Money was called: he had been in the service of France from July to December 1792, and produced his commission signed by the King and the Mareschal de Camp General; on his return to England, he had been graciously received at Court and had waited upon members of the cabinet. However, the judge ruled that whether the colonel's conduct was right or wrong, whether it was approved or disapproved, was immaterial, and he was not allowed to pursue the matter any further. Another officer, Captain William Tooke, of the Ninth Regiment of Dragoons, the nephew of Horne Tooke's friend, was called: he had known the defendant for many years, and had known him as a firm supporter of Parliamentary reform.

George Rous, a barrister, was called; he was a member of the Society of the Friends of the People, but started to give evidence about the London Corresponding Society. Garrow objected and submitted that the witness could not possibly give evidence about a society of which he was not a member. The Attorney-General joined in and Erskine spoke at length, more as a witness than an advocate, until the Attorney-General interrupted:

'You cannot state all your evidence in a speech'.
'Then you give up the present point?' inquired Eyre CJ.
'No, I do not', replied Erskine.

For once, Horne Tooke kept quiet, but the others went on tossing the point backwards and forwards, until Eyre CJ ruled that the evidence could not be produced. But Erskine said he was referring to a different piece of evidence, and they were off again. It was nearly 9 p.m., and everyone was tired, but it seems that Erskine was trying to ask Rous what had passed between him and Richter, another prisoner in Newgate. Eventually Eyre CJ closed the door:

The gentlemen will have the goodness to recollect the declaration I set out with in giving the rule in the morning – that the principle was, that declarations for a man's self are not to be received...; and this is so universally known in practice, that I think it cannot fairly be doubted.

Horne Took then said: 'My lord, the multitude of evidence which I had intended to call I wish to relinguish; I am very well satisfied with the evidence I have already given; but as the Bishop of Gloucester is in Court, I will call him now and conclude my evidence.'

And so Richard Beadon DD, the Right Reverend Bishop of Gloucester, came into the witness box. After the preliminaries, the examination proceeded as follows:

'Does your lordship remember my taking my master of arts degree?'
'I do, perfectly well.'
'Does your lordship remember that that degree was opposed?'
'I do....'
'Is not the degree of master of arts such a one as would be given to any creature that could answer a rational question?'
Eyre CJ intervened: 'For the honour of the University, you will not pursue that, Mr Tooke.'
'I beg your lordship's pardon – It is of some consequence to me, and does not affect the honour of the University ... for I mean no joke upon that University.'
'It is not put in terms that are quite so measured as you would upon consideration put it.'
'...Your lordship must perceive it is something extra-ordinary that that which is given to everybody for nothing, was refused to me, and never refused to anyone else.'
'I only object to the phrase.'

The Bishop then gave evidence that objections had been made to Horne Tooke receiving his degree because of the letters which he had written to

Wilkes, and that inquiries were made at the University to find something to lay to his charge – but no evidence was ever found which could form any charge against him in respect of his morality, knowledge, decency, quietness, or the respectability of his behaviour and conduct. His political sentiments had remained the same from the time they first knew each other until the present.

'...Must I have been very dissipated or tolerably studious?'
'I am inclined to think it has been studious.'
'Has your lordship ever assisted me with books, from the University of Cambridge?'
'I think I have.'
'Did your lordship discover for me some books no where else to be found, that were in the Bodleian Library at Oxford, *Caramuel* and *Campanella*?'
'Yes.'
'Did your lordship suppose that I was more employed in deposing the King, and overturning the state, or in hunting out for new words and new meanings? Which does your lordship think most occupied my attention?'
'I knew you was very much employed in the latter; I never did know that you were and I hope you never have been employed in the former.'
'And did you believe that I was?'
'I have no reason to believe it, from any thing I have heard you say, or any thing I knew you do.'

The Attorney-General had only one question to ask in cross-examination: 'Do you know anything of the proceedings of the Constitutional or the London Corresponding Societies, for the last three years?' 'Nothing at all.' Horne Tooke objected to this question, but Eyre CJ said it was impossible for him to rule that it was irregular. And so, it being now past 9.30 p.m., the Court adjourned.

The evidence was now complete, but there was one item which, regretfully, Horne Tooke had not been able to place before the Court. During Hardy's trial, a song, *Plant, plant the Tree,* had been put in evidence:

Plant, plant the tree, fair freedom's tree,
  Midst danger, wounds and slaughter;
Each patriot's breast its soil shall be,
  And tyrant's blood its water.

If this had been put in evidence against him, Horne Tooke used to say in later years, it had been his intention to have stated that, as nothing treasonable had ever been discovered in the words, then something of that kind might be supposed to be in the tune; and he had therefore decided to hum it before the judge and jury; 'and thus', he added, 'I should have afforded the example of being the first prisoner, tried for his life, who had ever dared to sing a song in open court!'

On his way back to Newgate that evening, Horne Tooke was accompanied by his nephew, John Wildman, who said that he had got Pitt down and might have done more with him (a somewhat uncharitable remark to make in respect of a witness who had come to give evidence on his behalf): 'Yes, I might', the old man replied, 'but never in my life did I choose to trample on a fallen foe'. And it may have been on the same night that a lady came up to him, pulled up the collar of his coat, and put a silk handkerchief round his neck; to which he responded, 'Pray madam, be careful, for I am rather ticklish at present, about that particular place'. And every night, after dinner in Newgate, he used to sing a song which he had learnt from his grandmother, and which had probably been written on behalf of the claims of the House of Hanover in opposition to the Jacobites:

> Here's a health to our old constitution,
>   Let the trumpets sound,
>   And the hautboys play.
>   Huzza!
>   Huzza!
> To the downfall of all tyranny;
>   I long to see the day.
>   Huzza!
>   Huzza! Huzza!

CHAPTER 17

THE END OF THE TRIAL OF JOHN HORNE TOOKE

The Court was in an end-of-term mood when it reconvened next morning at 10 a.m. for the final stages of the trial. Eyre CJ had remembered that, although references had been made to the acquittal of Hardy, this had never formally been proved. Erskine said that it had been his intention to prove it, but in any case it was a matter of common knowledge. Horne Tooke apologised to his counsel for having closed the case prematurely without consulting them. The Attorney-General said that, notwithstanding Horne Tooke had closed his case too early, he gave his consent to offer any additional evidence he pleased. Eyre CJ said that, unless the acquittal was properly proved, he would have to direct the jury to disregard it, which in the circumstances they would find difficult to do, and he went on to compliment the Attorney-General on 'that candour which has distinguished his conduct throughout the whole of the proceedings'. The minutes of Hardy's acquittal were then read by the Clerk of Arraigns.[1]

'Vinegar' Gibbs then addressed the jury. This time, he did not faint. He spoke for four hours or more. On the following day, Eyre CJ was to say that he had

> heard this speech with as much pleasure as I ever heard any speech in my life. I never heard a speech that was, in all respects, fitter to be offered to a jury, by a council (*sic*) assigned for the prisoner, in a case of high treason, where very much depends upon the counsel (*sic*) keeping themselves strictly within their line of duty, giving the Court and the jury effective assistance, in the discussion of the law, and in the examination of the fact....The putting the case in every possible light, in which it can be put for the prisoner...is not only the right of the prisoner, but is essentially useful to the public justice of the country, as it enables those, who are to decide, to see where the truth of the case lies.

And many years later, in his biography of Horne Tooke, Stephens was to write that it was on this day that Gibbs laid the foundation of his future fortune.

Quietly, methodically, with an acid irony which was so apt to his nickname, Gibbs set out to dismantle the case for the prosecution stage by stage, in law and on the facts. He discussed the significance of the word *convention*: was it not simply a synonym for *meeting*? They had no money, except ten guineas – 'and if this great national fund failed, there was nothing, and then they were to go to war without money'. They had no arms – 'nothing in the world but 12 pike-staffs', and those made for self-defence. The prosecution had produced a great mass of papers, which 'took thirty hours to read in court, and by which our attention was distracted and confounded – papers which it is utterly impossible for me to observe upon to you, because no human strength could be equal to it' – some of which could never have come to the knowledge of the defendant: 'and yet you will recollect that my two learned friends ... have had this business before them for half a year ... – there was not a paper in all these boxes and bags that they have not read over and over again'.

In most cases of treason, there was some pretender to the crown, ready with an army, to which the conspirators could attach themselves. Was there anyone here? It could not be Hardy – 'the great leader of the conspiracy, the secretary of the most obnoxious society, the man who is supposed to have been the generalissmo [*sic*] of those troops – the manager of all this, whose hand was in everything', because he had been acquitted.

He believed that the case called for no answer from the defendant; it had been destroyed by the witnesses called for the prosecution; but for the satisfaction of the world, and of the court, and of the jury, he would assert that his innocence had been abundantly proved by the witnesses he had called. Throughout his life, he had worked unswervingly for Parliamentary reform, with nothing but regard and reverence for the King; yes, he had rejoiced in the French Revolution – but only in so far as it affected France – he did not wish any part of it to be applied in England. In conclusion, he said:

> The proof to convict an Englishman of high treason must be plain; must be direct; must be manifest. The proof in this case is plain, is direct, is manifest: but it is all in favour of the prisoner. The proof offered to support the prosecution, furnishes a plain, direct, and manifest case for an acquittal.... I have no scruple to say ... that I think a ruder shock cannot be given to the constitution of England ... than by convicting the prisoner upon this evidence.

When Gibbs concluded, Eyre CJ asked Horne Tooke if he wished to say anything; for once, the defendant restricted himself to a single sentence: 'I very much fear that I have spoken already too much, and too often in this court, and I do not mean to trouble you with one word.'

The Attorney-General had opened the case for the Crown against Hardy; he now proceeded to close the case for the Crown against Horne Tooke. 'It has pleased the Providence of God', he began, 'in such of his dispensation as affect the situation which I am to hold in this world, to call upon me, at this moment, to execute a duty so awful and so important ... that I can only look to his support, to enable me to execute it, as I ought to the prisoner, and the country'. There was much more – long entangled sentences about the highest council of His Majesty, and the suspension of the Habeas Corpus Act, and his regret that he had been unable to conclude the case at the end of the evidence for the prosecution; but he had his duty to do:

And when I am laid in my grave, after the interval of life, that yet remains to me, my children, I hope and trust, will be able to say of their father, that he endeavoured to leave them an inheritance, by attempting to give them an example of public probity dearer to them than any acquisition of honour that this country could have given the living father to transmit to them.

At this point – it does not appear on the record, but there is a well-authenticated account of the episode[2] – the Attorney-General burst into tears. He was, apparently, accustomed to do so and this caused little surprise, but on this occasion, the Solicitor-General also burst into tears. 'Just look at Mitford', said someone to Horne Tooke, 'what on earth is he crying for?' To which Horne Tooke replied, 'At the thought of the little inheritance which poor Scott is likely to leave to his children.'

There must have been some in Court that day who feared that, over-whelmed by the strain, the Attorney-General was on the point of collapse; but he recovered his composure, and, like Gibbs, spoke for four hours or more. The defendant was a gentleman, undoubtedly, of great accomplish-ment, but it was the bounden duty of the jury to find him guilty, he said. He referred to the revolution in France – the monarchy had been destroyed; the societies in England had embarked upon a course designed to depose the King, and therefore to compass the death of the King. Gibbs's arguments were defective – there were vital omissions in what he had said. Whatever Horne Tooke's views may have been in the 1780s, in 1792 he himself had written the letter to Stockport referring to the 'vipers monarchy and aristocracy'. He was also personally participating in a scheme to compel the King by force to take a different Parliament from that which the law and the constitution had given him, so that he would be bound to resist such a scheme, even at the hazard of his life. And if it was true that Horne Tooke had not taken any part in the conspiracy, the best person to prove it was the man most closely associated with it, namely Hardy himself who had been acquitted; but he had not been called. Horne Tooke must have known all about the Chalk Farm meeting – and no one was called to prove that he had no connection with it. In the summer of 1792, when France still had a King, he had been corresponding with the Jacobins, and after the King had been deposed, he had been corresponding with the French government.

The Attorney-General has frequently been criticised for having instituted these proceedings at all; and even those who have accepted that there was some justification for launching the prosecution have been baffled by his decision to continue the case against Horne Tooke after the acquittal of Hardy. The Attorney-General never formally placed on record his reasons for this decision, but he made them fairly clear during the course of his closing speech: he blamed the judge. It was no part of his duty to speculate why the jury had acquitted Hardy, but 'I say, and speak with great deference to my lord, because there is no man who wishes to be more respectful than I do to courts, and more especially where I know it so well deserved from me – I say, upon a review of the evidence, there was a great deal more affecting him than was actually recalled to the consideration of the jury'.

Nevertheless, he closed his speech by saying that he ought to be counsel for those whom he prosecuted as well as counsel against them, and he was sure that if he had fallen into any error, it would be corrected by the judge; and finally:

> May God Almighty direct you to a right verdict, and whatever your conclusion upon the case is, may he grant that it may have a tendency to secure the peace and happiness of the country in which we live.

*   *   *

It was after dark that November evening when Eyre CJ started his final address to the jury, and at about 9 p.m. he told them that it would be impossible to conclude his summing-up that night, and he adjourned until 9 a.m. the following morning. He then addressed the jury throughout the Saturday until nearly 8 p.m., a total of some thirteen hours.

The trial of Hardy had been longer, but the summing-up had been shorter; following the Attorney-General's complaint, Eyre CJ was not going to make the same mistake again:

> Gentlemen, I perceive it is expected of me that I should undergo the fatigue and labour of summing up to you the whole of this case which has been laid before you in evidence ...

And this is what he did. He had a detailed note of everything all the witnesses had said, and this he repeated to the jury; the bulk of the documentary evidence was read again. He had been seised of this matter since at least the day of the Grand Jury hearing in September, probably since the proceedings before the Privy Council in the summer; but one can have nothing but admiration for the complete grasp which he had on every item of evidence, often interspersed with shrewd comments of his own. Thus, commenting on Hardy's and Margarot's address of 6 August 1792, he said, 'I discover in it something very inflammatory, licentious and libellous upon all the orders of the state...but I cannot say myself, that I do discover any distinct traces of a national convention ...; it would be difficult to collect more from it, than that ... they proclaim to the world, that grievances exist; and that they are determined to procure a reform of those grievances, by procuring a better representation of the people in parliament'.

When he came to deal with the Scottish Convention, their use of the word 'citizen' instead of 'gentleman', their use of the phrase, 'the first year of the British Convention', their appointment of a committee to draw up a declaration of the natural, unalienable and imprescriptible rights of man, and their resolution to use force in certain circumstances, he commented: 'To those who are acquainted with the history of the National Convention of France, this sort of resolution has an alarming aspect'; but then he reminded the jury that ridicule had been poured on their finances – a budget of £4.5.8d, including two bad shillings.

In commenting upon a letter found at Adams's, 'dated the twenty-sixth May, 1797, but probably it means 1792', he noted that the only word in Horne

Tooke's writing was the word 'from', from which it was permissible to deduce that the defendant was simply concerned in correcting the grammar; and he later added that there was little evidence to connect him with the resolutions passed at Chalk Farm. His comments on Jeremiah Joyce's letter were favourable to the Crown, without casting blame on Horne Tooke:

> It is supposed that these words were thought mysterious...and that apprehensions were entertained that some mischief was intended, and that, therefore, the government took some precautions. It does not appear in evidence whether any such precautions were taken or no, but if they were, I think no man can impute blame; but, on the contrary, that our acknowledgements are due to government for being ready to hold out protection; and, undoubtedly, the exterior of all this business was such as justified alarm, and made it necessary for government to be on their guard. A witness said that he understood that these words – 'Is it possible to get ready by Thursday?' – alluded to Mr Tooke's being ready with some extracts from the red book.... One might observe that this line, immediately following the account of Hardy's capture, certainly does not very well fall in with that turn given to it, and yet, at the same time, it may be, that it really ought to be so understood.

If the judge's review of the evidence had been exemplary, the same cannot be said of his direction on the law. As in Hardy's case, Eyre CJ peremptorily dismissed the arguments of counsel for the defence in a couple of sentences: a conspiracy to depose the King, he said, was a conspiracy to compass his death; that was a matter of law, and 'God forbid ... that a jury should doubt that he who means to depose the King, compasses and imagines the death of the King'.

The judge then commended the jury for the way in which they had tried the case:

> Gentlemen, the case for your consideration, is a case of fact; and a great satisfaction it is to me, that if, under the pressure and fatigue which I have undergone, any great omission may happen to be made by me, the attention which you have shown to the evidence, will enable you to supply those defects. The mass of the evidence is quite new to you, except so far as you may have read it, through the imperfect medium of accounts, which the newspapers may have given you of it; it is, to me, the second laborious investigation.

The case, he said, really resolved itself into two issues. First, was there a plan to establish a national convention which should usurp the powers of government? And secondly, was the defendant a party to such a plan? It was clear that there was a plan to hold a national convention for some purpose, and it could hardly be denied that the defendant was a participating party; but the avowed intention of the convention was a reform of the House of Commons, and that was an innocent intention; but, said the prosecution, the avowed intention was not the true intention – it was a disguise for a different intention:

> That is a thing which is not to be believed, or to be found by a jury, without very clear proof; it is not to be believed by you upon probabilities; in the common concerns of life men are obliged to act upon probabilities, but that is not the case with a jury; I might add that even in the common understanding between man and man, one ought not to believe such a thing, without its being more distinctly proved than it has been in this case.

Everyone knew that the national convention in France had taken possession of the government; the London Corresponding Society had become a portentous political monster, raising itself to power like similar societies in France; but the Society for Constitutional Information seemed to be a mere club. It is true that it had been in correspondence with the National Convention in France, and had congratulated them upon their success – but whether this was part of a plot to destroy the King and his government was a matter for the jury to decide. The Scottish Convention had imitated the proceedings of the French Convention, but 'whether all this form had really no bottom, and was only a piece of solemn mummery, meaning nothing at last ... is for your consideration'. The societies in England had magnified their numbers and their strength much beyond the truth; but the true state of the societies, and of the Society for Constitutional Information in particular, was material to deciding whether they really intended to usurp the government – it had 'neither numbers, money, nor even zeal' to embark upon such a scheme – a phrase picked up and repeated by Sheridan in a subsequent debate on the trials in the House of Commons.

Referring then to the defendant:

> Gentlemen, Mr Horne Tooke went into a very effective cross-examination, and he also examined witnesses on his behalf. I think he did well in so doing; for I myself cannot but think that this was a charge, which it became Mr Horne Tooke to treat most seriously, and to give the most satisfactory answer to it that evidence could furnish....
>
> I wish heartily that Mr Tooke had put this case really beyond all suspicion, because I see, with great regret, a man of his cultivated understanding, of his habits, of his capacity to be useful to mankind; a man supported by the evidence of that venerable prelate, the bishop of Gloucester, who, I am sure, would flatter no man; I say, I am heartily sorry to see him in such a situation, and I should have been heartily rejoiced if he could have put this case beyond all suspicion, but I cannot say that he has done so. There certainly is a great deal to be explained, which I am not able to explain, and I am at this moment totally unable to develop the character and conduct of this gentleman; but that goes but a little way upon the question, whether he is guilty or innocent of this indictment; that you will judge by the result of the evidence, and the clear impression that that result shall make upon your minds. I repeat that you have a very serious duty imposed upon you; but, after the pains you have taken to make yourselves masters of the case, it is a duty which you will discharge with satisfaction to your own consciences, and consequently, with satisfaction to your country.

It was 7.50 p.m.: the jury retired; they were back in Court before 8 p.m. The Clerk of the Arraigns said,

> 'John Horne Tooke, hold up your hand – Gentlemen of the Jury, look upon the prisoner – How say you, is John Horne Tooke guilty of the high treason whereof he stands indicted, or not guilty?'
> 'Not guilty.'
> 'Did he fly for it?'
> 'Not that we know of.'

*   *   *

Horne Tooke had had the first word; now he was determined to have the last word. He stood up to address the Court:

> My mind, my lord, is much better formed to feel and to acknowledge kindness than to solicit it. I desire to return my most sincere thanks to your lordship, and to the bench, for the conduct which you have held towards me, during the whole of this tedious trial.
>
> Gentlemen of the jury, you have afforded a just protection to my life: I thank you for it: and give me leave to tell you two things, which will increase your satisfaction as long as you live. We shall both have done good to our country. When I have told you two facts, one of which it was impossible I should tell you before, and the other it was unfit that I should tell you before. I am sure we shall never see such a trial as this again. My caution, and my virtue, for at this moment I will place it to myself, are the cause of those suspicions which dwelt upon his lordship's mind; his sagacity and integrity assisted him to clear many things up to you; but the whole suspicion has arisen from this – I was anxious for the proper conduct of other men; and if I could have foreseen, what I never could foresee, till the attorney-general made his reply –

At that moment, part of the students' gallery collapsed. It may have been during the ensuing interval that the Attorney-General took a pen and paper and wrote a message and passed it across counsels' table to Gibbs:[3] 'I say from my heart that you did yourself great credit as a good man, and great credit as an excellent citizen, not sacrificing any valuable public principle; I say from my judgment that no lawyer ever did himself more credit, or his client more service; so help me God!'

When the confusion had subsided, Horne Tooke went on to explain that when the secretary of the Society brought papers to him for publication he struck out words which might have given rise to a prosecution for libel; other people brought their work to him to be corrected:

> There was one paper, where the word 'government' was struck out, and 'country' put in. 'Radical reform of the government' might mean to pull the government up by the roots; 'radical reform of the country' could mean no such thing; – no man will be charged with pulling the country up by the roots.... To prevent the prosecution of other people for libel, I have suffered a prosecution for high treason. I return your lordship thanks – I return my counsel thanks, my noble friend Mr Erskine, who has been so nobly supported by Mr Gibbs; – and you, gentlemen of the jury, I return you my thanks. I am glad I have been prosecuted; and I hope this will make the attorney general more cautious in future; he said he would have no treason by construction; and there is no suspicion against me but by construction and inference.

Major Cartwright had stayed in London, and on the Saturday, while the judge was summing up, he wrote a hasty note to his wife: 'We expect the final decision almost every minute. Five days close attendance has fatigued me too much to stand the court, the bad air, and the bad accommodation this morning. From the evidence, it seems impossible to decide against him. During the whole time he has shewn himself a wonderful man.' Next day he added:

Sunday morning. On the words "not guilty", the air was rent with joyful shouts, and Felix trembled. As soon as the shouting subsided, Tooke addressed the Court, in a very few words, thanking them for their conduct on the trial.... I supped with Mr Tooke at his surgeon's, Mr Cline. About twenty in company. You may imagine the joy in every bosom. I would not but have been an evidence on this trial for the world...

It was Henry Cline after whom, many years later, Erskine named one of his pet leeches.

Horne Tooke went home the following afternoon: the last entry in his diary reads simply, 'Wimbledon. Arrived at 3 o'clock P.M.'; and by the following week, life was returning to normal. In a letter dated [Monday] 1st December, the Major wrote:

> A joyous dinner and afternoon yesterday at Tooke's. Four ladies, of whom two were his daughters, and a large party of men. We drank the King's health, which I dare say was not expected at the next door (Dundas's), where he had Pitt and a large party to dine. Hoffner, Banks the sculptor, and Sharp the engraver were there; busts, medals, etc., are under consideration...

Horne Tooke had a large fine tom-cat which he used to fondle and feed with his own hand; during his master's absence, the cat did not make its usual appearance at 4 o'clock every afternoon, but no sooner had he returned from prison, than it went into the parlour, and seeing him seated in his usual place at the head of the table, immediately perched on his shoulder and purred contentedly throughout the meal. Charlotte Harte drew the cat's portrait in black chalk and this was hung in her father's bedroom; its offspring were carefully preserved in the family, and Alexander Stephens remembers seeing its great-grandchildren playing about in the hall.

A week or two later, Horne Tooke met the Attorney-General in Westminster Hall, and walked up to him and saying, 'Let me avail myself of this opportunity to express my sense of your humane and considerate conduct during the late trials'; but privately, he said that if ever he was indicted for treason again, he would immediately plead Guilty, as he considered hanging and beheading would be preferable to the long speeches of Sir John Scott.

CHAPTER 18

UNFINISHED BUSINESS

A fortnight after the acquittal of Horne Tooke, the Court reassembled. Bonney, Joyce, Kyd and Holcroft were brought to the bar and the Attorney-General announced that he did not propose to proceed further against them. Eyre CJ directed the jury to bring in a verdict of Not Guilty, which they did. Bonney, Joyce and Kyd then bowed to the Court and withdrew; Holcroft, however, endeavoured to address the Court, and an argument ensued between him and the judge until the latter warned him: 'You had better take care of that, or you may get into another scrape as soon as you are relieved from this'. So he went to sit beside William Godwin who had gone to the Old Bailey to see what was happening; Thomas Lawrence the painter was there too, and left us a sketch of the pair of them (see Figure 15).

Having disposed of these four gentlemen, the Court then proceeded to the trial of John Thelwall (see Figure 16). Serjeant Adair opened the case against him; Major Cartwright was in Court, and in a letter to his wife he said that his speech 'nearly lulled me to sleep, and I was told that the Chief Justice[1] had been asleep the greatest part of the time'. Once again, Erskine was briefed for the defence. He had another difficult client; at one stage, Thelwall wrote him a note, 'I'll be hanged if I don't plead my own cause', and handed it down to counsels' table; and Erskine wrote back, 'You'll be hanged if you do'; so Thelwall allowed him to continue. The indictment included a reference to his parable of King Chanticleer – 'a very fine majestic animal, the game cock, meaning our Lord the King'; and there was the evidence of the spy Groves who had said that he had seen Thelwall blow the head off his glass of porter and heard him say, 'This is the way I would have all kings served'.

The prosecution closed their case on the third day of the trial, and Erskine displayed his usual ability and energy, and dealt firmly with the statement which his client was alleged to have made. Even if the phrase had not been exaggerated, he said, allowance ought to be made for infirmity of temper, and the faults of the tongue, in a period of intense excitement. Who would be safe, if every loose word, uttered in a moment of inadvertence or irritation, were to be admitted as evidence of a criminal purpose? Who had not, in an unguarded hour, inveighed against the government to whom he is most firmly attached?

Figure 15. Thomas Holcroft and William Godwin, sketched by Thomas Lawrence in the Old Bailey, immediately after Holcroft had been discharged. (From a private collection.)

> If there is such a man present so uniformly correct in expression, so guarded from mistake, so superior to passion, let him stand forth, let him claim all the praise due to a character so superior to the common state of humanity. For myself, I will only say, *I am not the man*.

It was Erskine's last speech in this series of cases, and again he saw his client acquitted. And so finally, on 15 December, the two remaining defendants, Richter and Baxter, were brought to the Old Bailey; the Attorney-General

Figure 16. John Thelwall, at one time attributed to William Hazlitt, who was trained as an artist, but now believed to be by his brother, John Hazlitt. (By permission of the National Portrait Gallery.)

said that he proposed to offer no evidence, and Macdonald CB, who was presiding that day, told the jury to bring in a verdict of Not Guilty, which they did. And so the great case came to an end.

At about the same time the Sheffield witnesses returned home; a great procession went out to meet them and escorted them for the last half mile of their journey; they carried a silk flag and flambeaux, and there was a coach decorated on one side with a painting of the sun, and on the other with a figure of liberty; and a 'monster dinner' was held in their honour on Boxing Day.[2]

A meeting, said to have been attended by 1300 persons, was held at the Crown and Anchor on 4 February to celebrate the acquittals; Earl Stanhope was in the chair; twenty-seven toasts were drunk, including, 'The Swinish Multitude and may the Honest Hogs never cease to Grunt until their Wrongs are Righted'.

The Earl also gave a ball at Chevening to celebrate the acquittal of the Revd Mr Joyce. Besides his tenants and neighbours, a number of the Earl's friends from distant parts of the country were invited. At 8 o'clock, the company was taken into the ballroom. In the centre of a large group of emblematic figures were displayed, in large letters, the words, 'The Rights of Juries'. After the ball, some two hundred persons withdrew to partake of every delicacy that Chevening Hall or the season could produce; and after a number of appropriate toasts and songs, they retired to give place to others at the tables. Dancing was resumed and continued until 6 o'clock in the morning.

*   *   *

In the autumn of 1794 Henry Yorke was in custody in the Castle at York, well aware that he had been singled out as the military leader of a planned insurrection. Following the acquittal of Hardy and Horne Tooke, the Crown realised that there would be little chance of securing his conviction on this charge – the thought of this young man, still in his early twenties, marching at the head of 10,000 Yorkshiremen, with pikes on their shoulders and *couteaux secrets* in their pockets, down the Great North Road to seize London and drive the King from his throne, could hardy be expected to stand up to examination in the cold light of day by a jury of their own countrymen.

So the Crown restricted the case against Yorke, along with Joseph Gale the printer,[3] to one of seditious conspiracy, based on the events at Castle Hill on 17 April 1794. The grand jury, which included William Fawkes of Farnley, one of Guy Fawkes's descendants, found a true bill against him at the Lent Assizes at York in 1795; and he appeared for trial there on 23 July. Rooke J. presided; the Treasury Solicitor briefed John Law; Yorke briefed Mr Hotham, but he conducted most of the case himself, with considerable skill and panache.

> 'What do you understand by the vile tools of government?' he asked William Frith, the surgeon, at one point.
> 'The persons concerned in the Assizes', replied the doctor, 'I suppose the same as they are here', at which the Court burst into a peal of laughter.
> 'You do not mean to say that Mr Law is a vile tool of government?'
> 'You might call him so perhaps.'

But, like many an inexperienced advocate, he asked one question too many; it was in answer to Yorke himself that Dr Frith described the conversation which he had had with Mrs Rhodes on the morning of the Castle Hill meeting, and thus virtually destroyed his defence that he was only in Sheffield by chance.

At the end of the case for the prosecution, Yorke made an unsuccessful submission that he had no case to answer, and then addressed the jury. He spoke for over three hours; it was a speech which rivalled even Gerrald's in Edinburgh. He answered Law's opening speech for the Crown by a learned lecture on jurisprudence and constitutional law, on the history of mankind, and the consequences of the invention of printing. In view of recent events in France, it was no longer possible to eulogize the Revolution, so he delivered a withering attack upon Robespierre. Rooke J. listened politely. Once, when the defendant was attacking the House of Commons, he intervened to say that he could not permit any sentiment to pass that was at all disgraceful to the House, and added, 'I have heard you with great pleaseure, and am very sorry to be obliged to interrupt you'. On another occasion, when Yorke was describing the annual parliaments held by the Anglo-Saxons, the judge broke in to explain, like a tutor to an over-enthusiastic pupil, 'You seem not at all aware that the Crown used to summon a parliament annually, but there was not an annual election. These words *annuo parliamento*, relate to their meeting, and not their election'.

Yorke dealt with the evidence of the witnesses for the Crown; he explained what he had intended to say, and what he thought he had said, at the meeting; he dealt with arms, and the manufacture of pikes and the right of the people to have arms according to their condition and degree; he dealt with the situation in Sheffield:

> Permit me here to observe, that while we are blackened as seditious conspirators, while I am denounced as the instigator of tumult and insurrection, the town of Sheffield, when almost every part of England has been a scene of riot, has remained in the most perfect tranquillity....
>
> I confess ... this is one great source of consolation ... that in these troublous times, when every part of the commonwealth is in commotion, I should stand here charged with irritating the passions of the people of Sheffield (a town too which has been stamped as the mart whence emanated all the treason of the land); that I should stand here, I say, the avowed leader of a tumultuous confederacy, when facts speak the direct contrary, is an event as astonishing as it is inconsistent ... and honours the character of that town which has been so much belied and calumniated.

He referred to Livy and Luther, to Dr Jebb and Dr Paley; he spoke of the slave trade and universal suffrage; he quoted passages from Burke and Junius; he told the jury that he was not asking for mercy but justice, and said that he understood that his own professional prospects were at an end; and finally:

> Already the minds of the people of England are veering towards the polar star of truth.... At such an epoch,... when thrones are vibrating on the precipice of destruction, it doth not bespeak wisdom in its government to cry down and punish the efforts of the well-intentioned. It is a measure hostile to its own security; but if I must yet be doomed to languish out the most precious moments of my life in a prison, fatal as it must be to my interest, blasting everywhere my hopes, and sinking me down completely into ruin, my mind shall be equal to the task – it shall bear with

calmness and serenity the worst of ills, in support of a cause whose basis is truth, and whose object is the liberty of my country.

Hotham and Yorke then called several witnesses to give the defendant's version of the Castle Hill meeting, and Law replied for the Crown. Rooke J. summed up: he explained to the jury that they were to consider whether it was Yorke's intention merely to enlighten the minds of the people upon a speculative point, or to carry them a step farther, and excite a spirit of discontent, disaffection, and sedition in their minds; in that case, he was guilty of seditious conspiracy.

The jury retired and brought in a verdict of Guilty. Yorke was brought up for judgment in the Court of King's Bench in the following Michaelmas term, and was imprisoned for two years in Dorchester gaol.

It is said that two of the objects of imprisonment are the reform and rehabilitation of the prisoner; if ever those objects were achieved, it was in the case of Henry Yorke. Shortly after his release from Dorchester gaol, he married the keeper's daughter, and shortly after that he was called to the bar by the Inner Temple. At York assizes he had demonstrated a talent for advocacy which rivalled that of Erskine himself, but regrettably he was taken ill and died in 1813.[4]

*   *   *

It will be recalled that Hamilton Rowan was in prison in the Dublin Newgate. On the day after he met William Jackson and John Cockayne, he persuaded the gaoler to go with him to his own home, where a rope was already slung out of a two-pair-of-stairs window; so Rowan went upstairs, climbed down the rope to the garden, took a horse out of the stables and made good his escape. He went to Buldoyle, four miles from Dublin, to meet the owner of a small pleasure boat, who managed to procure three sailors, two of whom were smugglers and knew well the coasts of both France and Ireland; and a few days later he landed at Roscoff.

Rowan was now outlawed, and therefore under sentence of death. He stayed in France for a year, and then went to America. Later he was permitted to meet his family – he had eight children – in Denmark, and for a time they lived together in Hamburg. During the Peace of 1803, a pardon was negotiated for him and this was granted in the Court of King's Bench in Dublin on 1 July 1805.

*   *   *

William Jackson had been arrested in Dublin on 28 April 1794, and was charged with treason by adhering to the enemy. His trial was postponed from time to time, first at the request of the defendant whose wife had gone to England in search of witnesses, and later at the request of the prosecution, some of whose witnesses had been stranded at Holyhead by a storm, and in particular because John Cockayne was ill and had been advised by his surgeon not to travel.

One evening during his long period in custody, Jackson was entertaining a friend in Newgate; when the time came for the visitor to go, Jackson took him to the gate where he found the turnkey fast asleep, so he borrowed the keys to let him out; he himself could easily have escaped, but rather than get the turnkey into trouble he locked the gates again and returned to his cell.[5]

The trial was fixed for 23 April 1795. On 22 April, Cockayne was back in Dublin. That night William Lawler (who told the story six months later, when he had turned King's Evidence and was a witness against a Defender), and two other men made a plan to kidnap Cockayne so that he would not be able to give evidence at the trial; but after walking round Dublin for some four hours without finding him, they abandoned the idea.

Cockayne was the principal witness for the Crown. Even from reading the bare text of the transcript, page after page, it is obvious that he was a very sick man. The Attorney-General for Ireland, Arthur Wolfe, took the examination himself, and had considerable difficulty in extracting the story – 'My spirits are so agitated at this moment', said the witness at one point, 'that I cannot recollect. I am very sorry to detain the Court; I have really lost every idea of where I was'. And later, in cross-examination by Curran, counsel for the defence, who had asked him if his memory had been shattered, he said, 'It grieves my mind more than I can describe, to see that gentleman in that situation'. He had to admit that he had come to Ireland to spy on his client and he thought that his own life was in danger. Later a witness was called by the defence to give evidence as to Cockayne's character, and told the Court that 'There was neither morality nor integrity in it'.

However, the documentary evidence against Jackson was incontrovertible, and there was little that Curran could say. Some time after midnight, the Earl of Clonmel CJ summed up; he allowed the defendant to interrupt him on several occasions to comment on various items of evidence – 'There is another circumstance I must mention', he said at one point, 'I am afraid I shall tire your lordship'. 'No, sir, go on', replied the Earl, 'nothing can tire me on this occasion'. At 4.15 a.m. the jury retired, and returned half an hour later with a verdict of Guilty, and a rider recommending mercy for the prisoner. The Court declared that four days must elapse before judgment could be pronounced, and the case was adjourned until Thursday 30 April.

＊ ＊ ＊

Early that Thursday morning, Mrs Jackson visited her husband in Newgate. When he was brought into Court, the Earl of Clonmel CJ noticed that he was ill and requested a surgeon to go into the dock and examine him; he did so, and reported that he thought that the prisoner 'would go off immediately'. An apothecary happened to be in the jury box, and he too went to examine the prisoner, and came back to report, under oath, that he was certainly dying. So the Earl adjourned the Court and ordered Jackson to be taken away and remanded until further notice; but before this could be done, the Sheriff reported that he had died.

And so the Court adjourned, and the body was left in the dock until the following morning, when two surgeons opened it and found 'near a pint of acrid matter in the stomach, which was entirely corroded'; they were of opinion that this was a metallic poison, and that no normal diet could have caused it. It was generally believed that Mrs Jackson had brought some poison into the prison that morning and that her husband had committed suicide.

❊   ❊   ❊

The trial of William Stone was postponed until Thursday 28 January 1796. The case had the feel of a piece of unfinished business left over from a different era. *R.* v. *Hardy* and *R.* v. *Horne Tooke* were already part of history; the reports of these cases were now in print, and counsel had the massive volumes on the table in front of them. On 29 October 1795, a shot had been fired at the King on his way to open Parliament, and the government immediately introduced, and Parliament passed, as often in times of crisis, a new Treason Act to extend the scope of the law. In France, hundreds had been shaved by the national razor, hundreds drowned in the national bath. Tom Paine, after a year's imprisonment, had only escaped death because the turnkey had made a mistake in failing to chalk the fatal cross on the door of his cell.[6] By now, as Erskine said during this trial, a man must be either a madman or a fool to wish for revolution.

Stone was tried at a regular sitting of the Court of King's Bench at Westminster Hall; Kenyon CJ presided, along with the other three judges of the Court, Ashurst, Grose and Lawrence JJ. The team of prosecuting counsel was the same as in 1794, but with one important difference: Serjeant Adair had changed sides, and was briefed as leading counsel for the defence; Erskine was his junior, an unusual part for him, and Gibbs was relegated to the silent role of assistant counsel. Stone was charged with compassing the death of the King, a formality, and with adhering to the enemy; and on this charge the evidence of the Crown was overwhelming. Hurford Stone, the defendant's brother, had thrown in his lot with France: that could not be denied, and was not denied. William Jackson was a traitor: an Irish jury had found him so. And William Stone was implicated beyond all doubt with both of them.

Much of the first day of the trial was taken up with reading the documents which had been found at Old Ford; witnesses were called in the evening, among them John Cockayne, evidently recovered now, and giving evidence like anyone else. At about 9 p.m., there was some discussion as to how long the case was likely to continue; the Attorney-General thought that the case for the Crown might last another four hours, and Kenyon CJ said: 'I hope four hours will not wear out either the strength or spirits of the jury'. And one of the jurors said: 'I am not a young man. I wish to understand this matter perfectly right; it is a case of life or death: I may be wearied out, and perhaps by-and-by be asleep'. They continued for another hour; by then the Court had sat from 9 a.m. without any interruption or refreshment, and the jury then spent the night at the Swan Tavern in Bridge Street.

The following morning Serjeant Adair addressed the jury and the defence called a string of witnesses, friends and acquaintances of the defendant who gave evidence as to his good character. As Erskine was junior counsel, he spoke after the close of the defence and spoke for a couple of hours, a relatively short speech for him. He analysed the evidence, item by item, in an endeavour to show that his client could never have had the intention of assisting the enemy. The Solicitor-General replied for the Crown; he had already embarked on his speech when Kenyon CJ remembered that he had failed to ask the defendant whether he wished to say anything on his own behalf, so he had to interrupt him; but Stone had nothing to say.

So the Solicitor-General proceeded, and demolished, one by one, all the arguments of Serjeant Adair and Erskine. The cornerstone of the case for the Crown was the detailed survey of the state of the nation, which Stone had prepared for Jackson to transmit to the French government. As the advice was that an invasion would be stoutly resisted, and was designed to avert, not to encourage, such a calamity, this was written, defending counsel had said, to assist England, not the enemy: not so, replied the Crown – any communication with the enemy necessarily involved giving them aid and assistance. Stone had sought the advice of the Prime Minister: yes, but the information given to him was incomplete if not positively misleading. Stone had consulted various distinguished men as to his course of action: indeed he had, and the Crown had called them to say that he had disregarded the advice which they had given him. Stone had genuinely believed that Jackson was an American gentleman and that their correspondence was on purely commercial matters: how could this be reconciled with the fact that Jackson had been introduced to him by his brother Hurford, an avowed supporter of the French government? Jackson, it had been argued, had used the name Popkins simply to disguise himself from his creditors: if so, then from whom was Stone trying to disguise himself in using the name Enots?

At about 7 p.m. that evening, Kenyon CJ started to sum up. After a few opening remarks, he referred to the length of the case and his own fatigue: 'I cannot but lament a little, that, in my own case, I certainly do feel a very considerable degree of fatigue; but the duty is cast upon me, and I will perform it as well as I am able'. He directed the jury on the law, to the effect that any correspondence with the enemy, to enable them to annoy us or to defend themselves, constituted the crime of treason by adhering to the enemy. He reviewed the evidence and the arguments on each side; towards the end, he referred to an observation which, he said, had been made by Erskine, and Erskine interrupted to say that he had been misunderstood; and the Attorney-General intervened and Grose J. joined in to say that counsel did not differ. But no sooner had that problem been disposed of when a juror asked whether the intention of the prisoner was not necessarily to be considered, or the mere act, and Kenyon CJ replied, 'You will consider the intention in the evidence'.

The situation was becoming increasingly confused; Eyre CJ would never have allowed himself to get into such a scrape. Lawrence J. intervened in an attempt to clarify the position:

> It has been stated by the counsel for the prisoner, as I understand (if I am mistaken I wish to be corrected) that the question was, whether he acted *bona fide*, or with the traitorous intention stated in the indictment.

But then he went off on a discussion as to whether and when the correspondence between the Stone brothers had been interrupted; Serjeant Adair said that it had been interrupted, and then the Attorney-General joined in:

> This is getting into great irregularity; but if counsel are thus to break in after the Court has summed up, I should wish to observe concerning the account of Popkins and Enots.

Lawrence J. and Erskine had a further discussion, and the Attorney-General said he thought that Lawrence J. had been accurate; and Grose J. read out his own note, and Kenyon CJ said that that was what he had told the jury. Grose J. said the question was now clear, and so, at 8.10 p.m., the jury retired. They returned at 11 p.m.; the verdict was Not Guilty. It was a perverse verdict, but it is the privilege of a jury to be perverse. Perhaps they thought that the prisoner had suffered enough: his business was in ruins, and Erskine had told them that if he was acquitted on the criminal charge, he would at once be confined in a debtor's prison.

When the verdict was announced, some people in Court clapped their hands and huzzaed; one gentlemen, Mr Richard Thompson, was particularly noted by the Court and was fined £20.

CHAPTER 19

THE AFTERMATH

I The Cordwainer and the Hoary Traitor

It was all over now. The papers were cleared away, back into their bags and boxes, back into the Treasury Solicitor's office. Some of those who had been through the ordeal found that any return to normal life was impossible. Holcroft's dramas were assailed by his political opponents, and he left the country to live in Germany; Thomas Walker was ruined by his business rivals; Thelwall was pursued by spies wherever he went.

For others, it was a time of triumph and rejoicing. Medals were struck; one bore on the obverse the profiles of Hardy, Horne Tooke and Thelwall, and on the reverse the portraits of Erskine and Gibbs and the names of all the thirty-six jurors who had acquitted them; it was engraved in Round Court, St Martin's le Grand, and sold there, in silver for £1.11.6 or in copper for 1/6d. There were others of Hardy, and of Lord Stanhope inscribed, 'Minority of One', and of Horne Tooke, and of Daniel Eaton with pigs and a cock. (See Figure 17.)

The Society for Constitutional Information, with its papers impounded and its secretary in custody, had virtually ceased to exist, and only met once more, in 1795, to protest against the new Treason and Seditious Meetings Act. The Friends of the People ceased to function. There is no record that the Sheffield society ever met again. The London Corresponding Society, on the other hand, in spite of the imprisonment of its secretary and other prominent members, and in spite of infiltration by spies, survived the events of May 1794; Francis Place, a journeyman breeches-maker, became a member at this time and took over its administration. The Society continued to meet throughout the summer and autumn of 1794, and raised at least £300 to support the defendants and their families.[1]

Hardy himself again considered the prospect of emigrating to America, but many of his friends promised him financial assistance and encouraged him to resume his business, which he did, on 29 November, at 36 Tavistock Street, Covent Garden. At first business boomed. For two weeks, he was fully employed in entering the orders in his book, while another man was fully employed simply in taking measurements. Many of his customers paid in

Figure 17. Medals celebrating the aquittals:
(i)   Obverse – Hardy, Horne Tooke and Thelwall. Reverse – Erskine and Gibbs,
        and the names of the 36 jurors who tried the three cases.
(ii)   Hardy, probably struck by a Birmingham token manufacturer.
(iii)   An example of Thomas Spence's political tokens.
(iv)   Four men dancing round a pole surmounted by the head of William Pitt.
(By permission of the Trustees of the British Museum.)

advance, some a guinea for two pairs of shoes, some even a guinea for one pair.
Crowds of people, of all ranks and both sexes, came to congratulate him, and
collected round his shop, curious to see him. The shop was full from morning
to night; at one time, he employed six men. However, the fashion soon
passed, and the crowds went away. Some shoemakers in those days employed

journeymen and apprentices, others set up shop in a garret or a cellar; 2/6d was enough to start in business, and sometimes half-a-dozen men would share a room. The shoemakers' Guild was the Cordwainers Company, so-called because they worked in cordovan, the fine leather from Cordoba in Spain, and they tried to squeeze the garret-masters out of business, but without success, so the trade was swamped.[2] Hardy's journeymen struck for higher wages, and promises of credit were not honoured; some of his so-called friends borrowed money and failed to repay it; and within 12 months, he found that there was enough work for only one shopman.

When Hardy had been arrested, the King's Messengers had seized his pocket-book which contained two bills of exchange, one for £136 and the other for £60. Some time after his acquittal, he set about the task of recovering the bills. He wrote to Secretary Dundas but was told that the Duke of Portland had taken over the Home Department; so he wrote to the Duke but received no reply. He then wrote to the King in Council – 'Your ministers have bereaved me of my wife and my child; they have attempted to take away my life and . . . have done everything in their power to destroy my good name in society . . . Your ministers have robbed me of my property – it is now in their hands . . .'. Again he received no reply, so he attempted to have the matter raised in Parliament, but this was the time when Fox and the rump of the Whig opposition had withdrawn from the House Commons. Eventually, in November 1797, Hardy had the whole correspondence published in the newspapers. The government had other financial problems to worry about, for the Prince of Wales was found to be in debt to the tune of £650,000; Hardy's £196 was never restored to him.

In the summer of 1795, Hardy went on holiday and toured the midlands. At Northampton, a gentleman happened to pick up one of his cards, which a lady had left on the parlour table while the travellers were having breakfast; as soon as he saw what it was, he threw it down and said that the jury which had acquitted Hardy were a set of villains; one of the ladies in the party reproved him for speaking in such a manner, and he said little more during the journey; the rest of the party kept up a cheerful conversation, in which Hardy, whose identity was unknown to them, joined. When the passengers alighted at the Bell Inn, Leicester, Hardy approached the ill-tempered gentleman, took his hand, and said: 'Friend, you have had the mortification to travel in the same coach with that Hardy whom you have been so illiberally abusing. I am that Hardy – farewell.' The stranger stood with astonishment, and went away without saying a word, to the great amusement of the other passengers. From Leicester, he proceeded to Nottingham and Derby; and the following summer he toured East Anglia.

On 29 June 1795, the London Corresponding Society held a mass meeting in St George's Fields, and another one in the fields next to the Copenhagen Tavern in Islington on 26 October; over 100,000 people are said to have attended these meetings, and they were addressed by John Binns, a young Irish American; it was these meetings that led to the government's decision to pass the Seditious Meetings Act. There were rumours that members of the

Society were in contact with the naval mutineers in 1797, and on 31 July, in defiance of the Act, they held another public meeting.[3]

In October of that same year, Hardy moved his business to No. 161 Fleet Street, and only a few days later illuminations were held to celebrate Admiral Duncan's victory at the battle of Camperdown. It was alleged, by 'an old inhabitant of Fleet Street', that Hardy had not only refused to light up his windows, but had sallied out of his house with a gang of ruffians, and set about the crowd outside; Hardy emphatically denied these allegations. Probably the truth of the matter was as recorded by John Binns in his own *Memoirs*, where he wrote that Hardy would not allow his windows to be illuminated, and the loyalist crowd threatened to break the windows and sack his home. About 100 men, members of the Society, many of them Irish, armed with shillelaks, took post close to Hardy's home; an immense crowd gathered in the street; many violent attacks were made, and many wounds were inflicted with fists and sticks. About 11 p.m. a troop of horses arrived, and soon after the crowd dispersed. 'I never was in so long-continued and well-conducted a fight', wrote Binns, 'as was made that night by those who defended Hardy's house against overwhelming numbers.'[4]

In the following year, the government obtained evidence that the Society was in league with the United Irishmen when Ireland was on the verge of rebellion; further arrests were made and the Society ceased to exist on 19 April 1798. Hardy agreed to act as the treasurer of a fund set up to support those who had been arrested, but otherwise he was no longer taking any active part in political matters.

*   *   *

In 1810 Maurice Margarot came home from Australia, the only one of the 'Scottish martyrs' to do so.

It was only in 1787 that the First Fleet of convicts had sailed to Botany Bay;[5] on their arrival, it was found that the site was quite unsuitable for a penal colony, and it was transferred a few miles north to Sydney Cove, although it was always referred to as 'Botany Bay' in this country. One of the ships which sailed in the Second Fleet in 1790 was the *Surprize* transport, built as a slaver and equipped with shackles; of 254 convicts on board, 36 died on the journey. This was the ship on which Margarot, Muir, Skirving and Fysshe Palmer set out in the spring of 1794. Almost at once, Margarot quarrelled with the others, and told the captain, Patrick Campbell, that 'good kind of man', that they were planning to murder him and his crew; as a result, the other three spent the voyage in chains, Fysshe Palmer suffering from dysentery throughout. However, they all arrived safely in Sydney on 25 October; as the first political prisoners in the colony, they were treated with special favours;[6] the number of convicts with any degree of education was very small and the Governor was glad to make use of their talents; Skirving, the farmer, was granted a hundred acres of land; Fysshe Palmer, who found a cure for his dysentery – cerated[7] glass of antimony and ipecacuanha – was the only man in the colony with an encyclopaedia and learnt to brew beer and make soap; and later contrived to build a boat.

Having been tried later than the others, Gerrald missed the sailing time; he travelled on a later Fleet and reached Australia in 1795, and died soon afterwards; Skirving also died of dysentery.

Muir managed to escape; early in 1796, he rowed out to an American ship in Sydney harbour and was taken to Alaska; there he transferred to a Spanish ship and sailed to California, and thence overland to Vera Cruz and so to Cuba where he was interned; later, he was put on another ship which encountered a British frigate off Cadiz and in the ensuing battle a shell exploded in his face and blinded him in one eye, so he was put ashore and taken to a prison hospital. There he stayed for several months until news of him reached his friends in France, and Talleyrand negotiated his release and brought him to Paris; there, it is said, he helped to plan an invasion of Scotland, in the belief that his countrymen would rise in arms to welcome the French.[8] He died at Chantilly in January 1799.[9]

Fysshe Palmer served his term of seven years, and bought a boat with the intention of sailing home with some friends; the boat was in a wretched condition, but they managed to reach New Zealand and thence set out into the Pacific; after numerous adventures and attempts to repair the boat, they landed on Guam, which was a colony of Spain, now at war with England; they were interned by the Spanish governor, and Fysshe Palmer himself died there in 1802.

There remained Margarot. He served his term of fourteen years, and there were stories that he was in league with the governor and spying on other convicts. In 1810 he returned home with his wife and a cat, at a cost of £450; he sought compensation for having served longer than his term, and gave evidence to a committee of the House of Commons which was inquiring into the running of the colony. There is a story that he travelled to Edinburgh and dined with one of the jurors who had convicted him. In spite of the way in which he had treated his fellow-prisoners, Hardy described him as a 'man of a strong philosophical understanding, ready wit, undaunted courage, and incorruptible integrity', and he raised a subscription for him. When he died, Hardy attended his funeral on 19 November 1815, and raised a further subscription of £200 for his widow.[10]

It was not quite the end of the story. In 1844, an obelisk was erected on Calton Hill in Edinburgh 'by the friends of Parliamentary Reform in England and Scotland' in memory of the five 'martyrs', whose names were engraved on the stone – upon which Lord Cockburn commented, 'How the judges' names are omitted I cannot understand. For it is, in truth, *their* monument'.[11]

*   *   *

Hardy himself continued in business until 1815, becoming a Freeman of the Cordwainers' Company and a Liveryman of the Needlemakers Company. Every fifth of November throughout all this time, and indeed until the end of his life, a dinner was held to celebrate the anniversary of his acquittal; his health was drunk, and he replied with a speech or, in later years, an address. Erskine was not invited to these dinners, so that his praise might be sounded more freely.

This was a time of depression; many tradesmen were going bankrupt, and Hardy was having difficulty in collecting his debts; he was now 63 and in declining health. He had managed to save £700, and at midsummer he retired; he still lived frugally and had no one to support except himself and his sister, and he thought that the £700 would suffice for the rest of his life. However, soon after retirement, his health rapidly improved. Macpherson, the author of the Advertisement to his *Memoir*, describes him at this time:

> In his person, Mr Hardy was of fine proportions, near six feet high, before he began to stoop; large breasted, broad shouldered, and muscular, without the least inclination to corpulence. He was, indeed, such a man, in body and mind, as we may suppose the patriots to have been who followed those immortal heroes, an Alfred and a Wallace, in their attempts to give freedom to their respective countries.

His frugal life stood him in good stead; apart from some slight rheumatic pains in his legs, he remained in good health throughout his 70s, and when his savings ran out, Sir Francis Burdett (to whom the *Memoir* was dedicated) and a few friends clubbed together and provided him with about £100 a year.

During this period, although he refused to join any societies or stand for any elections, Hardy was taking a renewed interest in politics. He retained his enthusiastic support for the French Revolution, and later for Napoleon. He often wrote letters to the press on a variety of topics and during the Peace of Amiens he wrote one to Napoleon which included part of his Address to the French Nation – 'Peace reigns on earth and this is the work of Frenchmen'.[12] One of his prized possessions was a piece of one of Napoleon's greatcoats which he acquired in the year after Waterloo.

For many years, Francis Place had been planning to write a history of the London Corresponding Society; the first part of the *Memoir*, written about 1798, had been intended as a contribution to this work. But the years, and the decades, went by, and although Place assembled no less than seven volumes of documents and other material, the history never came to fruition, so eventually Hardy decided to publish his *Memoir* separately.

✻   ✻   ✻

The health of Horne Tooke, the Hoary Traitor, continued to decline; frequent attacks of gout were so severe that he was unable to add to his income, even by his literary pursuits. He resolved to let his house and to move into a little white cottage, two hundred yards away on Wimbledon Common; but when news of his financial straits reached his friends, they rallied round and raised an annuity for him to enable him to stay in his home. The two Harte girls continued to live with him. He had them both taught drawing; he employed William Sharp to teach them engraving, and often had him to stay at Wimbledon for a week or more at a time for this purpose.

According to his biographer, he embarked on a period of cautious retirement and moderation of language; but this did not last for long. There was a general election in the spring of 1796, and Horne Tooke stood again, along with Fox and Admiral Sir Alan Gardner, as a candidate at Westminster.

He displayed all his old physical and mental vigour. His election address opened with these words:

> It is only in times like the present, when attempts are flagitiously made to murder innocent men, that the progress of a candidate can possibly be from the hustings to Newgate, and from Newgate back to the hustings ...

And he described the government as a 'tyranny ... under a temporary, elective dictator, dependant only upon his own corrupt and prostituted votes', and accused them of 'master-treason against the crown, the nobility, and the whole commons of the realm'.

The poll took place over fifteen days, in May and June. Horne Tooke spoke on every day of the poll with his old vitality and invective. He attacked the Admiral, the government candidate, for holding a sinecure as a Major General of Marines; he virtually accused the Prime Minister of perjury, alleging that he had endeavoured to take his life for

> following his own instructions. They certainly were his own instructions, for I have them in his own hand-writing. And yet I ought to be cautious how I say certainly, as I have no better authority for it than the minister's own oath in the late trials at the Old Bailey.

It was his next door neighbour (see Figure 18), however, who received the most savage onslaught. On the first day of the poll, the constable who had arrested Horne Tooke gave him his vote, and some days later the candidate explained why he had done so:

> The constable complains that Mr Dundas... – that this scoundrel – I desire to be clearly understood – let me be fairly understood. I mean that he is a *scoundrel* both as a secretary of state and as a man.... He complained that this secretary of state, who sends him to take up and put in dungeons better men than himself, never paid him a farthing for his trouble. He complains that they owe him near three hundred pounds.
>
> Mr Dundas, my next door neighbour, and who had been so for two years, knew perfectly well the situation of my family, with which others of the ministry might not, perhaps, be acquainted; but he knew it well. My family consists singly of myself, and two young women my children. He, a father of children himself, took me away suddenly ... and left my house and my family for twelve days and nights in the possession of four common thief-takers from the police-office.
>
> It almost overpowers me when I think of it. Look at the refinement of this man's malice; it was not enough that their father's head should be stuck upon a pole, that his body should be quartered, that his fortune should be confiscated, and that his children should be sent out naked and friendless, and beggars into the world, unless he could contrive that they should be sent out *dishonoured* too.

Another man who came to give Horne Tooke his vote was John Wilkes, now the chamberlain of London; he was an old man now, and it was one of his last public acts – he died a few months later.

Fox and the Admiral were elected, and in a letter to the constituents of Westminster the defeated candidate promised to present himself to them

Figure 18. Henry Dundas, Lord Melville. (By permission of the Wimbledon Society.)

again. But it was not to be, for five years later this life-long enemy of borough-mongers became the representative of Old Sarum, that miserable and deserted hamlet, which was and always has been regarded as the classical example of a pocket borough. He was nominated by Lord Camelford, an eccentric peer with a taste for science and an ungovernable temper. Horne Tooke only consented to accept the nomination after he had met his Lordship and had sat up three days and nights with him. The story was that the sole electors were Lord Camelford's butler and steward, but there were in fact six names on the roll. And so, on 16 February 1801, Horne Tooke took his seat in the House and shook hands with the Speaker; it was a most singular incident, for the Speaker was none other than Sir John Mitford, who, as Solicitor-General, had endeavoured to secure the new member's conviction on a capital charge: 'But [Sir John's] urbanity...', says Stephens, 'and the courtesy of the representative for Old Sarum rendered the scene less embarrassing, perhaps, than it would otherwise have been'. Hardly had he taken his seat in the House of Commons when a motion was put down to declare it vacant on the ground that, as an ordained priest, he was disqualified from membership. In the short time that he sat in Parliament, he took an active part in debates – on the poor law, the state of agriculture, and the recent unsuccessful attack on Ferrol. But it was in the committee set up to consider his own eligibility that he most distinguished himself, analysing all the arguments brought against him with the most meticulous care, and pouring scorn upon his opponents; the sub-committee appointed to examine the ancient records, he said, did not even understand the characters of the Saxon alphabet; as for the theory that a priest could not resign the priesthood, that doctrine must appear futile since there were so many canons on the deposition of priests:

> One of these states that if any clergyman attempted to cast out devils unlawfully, such person should be deposed. Now, for example, Mr Speaker, if I had attempted to cast the devil out of this House, I must have been deposed, and of course deemed eligible. But, in this case, my only crime is innocence – my only guilt, that of not having scandalized my order. I feel myself, sir, exactly in the situation of the girl who applied for reception into the Magdalen. On being asked the particulars of her misfortune, she answered, she was as innocent as the child unborn: the reply was, 'This is a place only for the creatures of *prostitution*; you must go and qualify yourself before you can be admitted'.

The committee dropped the issue but a bill was introduced to declare all clergymen of the established church to be ineligible to sit in the House of Commons. This led to the presentation of a petition by the Revd Edward Rushworth: not only had he sat in the House for many years, but a committee had declared unanimously that he was eligible to sit notwithstanding that he was a priest. But it was of no avail; the bill was passed by both Houses and became the Act now known as the House of Commons (Clergy Disqualification) Act 1801, which imposes a ban on clergy of the established Church from sitting as members of the House. Horne Tooke was permitted to retain his seat until Parliament was dissolved the following year; and he then addressed his final letter to the constituents of Westminster:

It has lately, for the first time, been discovered, that something (I know not what) mysterious, miraculous, and supernatural, was operated upon me nearly half a century ago, in this protestant country, which has divested me, at the close of my life, of the common rights of a man and a citizen. I am thus prevented, by a miracle, from keeping my word, and offering to you again my services in parliament.

He went on to say that in any event his infirmity already disqualified him from any considerable exertion in the legislature, and he thanked the electors for their past support.

*   *   *

Horne Tooke had many friends who dined with him at Wimbledon: there were his doctors, George Pearson and Mr Cline (the latter held a dinner at his home in Lincoln's Inn Square for many years on the anniversary of the acquittal of his patient); Joel Barlow, when he was in England, now back from the United States as ambassador to the court of Napoleon; the officers of the horse-guards and foot-guards who had conducted the Hoary Traitor 'with all the pomp and circumstance of glorious war' to Newgate, the Old Bailey and the Tower; Sir Humphrey Davy; Sir James Mackintosh. In addition, there was James Moody, a Carnaby Street shoe warehouseman who had been Horne Tooke's secretary at the Westminster election of 1796, and who was in the service of the government as a spy under the code-name 'Notary', and who kept reporting on his host's activities; in 1803 he reported that the Wimbledon circle was sympathetic to sedition, that Horne Tooke's house was its headquarters, and that Horne Tooke himself was its High Priest.[13] One Sunday, John Baxter (the author, now, of a major History of England)[14] arrived, uninvited, just as dinner was ready; the host had forgotten who he was, but asked him to come into the room where the guests were sitting, and the visitor reminded him that he had been a fellow-prisoner of his, and had taken the liberty of coming to Wimbledon to pay his respects. Horne Tooke remembered him at once:

> Ah, my good sir! I recollect you well! Gentlemen, permit me to introduce a brother sufferer to you; he is a little fellow, whom I never saw but once before; but he is at the same time a hero: for while we were in the *bail dock*, about to be arraigned, and as yet uncertain of our fate, he stepped forward to me, and exclaimed: 'Mr Tooke, our lives have hitherto been but of little service to our country; let us then behave like men, and see, if by dying bravely, we cannot prove of some service to the commonwealth'.

The company applauded, and the guest joined them for dinner.

It is safe to say that Horne Tooke's immediate neighbour was not one to receive invitations to these dinners, but Thomas Erskine kept a foot in both camps. On one occasion, he was talking in the garden with the other visitors, when he saw William Pitt in Dundas's garden next door, so he immediately sprang over the ha-ha to join him.

Another near neighbour, and a frequent visitor at the Sunday dinners, was Sir Francis Burdett, MP. In 1805, it is said, Napoleon had designated him as the President of England had a successful invasion been carried into effect.[15] He belonged to the new generation of radical reformers, a young man after Horne Tooke's heart, and he treated him like his own son.

If Horne Tooke was prevented from debating across the floor of the House of Commons, he had plenty of scope for arguing across his dinner table. He had a wide knowledge of many subjects: history; philosophy; literature; language; law – the law, he said, ought to be, not a luxury for the rich, but a remedy to be easily obtainable by the poor; when told that the courts were open to all, he replied, 'and so is the London Tavern – to such as can pay for the entertainment'.[16] Stephens records only one instance when Horne Tooke brought a conversation peremptorily to a close. The company had been discussing the identity of Junius, the notorious (but anonymous) political journalist of the 1760s, and someone asked if he knew who the author was; he immediately crossed his knife and fork on his plate, and said, 'I do'; his manner and tone were too formidable to admit of any further questions. It is, indeed, not outside the bounds of possiblity that he was Junius himself.[17]

Horne Tooke now devoted more time to his literary efforts, and in 1805 he published the second volume of his great grammar, *The Diversions of Purley*; it was dedicated to his counsel and jury, and consisted of a dialogue between himself and Sir Francis Burdett. The work was evidently a bestseller, and the author made a profit of £4000 or £5000 out of the two volumes. A third volume was planned, but during his last illness the author decided to burn his entire collection of papers; he and one of the girls spent a month carrying out this operation in a room upstairs, and everything was destroyed; his own greatcoat was badly singed during this process and was unfit to be worn again.

The author was also busy in his garden, coating his grass with manure which he had brought in from London at a guinea a load. In 1805 he wrote to Major Cartwright to tell him that he was about to send him some gooseberries, currants and strawberries of different sorts, and some fine red and white raspberry roots.

Horne Tooke's health continued to deteriorate, and in 1810 he was very seriously ill; on his recovery he became addicted to grapes; jars of Portuguese grapes were obtained from the importers in Thames Street, and when this supply failed, he purchased and devoured the entire crop of a hothouse in Chelsea; as well as jargonel pears from his own garden. 'What could this stomach be composed of?' Stephens used to ask himself; and indeed, like that of an ostrich, it seemed capable of dissolving iron:

> It was often occupied in digesting the most crude materials. He was accustomed to swallow cucumbers, melons, and pickled salmon, in great quantities, with impunity. Roast and boiled; white meats and brown; fish, either fresh or salted; pies, puddings, preserves, apples, pears, and walnuts, seemed all to be swallowed indiscriminately, without fear, and without danger.

In October 1810, Stephens visited Wimbledon. Horne Tooke was still ill, but he had made some degree of recovery. Two of his servants carried him to a wheelchair in the garden; Sir Francis Burdett was there, the two girls, and

John Wildman, his nephew, and they all went in procession to the kitchen garden where Stephens saw a mound of earth with a stone slab resting on it; he thought at first that it was the foundation for a summer house, but on further examination he saw that it was inscribed:

JOHN HORNE TOOKE
LATE PROPRIETOR,
AND NOW OCCUPIER OF THIS SPOT
was
BORN IN JUNE, 1736
and
DIED........
IN THE   YEAR OF HIS AGE
CONTENT AND GRATEFUL

The slab was black Irish marble, and beneath it was the vault intended for his burial. The party then returned to the parlour for dinner – turbot with lobster sauce, beef *en ragoût*, and a capon; walnuts, grapes, apples, pears and plums from the garden; Madeira and Port.

Figure 19. Horne Tooke in his old age. (By permission of the Trustees of the British Museum.)

During the next few months, the old man's health continued to decline (see Figure 19); he had gallstones; he became dropsical; he spent his time on a sofa, or in a bath chair; but he dressed well in a new suit of peach-coloured cloth. He told Stephens, much to his surprise, that he intended to make him one of his heirs; the 'legacy' turned out to be one of Boulton's copying machines,[18] which came in a cart a few days later, along with a mahogany table to put it on.

In the spring of 1811, he had his last brush with authority, in the person of the tax-gatherers. Back in 1799, when income tax was first introduced, the commissioner had written to him to say that he had reason to believe that his income exceeded £60 a year – 'I have much more reason than the commissioners can have to be dissatisfied with the smallness of my income', he had written in reply. And when a tax on hats was imposed, 'he conceived the strange and very extraordinary resolution of doing without them'; in those days, a failure to wear a hat was regarded as a health hazard by exposing the head to rheums and colds, but Horne Tooke propounded a theory that 'when the hair begins to fall, the skull at the same time begins to thicken; nay, it becomes thick and more hard, in consequence of exposure to the air, by being left without a covering'; so he refused to buy a new hat, and ostentatiously carried his old one under his arm.

In May 1811, Horne Tooke received a tax demand for 'himself, £3.11.0, tenantry $4^1/_2$d, stamp 2d'. On inquiring the reason for the $4^1/_2$d, he was informed that it was his share of a tithe to the clergyman, and he formed the opinion that it was illegal. Ill as he was, and in spite of the trivial size of the charge, he decided that it was an issue of public concern and refused to pay. The collector was a neighbour in Wimbledon who found himself in an embarrassing position, but he felt that he had no alternative but to enforce the demand by distraining on the tax-payer's property, so he visited his house and seized the item which he thought would least inconvenience the family, which happened to be a tea-chest belonging to one of the girls; but the collector lost his nerve, and returned the chest before the question could be tried in court. Everyone in the parish heard that Horne Tooke had refused to pay his $4^1/_2$d and so they all did likewise.

By now, the dropsy had become acute; the skin of the ankles ruptured and the liquid drained off, and painful dressings had to be applied; the patient became peevish and irritable, but his mind remained clear and whenever Stephens visited him, he was still able to converse on a variety of topics. And his appetite remained undiminished: on 11 February 1812, a relative wrote to a medical friend (both unidentified):

Our patient (or rather impatient) is wonderfully well – eating plenty of rich soup instead of coffee; in the course of the day, six dozen of large oysters, with wine, ale, imperial drink, milk, tea, muffins, and the juice of sixteen oranges; and on Sunday he drank the juice of twenty-eight! I wish you would tell me what his *stomach must be lined with*; I think it must be *gold*.

About a fortnight later, Horne Tooke heard that Dr Pearson had been bitten by a mad dog, and he wrote his last letter:

Wimbledon, Feb. 26, 1812.

My Dear Sir.

Though I have forborne to write, because I would not be troublesome, yet I am very anxious about your health. For God's sake, let some of your family tell me how you are.

J. H. Tooke

Early in March, one of the girls noticed a livid spot on her father's foot; Dr Pearson and Mr Cline were summoned, but there was nothing more that they could do, and he died, aged 76, in the evening of 18 March 1812. His wish to be buried in his garden was disregarded, partly because the vault had been flooded, and partly because the family feared that the presence of a grave would diminish the value of the property; instead, he was interred beside his mother and sister in the parish church of Ealing. He had always hated pomp and pageantry at funerals, and his was a simple one; the procession consisted of his nephew, John Wildman, Sir Francis Burdett, and a few close friends; 'Mr Pearson' was there, presumably George Pearson and evidently recovered from his bite; and 'Mr Hardy' and 'Mr Adams', whom Stephens does not further identify, but it is reasonable to suppose that they were Horne Tooke's colleagues from 1794.

II Lord Eldon and Lord Erskine

The Treason Trials are described about half way through the first of the three volumes of Horace Twiss's Life of Lord Eldon; to him, as to Lord Campbell, they were not the climax of his career, but merely the end of the beginning.

Sir John Scott remained, throughout the rest of that memorable decade, the principal legal adviser to the Crown. There were other cases of treason: Crossfield and the 'pop-gun' conspiracy in 1796, and O'Coigley, O'Connor and Binns at Maidstone Assizes in the spring of 1798. There was the attempt on the life of the King – it was Sir John who was responsible for passing through Parliament the legislation which followed. By the end of the century, he was, in his own words, 'worn down with labour and fatigue', so when Sir James Eyre died in 1799[19] he applied for his post, and the King agreed on condition that he would not refuse the Chancellorship when it became vacant. He was raised to the peerage, and chose the title of Baron Eldon; and on the following day he wrote to his mother:

My dear Mother,

I cannot act under any other feeling than that you should be the first to whom I write after changing my name. My brother Harry will have informed you, I hope, that the King has pleased to make me Chief Justice of the Court of Common Pleas and a Peer. I feel that, under the blessing of Providence, I owe this...to a life spent in conformity with those principles of virtue, which the kindness of my father and mother early inculcated, and which the affectionate attention of my brother, Sir William, improved in me.... I am anxious to express my love and duty to my mother, and affection to my sisters, when I first subscribe myself

Your loving and affectionate Son

'Eldon.'

The new peer now had a domestic problem to contend with. In those days it was *de rigueur* for judges to wear wigs, but Bessy preferred her husband in his own hair (and had arranged for him to have his portrait painted by Thomas Lawrence while he was still Attorney-General, 'to make sure of preserving a record of his features undisguised by the obnoxious peruke').[20] So Lord Eldon applied to the King to allow him to dispense with wearing a wig, except when he was sitting judicially, pointing out that some of the judges in earlier reigns had not worn them: 'True', the King replied, 'and I am willing, if you like, that you should do as they did; for though they certainly had no wigs, yet they wore their beards'. Given this choice, Lord Eldon, for two years, wore a wig.

There were other family troubles of a more serious nature. Henry died in 1799, and a few months later their mother followed him; she was 91. She had lived, in full possession of her faculties, to see her eldest son William appointed a judge in the Court of Admiralty, and John a Chief Justice and a Peer of the Realm: 'To think', she exclaimed, 'that I, in this out of the way corner of the world, should live to be the mother of a Lord!' Of her thirteen children, seven, including John's twin sister, had died in infancy.

Lord Eldon sat in the Court of Common Pleas for two years until Addington became Prime Minister; Lord Loughborough resigned the Great Seal and Lord Eldon replaced him. He attended the King on 15 April 1801; the King was very fond of Lord Eldon, and when the new Lord Chancellor approached him, he saw that the King had his coat fastened at the bottom, and he put his right hand inside the coat and drew out the seals of office, saying, 'I give them to you *from my heart*'. When the news of the appointment reached Newcastle, there was a general rejoicing; the church bells there and in Gateshead were rung from the arrival of the mail until late in the evening, and parties of friends and relatives gathered to celebrate the event; the ships in the Tyne hoisted their flags. One of the new Lord Chancellor's first actions was to appoint his old master, Mr Moises, as his chaplain.

The King's health was rapidly deteriorating at this time, and Lord Eldon regarded it as his duty to call at Buckingham House every day. On one occasion, the King took a watch, and desired Lord Eldon to accept it as a gift; he refused to do so, but about a year later, a red box was delivered to him; it contained the same watch, together with a seal which, according to the *Anecdote Book*, 'is a curious one. It contained a figure of Religion looking up to Heaven, and a figure of Justice with no bandage over her eyes, His Majesty stating that Justice should be bold enough to look the world in the face'.

The Eldons had had six children, the last having been born in 1798; two had died in infancy. John, the eldest son and heir, married Henrietta Ridley, from Northumberland, in 1804, and just over a year later she bore him a son. John had a bad cold at the time, and within a few days he became seriously ill and died on Christmas Eve at No. 2 Bedford Square, where Lord Eldon was now living.

A month later, William Pitt died. The King summoned Lord Grenville to form a ministry, with Fox as one of its leading members. On 7 February, Lord

Eldon went to the King to surrender the seals of office; he has recorded – 'The King appeared for a few minutes to occupy himself with other things; looking up suddenly, he exclaimed, "Lay them down on the sofa, for I *cannot*, and I *will not* take them from you."'

✳ ✳ ✳

A few weeks after the Treason Trials, Erskine wrote to Dr Parr:

> I am now very busy flying my boy's kite, shooting with the bow and arrow, and talking to my old Scotch gardener ten hours a day, about the same things, which, taken altogether, are not of the value or importance of a Birmingham halfpenny,[21] and am scarcely up to the exertion of reading the daily papers. How much happier it would be for England and for the world if the King's Ministers were employed in a course so much more innocent than theirs, and *so perfectly suited to their capacities*.

Relaxation with his children on Hampstead Heath was not a pastime that would last for long. Erskine's career at the bar continued unabated. He defended James Hadfield, who had attempted to kill the King, and succeeded in satisfying the Court that his client was insane when he fired the shot; he was appearing in practically every civil case which was heard at Westminster Hall – seduction of wives and daughters, assaults and defamation, breach of promise of marriage, the validity of wills, insurance claims. On 5 January 1795, he was back in the House of Commons. His forensic successes seem to have gone to his head, and his speeches in Parliament became increasingly intemperate, and so egotistical that it was a standing joke in the press that the printers ran out of letter 'I's when reporting them; and there was a story going round (although it was later categorically denied by his family) that he was taking opium; it was also, and rather more reliably, asserted that he used to carry a flask of madeira with him when he was speaking.

But as the century came to a close, Erskine gradually withdrew from politics (see Figure 20). When Addington became Prime Minister in 1801, he gave him his support, and his approval to the Peace of Amiens. During the armistice, he and Fox went to Paris where they were both presented to Napoleon, but war broke out again soon afterwards and Erskine pledged his support to the government in their resistance to the aggressor. He demonstrated his personal loyalty by joining a volunteer regiment. There were two such regiments in the Inns of Court, the Bloomsbury and Inns of Court Association (BICA or the Devil's Invincibles), and the Temple Corps or the Devil's Own. In view of his military experience, Erskine was given the command of the latter, but he had long forgotten how to drill his men. Lord Campbell was a student barrister at the time; he had enrolled in the rival regiment and remembered seeing Erskine putting his troops through their manoeuvres one summer evening in Temple Gardens, giving his commands from a piece of paper as if they were instructions written out in a brief. They drilled every morning, and one wet day they were all reviewed by the King; when the King asked Erskine what was the composition of the Corps, he replied, 'They are all lawyers, Sir', and His Majesty exclaimed, 'What! What!

Figure 20. Thomas Erskine, by Sir Thomas Lawrence (c. 1802) (From a private collection; photograph by the Courtauld Institute.)

all lawyers? all lawyers? Call them the Devil's Own, call them the Devil's Own'.

It was at about this time, in December 1805, that Erskine's wife died. Little is known of her; Lord Campbell says that she had been a faithful companion in her husband's early struggles against penury, and that she enjoyed more than he did the fame and high position which he had achieved; Mrs Mure once said: 'His wife I like very well; in his adversity she was most contented and uncomplaining, and in his prosperity is kind and unassuming'. On the other hand, Fanny Burney[22] said, 'His wife seems by no means to admire him as much as he admires himself, if I may judge by short odd speeches which dropped from her'. Whatever the truth may have been, the widower erected a tablet in Hampstead Church to 'the most faithful and most affectionate of women'.

*   *   *

After the death of Pitt, when the leaders of the new coalition government were looking for a Lord Chancellor, they asked the King for his permission to offer the Great Seal to Erskine, and he replied, 'What! What! Well! Well! – but remember, he is your Chancellor, not mine' – an observation which may have been motivated by Erskine's outspoken Whig principles, or alternatively because he thought that Erskine was professionally unqualified for the position.

The Chancellor in those days presided in the House of Lords and in the Court of Chancery. In spite of his immense practice in the courts of Common Law, Erskine had never once appeared in the Court of Chancery; he had no knowledge of the principles of Equity, or of the complexities of land law, which was the principal subject-matter of its jurisdiction. His reputation as an advocate was unsurpassed, but his judicial experience was nil; and his notoriety for egotistical volubility augured ill for someone on the bench.

Erskine received the Great Seal on 7 February 1806. On the same day, he was raised to the peerage; it was suggested that it would be appropriate if he assumed the title of Baron Ego of Eye in the County of Norfolk; instead, he styled himself Baron Erskine of Restormel Castle in the County of Cornwall in honour of the Prince of Wales, whose predecessors had resided there. He retained the family shield and crest, but his father's motto, 'Judge Nought', was clearly inappropriate, and was replaced by 'Trial by Jury'. The Prince presented him with a topaz in the form of a seal; the stone was uncut at the express desire of the Prince, who said that he hoped one day to have it engraved with an earl's coronet – a promise which was never fulfilled. Erskine's brother Henry was appointed Lord Advocate at the same time.

Lord Erskine immediately set about the task of disproving that he was unfit for his post; he succeeded in winning the respect of the chancery practitioners by his courtesy, patience and politeness; he said little on the bench, and listened meticulously to counsel. It so happened that Henry Dundas, now Lord Melville, was impeached before the House of Lords at that time, charged on ten articles of corruption while he had been Secretary of the Navy. The previous impeachment, of Warren Hastings, had lasted no less than seven years and had brought the procedure into disrepute; Lord Erskine was determined that there should be no repetition of this mismanagement. He insisted that the House should sit every day until the case was concluded; he presided with a firm hand; his decisions on matters of evidence, the examination of witnesses, and the admissibility of documents were received with respect by everyone concerned. The trial was finished in fourteen days; he summed up in a single sentence – 'My lords, your Lordships having heard the evidence and the arguments in this case, have agreed upon several questions which are severally to be put to your Lordships, and the first question is this:'. Then he put each article to the House and asked them if they found the defendant Guilty or Not Guilty. The majority of the peers acquitted the defendant on all charges, although Lord Erskine himself had voted Guilty on four of them; and he then formally concluded the last case of its kind in our history by informing Lord Melville that he had been acquitted on all charges. Nevertheless, Lord Melville had to leave his mansion next door to Horne Tooke, and, ironically, went to live in the little white cottage where his neighbour had at one time planned to go.

During the summer recess of 1806, Charles James Fox died; Lord Erskine felt the blow severely, for the two men had been friends for many years. Lord Grenville continued in office, but the administration was not a success. The only major item of legislation was a bill to allow Roman Catholics to hold commissions in the Army; the bill had been prepared without Lord Erskine's knowledge, and the King found it obnoxious; it was withdrawn, and the King then demanded an undertaking from his ministers that they would never again propose any measure for relaxing the laws against the Catholics. Thereupon, the Lord Chancellor, the Keeper of the King's conscience, went to His Majesty and delivered a long harangue on his constitutional duty to abide by the advice of his ministers. The King listened in silence until his Chancellor had concluded, and then said, 'You are a very honest man, my Lord, and I am most obliged to you.'

Less than a week later the government resigned and the Chancellor received a summons to attend the King and deliver up the Great Seal; he had held the office for little more than a year.

*   *   *

When Lord Grenville's ministry collapsed, the King invited Lord Portland to replace him, and Lord Eldon was re-appointed Lord Chancellor. Most of the ministers took office on 25 March 1807, but, in order to enable Lord Erskine to complete his unfinished business, his successor was not sworn in until 1 April – 'an ominous day', he said in a letter to his brother, Sir William, and added that he did not think that the new government would last a month. In fact, Lord Eldon was to remain Lord Chancellor continuously for a period of twenty years, and throughout the whole of this period, he had to carry out his judicial functions, with a case load which was increasing year by year. In 1825, when defending him against criticism for his handling of the work of the Court of Chancery, Sir Robert Peel said that the Chancellor devoted twelve hours a day, without remission, to his public duties, with only three weeks vacation every year; and he always spent Sundays preparing his work for the week ahead.

It was soon after his re-appointment to the Chancellorship that Lord Eldon purchased the Encombe estate, near Corfe Castle and the Dorset coast. It was a reckless scheme: he paid over £50,000 for the property, although neither he nor Bessy had ever set eyes on it; when they went there for the first time, they thought they had been very unwise, until they saw the fine sea view at the entrance to the valley. It was here that Lord Eldon used to spend his vacations. It was here that he nearly lost the Great Seal. There was a fire which destroyed two bedrooms – 'It really was a very pretty sight', he told his niece, Mrs Forster, 'for all the maids turned out of their beds, and they formed a line from the water to the fire-engine handing the buckets; they looked very pretty all in their shifts' – so he buried the Great Seal and forgot where he had put it; next morning the whole family were probing and digging until it was found.

Lord Eldon was a voluminous letter-writer: some 2000 letters were made available to Horace Twiss when he was preparing his biography, many of them, according to Lord Campbell, written on the bench while the Chancellor was listening to the arguments of counsel; and he would read the replies during the daily prayers in the House of Lords. Most of those written to his wife were lost, but one batch, dating from 1809, survived and describes the events following the resignation of the Duke of Portland and the formation of a new ministry. 'My ever dear life', they began, or 'My ever loved Eliza'; one ends 'May God's best and kindest providence watch over her who has the whole heart of *her* Eldon.'

It was Perceval who became Prime Minister; he had been the Chancellor's junior counsel in *R. v. Horne Tooke* fifteen years earlier. The health of the King was one of the first problems to be encountered by the new government. Plans for establishing a regency were renewed; in 1811, the necessary legislation was passed and the Prince of Wales became Prince Regent; his friends hoped that he would replace his father's ministers, but he decided to retain them in office. So Lord Eldon began to cultivate the friendship of his new master.

Hardly had the Regency problem been resolved when the Ministry suffered a devastating blow in the assassination of the Prime Minister by a man named Bellingham, who believed he had received a slight from the British minister at St Petersburg and decided to take his revenge on some member of the government. The Prince instructed Lord Eldon to take soundings for the formation of another ministry; it remained much the same as Perceval's under the premiership of 'that skipjack' Lord Liverpool, who remained in office for the remainder of the war and for many years afterwards.

In those years, England was plagued by riots. On one occasion in March 1815, the crowd proceeded to Bedford Square and broke the windows of Lord Eldon's house; they tore up some iron railings and smashed their way in. The back of the house led on to the British Museum, and there the family fled. Lord Eldon persuaded a Scotch corporal and four soldiers from the Museum guard to come back with him, and he suggested that they should surprise and seize the intruders. But the corporal said that he had not enough men for that, so instead, he ordered them to fix their bayonets and they all charged through the house; the mob fled, but kept milling around outside. According to one version of the story, Lord Eldon collared one of the intruders and said, 'If you don't mind what you are about, my man, you'll be hanged'; to which the visitor replied, 'Perhaps so, old chap, but I think it looks *now* as if *you* would be hanged *first*'. 'And I had my misgivings', said the old peer when relating the story later, 'that he was in the right.'

For several nights Lord Eldon's house was besieged; Lord Eldon himself was given the protection of a police officer, a man called Townsend, who took him to Westminster through the Museum gardens and a series of obscure streets and alleys; and Townsend spent the nights sitting in the library at Bedford Square reading Hale and Holt, and discussing them with the corporal. In the evenings, Bessy used to go to the House of Lords in her carriage to meet her husband; one day, some of the crowd were about to attack the carriage, but when they saw who was inside, they gave her a cheer and let her through. The corporal was killed later that same year at Waterloo.

In 1816 there were more riots in London and the northern counties; and there was the Peterloo Massacre in 1819. In the following year, there were riots in Birmingham; Major Cartwright, 80 years old now, was involved and was successfully prosecuted, and fined £100, at Warwick assizes for taking part in a seditious meeting; (four years later, on his death-bed, he was conducting a trans-Atlantic correspondence with Thomas Jefferson then aged 81). 'Prosecutions for *sedition*,' wrote Lord Eldon to his brother after Peterloo, '... are not worth a straw; and, blamed as I was in 1794, for prosecuting for *High Treason*, all are convinced here that *that* species of prosecution can alone be of any use. I think, however, that it won't be attempted; the case is as large and complicated as mine in 1794, and nobody has the spirit to attempt it.' The riots culminated in the Cato Street conspiracy; this was a much more sinister affair, for the conspirators planned to murder the entire cabinet at a dinner party, and to set fire to the cavalry barracks, and to proclaim a republic; two members of the gang betrayed their colleagues to the government who arranged for their arrest in Cato Street as they were setting out to give effect to their plan. Five of the leaders of the conspiracy were convicted of treason and hanged.

*   *   *

Lord Erskine's dismissal had been a calamity for him. As an Ex-Chancellor, he could not go back into practice at the Bar; he came to regret that he had ever accepted office, for he was now unemployed and unemployable, except for laying foundation stones and making speeches at anniversary dinners. For a time he continued to attend the House of Lords. He attacked the government's proposal to ban the export to the enemy of Jesuits' bark, later known as quinine, a remedy for many wartime diseases; he criticized the armed forces. There was however, one measure of reform which he himself instituted, the first bill for the Prevention of Cruelty to Animals; the bill, having passed the Lords, was rejected in the lower House, but Lord Erskine lived to see it reach the statute book.

Although his professional career was closed, Lord Erskine lived the life of a man of wit and pleasure, outwardly cheerful and happy – inwardly listless and melancholic. He was still living at Evergreen Hill, and Sir Samuel Romilly has left an account of a dinner party where the conversation turned to the Prevention of Cruelty bill, and the host's own menagerie of pets – Phoss was still alive, and another dog he had rescued while Lord Chancellor from a gang of youths in Holborn; a goose which followed him round the grounds, and sometimes accompanied him in his carriage; a macaw; and two leeches which had blooded him when he had been ill and had saved his life – he called them Howe and Cline after two celebrated surgeons, and he fetched them from his library and placed them, in their glass, on the dinner-table, and told his guests he was sure they knew him and were grateful to him.

It was about this time that he sold Evergreen Hill and bought a farm at Holmbush near Crawley in Sussex, but the soil was poor and grew nothing but stunted birch trees; so he set up a factory for making brooms and had them hawked round the country. He dabbled in verse and wrote a book, *Armata*, modelled on *Gulliver's Travels*. In 1814 the Prince Regent conferred upon him the 'Green Ribbon', the Knighthood of the Thistle. This was an honour of which he was particularly proud, since he claimed descent from the House of Stewart which had founded the Order, and he ostentatiously wore the Star of the Order upon his breast.

Lord Erskine had now been widowed for some years, and in 1816 he married a second time. His new wife was a woman of humble birth called Sarah Buck, and, disguising himself as an old nurse, he took her and four children off to Gretna Green where they were married by 'Bishop' Lang. It was usually the parents of the bride who tried to prevent runaway marriages, but on this occasion it was the eldest son of the bridegroom who pursued the couple; it is said that he arrived just after the ceremony, and engaged in a shouting match with Sarah in the village street.[23]

Only a few months later, he received a formal invitation to return to Edinburgh to attend a public dinner.[24] The Tories, including Sir Walter Scott, refused to attend, but one Tory lady, who had evidently seen him before, left this description of him:

> I was asked to meet him last Saturday night, and saw him surrounded by all his satellites. He is a shattered wreck of a man, decked with a diamond star. This decoration he wore, I was told, as a Knight of the Thistle. I always thought of him with the deep straw bonnet which he wore on his Gretna Green expedition.

Many Whigs went to honour their guest, and his forensic triumphs were celebrated. He replied with a typical after-dinner speech, with praise of Scotland, and anecdotes of playing fives at St Andrew's, and a variety of other topics. On the following day he visited the Court of Justiciary and sat on the bench; and then in the evening went to the Theatre to see *The Heart of Midlothian* – the author, Sir Walter, and Lord Erskine entered and departed at different times and sat on opposite sides of the house; both were applauded, and Sir Walter resented the fact that on this occasion the visitor received more applause than he did. The two men were not on good terms; Sir Walter had written a poem to celebrate the Battle of Waterloo (where Esme Erskine had been severely wounded at the Duke of Wellington's side whilst serving on the Headquarter Staff) and his lordship wrote in reply:

On Waterloo's ensanguined plain,
Lie tens of thousands of the slain;
But none, by sabre or by shot,
Fell half so flat as Walter Scott.

＊　　　＊　　　＊

Throughout this period, both Erskine and Eldon had been involved in the domestic affairs of the Royal Family. The Prince of Wales and Princess Caroline of Brunswick had separated very soon after their marriage in 1795, and for many years Lord Eldon was on friendly terms with the Princess. When she was accused of adultery with an Italian called Bergami, and a commission, of which Lord Erskine was a member, was set up to carry out a 'Delicate Investigation' into her conduct, she sought Lord Eldon's advice. After she had been acquitted of the charge, she dined with him at Bedford Square, although Bessy refused to join the party.

The Prince and Princess had one daughter, Charlotte, who married Prince Leopold of Saxe Coburg; Lord and Lady Eldon attended the wedding. In the following year, Princess Charlotte died in childbirth, and the baby died too. The Dukes of York and Kent were now next in line of succession. It was still the practice for senior statesmen to be present at the birth of all children who were close to the throne, and on 24 May 1819 Lord Eldon was summoned to Kensington Palace to attend the confinement of the Duchess of Kent; later that day, he returned home to Bessy with the news of the birth of Princess Victoria.

During the remainder of the Regency, the Princess of Wales lived abroad, but on the death of the old King in 1820 she returned to England and demanded to be given her rightful status as Queen Consort. An attempt to buy her off failed, and by midsummer she was back in London – which was illuminated three nights in her honour. Lord Eldon was now in close contact with the new King and had severed his links with the Queen; but she decided to purchase a house in Hamilton Place, next door to the Eldons who had recently moved there from Bedford Square. He was so angry at this both on his own and his wife's account, that he told the Prime Minister that if the purchase was completed, he would be bound immediately to vacate both his home and his office. The Prime Minister instructed the Office of Works to prevent the purchase, but, undeterred, the Queen arranged to buy the house through private contributions which were being raised for her; eventually, the Chancellor only stopped her by buying the house himself in the name of a friend.

The problem of the royal marriage was frequently discussed in Cabinet until late at night (and Bessy never went to bed until her husband came home) and eventually it was decided to deprive the Queen of her rights by a Bill of Pains and Penalties, incorporating a clause for divorce. It was arranged for the bill to be introduced into the House of Lords in the form of a trial, with counsel and witnesses being heard on both sides. As Chancellor, Lord Eldon was supposed to be presiding over a judicial inquiry, but the people regarded him as hostile to the Queen. On 16 August, the day before the hearing in the House of Lords began, Townsend came to see Lord Eldon and urged him to go to Westminster by way of Birdcage Walk rather than along the Mall and through the Horse Guards; but the Chancellor refused to accede to this advice. He insisted on driving along his usual route, and he went accompanied by his grandson and heir, and his younger son William; he faced the danger in the same way as he had in 1794, and he arrived safely.

When the case was proceeding in the House of Lords, Lord Erskine demanded that the Queen should be treated in the same way as a defendant in a criminal trial; for the last time, he marshalled his ancient knowledge of the law of evidence on behalf of the accused, and strove to ensure that the rules were properly enforced. During one speech, he collapsed with a stomach cramp; it was thought that he was dying, but he recovered and was back in the House next day.

The hearing continued until early September, when the House adjourned. Lord Eldon went to Encombe for a short vacation, and all along the way the people kept coming up to his carriage shouting, 'Caroline for ever'. The hearing was resumed in October, and on 5 November the bill passed its second reading by a majority of 28; three days later, after the committee stage, the majority dropped to nine. This, coupled with the Queen's continuing popularity, made it inevitable that the measure should be abandoned; and so it was. Lord Erskine's comments were:

> I see the fate of this odious measure consummated, and I heartily rejoice at the event. My Lords, I am an old man, and my life, whether it has been for good or evil, has been passed under the sacred rule of the law. In this moment I feel my strength renovated by that rule being restored. The accursed charge wherewithal we had been menaced has passed over our heads. There is an end of that horrid and portentous excrescence of a new law – retrospective, oppressive, and iniquitous. Our constitution is once more safe.

The time was now approaching for the Coronation, which was fixed for 19 July 1821. The King gave public recognition to Lord Eldon for his long service to the nation by promoting him Viscount Encombe and Earl of Eldon; his grandson was soon to assume the courtesy title of Lord Encombe. At the same time, Sir William Scott, who had presided for many years over the Court of Admiralty, was raised to the peerage under the title of Baron Stowell.

The Queen still believed that she was entitled to be crowned beside her husband, but she received no invitation, so she went to the Abbey uninvited, and was turned away. Popular support for the unhappy woman rapidly disappeared, and she was taken ill and died a few weeks later.

While the Queen's trial was proceeding in the House of Lords, Lord Erskine, at the instigation of his sons, tried to have his marriage to Sarah annulled, but on finding that it was valid under Scotch law, he gave up the suit and took her back, as she had always been 'chaste and virtuous'.[25] She later bore him a son called Hampden. At the same time, his championship of the Queen had revived his popularity to a degree which he had not known since the aftermath of the treason trials: he was cheered wherever he appeared in public; gold boxes, containing grants of the freedom of corporations, poured in upon him from all parts of the country; his pictures and busts were to be found in workshops and cottages. But as so often in Lord Erskine's career, triumph was followed by disaster.

The fortune which he had built up at the Bar was wasted away; he had lost a large sum on his farm, and more in an investment in American funds; a gentleman in Derbyshire left him a considerable landed estate in admiration of his public character (and also a legacy to Thomas Hardy), but the attorney who drew up the will committed a blunder and the legacies were invalid. The stories that he was taking opium were revived. In the autumn of 1823, he was minded to pay another visit to Scotland, to meet again his eldest brother, the 11th Earl of Buchan, and Henry's widow, and their children. He decided to go by sea, and when it was pointed out to him that it was the season of the equinoctial gales, he replied, 'What is a puff of wind on the German Ocean to an old sailor who has often combated a tornado in the West Indies?' And so, accompanied by one of his sons, he set sail from Wapping in a Leith smack. There was a violent storm off Harwich, but the 'old sailor' – he was nearly 73 – insisted on remaining on deck to show his hardihood. He became seriously indisposed with an inflammation of the chest, and by the time the ship reached Scarborough he was so ill that he had to be taken ashore. He recovered sufficiently to travel north to his sister-in-law's home at Ammondell in the valley of the Almond, close to the family home at Uphall in West Lothian, but shortly after his arrival he suffered a relapse and died on 17 November 1823. The parish clergyman gave an address, and then, with a few relatives and friends, accompanied the hearse to the family home at Uphall, where the coffin was laid to rest beside his brother Henry in a narrow vault near a little country church.

He left little enough for his family, and Sarah and Hampden were destitute; during the 1820s, there were sad stories of the widow and child hanging round the Mansion House in London, begging for the necessaries of life. It was a tragic postscript to the life of the illustrious advocate.[26]

✻   ✻   ✻

III Eldon, Hardy, and the Great Reform Act

Previous Chancellors had entertained on a lavish scale; but not the Earl of Eldon. Partly from ill-health, partly from shyness, Bessy had a great dislike of entertainments, and the Earl renounced visiting society for her sake, thereby acquiring the reputation of stinginess. When they were living in Hamilton Place, she herself cut his hair, and arranged his linen and clothes; and she used to steal to the window when he went out, to see, so neat in his appearance, her Lord Chancellor pass by. William Hazlitt used to meet him in the street, plodding along with an umbrella under his arm, without any trace of pride, with an almost rustic simplicity and honesty of appearance.[27] On the rare occasions when Bessy did hold a dinner party, it was a cause of special comment, as when the Earl wrote to his daughter Frances one day in November 1820:

> We are all well, safe, and quiet, only in a fuss, the morning after our cabinet dinner, which was by far the handsomest that any Minister has given in my time. Mamma really did this most magnificently.
> Sir William himself heard so much of my cabinet dinner, that he invited himself to dine yesterday on the *scraps*...

During the vacations at Encombe, Lord Eldon made it a rule never to transact any business. He spent his time there shooting partridges and hares, and he had a sailing vessel built in which he sailed round the Dorset coast.

In 1827, Lord Liverpool, the Prime Minister, was taken seriously ill and the government had to be re-constructed. When Lord Eldon surrendered the Great Seal, the King was as demonstrative as his father, and gave him a tankard of silver gilt, its lid embodied with an accession medal, and its side inscribed with these words:

> The Gift of His Majesty King George IV
> To his highly valued and excellent friend
> John Earl of Eldon
> Lord High Chancellor of England, &c.
> Upon his retiring from his official duties in 1827.

The Earl was now approaching 77. Nevertheless he still hoped that he would be recalled to the Woolsack; or that he would be offered a seat in the cabinet; or that at least he would be consulted on its composition; but the invitation never came.

Three governments were formed in quick succession – by Canning, Castlereagh, and the Duke of Wellington – and he wrote a long letter of complaint to Frances when he realised that the Duke was not proposing to offer him any place in the new ministry. And his resentment was aggravated by the fact that his successor, Sir John Copley, Lord Lyndhurst, had in his youth, and before he became a Tory, been a Jacobin who had sung *Ca ira*, and danced round the tree of liberty, and had attended the anniversary dinners of Hardy and Horne Tooke.

At the same time, the long love affair which had started in Sedgefield Church some 60 years before was drawing to its close. Bessy was unwell in 1827; in September, the Earl wrote to his brother, saying that he had brought her to Encombe and that she was somewhat better; a year later, also from Encombe, he told his grandson, 'We are living in seclusion, and mamma's state renders that matter [*sic*] of necessity'. Then in October, she had what Twiss describes as 'a violent affection of the brain, arising from a determination of blood to the head'. She failed to recognise the Earl, and the doctor feared that she would not survive more than a few hours; but the Earl and his grandson stayed up all night, applying 'a strong blister' at the back of her head, and she recovered sufficiently to return to London. She never went back to Encombe, and about a year later the Earl was writing to his brother: 'I see nobody – I seldom, very seldom, stir out, except to bear Lady Eldon company in the coach when she goes out'. She survived until 28 June 1831, and was buried in specially consecrated ground at a chapel at Kingston between Corfe Castle and Encombe, and the Earl erected there a tablet:

To the Memory of a Wife
To whom he was most devotedly attached
And with whom he lived in marriage
Nearly fifty-nine years

During the last illness of the Countess, William IV had succeeded George IV, and there had been a general election in which the Duke had been defeated. So Earl Grey became Prime Minister, with a programme, delayed for so many years, of parliamentary reform. Lord Eldon sought to bury his grief by devoting himself once again to public affairs.

The Earl had never been a keen advocate of change for the sake of change: he had opposed the abolition of the slave trade on the ground that it would be worthless without international agreement; he had opposed Roman Catholic emancipation on constitutional grounds. He now opposed the reform of Parliament on the ground that the boroughs were property rights conferred by purchase or charter and not to be confiscated, and that it would lead in turn to universal suffrage, annual parliaments, and vote by ballot. The Reform Bill was debated in the House of Lords, in October, night after night; and the Bill was rejected. In some quarters, the news was received with pleasure: in others, there were riots. In London, the rioters smashed the windows of the Dukes of Wellington and Newcastle; the Earl decided that it would be safer to go to Dorset; he travelled safely, but hardly had he arrived when he was warned that a mob was assembling at Poole to attack Encombe. The magistrates were warned, and the labourers were armed; special constables were alerted, and twelve muskets were put in order. However, a neighbour discovered that the insurgents were planning to cross Poole Harbour to Purbeck in some flat-bottomed canoes, and he managed to bore holes in the boats; so they gave up their scheme.

The Reform Bill was re-introduced, and during April it was again debated in the House of Lords; and between 6 and 7 a.m. on 14 April – the 38th anniversary of Chalk Farm – it was carried by 184 votes to 175. Lord Campbell was present when the result was announced; it was a beautiful spring morning, and Palace Yard was filled with the crowds; Lord Grey was rapturously cheered, and Lord Eldon was led to his carriage and driven off looking more dead than alive. Thereafter he and the majority of the Tories refrained from further opposition to the Bill, which became law in the summer.

*   *   *

Hardy's views on these events was rather different from those of his old adversary. When the Great Reform Bill was well on its way through

Parliament, Hardy wrote his last letter to Sir Francis Burdett, and the first letter in which he had ever expressed approval for a British government; it was dated 7 March 1831:

Dear Sir,
   I hope you are quite well. I congratulate you on the pleasing prospect before us, which I hope we shall before long fully enjoy, that great national blessing – a *Parliamentary Reform*, which your great talents, years ago, were often exerted to obtain. Although not then successful, yet your efforts were not lost, for you then sowed abundance of good seed, which has been springing up ever since, and which I hope will now produce a plentiful harvest for the benefit of your fellow countrymen. I am much pleased with the present Government; I believe they are sincere, and will be active in their exertions to promote that great object to its completion. I am pleased to see so many converts to the important cause of Parliamentary Reform; some from conviction of its justice, and others from necessity. I hope the Ministers will be well supported by all the *old* and *true* Reformers. Perhaps, you may smile when I tell you, that I am now, *for the first time*, in my humble measure, a supporter of Ministers. I greatly rejoice to see the great cause of Civil Liberty prospering, not only in this country, but all over Europe, and that I have lived so many years to witness it, having entered on the 80th year of my journey of life, the 3rd of this month of March. I hope you will excuse me for troubling you with this, and accept my best wishes that you may enjoy long life in health and happiness.

                                                            Thomas Hardy,
                                                 30, Queen's Row, Pimlico.
           7th March, 1831.
   Sir Francis Burdett, Bart. MP

About a month later, he wrote another letter to another statesman, another survivor from a previous age who had taken part in the American Revolution, and the French Revolution, and had survived imprisonment and the ravages of war, a long letter which was reminiscent of earlier times:

Dear and Respected Sir,
   Although I have not had the happiness to see you, yet you are no stranger to me, for I have followed you in all your peregrinations with my good wishes, high approbation, and esteem, for your unwearied exertions to promote the happiness of your fellow men. Ever since the beginning of the American Revolution, I remember well your laudable efforts, together with that extraordinary man Washington, to gain that great object for which the brave Americans were contending – their emancipation from a foreign yoke, which they at last effected; and now they are a great and prosperous nation. I have great pleasure to remark, that you and I have been fellow labourers in the great cause of Civil Liberty, ever since that important period. We may now be permitted to rejoice together with the great body of the friends of liberty, that their honest efforts have not been lost. It was a maxim of the celebrated Reformer, Dr John Jebb, that *no effort is lost*. Permit me now to congratulate you on the late glorious Revolution in France, in July last; it has no parallel in ancient or modern history. I also well remember the first Revolution in France, about forty years ago; and I am very happy when I recollect that I was instrumental in sending the *first* Congratulatory Address from this country, from *The London Corresponding Society*, to the *National Convention of France*, with which they appeared to be so well pleased, that it was read in the Convention,

ordered to be printed, sent to the eighty-four Departments, and to be read at the head of the Armies of France. When the Paris newspapers, having that Address, came to London, it astonished and highly pleased the people; but not so the Government. When that useful and important Society, the fruit of whose labours the British nation are reaping at this day, unanimously voted that Address, they deputed four trusty friends to convey it in the safest and quickest way possible. Being the *Secretary*, and in fact the *founder* of the Society. I waited on *Monsieur Chaveline, privately*, to know whether he would convey it. He readily consented, and ordered the deputation to wait on him the next day, at 11 o'clock: they, of course, punctually attended, and read the Address to him, with which he was much pleased, and promised to send it speedily. The Address was signed the 27th of September, 1792, *Maurice Margarot*, Chairman, *Thomas Hardy*, Secretary. That period is worth referring to, were I in Paris, if any of the records of the Convention are now in existence.

I cannot help mentioning to you how much I am pleased with the Revolution which has taken place in this country, for *revolution* it is. *The King, and his Ministers, are now turned Parliamentary Reformers!* They are guilty of the very crime, if crime it be, with which Parliamentary Reformers, in the year 1794, were charged by the infamous Government of *Pitt, Dundas,* and *Grenville*, the greatest crime known in our laws – *High Treason*. Many were imprisoned, some were banished, and three were tried for it; but an English jury had a very different opinion of the criminality of their conduct, and honourably *acquitted* them. I rejoice that it has pleased God to spare my life so long, being now in my 80th year, to witness this grand and beneficial change which has taken place in this country; and also changes all over Europe. I ardently wish the oppressed people of every country may be relieved from their oppressors.

Political knowledge is making a great and rapid progress; it is now diffused among all classes. The press – the printing press is performing wonders. It was a maxim of the great *Lord Bacon*, that *knowledge is power*. I fear that I have encroached upon your valuable time with my garrulity, if you will condescend to take time to read this long letter. I shall now conclude with my sincere best wishes, that you may enjoy long life, in health and happiness.

Thomas Hardy,
30, Queen's Row, Pimlico.

11th April, 1831.
Lafayette, France.
My friend, Mr Lewis, has been kind enough to say that he will convey this to you.

Some time later, the old Marquis replied:

La Grange, July 3rd, 1831

My Dear Sir,
Your much valued favour, April 11, has but this day been delivered to me. The wishes of the London Corresponding Society, for universal freedom, have been expressed in the beginning of the French Revolution; and now we can congratulate each other on the electric stroke of the French week of last July, and upon the happy spirit of Parliamentary Reform which is now prevailing in England. This mutual fellow-feeling must take place of the prejudices which aristocracy and despotism have so long kept up between nations. Be pleased to accept my acknowledgements for the sentiments you were so kind to express in my behalf, as well as the assurance of my good wishes and sincere regards.

Lafayette.
Thomas Hardy Esq.

It was a fitting epilogue to the correspondence which had taken place between Hardy and the French Convention forty years earlier.

It must have been about this time that 'when going to the city in a stiff-springed *omnibus*, he was so violently shook, that it brought on a stranguary, which, after much suffering, proved fatal to him'.[28] The closing words of his *Memoir* read:

> Like all human creatures, he has, in many things, failed, and come short; but he commits himself with confident hope to the mercy of his Creator and Redeemer, and awaits the period of his release from this state of mortality with patience and resignation.

He lived to see the last sheet off the press and the Great Reform Act on the statute book, and died, after some months of suffering, aged 80, on 11 October 1832. A member of the London Corresponding Society, Alexander Galloway, wrote this epitaph for him:[29]

> He was a plain upright man, a steady and inflexible Patriot ...; by his excellent conduct through a long life he demonstrated that the most Humble in Society, when guided by Integrity, and aided by Perseverance and Judgement, are sure to add to the happiness and advance the liberties of mankind.

One week later, he was buried at Bunhill Fields. At his graveside, John Thelwall, the last survivor of the defendants of 1794 – 'highly esteemed', Hardy had written, 'as a public lecturer on politics, classical literature, and general education.... He is also the author of many valuable works in prose and verse, and still lives highly and deservedly respected by a great number of his countrymen' – delivered a funeral oration to 'an immense multitude which was variously estimated from 20,000 to 40,000 persons'.[30]

*   *   *

Lord Eldon's health had in the past been remarkably good, except for the removal of a nasal polypus in 1822 and an occasional attack of gout. However, the death of his wife, the threats of riots, the problems of the Reform Bill, had affected him, and at the same period his son, William, died; he was the child that Bessy had been carrying during the Treason Trials, and his body was laid beside his mother at Kingston. William had a dog called Pincher, and his last request was, 'Father, you will take care of poor Pincher'; Pincher became the Earl's constant companion for the rest of his life. His doctor prescribed 'frequent movements through columns of air', and so he spent more and more time travelling around the country. For the first time for many years, he travelled north, and met Mary Forster, his brother Henry's daughter. He stayed at the inn at Rusheyford, on the Great North Road about eight miles south of Durham, and entertained his Eldon tenants to dinner. His friends pressed him to visit Newcastle, but No, he said, 'How can I pass that bridge?' The bridge looked upon Sandhill, where Lady Eldon had lived with her parents and his eyes filled with tears, and he exclaimed, 'Poor Bessy! If ever there was an angel on earth, she was'.

The Earl (see Figure 21) spent spent more time at Encombe now; he had a study which he called his 'shop' where he had a painting of George III, a drawing of Pincher by George Repton who had married his daughter Elizabeth, and a Greek testament which had belonged to Mr Moises. He used to wander round his estate wearing an old shabby jacket and a weather-beaten hat, chatting to the poachers ('Who are you? I suppose you are one of old Bags' keepers.' 'No, I am old Bags[31] himself'). He gave up shooting, which had been his favourite pastime during the vacations, although largely a waste of ammunition, and carried out chiefly to please the dogs.

In the summer of 1833, the Earl dined in Middle Temple, and was received with acclamation by the bench, the bar, and the students; his health was drunk, and in the course of his reply he expressed the hope that 'the Bar might continue to maintain that high and honourable and independent character, which was essential to the administration of pure justice, and which was ... one of the main sources of the prosperity which this country had hitherto enjoyed'. He continued to attend the House of Lords, although his appearances there dwindled as the years went by. His last speech was in July 1834, when he denounced railroads as 'dangerous innovations'. He took the oath of allegiance to the young Queen in June 1837, and his last visit was on 15 November, when he went supported by his mace-bearer and his butler; but he was too exhausted to return to hear Victoria's first speech from the throne.

He continued, too, to make annual visits to Rusheyford and Eldon, accompanied by Pincher; he was always accompanied by Pincher now – when they were travelling, the dog ran ahead of the carriage, always waiting on the brow of the hill to keep his master in sight; a bookseller used to pat him on the head and say he was very like *old Eldon*, particularly when he wore a wig. Pincher was painted by Edward Landseer, and also appeared in some of the portraits of his master.

At home, the Earl was suffering from boredom, alleviated by writing letters to his family, and re-writing his will (which eventually ran to more than 70 pages), and by dinner – his favourite food was liver and bacon, and his favourite drink was Newcastle port (of which he never took less than three pints, said Lord Campbell), but his drink never disturbed his understanding or impaired his health, or affected the discharge of his duties.

He continued to enjoy his visits to Durham and meeting his family. He was particularly fond of his great niece, Ellen Forster, herself nearly 40 now. 'When you and I meet in the Newcastle Assembly Rooms', he used to say, 'we will open the ball'. 'Yes, uncle, remember you are engaged to me', she would reply. 'I will not forget it; and we will call for "Jack's Alive" – that will be the proper one, "Jack's Alive".'

In the summer of 1837, the Forsters noticed a change. His brother William, Lord Stowell, had just died, after a long illness; he never took any exercise, the Earl used to say, except eating and drinking, but he had lived to the age of 90. The Earl's daughter Frances's marriage had broken down, and she had left her husband. The old man visited Eldon and again entertained his tenants at Rusheyford; but they knew it would be the last time. In December, his eldest

Figure 21. Lord Eldon in his old age, from the studio of Sir Thomas Lawrence. (By permission of the National Portrait Gallery.)

son's widow and her second husband came down from Clapham, under Ingleborough, to visit him; he was declining physically and his mind was wandering; but he still talked of his old cases, and made sure that Pincher, who never left his master's side, got his favourite biscuits when he came and scratched his knee. By January, he was confined to his bedroom, overlooking Piccadilly; there was a sharp frost on Friday 12 January, and his doctor said, 'It is a cold day, my lord', to which he replied that it mattered not to him, where he was going, whether it was hot or cold; his grandson and his two daughters were with him when he passed away the following afternoon. He was 86.

On Monday 22 January, the funeral procession set out from Hamilton Place. A vast crowd had assembled in Piccadilly, and the cortege, which included the Duke of Cambridge and many lawyers and peers, proceeded along Hammersmith Road, where it halted, and the private carriages returned to London. The procession then proceeded to Encombe and the Earl was interred beside his wife and son in the family vault.

CHAPTER 20

EPILOGUE

Lord Eldon was the last survivor of the protagonists of 1794. Sir John Mitford had become Lord Chancellor of Ireland under the title of Baron Redesdale; he died in 1830, leaving it to a later generation of Mitford girls to bring the family name back into the limelight. John Law, Lord Ellenborough and Chief Justice of the Court of King's Bench, died in 1818. 'Vinegar' Gibbs went into Parliament and became Sir Vicary and Attorney-General; his repressive measures made him unpopular, and he was no longer invited to the anniversary dinners of his erstwhile clients, but Horne Tooke would hear no word against him – 'He was my counsel, and knew nothing of the law of treason, as he confessed to me when I first employed him; but he soon obtained a masterly notion of the subject, and he did me ample justice – I never can, I never will speak ill of him'; he became Chief Justice of the Court of Common Pleas and died in 1820. John Thelwall, Gibbs's sole surviving client from 1794, continued his lectures and his efforts to obtain Parliamentary reform until his death in 1834.

It now remains to consider the question: Why were they prosecuted? At the time of the trials much of the press and public opinion supported the Crown; the successful defendants were even referred to as 'acquitted traitors'. John Gifford, in his *Life of Pitt*,[1] published very shortly after the latter's death, declared that it was impossible to read the accounts of the trials without being impressed with a conviction of the existence of a treasonable conspiracy, which had as its object the utter subversion of the constitution and government; and he agreed with the opinion of the Committee of the House of Lords, that 'The ostensible object of the several meetings, whose members were to be the followers in this conspiracy, namely Parliamentary Reform, is a pretext that could impose on none but the most credulous, ignorant and unwary'; and for good measure he asserted, on the authority of one of the jurors, that the jury themselves were fully satisfied of the existence of such a conspiracy, and that they would undoubtedly have convicted the defendants if they had been prosecuted for a misdemeanour.

In later years, the pendulum swung the other way, and the prosecutions came to be regarded as little more than an attempt to secure the death of innocent reformers, with Pitt cast in the role of principal villain – although this would have involved him, along with the Law Officers and the Judiciary, in a conspiracy to commit judicial murder.

Hardy, who, for several months in the Tower, in Newgate, and in the dock at the Old Bailey, had had the Great Axe suspended by a single thread over his neck, can be forgiven for regarding himself as the innocent victim of a malicious persecution; it was Erskine's duty so to convince the jury. And Sheridan developed this theme in Parliament[2]:

> Having but one neck to lose, I would be as sorry to find *mine* undergoing the operation of the lamp-post as any honourable gentleman in this house; but I must confess I felt myself considerably cheered by the discovery that the danger existed all within the vision of the treasury bench. I cannot help thinking, with the chief justice, that it was much in favour of the accused, that they had *neither men, money, nor zeal.*
>
> I own that there was something in the case, quite enough to disturb the virtuous sensibilities and loyal terrors of the right honourable gentleman. But so hardened is this side of the house, that our fears did not much disturb us. On the first trial *one* pike was produced. That was, however, withdrawn. Then a terrific instrument was talked of, for the annihilation of his majesty's cavalry; it appeared, upon evidence, to be a *tee-totum in a window in Sheffield.* But I had forgot, there was also a camp *in a back shop*; an arsenal provided with *nine muskets*; and an exchequer containing the *same number of pounds*, exactly nine, no, let me be accurate, it was nine pounds and *one* bad shilling.
>
> In Edinburgh an insurrection was planned; the soldiers were to be corrupted; and this turned out to be – by giving sixpence for porter. Now, what the *scarcity of money may be in that country* I cannot tell, but it does not strike me that the system of corruption had been carried to any great extent. Then, numbers were kept in pay, they were drilled in dark rooms by a sergeant in a brown coat, and on a given signal they were to sally from the back parlour and overturn the constitution.

Others should have taken a more objective view.

It has already been observed that Lord Brougham virtually accused Sir John Scott of failing to read his brief,[3] although anyone who actually reads the transcript of the proceedings will at once recognise Scott's total grasp of the evidence. Then Lord Campbell declared that Scott should have prosecuted for misdemeanour only; but both Parliament and the Privy Council had formed the opinion that a treasonable conspiracy was in existence – it would have been a brave Attorney-General indeed who would have disregarded such clear advice from such sources as these, quite apart from the technical legal problem[4] involved which seems to have escaped Lord Campbell's notice. Sir John's own explanation is quite different. In his *Anecdote Book* he said that he decided to prosecute for treason both to obtain the opinion of a jury whether the conspirators were guilty of treason or not, and also to lay the whole evidence before the public to acquaint it of the dangers to which it was exposed if they had held their convention; it appeared to him to be more essential for securing public safety that the whole of their transactions should be published than that convictions should be secured. It is to be noted that he accepted full responsibility for the decision;[5] there is no suggestion that he made it under pressure from Pitt.

There was also the persistent belief that the Crown's case was based upon the doctrine of 'Constructive Treason', a belief which probably originated in the *Cursory Strictures* of Eyre CJ's charge to the grand jury. Sir John Scott repudiated this when he expressly disavowed constructive treason, but this was not good enough for Lord Campbell, who roundly declared that 'it was thought better to resort to the law of "Constructive Treason"... and therefore to insist that all who belonged to [these societies] were to be considered guilty of "Compassing the death of our Lord the King" and ought to die the death of traitors.'

Lord Campbell went even further in accusing the Prime Minister of instigating the prosecutions:

> The blame for these prosecutions rests chiefly with Mr Pitt.... If he had sincerely changed his opinion on parliamentary reform, it was not right in him to try to bring his former associates to an ignominious death for zealously treading in his footsteps.

This is an unfounded allegation. The Committee of Secrecy, of which Pitt was a member, and whose report he himself presented to the House of Commons, came to the conclusion that the reforming societies were planning to call a convention, not for parliamentary reform, but for a quite different purpose; Eyre CJ told the grand jury to throw out the indictment if they were satisfied that the genuine purpose of calling a convention was to petition for parliamentary reform. The case for the prosecution throughout the trials was conducted on the basis that the plans for holding a convention were not restricted to the lawful purpose of petitioning Parliament.

Lord Campbell's work on the *Lives of the Chancellors* is a massive achievement, and no one who has read it can doubt his industry and erudition; but it has not escaped criticism. Lord Lyndhurst expressed the opinion that the *Lives* added a new terror to death; and Lord Brougham once said in the author's presence, 'Don't mind what Jack Campbell says; he has a prescriptive privilege to tell lies of all Chancellors, dead and living'; and one recent writer has gone so far as to say that 'Historical truth and accuracy are constantly sacrificed for literary effect and the snide prejudicial remark'.[6] Nevertheless Lord Campbell's views on the trials of 1794 have been embodied in the national folklore and have been repeated down the years.[7]

In the early years of the present century, the events of the 1790s were investigated by three young men: George Veitch, Walter Hall and Philip Anthony Brown. None of them was legally qualified; none of them considered the ingredients of treason under English law, or the functions and duties of the principal law officers of the Crown, or the evidence which would have been required to secure a conviction. Veitch gave a detailed account of the reform movement during the 1780s and the early '90s, but had little to add on the trials themselves. Hall did call in question the conventional view; he thought that planning an armed revolt would have justified a conviction, and indeed such conduct, under the legal phrase of 'planning to levy war in the realm', would have amounted to an overt act of treason; unfortunately, the evidence which he then set out, in the form of riots and mutinies, disaffection and disturbances, related mostly to events which occurred *after* 1794, and therefore throw little light on the guilt or innocence of those who were put on trial in the autumn of that year.

By the summer of 1914, Brown had virtually finished his book. He had investigated the evidence with considerable care (although relying principally on the Treasury Solicitor's papers, and the statements given to the Privy Council rather than the records of the trials themselves); he pointed out that the fact that the defendants had been acquitted did not mean that they should not have been prosecuted – anyone who has had experience of the criminal courts knows that witnesses do not always repeat on oath what they have said earlier, and that evidence can evaporate under cross-examination. He then dealt with each of the principal participants, Hardy, Horne Tooke and Thelwall, in turn; and he concluded his observations with the words: 'The general result of our examination is to acquit the responsible leaders of the reform societies between 1790 and 1794 of the wish to use force'. That, of course, is not the whole story; there was much that he left unsaid, and in particular he made no mention of the Stone brothers or of William Jackson; this was an omission which he must surely have remedied had he lived. Sixty years later, Professor Goodwin investigated the events of this period in considerable detail, and devoted some twenty pages to an account of the trials of Hardy, Horne Tooke and Thelwall (but said very little about the trials of Watt and Downie, Jackson and Stone). His discussion of the law, and of the reasons for the prosecutions, added little to what had gone before.

What then, was the position in the summer of 1794? It is true that the whole affair had an atmosphere of *opéra bouffe*, in marked contrast to the terrible tragedy which was unfolding on the other side of the English Channel. Nevertheless, taking into account the schemes of Watt and Downie in Scotland, and of the Stone brothers and Jackson in France and Ireland; the 'pop-gun' conspiracy; the evidence of the manufacture of weapons; the correspondence between the London Societies and France; and the plans to hold a convention – it is hardly surprising that the government was alarmed. These matters clearly constituted *prima facie* evidence of overt acts of compassing the King's death within the provisions of the Act of 1351, and the government would have been guilty of a grave dereliction of their duties had they turned a blind eye to all that was going on.

Not all of this evidence was admissible against Hardy, but some of it was, together with the evidence of Jane Partridge, which went unheard. Even if the case had been tried under stricter rules, and those matters over which Hardy had no control and of which he had no knowledge (covering most of the events which had taken place in Scotland and Sheffield) had been excluded, there remains a hard core of evidence, including in particular his address to France after the deposition of the King. However restrained Hardy may have been in his use of the spoken word, his personality changed once there was a pen in his hand; and then there was Samuel Williams's evidence (which went unchallenged) that Hardy was acting as an arms broker for the Loyal Lambeth

Association. On the strength of this it would have been open to the jury to hold that he was, at the least, recklessly indifferent to what happened to the King.

As for Horne Tooke, in spite of his constant protestations that he never knew on what grounds he was prosecuted, he had, on the admission of his own biographer, been holding himself out as the leading spirit in a planned insurrection (although evidence to this effect never materialised at his trial); Thelwall, who knew him well, went so far as to say that he was one of the most violent spirits of the age – 'a strenuous advocate of the decapitation party, he was for having kings but for cutting off the head of one of them every 50 or 100 years'.[8] And on the day after Hardy's arrest, the very day on which the government intercepted Joyce's letter – written from the home of Earl Stanhope, one of the most ardent supporters of the French revolution – which indicated that an insurrection was to start that very week, he went to Spitalfields which was as likely to be a centre of insurrection as anywhere. He was asking for trouble.

Additionally, according to the spy, Groves, Thelwall had blown off the head of his porter and said, 'This is the way I would have all kings served'; anyone who said that in 1794, did so at his peril.

In the face of this evidence, why were the defendants acquitted? Hazlitt[9] expressed the view that William Godwin could claim a major share of the responsibility for the successful outcome of the cases; Godwin's 'Remarks on Judge Eyre's Charge to the Jury', he wrote (not even prepared to give the Chief Justice his proper title), 'gave a turn to the trials for high treason in the year 1794, and possibly saved the lives of twelve innocent individuals, marked out as political victims to the Moloch of Legitimacy, which then skulked behind a British throne, and had not dared to stalk forth (as it has done since) from its lurking place, to brave the opinion of the world'. Hazlitt, it seems to me, was more concerned with fine phrases than with logic or law; I find it hard to believe that these *Cursory Strictures* could have had much impact on the minds of the juries.

The generally accepted view is that Hardy and Horne Tooke were acquitted because of the common sense of the jury, and the eloquence of Erskine (Gibbs's contribution is usually overlooked, but his closing speeches, particularly in the case of Horne Tooke, certainly merited the commendation which he received from his principal opponent).

Once again, it is useful to ascertain the views of those who actually participated in these proceedings. Sir John Scott's explanation[10] was that the jury were so perplexed by the great mass of evidence (and anyone who has endeavoured to read and digest the transcript will surely agree with him) that they were unable to draw the proper inferences from it; and this is corroborated from Hardy's jury itself, one member of which said to Adolphus: 'Sir, if the evidence had been much stronger than it was, I should have had great difficulty in convicting men of a crime, when it occupied the Attorney-General nine hours to tell me what it was'.

Even if the part which Erskine played in securing the acquittals has been exaggerated, nevertheless his contribution to the events of the decade remains immense. The very fact that a man who was both the leading advocate of his day and an aristocrat of royal blood was prepared to defend men who were charged with plotting against the Crown, to defend them free of charge,[11] to the very limits of his physical endurance, was an example of professional courage of the highest order. 'His sword and buckler', wrote Lord John Russell,[12] 'protected justice and freedom. Defended by him, the government found in the meanest individual whom they attacked, the tongue of Cicero and the soul of Hampden, an invincible orator, and an undaunted patriot'. He was, indeed, a benefactor to the whole state – the Crown, the government, and the people – the people were alarmed by fear of the Crown; the Crown was alarmed by fear of revolution. The success of his appeals to the law showed the people that they had in the law a sure defence, and, by soothing the fears of the people, he gradually soothed the fears of the government; by exalting the law, he gave both the King and the people a common security.[13]

Sir John Scott has not fared well at the hands of posterity. He and his wife are still commemorated in their home town,[14] but elsewhere he is hardly remembered except as the aged, dilatory and reactionary chancellor and politician. But to him too the nation owed a great debt; there fell upon him that year a burden as great as ever befell any member of the legal profession: that of piloting the state through a time of unprecedented peril – and he never faltered.

As for Sir James Eyre, he may best be remembered in the closing words of his obituary in the *Gentleman's Magazine*:

> Regretted by the Bench, by the Bar, and by the Public … this valuable and excellent Judge has left a character behind him, which as it was formed on the best examples of our legal history, so it will survive to be itself an example hereafter, recorded alike by his profession and his country.

*   *   *

John Adolphus did not practise as an attorney for long, and spent his time writing histories of France and the opening volumes of his *History of the Reign of George III*, which were so well regarded that he was appointed a salaried adviser to the cabinet. In 1805, he realized his boyhood ambition of being called to the bar, and soon acquired a large practice at the Old Bailey. After the Cato Street conspiracy, on the very day before the trial, he was briefed for the defence; he stayed up all night to assimilate the vast mass of papers, and so joined the select body of counsel who have acted for the defence in a case of treason. His conduct won the admiration of everyone concerned, even though his clients were convicted.[15]

Towards the end of his life, when his practice at the bar was dwindling, he resumed his work on the Reign of George III. He examined the events of 1794 with some care, and he too expressed the opinion that a charge of treason should not have been brought, but then went on:[16]

On the whole, these trials were of the utmost benefit to the public interest. The unimpassioned fairness of the prosecution, the freedom of defence, the candour of the judges, and the integrity of the juries, afforded to the people of this realm, convincing proofs that their liberties were amply protected by a system which affords such, and so many, means of security.

This may be regarded an an appropriate verdict on these trials.

THE TREASON ACT 1351

This Act was originally written in French, but the generally accepted English version (which I have divided into sections for convenience of reference) reads as follows.

1. Item, whereas opinions have been before this time in what case treason shall be said, and in what not: the King, at the request of the lords and commons, hath made a declaration in the manner as hereunder followeth, that is to say:

    (i) When a man doth compass or imagine the death of our lord the King, or of our lady his Queen or of their eldest son and heir;

    (ii) or if a man do violate the King's companion, or the King's eldest daughter unmarried or the wife of the King's eldest son and heir;

    (iii) or if a man do levy war against our lord the King in his realm;

    (iv) or be adherent to the King's enemies in his realm, giving to them aid and comfort in the realm or elsewhere, and thereof be probably attainted of open deed by the people of their condition;

    (v) or if a man counterfeit the King's great or privy seal;

    (vi) or if a man counterfeit the King's money....;

    (vii) and if a man do slea the chancellor, treasurer or the King's justices...;

and it is to be understood, that in the cases above rehearsed, that ought to be judged treason which extends to our lord the King, and his royal majesty....

2. And because that many other like cases of treason may happen in time to come, which a man cannot think nor declare at this present time: it is accorded, that if any other case doth happen before any justices, the justices shall tarry without any going to judgement of the treason, till the cause be shewed and declared before the King and his Parliament, whether it ought to be judged treason or other felony.

Subsections 1 (i) to (iv) and (vii) (which includes a definition of justices) are still in force; subsections (v) and (vi) were repealed in the nineteenth century. Section 2 was repealed by the Criminal Law Act 1967.

THE COURTS AND THE LEGAL PROFESSION

In the eighteenth century, the 'superior' courts in England were as follows:

The Court of Chancery, otherwise known as the court of equity; cases in this court were usually tried by the Lord Chancellor sitting alone; its principal function was in the administration of trusts and estates, etc.

And the three courts of common law:-

The Court of King's Bench; this court consisted of a Chief Justice and three justices (usually sitting together); its principal functions were the trial of certain civil cases, and the supervision of inferior courts.

The Court of Common Pleas; this court consisted of a Chief Justice and three justices (usually sitting together); its principal function was the trial of certain civil cases, particularly relating to land.

The Court of Exchequer; this court consisted of a Chief Baron and three Barons (who had the same qualifications and status as the judges of the other courts); the original function of this court was to try disputes between taxpayers and the Exchequer, but its jurisdiction was extended to the trial of other civil cases, especially relating to the recovery of debts.

There were also:

The Court of Exchequer Chamber, consisting of the Lord Chancellor and the Twelve Judges of the common law courts, was a court of appeal; and a final appeal lay to the House of Lords. By the eighteenth century, it was a convention that only legally qualified Peers sat when the House was acting in its judicial capacity.

Assizes: justices of the three common law courts, and Serjeants-at-law (see below) visited all counties and held assizes once or twice a year. The assizes for Middlesex sat at the Old Bailey. Serious criminal cases were normally heard on assize, but important cases could be removed for trial to the Court of King's Bench at Westminster; alternatively, the Crown could appoint a Special Commission for the trial of a case of exceptional difficulty or importance.

In Scotland, the principal criminal court was the Court of Justiciary: the nominal president of this court was the Lord President (or Lord Justice General), but his deputy, the Lord Justice-Clerk, usually presided; the other judges in this court were (and are) referred to as Lords.

The legal professions in England were organised along similar lines as today. Members of the Bar, who were called to the Bar by one of the four Inns of Court, had the sole right of audience in the superior courts; senior barristers could apply to be appointed King's Counsel ('to take silk') but it was not then customary to add the letters K.C. after their names. There was also the senior rank of Serjeants-at-Law who had certain privileges and from whose ranks the judges of the superior courts were appointed; the 'King's premier' or 'prime' serjeant was head of the profession; although the rank of Serjeant has never been abolished, no new Serjeant has been appointed since 1868. The principal legal advisers to the Crown were the Attorney-General and Solicitor-General, who (then as now), in spite of their titles, were barristers (and Members of Parliament). (There was also the Advocate-General, who advised the Crown in Admiralty and certain other matters; no Advocate-General has been appointed since 1872, and most of his functions have been taken over by the Queen's Proctor).

Solicitors (who practised in the Court of Chancery) and attorneys (in the common law courts) were, strictly, separate professions; but in practice, any qualified solicitor was admitted as an attorney and vice versa. Before the institution of the office of Director of Public Prosecutions, the Treasury Solicitor prepared criminal cases for the Crown and briefed counsel.

In Scotland, barristers were, and are, known as advocates, and are members of the Faculty of Advocates; the elected head of the profession is the Dean of the Faculty; and the Crown's legal advisers are the Lord Advocate and the Solicitor-General for Scotland. In the eighteenth century, the Lord Advocate was effectively the government's manager for Scotland and responsible for its administration.

In Ireland, the court system and the professions were based on those of England. Serjeants-at-Law continued to be appointed for some time, and Sjt Sullivan, who defended Sir Roger Casement, was the Last Serjeant.

CA IRA AND LA CARMAGNOLE

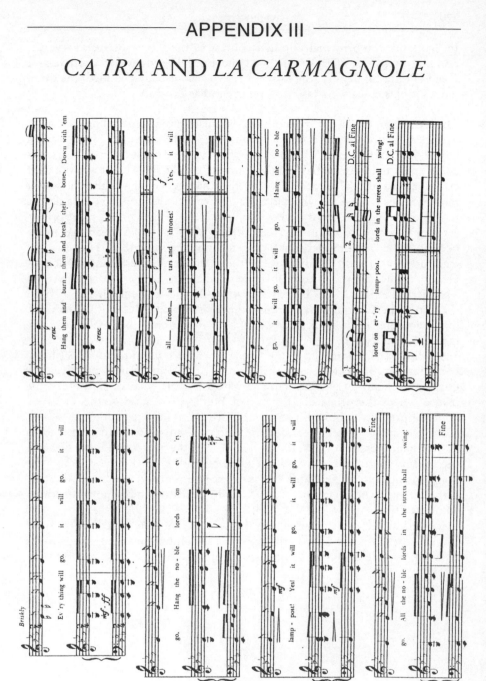

LA CARMAGNOLE

NOTES

Preface

1. [1967] *Cambridge Law Journal*, 189.
2. Thus Thompson *The Making of the English Working Class*, 21, describes the penalty for treason; but I cannot find in his book any account of the ingredients of treason under English law.

Sources

1. DNB; *Memoirs of John Adolphus*, by his daughter, Emily Henderson.
2. Gilbert Murray's Introduction to Brown's book; the citation to Kenny's V.C.; Brown's Letters to his Mother from France. According to Murray, Brown's friends were preparing a *memoir* of him, but if this was ever published I have been unable to find a copy. I am grateful to Mr Stephen Shannon of the Durham Light Infantry Museum, Dr J.T. D. Hall, the Librarian of the University of Durham, Mr Michael Standen of the Northern District of the WEA and Mr Simon Finch of the Beckenham Library for supplying me with such information relating to Philip Brown as exists.
3. DNB.
4. I am grateful to Professor A.H. Hudson, of the Law Faculty of the University of Liverpool, for supplying me with information relating to George Veitch.

Chapter 1

Note: Much of the material in Chapters 1 to 4 is to be found in the State Trials; other sources are listed *ante*.

1. In Cornwall, a particularly notorious example, 42 out of 44 members were returned by 453 electors.
2. *History of England,* ch. 11.
3. Veitch, 63. In a letter to France dated 1 December 1780, and printed in translation at 21 St. Tr. 760, the spy de la Motte reported that the county associations were aiming to dispose of their militia and volunteers in support of their political objectives.
4. The use of the word 'Scotch' is now regarded as incorrect, but was in regular use in the Eighteenth century.

5. Adolphus (England) III, 281 (8 March 1780).
6. Various conferences, meetings, and conventions were held in the early 1780s, but there is no doubt that one of them, with delegates from many parts of the country, met at about this time at the Guildhall.
7. Brown, 13.
8. Per Wallace A.-G. and Loughborough C.J., 21 St. Tr. at 504 and 489 respectively.
9. At this time Mansfield was Chief Justice of the King's Bench, Loughborough of the Common Pleas.
10. Hereafter referred to as the King.
11. Printed at 22 St. Tr. 492.
12. Moody and Vaughan, *A New History of Ireland,* (1986), vol. IV.
13. The whole letter is printed at 24. St. Tr. 1048 ff.
14. Brown, 82.
15. A medical encyclopaedia in 18 volumes.
16. This was a special procedure, already nearly obsolete, in which the victim of a crime, or the relative of a victim of murder, could 'appeal' the defendant; the appeal could either be tried in court, or fought out in battle between the victim (or, in the case of a widow, her representative) and the defendant.
17. Or according to Stephens, the Lord Mayor himself.
18. Many societies with similar names were being set up at this period. The Constitutional Society and the Society for Constitutional Information have often been confused; however, the Constitutional Society was definitely founded by Horne Tooke in or about 1770 and the Society for Constitutional Information by Major Cartwright in 1780. There was also the Constitutional Club, of which both Horne Tooke and Pitt were members.
19. The Rules or Liberties were districts round a prison in which a prisoner might live if he could afford to do so: Bayne-Powell, 217.
20. Jail fever, or typhus, is a lice-borne disease, causing a high fever, skin-rash and headaches. The usual treatment, according to Bayne-Powell, 227, was 'to keep the patient in a warm dark room from which fresh air was rigidly excluded, to bleed and purge drastically and to support the strength by giving plenty of wine and red meat.' In 1774, Dr Lettsome recommended the very reverse – nursing in the open air, no wine or meat, and water, lemonade or fresh foods instead; but it was some time before his methods came to be accepted: George, 54 & 338. Horne Tooke evidently did not suffer a severe attack; in many epidemics, the death rate was very high.
21. Gout was prevalent, and often terminal, in the 18th century: Boerhaave, vol. 13.
22. Mr Ian Murray, the archivist of Inner Temple, assures me that the records of the Inn simply state: Ordered – that Mr John Horne be not called. Stephens gives a long account of the alleged ineligibility of the clergy to be called to the bar.
23. Brown, 31: Goodwin, 108.
24. Veitch, App. I, lists more than 50 French societies which were in correspondence with the English Revolution Society in 1789/92; some French societies mistakenly believed that it had been founded in honour of their own Revolution, and some believed that the Jacobin Club had been modelled on it: Veitch, ch. VI. And see also Goodwin, 112, 128–129.
25. The Godwins' daughter, Harriet, married Shelley.

Chapter 2

1. Torrington's Diaries, 22 June 1790; and see Goodwin, 139–47.
2. Veitch, 183.

3. Accounts of the Birmingham riots may be found in biographies of Priestley and other standard works.
4. The Society seems to have been moribund during the late 1780s, but started to thrive again at this time: Brown, 53.
5. Hardy gives no date for this incident, but it was probably before the Gordon Riots.
6. Hardy never mentions the name of his wife, nor have I seen it in the literature; however, a Thomas Hardy married Lydia Priest of Chesham at St Martin's in the Fields, Westminster, on 21 May 1781; it is very unlikely that this is a different couple.
7. This was where Piccadilly Circus is now. The end of the street was demolished about 25 years later when Regent Street was built.
8. Edmund Vale, *The Mail Coach Men*, time-bills 4 to 6 (pp. 230ff.); Bayne-Powell, 31.
9. Hall, 11.
10. Veitch, 192, gives this as the date of the first formal meeting of the Society; he says that the original meeting had been in October.
11. Baylen and Gossman, *Biographical Dictionary of Modern British Radicals*.
12. Another form of *pasha*, or an imperious person.
13. Brown, 57; Cone, 121; Veitch, 205–207.
14. Cone, 117; Veitch, 194–195.
15. Bindman, 66.
16. Trevelyan, *English Social History*, ch.12; David Dymond, *The Norfolk Landscape*, 171; Barbara Green and Rachel M. R. Young, *Norwich*, 25–30; Goodwin, 148–58.
17. On his first arrival in London, the Prince of Orange invited some peers and MPs who had previously sat in the House of Commons, and two Aldermen of the City to advise him; this was not the Convention, which was summoned later, and was elected like an ordinary Parliament: Macaulay, *History of England*, ch 10.
18. Bindman, 19 (54); Hall, 85–86.
19. Bindman, (67b).
20. *Ibid.*, (69)
21. A report of the Prince's speech is given in Croly, 78–79; there seems to be some uncertainty as to the occasion, but it was most likely given on 21 May 1792.

Chapter 3

1. During the years after the Revolution, there was a fashion in France for planting symbolic Trees of Liberty; some 60,000 are said to have been planted between 1789 and 1793. The tree almost invariably selected for this purpose was the Lombardy poplar, possibly because of its association with the word for 'people' – *peuple/peuplier* in French, *populus/populus* in Latin; and it became a regular feature of the broadsheets of the period; the fashion was revived in 1848, and again in 1889; and two years later Monet painted his series of Poplars on the Epte: Prof. Paul H. Tucker, *Monet in the '90s*. In England, any sort of tree, or even a pole, seems to have sufficed; the trees were sometimes decorated with symbols of liberty, rather like a Christmas tree: Bindman, (124, 190, 206p).
2. See Appendix III.
3. This account of the Marseilloises is based on Adolphus (England, V); he hardly mentioned the episode in his own *History of France* published forty years earlier; it may be that the ill-repute of the Marseilloises had grown over the years.
4. Carlyle, *French Revolution*, VI, ch. 5. It was the regular practice for a regiment returning to Paris to be entertained to dinner: Schama, 459.

5. Schama's account of the revolution of 10 August is very brief; there is a vivid description in Carlyle, *op. cit.*, book VI.
6. A replica of the 'Halifax gibbet', incorporating the original blade, is on view at the Halifax Piece Hall.
7. Horne Tooke lived at Chester House, Westside (now Barclays Bank's training centre); strictly speaking, it was Secretary Dundas's son, Robert, who lived next door at Westside House, and the Secretary of State himself lived next door but one in Warren House (now known as Cannizaro Park), but Horne Tooke always referred to the Secretary of State as his next door neighbour. I am indebted to Mr Richard Milward for supplying me with this information; see his books, *Historic Wimbledon* and *A Georgian Village – Wimbledon, 1724-1765.*
8. Petion replied, *post;* but Veitch, 228, points out that there is no record of his ever appointing an agent. Veitch describes how a meeting for raising this money was convened in Portland Square at the house of a Dr Maxwell, but a Col. Glover came and threatened to cut off his nose and ears, and a howling mob collected; when Horne Tooke arrived, he challenged the Colonel who beat a retreat, and the subscribers adjourned to another house in Soho Square. Dr Maxwell went to France and is believed to have been killed in the Vendée. Petion had visited London in the autumn of 1791, and had attended a dinner at the London Tavern: Goodwin, 186–188.
9. It was not until a year later, on 5 October 1793, that the French Convention formally abolished the Gregorian calendar and replaced it with a new one, back-dated to 22 September 1792 (Bindman, 227); however, a new calendar was in practice in use from the start of the Republic.
10. According to Carlyle; wolves, according to other sources.
11. Brown, 89.
12. See *post*, Ch. 9 (iii).
13. Veitch, 226–227, was unable to ascertain the truth of the story about the shoes (except that Frost took a pair in his pocket to the Convention and deposited them on the bureau, where they were much admired); but Goodwin, 254 and 511, asserts, on the strength of documentary evidence both in France and England, that 7000 were ordered, and purchased from Hardy at £3 per dozen pairs, and that 6000 reached France; the money was raised in the autumn of 1792 and the scheme was wound up in April 1793.
14. Bindman, (88–122).

Chapter 4

1. Bindman, 32; Cone, 146–148.
2. Cone, 115; Veitch, 233; the proclamation was issued under the provisions of the Militia Act, 1786.
3. Throwing is the process by which raw silk is wound from the skein, twisted, doubled and twisted again. Sarah Bush, *The Silk Industry,* (Shire Publications); Bayne-Powell, 78–79; George, ch.IV.
4. Brown, 102; Hall, 37.
5. Moody and Vaughan, *A New History of Ireland,* vol. IV.
6. *Culottes* were the short breeches worn by the French aristocrats; the peasants wore trousers, i.e. *sans culottes;* but before long, the term came to be used by caricaturists as meaning without any lower garments: Bindman, (81, 82b).
7. Not at this time; strong links were developed towards the end of the decade.

Chapter 5

Note: The trials of the 'Scottish Martyrs' are fully reported in vol. 23 of the State Trials, and are discussed in detail by Cockburn.

 1. When Henry Erskine was appointed Lord Advocate in 1806, Lord Lauderdale organised his election for the Royal Burghs of Dunbar, Lauder, North Berwick, Haddington and Jedburgh; the procedure was that the magistrates and council of each burgh chose delegates, who in turn elected the MP, but in practice Lord Lauderdale controlled Lauder and Dunbar, and the Dalrymple family controlled North Berwick, and they so arranged matters that a Lauderdale nominee sat during two parliaments, and a Dalrymple nominee for one parliament; Haddington and Jedburgh were always in a minority, and for generations were never represented; Erskine, apparently without visiting any of the five burghs, went to London and his election was completed after his departure. Ferguson, 436–437.
 2. Veitch, ch. X.
 3. Brown, 67–68.
 4. Veitch, 288.
 5. *Ibid.*, 247.
 6. DNB (Robert Macqueen).
 7. A somewhat similar procedure was employed when a case was tried on circuit.
 8. During the 1780s and '90s, two Surveyors of Mails, John Palmer and Thomas Hasker, were making marked improvements in the Royal Mail service. The Edinburgh coach left the General Post Office at St Martin le Grand at 8.0 p.m. every evening and arrived at the Edinburgh Post Office at 6.0 a.m. on the third morning – 396 miles in 58 hours; the return coach left at 3.45 p.m. and reached London in a little over 60 hours; the timetables were strictly adhered to except in very bad weather. No cases of highway robbery were effected on mailcoaches during the decade, and only one case of theft by a dishonest passenger (*R.* v. *Thomas*): Edmund Vale, *The Mail Coach Men*, 244–245 – the 1797 time-bills (the only set to have survived; the times may have been slightly quicker in 1797 than in 1794). The price of a letter from London to Edinburgh was $1/1\frac{1}{2}$d per sheet: Bayne-Powell, 37.
 9. Brown, 103–104. Immediately after the meeting, Briellat was arrested, prosecuted for seditious words spoken in the previous year, convicted and imprisoned in Newgate for two years: Goodwin 291–292.
10. Veitch, 284.
11. According to Goodwin, 294, Sinclair was the son of Sir John Sinclair, the first President of the Board of Agriculture.
12. Hall, 112.
13. A word of Spanish or Arabian origin – a minister of state.
14. The clearance of the Highlands took place after the '45 Rebellion; but even as late as the 1790s, hundreds of Highlanders were emigrating every year: Ferguson, 229n.
15. He was also the great great great grandfather of President Reagan: *The Times*, 21 Oct. 1991.
16. J. Holland Rose, *William Pitt and the Great War*, 182.
17. C. Cestre, *Life of John Thelwall*.
18. Veitch, 287.
19. Brown, 111.
20. The Royal Mail held a monopoly for the carriage of letters, but not of parcels; there was nothing to prevent anyone from wrapping up a letter as a parcel and sending it by a commercial carrier; it would take longer, but was less liable to interception: Vale, *op. cit.*, 15.

Chapter 6

1. Mackenzie, book I, title 7; Forbes, book I, title 2; Boyd, book I, title 5; but Cockburn had some doubt as to whether the offence existed at all.
2. Trying to ascertain the meaning of treason under Scotch law prior to 1707 is a difficult task; probably, it was as vague as treason at common law in England before 1351. Stair, in the 1693 edition of his *Institutions of the law of Scotland*, III, 3, § 29, states that it included, *inter alia*, raising a fray in the King's host, impugning the dignity or authority of the three estates of Parliament, or procuring any innovation or diminution of their power.
3. 23 St. Tr. 903.
4. This was the procedure for appealing to the House of Lords; but in fact the House had recently decided in *Bywater* v. *R.* (1781) that it had no jurisdiction to hear appeals in criminal cases from Scotland.
5. DNB.

Chapter 7

Note: This chapter is based on the State Trials and other sources listed *ante*.
1. Torrington's Diaries, 13 June 1793.
2. In the Eighteenth century a staircase was regularly referred to as a 'pair of stairs', the word 'pair' indicating a set rather than a couple, as in the phrase 'pair of steps' for a step-ladder; a room on, for example, the second floor was described as 'up two pairs of stairs' or 'a two-pair-of-stairs room'.
3. At Horne Tooke's trial, he said he had never been paid.
4. Toulon had been captured by the British fleet in 1790; it was retaken by Napoleon in December 1793.
5. See *post*, ch. 9 (iv).
6. In those days, most tradesmen took Mondays off work, so public meetings were usually held on Mondays: John Belchem, *Industrialism and the Working Class*, 49–50.
7. One of the King's ancestors was called Guelph: Croly, 6.
8. Peter Smithurst, *The Cutlery Industry* (Shire Publications); and see Goodwin, 158–69.
9. Law's opening speech in *R.* v. *Walker*, see *post*, ch. 9 (iv).
10. *sic*: 26 St. Tr. 1069n.
11. Henry York Rhodes, the son of John and Elizabeth Rhodes, was baptised in St Peter's Church, Sheffield, on 21 May 1794.
12. In those days, the House of Commons used to sit in St Stephen's Chapel; there were 558 members.
13. The sign of the Bunch of Grapes indicated a wine-house as opposed to an ale-house: John Wittich, *London's Inns and Taverns* (Shire Publications).
14. That is, Lambeth.
15. A hot drink made of salep or sassafras.
16. Bindman, 56, 198, (205, 206).
17. Bryan, *Dictionary of Painters and Engravers*.
18. Brown, 135–136; Nodder did not repeat this evidence at the trial.
19. Chalk Farm was a pleasure ground by Hampstead Road at the foot of Primrose Hill: E. Beresford Chancellor, *The Pleasure Haunts of London*; Goodwin, 328.
20. Trap-ball was a game in which a ball was placed on a 'trap', a piece of wood balanced on a pivot; the player struck one end of the trap with a bat, thereby throwing the ball into the air, and then hit the ball.

21. These were almost certainly 'lockback' knives, similar to penknives but where the blade can be locked into an open position 'to prevent the blade from closing on your hand during a fight': Simon Moore, *Penknives* (Shire Publications) and private correspondence.

22. See *post*, ch. 9 (iv).

23. This was a statement of fact; as Veitch pointed out, 302n, words to this effect had been part of the oath of allegiance prior to 1688, when they were removed by statute.

24. Brown, 115, found the accounts for this dinner in the Treasury Solicitor's papers; 260 people were present, and £37 was spent on wine, strong beer, and ingredients for negus.

25. I have not been able positively to identify this item of 'bad news'; however, military operations were in progress in the Low countries; on 26 April, the French under General Pichegru were defeated by the Allies, but on 29 April he counter-attacked and captured Moucron and Courtray (Adolphus (England) V, 634); it is possible that news of these events could have reached London by the afternoon of 2 May.

26. Robert Jenkinson, later Lord Liverpool; there are various meanings of skip-jack – a hair-brained fellow or fop, a horsedealer's boy, a toy made of a bird's wishbone, a fish which leaps out of water, a click beetle; no doubt Horne Tooke left it to his audience to decide which to apply.

27. There are various Newingtons in or near London; this is probably the one in south London.

28. The Vendée was the centre of a counter-revolution in western France which was crushed with ruthless brutality: Adolphus (France), and Schama, (particularly 787–792).

29. Talleyrand had been in England during the spring of 1792, and had submitted, *via* M. Chaveline, a report to the French government in very similar terms: Veitch, 209.

30. King's Messengers were (and Queen's Messengers are) a corps of couriers, now attached to the Foreign Office: see Wheeler-Hoolohan, *The King's Messengers*; they were used as a police force during this period: see *Leach* v. *King's Messengers* (1765).

Chapter 8

Note: the principal sources for this chapter are the State Trials and the Journals of the House of Commons, May–June 1794; other sources are listed *ante*.

1. This passage does not appear in Hardy's own *Memoir*, but is quoted by Veitch, 305.

2. Hall, 195n.

3. When Ghita Stanhope was carrying out her research into the Earl's papers a century later, she found some evidence that he was corresponding with the enemy; but it is most unlikely that this came to the notice of the government at the time.

4. Seven police or public offices had recently been established under the Middlesex Justices Act 1792: see Hone, 66–67.

5. 1 Bl. Comm. 231.

6. Veitch, 310.

7. *Ibid.*, 311–312.

8. *Ibid.*, 305.

9. Brown, 122; Thompson, 20–21.

10. Thompson, 21.

11. J. Holland Rose, *William Pitt and the Great War*, 185.
12. At the subsequent trials, no evidence emerged of any plan to seize Newgate or the Tower.
13. The House of Lords also appointed a committee which carried out an enquiry and presented a similar, although not so detailed, report: Journals of the House of Lords, May–June 1794.
14. Bryan's *Dictionary of Painters and Engravers*.
15. Brown, 119ff; Veitch, 305ff.
16. Goodwin, 333: Introduction to Henry Yorke's Trial, published by himself.

Chapter 9

Note: This chapter is based on Campbell, Eldon, Ferguson, Lovat-Fraser and Twiss. Many of the stories are anecdotal and I have borne in mind Lovat-Fraser's warning that a long study of the Eighteenth century had made him extremely sceptical of its picturesque stories and he quoted de Quincy: 'all anecdotes are false, and all dealers in anecdotes are tainted with mendacity'. However, in the case of Scott (Lord Eldon) the accounts of his early life given by Campbell and Twiss (and by Lord Eldon himself) are virtually identical, and are based on long-established family tradition and contemporary letters; in the case of Erskine, on the other hand, there are often discrepancies between Campbell and Ferguson who clearly had access to material which was unknown to Campbell; where they differ, I have followed Ferguson. Erskine himself had a reputation for romancing.

 1. There seems to be some dispute as to when the name Geordie originated – possibly not until the following century.
 2. The population of Newcastle in the middle of the Eighteenth century was probably about 20,000, rising to 28,000 in 1801: S. Middlebrook, *Newcastle upon Tyne*, 116 and 150.
 3. The Forth was a pleasure garden: *ibid., 85.*
 4. The approved method of marriage in Scotland were before either a magistrate or a minister of the kirk; but a declaration by a man, in the presence of witnesses, that a woman was his wife sufficed to constitute a binding marriage. When eloping couples started to run away to Scotland after 1753, Joseph Paisley, a farmer at Gretna Green, started to make arrangements for marrying them as soon as they set foot in Scotland; he came to be called 'the blacksmith' because of his quickness in uniting the eloping parties – 'Strike while the iron is hot, Joseph'; after a short ceremony, the couple were ushered into the 'nuptial chamber' of the inn so that the marriage could be consummated there and then. 'Parson' Paisley carried on his business for some 60 years (c. 1753 to 1811) when it was passed on to his son-in-law 'Parson' Elliott. Elliott, *The Gretna Green Memoirs*.
 5. The Scottish law courts.
 6. Flip – a hot drink made of beer, spirit and sugar; salmagundy – a dish of chopped meat, anchovies, eggs and onions.
 7. 'A good old Scotch phrase....' Ferguson, 94–95, *à propos* a poem written by Henry Erskine to the daughter of the landlord of the Golden Lion at Liverpool.
 8. Broughton's *Recollections*; the assize town is not mentioned by other biographers.
 9. Littleton's *Tenures* was an early work on land law; *Coke on Littleton* was Coke's commentary on this book.
10. *Ackroyd* v. *Smith*.
11. A copy of the proceedings in Keppel's case, based on Blanchard's shorthand note, was published by Almon in 1779.
12. i.e. to send letters free of charge.

13. This was, in effect, a plan to nationalize the East India Company, and to place the government of India in the hand of commissioners appointed by Parliament.
14. There is a long-standing tradition that Erskine's maiden speech was a disaster; but Sir Thomas Dundas heard it, and described it as 'excellent' in a letter written to Henry Erskine on the following day: Ferguson, 248.
15. i.e. the fee payable to a barrister for appearing on any circuit other than his own.
16. Toss according to Campbell; but Ferguson explains that he was called after a character in Henry Carey's burlesque *Chrononhotonthologos*.
17. In the twentieth century, the King's illness was retrospectively diagnosed as porphyria, an abdominal malady; but to outward appearance, it seemed to be a case of insanity, attributed by Dr Willis, the King's doctor, to 'twenty-seven years of study, abstinence and labour'; Croly, 210.
18. See Appendix II.
19. Small-pox had been a relatively mild disease, but became widespread and virulent in the eighteenth century. In 1720, Lady Mary Wortley Montague introduced into England from Constantinople a method of inoculation, by injecting matter from small-pox pustules into the patient, e.g. by drawing an infected thread under the skin; the success rate for the patient was good, but in the meantime the patient became highly infectious; some doctors provided nursing-homes where the patients could be kept until they became immune: Bayne-Powell, 225; Buchan, *Domestic Medicine* (1783), 175. Jenner started to practise the modern method of vaccination with cow-pox in 1796.
20. Veitch, 121n, pointed out that this cannot be true – the Jacobins never had a uniform.
21. *sic*; Christopher Wade, the curator of the Hampstead Museum, assures me that this is the correct name, not Evergreen Hall; Erskine's home has been demolished, and the present Evergreen Hill is modern.
22. Albert Crew, *The Old Bailey*, 12–13; Dick Hamilton, *Foul Bills and Dagger Money*, 91.
23. Veitch, 270.
24. The Collegiate Church later became Manchester Cathedral.
25. Brown, 124.

Chapter 10

Note: Horne Tooke's diary was found in the British Museum and was published in *Notes and Queries* (8th series), vol. 11, 1897. An account of Holcroft's involvement in the case appears in his own autobiography, edited by Hazlitt.
1. Adolphus (France), I, 516.
2. Schama, *passim*; in his *History of France*, written before the end of the century, Adolphus estimated that 900,000 people had been killed, and 20,000 dwellings destroyed, during the period of the Terror.
3. A chamber pot, (or, as the Shorter Oxford Dictionary puts it, a chamber utensil) enclosed in a box or stool.
4. The street at the back of Piccadilly, demolished to make way for Regent Street, was named Shug Lane in Rocque's Atlas, Titchborne Street by Horwood.
5. At 24 St. Tr. 132, the editor inserted a note relating to Horne Tooke's infirmity; he quoted a passage from Stephens referring to the defendant's 'complaint', adding '[in the rectum]'. The doctors may have been carrying out a digital examination of the rectum to see if the neck of the bladder was blocked; but it is difficult to see what obstruction could have caused the patient to be 'up four or five hours before' he came into Court (see p.203).

6. Thompson, 88.
7. The proclamation was scheduled to the Riot Act 1714; reading the proclamation was colloquially known as 'reading the riot act'.
8. Both Brown, 116, and Veitch, 304, thought that Ward had submitted a report to the government in May; this may be an error, or there may have been two reports. Crossfield, a member of this conspiracy, was subsequently prosecuted and acquitted.
9. Eldon § 96. According to Goodwin, 338–339, Scott had obtained counsel's opinion from Perceval in March and Lowndes in April that there was insufficient evidence to support a charge of treason: but much more evidence came to light in May and June.
10. 4 Bl. Comm. 75.
11. The text of the Act is printed in Appendix I.
12. Reprinted at 1 St. Tr. xxvi. I have not found this passage quoted in any of the documents of the period – indeed it seems to have disappeared from the literature until I revived it in defence of my own relatives in [1967] C.L.J. at 191.
13. 4 Bl. Comm. 79.
14. *Patrick Harding's Case*, (1691). In his *Anecdote Book*, § 226, Lord Eldon relates that when he was asked by Fox whether a plot to depose the King was an overt act of treason, he replied that it was and referred to (an unnamed) case in Ventris; I have no doubt that this was the case.
15. Thus Brougham, in his *Historical Sketches of the Statesmen of the Time of George III*, essay on Lord Eldon, wrote: 'If he had only examined the proofs with a steady eye, he must have seen at once the merely seditious character of the whole matter, the certainty of defeat if he prosecuted for treason, and the probability of conviction if he had gone upon the misdemeanour'.
16. see 4 Bl. Comm. 150.
17. Murder and manslaughter is an obvious example. In the eighteenth century, the theft of any article worth 12d or more was a capital offence; it was a regular practice for juries to find that the article stolen was worth less than 12d.
18. §96. As far as I am aware there was no judicial decision on the point, but it was raised by Heath J. in *R. v. Walker*, 23 St. Tr. 1148ff. The proposition was not devoid of reason, for a person charged with treason had many procedural advantages – the rights to see the indictment and list of witnesses and jurors ten days before the trial, to challenge 35 jurors, to have the offence proved by at least two witnesses, to have the same compulsory process as the Crown for calling witnesses, and to have counsel assigned to him – which were not available to persons charged with felony or misdemeanour.
19. It may be noted that when Yorke was charged with seditious conspiracy, the case was limited to his speech at Castle Hill; the Crown did not present the much stronger evidence of treason against him: see *post*, ch. 18.
20. 24 St. Tr. 200–210.
21. *ibid.*, 210–232. Adolphus (England) VI, 47, was also of the opinion that the *Strictures* were written by Vaughan; there was also a rumour that they had been written by Lord Thurlow.
22. It must be conceded that the author, whoever he was, wrote in a hurry (according to Goodwin, 341, Godwin hurried home from Warwickshire), and admitted that he was waiting to see an authentic copy of the Charge; this may explain why he used his imagination to conjure up such passages as these: 'The remainder of the charge is made up of hypothesis, presumption, prejudication, and conjecture. There is scarcely a single line which is not deformed with such phrases as "public notoriety", "things likely", "purposes imputed", "measures supposed", and "imaginary cases".... It may be doubted whether, in the whole record of the legal

proceedings of England, another instance is to be found of such wild conjecture, premature presumption, imaginations so licentious, and dreams so full of sanguinary and tremendous prophecy.'

23. When *The Marriage of Figaro* was first performed in Paris, he sat in the theatre, night after night, until he had memorized the entire text, and then translated and adapted it for the English stage.

24. A Jane Partridge is recorded as having been baptized at St Mary's Church, Nottingham, on 23 January 1760.

25. Albert Crew, *The Old Bailey, passim.*

Chapter 11

Note: These cases are reported in volumes 23 and 24 of the State Trials.

1. Veitch, 292, quotes a letter from the Lord Advocate to Secretary Dundas in which he expressly requested the appointment of a commission to be presided over by the President and the Chief Baron 'in place of the violent and intemperate Great man who sits in the Judiciary, and whose present state of Health and Spirits is such as to afford no chance of his being more soberly inclined in his demeanour than he was last winter'.

2. i.e. a carving knife; Downie's niece remembered playing with some pikes in a lumber room over her uncle's shop: Brown, 125.

3. According to the State Trials, Downie appears to have received a free pardon, but Adolphus (England) VI, 43, said that he was pardoned on condition that he transported himself for life; Cone, 186, says that he was sentenced to one year's imprisonment followed by exile for life; *The Times*, 21 October 1991, says that he was 'deported' (*sic*) to Amsterdam.

Chapter 12

Note: Hardy's trial is reported in volume 24 of the State Trials.

1. 24 St. Tr. 221 and 1385; Gurney's report of the first day's proceedings are brief; a full account is found in the Addendum, 1385ff.

2. At common law, there was a right to challenge 35 jurors, and this survived in cases of treason when the number was reduced to 20 in cases of felony in 1523; the Crown was entitled to ask jurors to 'stand by', i.e. they would serve on the jury only if there was no one else left: 4 Bl. Comm. 352–353.

3. It has regularly been stated that Scott's speech lasted nine hours, and Erskine's seven hours, and they occupy 129 and 93 columns respectively in the report – roughly 13 or 14 columns to the hour; this provides an approximate guide to the length of other speeches and other proceedings.

4. *sic.*

5. See *Gentleman's Magazine*, 1799, II, 709; *European Magazine*, No 36 (1799), 7; Foss, *Lives of the Judges.*

6. Brougham, *Historical Sketches of the Statesmen of the Reign of George III*, essay on George III.

7. This remark led G. T. Kenyon to write his *Life of Lloyd, First Lord Kenyon* to refute it – but regrettably his book throws no further light on the appointment of Eyre rather than Kenyon.

8. It appears to be a very strange decision – as Hardy himself said, 'No means, however unjustifiable, were spared that could effect his ruin. Letters written by others to different persons, without his knowledge or consent, and which he had

never seen or heard of, until they were produced in court, were attempted to be read in evidence against him....' Nevertheless, the decision has recently been upheld by the Court of Appeal in *R.* v. *Walters* (1979) and *R.* v. *Donat* (1986); it seems unlikely that anyone in the Court of Appeal realized that the origin of this rule lay in a letter describing how a girl threw a clog at King George III's carriage.

9. After holding many high offices of state, Huskisson was present at the opening of the Manchester and Liverpool Railway in 1830; he slipped on the line, and the engine ran over his foot; he died few hours later.

10. There are believed to be in existence no less that four reports of Hardy's trial, but the editor of the State Trials relied on Gurney.

11. DNB.

12. 24 St. Tr. 1386ff.; I have been unable to find out who this lady was.

13. But it never was proved.

14. Thompson, 147n, was evidently unaware that Groves was called as a witness.

15. When I wrote my article, *Crown Privilege in Criminal Cases*, [1971] Crim.L.R. 675, *R.* v. *Hardy* was still the principal authority on this issue; since then the ruling has been confirmed by the House of Lords in *Rogers* v. *Home Secretary* (1973).

16. The spies were probably reporting to Evan Nepean, an under-secretary at the Home Office: Hone, 67–68.

Chapter 13

1. This was true; Groves continued to spy for the government until mid-October 1794; Thompson, 147n.

2. Brown, 127.

3. Newgate had replaced Tyburn as the place of public execution in 1784: Bayne-Powell, 221–222.

4. John Wittich, *London's Inns and Taverns* (Shire Publications).

5. DNB.

6. DNB.

7. At this time, a person accused of treason or felony had no right to give sworn evidence, but was entitled to make an unsworn statement from the dock.

8. Eldon, §173.

Chapter 14

1. DNB.

2. The grassed area between Clifford's Tower, the Assize Court (which had been built in the 1780s), and the prison (now the Castle Museum) was then known as the Eye of York; by the eighteenth century, executions took place at Knavesmire, beside the racecourse: P. R. Newman, *The Royal Castle of York*; Torrington's Diaries, 4 June 1792.

3. This is doubtful. Parliament had over the years passed many acts to extend the law of treason in times of crisis; it is a matter of considerable difficulty to ascertain which, if any, of these were in force in 1794, but it is likely that the Crown could have resurrected some Tudor legislation if they had really been determined to do so.

4. *History of England*, ch. 2.

5. In my article, *Treason in Rhodesia*, [1967] C.L.J. at 205, I submitted that Eyre CJ's direction to the jury was erroneous. I was at that time under the impression that

no one else had commented upon it (Stephen, in his *History of the Criminal Law*, thought that Eyre CJ had not given any direction to the jury on the law, so he had evidently failed to find the passage). It was not until more than twenty years later that I discovered that Cockburn, I, 229–231, had made a similar criticism, citing in turn Samuel Phillips, *State Trials*, II, 78–80 where the matter is discussed in some detail. There were, in 1794, various grounds for appealing against a conviction, but a misdirection to the jury was not one of them, so there was no means by which this error could have been corrected.

6. Bayne-Powell, 304.
7. Hall, 233; Goodwin, 353. The troops were left standing in the rain until 10.30 p.m.
8. At one time a person, even if acquitted of the offence charged, could nevertheless be punished for running away from his accusers; but by the eighteenth century, the finding had become a formality.
9. Vincent, 75n.

Chapter 15

Note: The trial of Horne Tooke is reported in volume 25 of the State Trials.
1. Presumably a reference to Lord Mansfield CJ.
2. Adolphus (England), VII, 74; Albert Crew, *The Old Bailey*, 42.
3. This issue was raised again in *R. v. Mason* (1980).
4. Mugs, cameos, etc., were being manufactured at the time, inscribed or decorated with revolutionary and counter-revolutionary motifs: Bindman, *passim*.
5. Verrall's relationship with the third member of the Trinity was never explained.
6. See ch.10 note 5, *ante*.
7. For readers who ask the obvious question, the answer is that there was a large vase in the corner of the court: *The Oxford Book of Legal Anecdotes*, § 226.

Chapter 16

1. Cone, 207–208, has alleged that Horne Tooke conducted his defence in such a way as to make things worse for his co-defendants; this suggestion appears to be based solely on a statement by Hazlitt (*The Spirit of the Age*, 117) and is quite contrary to what Erskine said.
2. As far as my own research goes, it seems that such submissions were rarely made until towards the end of the following century, or even the establishment of the Court of Criminal Appeal in 1907; but Yorke made a similar submission at York Assizes: see Ch. 18 *post*.
3. 'I think somewhere about the year 1785; I think it was very soon after one of Mr Pitt's motions for parliamentary reform; in the year 1785, to the best of my remembrance': 25 St. Tr. 370.

Chapter 17

1. In *Hui Chi-ming v. R.* (1991), the Judicial Committee of the Privy Council, unaware of what had occurred in *R. v. Horne Tooke*, ruled that the acquittal of one defendant was not admissible in later proceedings against a co-defendant; Hui Chi-ming had been sentenced to death and his appeal was dismissed. At the time of going to press, a Petition for Clemency is being prepared on behalf of the appellant.
2. J. A. Lovat-Frasesr, *Erskine*, 56–57.
3. DNB (Gibbs).

Chapter 18

Note: The editor of the State Trials said that the report of Thelwall's case was lost (but Cestre, *Life of John Thelwall*, managed to find a copy); the trials of Yorke, Jackson and Stone are reported in volume 25 of the State Trials; other sources are listed *ante*.

1. *sic*; but in fact Macdonald CB took the place of Eyre CJ.
2. Hall, 233. Goodwin, 380.
3. Gales fled to America: Thompson, 144–145.
4. DNB.
5. DNB.
6. Paine subsequently emigrated to the USA.

Chapter 19

Notes: The principal sources for this chapter are Campbell, Eldon, Hardy, Stephens and Twiss.

1. Brown, 150–151; Veitch, 322–333.
2. June Swan, *Shoemaking* (Shire Publications); George, 195–202; Hardy himself says virtually nothing about his work.
3. Brown, 154–156; Cone, 217, 222; Hall, 177–178; Veitch, 318, 322–333.
4. Vincent, 94–95; Cone, 198, confuses this incident with the attack on No. 9 Piccadilly in June 1794, but they are clearly separate occasions.
5. For a detailed account of the convict colony, see Robert Hughes, *The Fatal Shore*; an account of the 'Scottish martyrs' also appears in the State Trials; and see Veitch, 294–297.
6. In later years, the political prisoners, especially the Irish, were treated much worse than the criminals.
7. waxed.
8. Brown, 154; and see Marianne Elliott, *Wolfe Tone*, 367.
9. Accounts of Muir's escape appear in the State Trials, and in Veitch, 294–296, and Hughes, *op. cit.*, 179–180; Veitch mentions a story that an American ship was sent to rescue Muir, but this seems unlikely. According to the State Trials, he died in Bordeaux; other writers say Chantilly.
10. Veitch, 297; Vincent, 69; Hughes, *op. cit.*, 181.
11. Veitch, 297–298.
12. Hone, 98.
13. Hone, *passim*.
14. In 1796, Baxter published a work listed in the British Library catalogue as *A New and Impartial History of England from the earliest period of genuine historical evidence to the present important and alarming crisis* (806 pages): copies were bought up and rigidly suppressed by the government: Goodwin, 371.
15. 'Of this republic [i.e. England], Sir Francis Burdett had the burlesque honour to be, in the judgment of Napoleon, "the fittest man in England" to fill the presidential chair': Croly, 285.
16. Paine is also credited with having coined this phrase; the modern version, which usually refers to the Ritz or the Savoy, is attributed to Mathew J.: Megarry, *Miscellany at Law*, 254.
17. Croly, 169ff, discussed several of the possible candidates; of Horne Tooke he says that 'he had the virulence and the disloyalty in superabundance; but he wanted the cool sarcasm and the polished elegance, even if he could have been fairly supposed to be at once the assailant and the defender'.
18. Matthew Boulton the engineer devised a system of mixing ink with sugar or gum arabic; he pressed the paper on which this was written against unsized tissue and

obtained a copy which could be read by looking through the sheet; he also designed a roller press for taking impressions which was patented in 1780: F. W. Gibbs, *Joseph Priestley*, 143. He also minted coins for the East India Company and the colonies (DNB), and was suspected of faking Roman coins (Torrington's Diaries, 30 May 1789).

19. Eyre CJ died at Ruscombe, Berkshire, on 6 July 1799.
20. This is probably the portrait which appears as the frontispeice of Lord Eldon's *Anecdote Book*.
21. The minting of coins is the responsibility of the Crown under the royal prerogative; but in the eighteenth century, the private manufacture of tokens or coins of small value was permitted.
22. (Mme D'Arblay); quoted by J.A. Lovat-Fraser, 144.
23. Olga Sinclair, *Gretna Green*, 38–39. 'Parson' Elliott, *The Gretna Green Memoirs*, 19, also claimed to have married Erskine, but his account is believed to be a fabrication. It is significant that Campbell feigns ignorance of all this, simply stating that 'He had contracted a second marriage – when, how, or with whom I have not learned upon any authority'; it is very difficult to believe that he was unaware of what must have been a matter of common gossip.
24. According to Campbell, this dinner was held in 1821; but Ferguson, 160n, gives the precise date, 21 February 1820.
25. Elliott *ibid.*.
26. J.A. Lovat-Fraser, 107.
27. *The Spirit of the Age*, essay on Lord Eldon.
28. Macpherson, Advertisement to Hardy's *Memoir*.
29. Hone, 362.
30. Vincent, 29.
31. The Great Seal is carried in a bag, and 'Bags' was the traditional nickname for the Lord Chancellor and the Keeper of the Seal.

Chapter 20

1. II, 416.
2. Quoted in Croly, 151–153.
3. See Ch. 10, n.15, *ante*.
4. See Ch. 10 and n.18, *ante*.
5. §96, and in open court, 25 St. Tr. at 498.
6. Prof. Gareth Jones, *Biographical Dictionary of the Common Law*, (ed by Prof. A.W.B. Simpson) (1984). Most of the *Lives* were published in 1845–47, but the *Lives* of Lords Brougham and Lyndhurst were published after the writer's death in 1861. Ferguson, in commenting on Campbell's account of Henry Erskine, preface, x, said, rather more politely, 'the facts regarding [Erskine and his career] and Scotch affairs generally, as given in the *Lives*, are not always quite accurate'.
7. Thus Trevelyan, *History of England*, Book V, ch. iv, wrote: 'Pitt's Attorney-General ... demanded in 1794 the condemnation of the Radical shoemaker Thomas Hardy for High Treason on the ground that he had advocated "representative government, the direct opposite of the government which is established here"'; no citation is given for the passage quoted in inverted commas; and three pages later: 'The government was so far blinded by panic that it sought the lives of the reformers'. And Sir Charles Grant Robertson, in an appendix to his *England under the Hanoverians*, 15th ed., 530: 'The trials for "treason" [his inverted commas] in both countries [i.e. England and Scotland], in fact, make a soiled chapter in the history of the British Judiciary, which distinguished lawyers since are only too glad either to scourge or forget'.

8. Brown, 137.
9. Hazlitt, *The Spirit of the Age*, essay on Godwin.
10. *Anecdote Book*, § 96.
11. It was contrary to professional etiquette for defence counsel to accept a fee in a case of treason: Campbell (Erskine) 678n; and see Erskine's own letter to the London Corresponding Society, Hall, 233. The rule did not survive into the twentieth century; Sjt Sullivan and Artemus Jones charged £530 and £325 respectively for acting for Casement, although Prof. J.H. Morgan gave his assistance free of charge: Notable British Trials, *Sir Roger Casement, passim*. William Joyce's counsel were paid out of the Poor Prisoners' Defence fund.
12. Quoted by J. A. Lovat-Fraser, 110.
13. This passage is paraphrased from Croly, 121; Lovat-Fraser, 110–111, has a similar passage, but without acknowledgement to Croly.
14. Eldon Square is the principal shopping centre in the City; Bessie Surtees House has been renovated and is now the headquarters of the North region of British Heritage.
15. *Memoirs of John Adolphus*, by his daughter, Emily Henderson.
16. Adolphus (England), VI, 77.

Index